THE SILENT
SOCIAL REVOLUTION,

AN ACCOUNT OF
THE EXPANSION OF PUBLIC EDUCATION
IN ENGLAND AND WALES
1895–1965 ,

2nd. ed.

BY
george alfred norman
G. A. N. LOWNDES

OXFORD UNIVERSITY PRESS
1969

Oxford University Press, Ely House, London W.1

GLASGOW NEW YORK TORONTO MELBOURNE WELLINGTON
CAPE TOWN SALISBURY IBADAN NAIROBI LUSAKA ADDIS ABABA
BOMBAY CALCUTTA MADRAS KARACHI LAHORE DACCA
KUALA LUMPUR SINGAPORE HONG KONG TOKYO

FIRST EDITION 1937
SECOND EDITION 1969

1. Education — Great Britain
2. Education — Wales

I. Title

370.942
L 919 A

PRINTED IN GREAT BRITAIN BY
BUTLER & TANNER LTD, FROME AND LONDON

FOREWORD
by the Rt. Hon. Lord Butler of Saffron Walden, P.C., C.H.

A T first sight, when one reads of a new book on Education, one feels a certain 'drawing back' since so much has been written. But with this book I became, as a keen educationist, quite absorbed, and would like strongly to recommend a close perusal of its contents.

It is a pity the work has even to stop at 1965 since I have little doubt that the present Administration will try to find time to legislate on education, even though the 1944 Act has made everything possible that really needs doing at the present time. However, any modernization of the education system that can be brought in would be examined by me in a favourable light.

The author brings his work sufficiently up to date to describe comprehensive schools on page 307 seq. It is clear that these schools and the demise of the 11 + have been perfectly possible to introduce very widely indeed under the Act of '44. The author very sensibly regards these schools as having come to stay and stresses the importance of their sixth forms.

The book is related almost entirely to the public system of education and therefore there is nothing about what is known as the Public Schools. These form, however, so minute a proportion of the whole that their omission is to be understood. However, it is partly with them that some of the modern legislation may have to do.

The book stresses the importance of the Act of 1902 and perhaps makes a more impressive case for it than has been made before, particularly in its mention of Higher Education. On page 66 there is a quotation by Mr A. J. Balfour and one by Mr Dillon. The latter said, 'If you could eliminate the religious difficulty, your Education Bill would pass the Second Reading in a single night and the Committee stage would not take a week.' This was precisely the difference between my Act of '44 and the Education Act of 1902. Although my Act took quite a long time to get through Parliament, the religious animosity had died down and it was possible to reach a settlement of the religious issue which would have seemed quite out of the question in 1902.

There is one statement in the book, on page 384, in the bibliography of Chapter 14, in which the author says that the 'Green Book' of June 1941 could not have differed as to its contents very materially from those in the White Paper of July 1943. This is true of a proportion of the lay-side of the proposals, but it is quite untrue in regard to the religious settlement. If we in 1942 had accepted the solution of the Green Book, we should not have had an Education Bill at all. This is made quite clear in Dr Cruickshank's story of the religious settlement of 1941–4.

Before I leave the act of '44 and acknowledge the generosity of the comments, I would agree with page 268 where it is stated that one of the main losses must be the failure of the country to implement the County College proposals.

What is impressive about the book is its description, first of all on page 105, of how secondary education lagged behind other countries at the beginning of the twentieth century. The author thinks we were sixty years behind other countries. He also points out on page 72 how far behind America and Germany we were in technology at the turn of the century. Mr Sadler said, 'The very existence of the Empire depends upon sea power and school power', and it has been held by a recent historian that if our school power had been more developed prior to the Battle of Jutland, especially in relation to our technical efficiency and the recruitment of the Royal Navy, the battle might have had a more conclusive result in our favour. The two chapters on the development of technical education, numbers 9 and 18, show what a wide grasp the author has. These show that it was not really until 1956 that a big drive on technical education took place. We are now less behind than we were, but we still have an enormous drive to make, and the tables on page 354 give some idea of the progress we have made.

The book has one great distinguishing feature in that the author does not talk about education in a water-tight compartment. The history of wars and struggles of one sort and another permeate the chapters. There is also humour and on page 74 a delightful mixed metaphor: 'The Government has thrown down an apple of discord which has burst into flames and flooded the country.'

I find this book a most valuable commentary on the history of education in modern times in Britain.

PREFACE TO THE SECOND EDITION

ANYONE who, having essayed to write a thesis in his thirties, has to his astonishment seen it turned into a book which has been selling over a period of nearly thirty years, may perhaps be forgiven if, in his seventies, he is seized with a desire to carry the story forward over the intervening thirty years. Before deciding to make the attempt, however, he will do well to reflect that however willing his pen the flesh may be weak, and the critics liable to ask why he could not have left well alone; and also to reckon up the cost in visits to libraries, colleges of education, and schools which his pension or other savings will have to meet.

It is one of the more questionable features of the activities of that section of the Department of Education and Science which administers educational trust funds that their Schemes have always limited their beneficiaries to those who are under twenty-three years of age. Thus, except in the sphere of medicine, a considerable accumulation of perishable knowledge dies with each generation. Fortunately there is one Trust, the Leverhulme Research Awards, which is not governed by this quaint restriction, and it is to their generosity that I owe the chance to write this book.

One of my many friends who constantly urged me to continue my *Silent Social Revolution* was Hammond Jenkins who devoted the remaining twenty years of his long life after retirement from the Board of Education to sterling service to the Essex L.E.A. During the memorial service to him on 12 November 1965 in the chapel of St John's College, Cambridge, one of the prayers used was that of Sir Francis Drake before Cadiz. This seemed a direct message to me to make the attempt, and it is in the spirit of that prayer that I have forced my 'heart and nerve and sinew' to 'continue the matter until it be thoroughly finished'.

I have received much friendly help from such varied sources as the Department of Education and Science, the Ministry of Health, the Treasury, the Registrar General, the University Grants Committee, the Wiltshire Education Authority, the Catholic Education Council, and the research department of the Conservative Central Office. I owe a special debt to the librarians of the Department of Education and Science, Miss Phyllis Downie and Miss D. M. Jepson, and those at the Teachers' Reference Library of the Inner London Education Authority. Dr Alec Hay, lately Chief Inspector, and Mrs G. M. Goldsworthy, lately Inspector of nursery schools, at the London

County Council have generously allowed me to quote a few delightful examples of children's sayings and writings which they have collected.

No book on the history of education can ever be entirely up to date on publication because of the time-lag in the production of the Department's statistics and reports. I have thought it well in the circumstances to confine myself, substantially, to the years 1935 to 1965. These years in themselves constitute a kind of watershed between the post-war years of resurgence and the restrictions induced by the national 'balance of payments' freeze.

1968

PREFACE TO THE FIRST EDITION

'IF all the nonsense', remarked the Rev. Dr Opimian in Thomas Love Peacock's *Gryll Grange*, 'If all the nonsense which has been talked on all other subjects were thrown into one scale, and all that has been talked on the subject of education alone were thrown into the other, I think the latter would preponderate.'

The author who would add to the already weighty pile of works upon education therefore incurs a heavy responsibility—a responsibility which becomes all the heavier if he happens to share the Rev. Doctor's views.

In extenuation I can only offer two pleas. The first is that it is my first offence; the second, that this book began as an expensive opportunity for repentance in that, owing to the war, I had omitted that rather necessary preliminary to a life-time of educational administration, the taking of my university degree. To these pleas the critic might, and probably will, reply that as a member for fourteen years of a service which, on Mr Baldwin's authority, is 'as silent in public as it is garrulous in private', I could hardly have made an earlier incursion into print; and secondly that I should never have allowed what began as a rather belated attempt to obtain a degree to develop into a book. I had, however, felt for some years that a need existed for some brief, and if possible readable, account of the steps which this country has taken to build up a public system of education since the first generation to receive compulsory education was disciplined by 'payment by results'. With a few—too few—brilliant exceptions, the existing literature of public education is, as anyone who has to read it knows, voluminous, well intentioned, accurate, and cautious. But even in those cases where it is not intentionally soporific, owing to the fear of provoking religious controversy, it has often seemed to me to be duller than the intrinsic interest of the subject warrants. I wondered if by reading widely enough and yet keeping, the while, a firm check on a sense of humour which my elders and betters at the Board of Education used, I believe, to stigmatize as flippant, I could contrive to bring the blue books to life. For blue books are particularly prone to use their statistics not as a living record of social progress but (to quote a deservedly immortal phrase of Andrew Lang) 'as a drunken man uses lamp-posts—for support rather than for illumination'.

I find that under the standing orders of the Local Education Authority which I serve I am required to state that any views I have expressed are entirely my own and do not in any way commit my employers. That this is the case will, I think, be obvious to anyone who reads what I have written. I have in fact been at some pains to eliminate any direct mention of that Local Education Authority except where absolutely necessary. I would, however, like to acknowledge my very deep sense of gratitude to Mr E. M. Rich, the Education Officer to the London County Council, and to Mr H. E. M. Icely, Reader in Education at the University of Oxford, for the encouragement I received from them to persevere with an attempt to do two full days' work in one for more than a year; to Miss Shuckburgh, the Librarian at the Board of Education, for much advice as to the books I must read; to Mr H. Ward who, actuated by that charming friendliness which exists between former members of the administrative staff of the Board and former members of the Inspectorate, hastened to send me a number of notes for the early chapters of a similar book which he had once contemplated himself. Lastly, to Mr Brentnall, lately headmaster of Lancaster Road Senior Boys' School, London, for his account of the life of a teacher working under the system of 'payment by results'.

I am told that dedications, even in one's first book, are out of fashion. But even if it cannot have a page to itself I cannot refrain from inserting mine. For to write this book at all it was necessary for me to live the life of a hermit, travelling daily between Oxford and London for a year and devoting every minute of my private time to it. What sacrifice this entailed for my family only they know. And if I were allowed a dedication it would be to my wife, without whose loyalty this book could never have been written, and to one who, had he lived, would have entered school this year.

1937

CONTENTS

LIST OF ILLUSTRATIONS

LIST OF GRAPHS

THE Graphs illustrate the proportion of children and individuals of any given age who were attending different types of school or educational courses in the years named. The actual numbers are shown, but they are not so important as the relative proportions because the size of an age-group may vary with each year.

It will be noted that comparing Graphs A, B, and C there were just over 5½ million in the public system of education in 1895; 6·2 million in 1935 and just over 10½ million in 1965. In arriving at these totals the men and women students in initial training courses for entry to the teaching profession and also students attending courses of adult education have been included. These do not appear separately in the graph because their age distribution is uncertain. The University population (140,500 in 1965) is not included because the Universities are outside the public system.

Two further figures may surprise anyone who examines the graphs:

(1) 60·4 per cent of all children in the age-groups two to nineteen are now attending school. If the calculation is made on the basis of the age-groups five to nineteen the percentage becomes even higher, e.g. about 77 per cent, and this figure does not take into account the 16-, 17-, 18-, and 19-year-old students attending full-time or sandwich courses in colleges of technology and art.

(2) Despite the apparent narrowness of the column representing full-time technological education in the 1965 Graph, when the University students who are studying science and technology are added, England and Wales, according to a recent O.E.C.D. report, had the highest proportion of full-time students studying science and technology of any O.E.C.D. country. 5·1 per cent of our 20–24 year olds graduated in these subjects compared with 4·2 per cent in the United States and 3·2 per cent in France.

Other points which will be noted are:

(a) The virtual completion of 'Hadow' reorganization by the elimination of 'all-age' schools. A column showing the 9,758 pupils over 11 remaining in such schools in 1965 would be too narrow to appear on the graph, and practically all such schools have now been brought to an end.

(*b*) The emergence of the column representing comprehensive schools and that of the group described as 'Other secondary schools.' These are in most cases Bi-lateral schools.

(*c*) The post-war 'bulge' age-groups now passing out of the school population but being replaced by a new 'bulge' formed by those aged 2–6.

ABBREVIATIONS USED IN THE FOOTNOTES

R.E.D. Report of the Education Department of the Privy Council (issued annually till 1899).

C.C.R. 5687. Report of the Cross Commissioners 1886–9, Answer 5687.

H Hansard.

B.C.R. Bryce Commission Report (Royal Commission on Secondary Education 1895).

B.E.R. Annual report of the Board of Education for the year shown.

E.P. No. 94. Educational Pamphlet No. 94. The series of Educational Pamphlets prepared by the Board of Education and published by Her Majesty's Stationery Office.

R.C.E. 1868. Royal Commission on Education 1868, usually referred to as the 'Schools Inquiry Commission'.

R.C.C. 1909 etc. Report of the Consultative Committee appointed by the President of the Board of Education.

C.M.O. 1909 etc. Report of the Chief Medical Officer of the Board of Education for the year 1909 etc.

PART I

Towards the System of Public Education

CHAPTER I

THE ERA OF 'PAYMENT BY RESULTS'

The State concerns itself with the supply of elementary schools.—The Education Acts of 1870, 1876, 1891, and 1893 conscript a huge army of infants and juniors.—Their 'militia' training.—The small 'professional army' in the grammar schools.—The reluctance of the State to concern itself with secondary education.—The untimely fate of the Endowed Schools Commission.—Progress between 1870 and 1895 in building elementary schools.—The singular educational device of 'payment by results'.—Its origin.—A description of its working.—Its demerits as an educational instrument.—Its one achievement, the disciplining of a far from civilized child population.—The system abandoned 1895.

B Y 1935 successive British governments had been engaged for just over a century in an endeavour to extend a modicum of schooling to the whole mass of the child population of England and Wales.

A coiner of epigrams—unfamiliar with the chequered history of public education—might indeed be tempted to remark that they had been endeavouring to purchase an educated democracy on the instalment plan; that for the first forty years of that century (1833–70) they paid the premiums to men of goodwill wherever they might be found who showed themselves ready to undertake the building and maintenance of voluntary schools; but that in 1870 when voluntary initiative had failed to provide a school place for more than one child in two in London or one in three to five elsewhere, the State itself had to enter the field and pay larger instalments in the form of Education Acts. For an Education Act is in a very real sense an instalment in the education of a whole people.

First Mr Forster's Act of 1870—in its ultimate social results one of the greatest measures which has ever received parliamentary endorsement—established once and for all the State's concern with school 'supply'. Next Lord Sandon's Act of 1876 prohibited the employment during school hours of children under 10 years of age who lived within two miles of a school, thus virtually introducing the first comprehensive measure of compulsion. A third Act passed in 1891 abolished the payment of fees in all schools charging less than 10s. a year, extended the prohibition to all schools to be opened in the future, and took power to modify fees in those schools charging more than 10s.

Finally, the Elementary Education School Attendance Act of 1893 passed by Mr Gladstone's short-lived fourth ministry raised to 11 years (from 1 January 1894) the age at which a child might obtain total or partial exemption from the obligation to attend school.

To appreciate just how much had been achieved by these first four instalments it is necessary to take stock of the extent of educational provision in England and Wales at the end of the nineteenth century. The year 1895 suggests itself as a suitable point for this stocktaking for a variety of reasons which it will be the purpose of this and the succeeding chapters to trace. Moreover, an attempt to present a fairly complete picture of the state of public education in 1895 will render it possible, by contrast, to illustrate the remarkable expansion which took place in the next forty years.

In the first place it should be noted that the four Acts had, as it were, placed the State in a position of responsibility to a huge conscripted army of quite young children. This army to be precise numbered 5,235,887 in 1895, 4 million of its units being under 10 years of age.

It is difficult to get back to what may be described as the greatest common measure in the public attitude towards education at any given period. Probably, however, it is not far short of the truth to say that, during the twenty-five years which preceded 1895, it must have appeared a sufficient task to teach mastery of the mechanical tools of education, the three R's, to this conscripted army of children up to their tenth or eleventh year. As Mr H. G. Wells remarked in his *Experiment in Autobiography*—'The Education Act of 1870 was not an Act for common universal education, it was an Act to educate the lower classes for employment on lower class lines, and with specially trained, inferior teachers who had no university quality.'

In other words the primary concern of the State in discharging the new responsibilities it had undertaken must be to afford to this army of children a militia training directed to the acquisition of quite general powers such as the arts of speech, reading and writing, and the fundamental ideas of magnitude and number. A militia, it was recognized, must be supplemented by a small professional army; and this must have received post-primary education. Was the task of providing this post-primary education also regarded as the concern of the State? Might it not quite safely be left to the ancient grammar schools? Advanced thinkers such as Matthew Arnold had for years urged that it could not. An authoritative but politically inconvenient Royal Commission, the Schools Inquiry Commission of 1867, had been of the same mind. But the Endowed Schools Commission, the executive body created to give effect to the Royal Commission's findings, had come to an untimely end. It had in fact been too successful in its efforts to rescue the endowed schools. It had displayed such energy in its handling of moribund or misapplied endowments that it had become unpopular with a section of the Tories. These, on Disraeli's accession to power in 1874, secured the dismissal of Lord Lyttelton and Mr Roby, two of the paid commissioners, and the submergence of the functions of the commission in those of the Charity Commission, a government Department which could be trusted to repress its enthusiasm. The lot of inconveniently earnest executive bodies during the reign of the Great Queen was never an easy one. Twenty years earlier Edwin Chadwick's Public Health Commissioners had suffered a like fate. 'Master John Bull', as *The Times* put it, had preferred to 'take his chance of cholera' to being 'scrubbed and rubbed and small tooth-combed till the tears ran into his eyes and his teeth chattered and his fists clenched themselves with anger and pain'. Perhaps we ought not to smile too readily at the Victorians. For as lately as the 1930s we witnessed that singular act of Imperial Statesmanship which destroyed the Empire Marketing Board, not, be it noted, because it had failed but because it was becoming too successful.

The peculiar genius of the British people for large-scale and more or less spontaneous organization, the product, as some believe, of the fusion in their make-up of Norman administrative ability, Celtic imagination, Nordic 'practicality', and Roman respect for law, had by 1895, as we shall see, made a success, up to a point, of the vast task which the four Acts had imposed. Here an interesting parallel occurs, for in the years between 1914 and 1918 this country had to raise, house, clothe, feed, equip, munition, and train an army of 8 million men and put it into the field to meet the finest continental army ever assembled. In the years which followed 1870 the country had had to encompass a similar, though a more enduring, piece of organization. In each case the Continent was many years ahead of this country. But the founders of our public educational system, so far from being able to enjoy the unlimited financial backing which assembled and sustained the armies between 1914 and 1918, were constantly expected to produce 'results' in an atmosphere of parsimony which made their attainment chimerical.

Thus between 1870 and 1895 the School Boards provided new school accommodation for 2,211,299 scholars for £29,468,477 and the voluntary schools seats for 1,475,000 (between 1870 and 1891) for £7 million.[1] The School Board for London built, at a cost of £6 a head for sites and £12 a head for buildings, three-storey erections of such permanence and utilitarian ugliness that generations of local administrators have lived to regret that they did not spend the £12 on the site and the £6 on less regrettably indestructible buildings. Their record, considered as a piece of organization, was, however, a most remarkable one, for between 1872 and 1880 they built 197 schools, between 1881

[1] *R.E.D.*, 1894, p. xxv.

and 1890, 151 schools, and between 1891 and 1902, 90 schools. Moreover, while these schools were being built, against a roll increasing by 8,000 a year, they were often able to organize temporary schools in mission halls, chapels, and even under railway arches.

That the edifice which was erected was in certain respects a makeshift one, and that the militia training was more thorough in its disciplinary than its lasting educational qualities, is perhaps in the circumstances hardly a matter for wonder. The real matter for astonishment is that, in the light of the resources applied to it, it was erected at all!

The 'educational' means employed was a singular one, without parallel—until the educational 'reforms' of the early thirties in Russia[1] —in continental or American practice: the system of 'payment by results'. By 1895 this system stood condemned—and rightly so—by most contemporary as by nearly all subsequent educational thought. Thus to the modern student of educational method it is now of little more than cautionary interest as the negation of everything for which true education should stand. To those concerned to trace the successive factors which have made for the growth of the English educational system, it is, however, deserving of closer study. For our modern educational system can be said to have been grounded upon it, and when it was relaxed, teachers' thoughts were directed from the static present to the dynamic future. To understand some of the most important features of English education, and the rapidity of its development since 1895, the genesis, main outlines, and lasting influence— both good and bad—of this singular educational device must therefore be grasped.

The origin of the system does not, as some historians have too readily assumed, appear to have been entirely due to the blind demand of mid-Victorian parliamentary thought for a visible demonstration of value received for money expended. This demand no doubt played a substantial part. It was Matthew Arnold's contention that the Newcastle Commission (1858) had to have a point; that they thought they had found one in the neglect of a body of backward children in favour of the brighter scholars; that a commercially minded Parliament had fixed upon this point to demand a ledger account of educational progress; but that the pre-1862 system had never had a fair trial because the teachers were not properly trained at the time.[2]

On the other hand this opinion was not altogether shared either by his contemporaries or by subsequent Inspectors. As one of his contemporaries told the Cross Commission:

'The teaching and influence of the national school of that era [i.e.

---

[1] *The Times*, 6 November 1935, 'Soviet School Reform'.
[2] *C.C.R.*, 5687–819.

the era before the establishment of "payment by results"] was quite partial and eclectic. The *people* were not being educated; those of the people who were actuated by parental ambition for their children's education secured a really good education for them; the mass of the children of the struggling poor remained (sometimes in spite of being at school, generally from the fact of not attending school) quite uneducated.'

This view was echoed by another of Her Majesty's Inspectors, Mr Du Port, writing, in 1895, 'from a very large experience of the life of the schools as observed by me at visits of inspection without notice. Our schools', he said, 'have learned one lesson from the old annual examination. The radical defect of the pre-Revised Code days has been cured. Every child, however backward, young, or dull, has had its full share of conscientious attention.'[1]

It is probably nearer the truth to say that the originators of the system were aiming at the removal of a political danger and the establishment of a tidier administrative system than at the creation of a balance sheet in which progress could be recorded. In other words Robert Lowe and his advisers were impelled first by irritation and secondly by alarm. They were irritated because the increasing centralization of the educational system was daily creating fresh routine work in Whitehall, and fresh pressure by the Treasury to decentralize— backed no doubt by resistance to all demands for additional staff. They were alarmed because they felt themselves to be living on a volcano, and that at any time the Englishman's innate distrust of an educational system liable to capture and control by a political party might call them to face an awkward situation in the House. For this was not by any means an imaginary danger in 1862. Kay Shuttleworth, who controlled the destinies of the Education Department up to 1849, does not seem to have displayed any fondness for decentralization. In fact there is some evidence for the view that he had believed that education could be controlled from Whitehall. 'I understood your Lordship's Government to determine in 1839', he had written some years previously, 'to assert the claims of the civil power to control the education of the Country.'

Certainly this view as to the politico-administrative origin of the scheme is supported by authority no less respectable than that of Lord Lingen, who succeeded Kay Shuttleworth in 1849, and was actually serving as Secretary to the Education Department when the system was instituted. His evidence to the Cross Commission on the point is remarkable. While at first stating the orthodox view that the Newcastle Commission had considered that they were justified in stating that the great bulk of the children were quitting school with no real

[1] *C.C.R.*, 5822; *R.E.D.*, 1895.

knowledge of the elementary subjects of instruction, he later changed his ground.

Mr Lowe in 1862 dwelt in his speech upon the consideration that the proportions which the grant was taking threw far too much power into the hands of the Government of the day. . . . I think that at the time the particular consideration he had in view was this; the grants were not made as they are now, exclusively to the treasurers of the schools, but very largely to individuals. For instance all the pupil teachers were directly paid in their own names by Post Office orders (despatched from Whitehall). The schoolmasters in the same way were paid their grants of augmentation. Mr Lowe very strongly felt that as this vast number of persons increased it became a serious public consideration to put some check upon that system. Taking the recommendations of the (Newcastle) report seriatim, the first in importance was felt to be to get rid of the direct personal claims of the teachers upon the State and for that purpose it was necessary to pass to some different system of payment such as the payment by results. But that process led to such storms that I think by the year 1864 the Government having in the main carried its point had had about enough of it, and was glad to rest.[1]

A reference to Mr Lowe's speech (13 February 1862) confirms this view, although Mr Lowe inverted the argument, representing that the teachers would capture the political parties if they continued to be paid by Whitehall.

May it not be that Lord Lingen's memory grew clearer as his examination proceeded and that Robert Lowe's primary intention was in fact to secure a measure of decentralization? With other difficulties pressing upon him he would no doubt be glad to enlist the support of members who saw in his proposals the means to satisfy their demand for some such annual stocktaking as their business experience and habits of thought could appreciate.

If so may it not also be that those 'storms' of the 1860s are still more important to us than we think?

For we can now appreciate after 100 years' effort to build an educational system fit to be the servant of the nation, not the servant of the political state, that the infinitely diverse needs of modern civilization can never be met by one system of schools unified under rigid public control, still less by a system at the mercy of successive party machines. Perhaps Robert Lowe, in apparently doing a grave injustice to a whole generation, in reality by this early measure of decentralization saved English education once and for all from the pitfalls which have ensnared the systems of so many other countries; notably Germany, Italy and, to a less extent, France.

The essential principles of the system itself can be described quite

[1] *C.C.R.*, 56,209; 56,276; 56,284. *H*, Vol. 165 (Third Series), cols. 199 and 210–13.

briefly, although many modifications were introduced in the thirty-three years during which it existed.[1]

The school population was classified, after passing through the infant school, into 'standards', age being the primary consideration. Just as many American children even today are placed in a class with all the other entrants whose name begins with the same letter of the alphabet, and will remain with the self-same class, irrespective of their attainments, throughout their school life, so those children who passed the examination for their standard were promoted 'en bloc' after the Inspector's visit. A minutely detailed schedule of work was laid down for each standard by the Code of the Education Department.

The children were drilled in this throughout the year and examined on a previously determined day by H.M.I.

In arithmetic three straightforward sums were set to each standard, and one problem. 'A school containing 568 scholars is put into 43 desks, and there are 9 scholars over. How many scholars are seated in each desk?'[2] 'It really sometimes looked (as one Inspector remarked) as if teachers would hardly rest satisfied till they had obtained five right answers out of four sums set!'

In 'reading' the examination took place from one of three books in Standards III to VII, from one of two in Standards I and II.

These books contained a number of stories, poems, and general knowledge extracts each preceded by lists of difficult words and followed by a list of 'meanings' of different words and phrases. In Standard I for instance there would be a reader of this type and a geographical reader descriptive of 'The Ball on which we live'. At the examination each child had to read to the Inspector (it took 30 hours in a school of 1,000 pupils), and his reading was marked in the schedule, X for an excellent, T for a good pass, / for a bare pass, and O for a failure.

How far the poems and meanings 'were within the comprehension of the children' it is difficult today to estimate. The poems of course were frequently supplemented by the learning of hymns, including no doubt that hymn which contained the remarkable entomological revelation that 'Even the worm will bend the knee'. The author's mother, who was at school in the 1880s, used to recall discussing with a bosom friend whether the words of the hymn they had been learning,

---

[1] I am indebted for much of this description of the system of 'payment by results' to the late Mr E. J. Brentnall, M.B.E., a former headmaster of Lancaster Road Senior Boys' School, Kensington. I have verified his account where necessary by reference to the Elementary Education Codes and evidence of witnesses before the Cross Commission. 'Payment by results' has become a household phrase in education circles, but there are no teachers left who actually worked under it.

[2] For this and other problems set to various standards, see C.C.R., 23,647 and 23,693–8.

by repetition, ran 'Pity me a simple T' or 'Pity mice and plicity'. Mice were obviously to be pitied because they got caught in traps and 'plicity' was believed to be some unlucky type of lizard.

A child who possessed a good memory would often pass, although he could not read at all, if he were given the first word and not told to skip a paragraph, through knowing the set books by heart. Occasionally such children were detected because they held the book upside down!

Even the choice of suitable reading matter was not always so simple as might be assumed, for parents and school managers were often narrow, suspicious, or ignorant.

'I beg to call your attention to a book that is being read at the Pangbourne School titled Ivanhoe', wrote an incensed parent to the Education Department as late as 1886. 'It is a book I cannot allow my Daughter . . . to read. I object to her reading it on moral and religious grounds. Trusting you will use your powerful influence and stop the reading of such novels at School. I don't allow my children to read such books at home and I will not allow them to read them at school, for I believe them to be very injurious to children.'

Similarly *John Gilpin* was objected to by other parents on temperance grounds, and Scott's *Lady of the Lake* as having an immoral tendency, while even Matthew Arnold himself was once reproved by their lordships for setting to fourth-year pupil teachers (aged 18) a passage in which a reference occurred to hinds dropping their young.

Writing was tested in Standard I by a ten-word spelling test, in Standards II to V by a prescribed number of lines of 'Dictation', in Standard V by the reproduction of a short story read twice by the Inspector, in Standards VI and VII, which few reached in 1895, by an essay. So great an impression did the examination make on the children's minds that teachers who retired in the 1930s could still relate how they spelt 'farmer' with three 'rs', to the mortification and disgust of their harassed class teachers. For they knew that they would spend another full year on the same readers if they failed to pass!

Recitation, grammar, geography, and music were also introduced as the system drew to its close, the number of lines to be learnt and the amount of knowledge in grammar to be assimilated in each year again being minutely prescribed from Whitehall by the Code. But it was not the modern geography of trade winds and map readings. It merely consisted of maps and lists of towns, capes, islands, etc. There must be thousands of people still alive who can recite the towns of France in alphabetical order: 'Dieppe, Dijon, Dunkirk (querque was too difficult), Havre, Lille, Lyons (pronounced Lions), Marseilles, Montpellier, Orleans, Paris' (pause, then on again).

Drawing and very elementary everyday science in the form of

'object lessons' were late introductions. History was not usually taught at all except as a 'specific subject'.

In 1891 'examination by sample' was introduced, the classes being divided into thirds to save the Inspector's time.

That such a system was bad for the Inspector, bad for the teacher and, above all, bad for the schools, goes without saying. Its condemnation on moral, educational, and psychological grounds, by Mr Edmond Holmes in *What is and What might be*, written immediately after his retirement from the Chief Inspectorship, is a landmark in educational literature. It only remains therefore to note briefly its defects and its one merit from the point of view of the growth of the public system of education.

The teacher was put in the false position of having to outwit the Inspector, whose sums were passed quickly from school to school or sometimes published in 'The Teacher's Aid'. Some teachers employed an elaborate code of signs to tell their class what was expected of them, e.g. hands in pockets = multiplication, hands behind back = subtraction, etc. The Inspector on his part was forced to look for subterfuge and became the enemy of the teacher instead of his counsellor and coadjutor in securing educational advance. Many Inspectors—as their general reports show—were men of vision and courage. Moreover, their reports were published. It does not therefore seem too much to claim that many far-reaching reforms might have been brought about earlier if they had been able to count on the whole-hearted co-operation of a united teaching profession. This is not to suggest that an Inspector's life was arid and without compensations. The opportunities it afforded for rewarding social service were often striking. One of the most poignant stories in the annals of the Inspectorate concerned a murderer who was awaiting execution for a series of the most brutal murders. He refused to receive the prison chaplain, but asked if he might see that young man (the local Inspector) who had done so much for his boy and, on his request being granted, he begged the Inspector to look after his boy after he had gone.

Again the problem of over-large classes might have been tackled many years earlier if the salary of the teachers had not, in far too many cases, been paid out of the grant earned, making it to their interest to attempt to teach as many children as they could secure rather than share the grant with additional teaching staff.

Finally children hated their schooldays, left them behind as soon as possible, soon forgot what they had learnt, and when they became the parents of the next generation (and marriages took place early) in all too many cases could neither contribute culture to their own children in the home nor readily modify the attitude which they had learnt towards their teachers in their own schooldays. For in some parts the teachers of those times would hardly dare to go home alone owing, as one teacher whimsically expressed it, to 'the pelting tendencies and rough humour of the neighbourhood'. When it is recalled that the sole form of local traction was still the horse, 'pelting tendencies' takes on a peculiar significance.

The one substantial contribution of the system to the building of our modern educational system was, as noted above, its disciplinary effect. In Dostoevsky's *Winter Notes on my Summer Impressions* (tr. by R. Gill in *European Quarterly*, August 1934) we have a picture of London in 1863, at the start, that is, of the 'payment by results' system.

After describing the city with its millions and its world-wide trade, the Crystal Palace, the Great Exhibition, and contrasting these emblems of Victorian prosperity with the terrible dens (such as Whitechapel) and their 'half-naked, savage, and starving population', he gives us some of the most revealing pictures of the child population which it is possible to imagine.

For instance I was told that on Saturday night half a million working men and women with their children spread like a flood over the whole town, for the most part gathering in certain districts. All night, it is said, up to five o'clock in the morning, they celebrate their holiday, that is, they fill themselves like cattle with food and drink and so make up for the whole week past. The beer houses are decorated like palaces. Drunkenness is everywhere, but it is joyless, sad, and gloomy; a strange silence seems always to prevail. Only now and then do abuse and brutal fights disturb this weary silence which weighs upon you so heavily. The women are in no way behind, and get drunk along with their husbands while the children crawl and run about among them. Many of these husbands thrash their wives dreadfully.[1] The children of these people, almost before they are grown up, go as a rule on the streets, mingle with the crowd, and often do not return to their parents. At the Haymarket I observed mothers who brought their young daughters to trade with. Little girls, about twelve years old, catch you by the hand and beg you to come with them.

A grim picture, especially when it is remembered that there were many cities which could, and still can, show slums far worse than London. That it was not overdrawn can readily be confirmed by any-one who reads the horrifying reports of the divisional superintendents of London Attendance Officers.

It was this state of affairs which the 'payment by results' system was largely instrumental in sweeping away. For just as the heterogeneous and loosely knit races which inhabited these islands before the Conquest found a new discipline and sense of unity under the impartial rigours of their Norman masters,[2] so the child population of England

---

[1] Elsewhere he refers to the poker as the readiest instrument for such chastisement.
[2] Professor Pollard's *Short History of England*, in Home University Library series, 1912, p. 33.

and Wales found a new discipline and sense of membership of a social community under the impartial rigours of 'payment by results'.

Unfortunately 'discipline' in its narrower sense too often seems to have taken precedence over the social aim, for the times were hard, the children lawless and the teachers hard-pressed.

A few photographs and one description of the children to be met with in many of the early schools have come down to us. The description is worth quotation in full:

They were a wild lot gathered in the Willow Alley shed. Not one boy had experienced any but parental discipline before, and most of the little fellows had been used to blows. When the teacher spoke to a lad the youngster's hands were instinctively made ready to protect the head. Their minds were in a turmoil; their curiosity was at fever pitch. Some were hardy enough; some were very intelligent in appearance; some were cowed and sly but vicious, and some were dulled into semi-imbecility by hunger, disease, ill-usage. They had no conception of the meaning of an order and the teacher was obliged to drill them again and again in the simplest movements. The power of paying attention was almost wanting in them. So far as attainments were concerned, the boys were tolerably level. Not one knew the entire alphabet and those who had picked up a slight idea of the letters from the street hoardings were decidedly vague. The teachers found it impossible to interest them in any subject for more than five minutes. They had the fluid mind of the true barbarian and it was quite useless to attempt any species of coercion.

To look at a photograph of a class in a school of those days—hands folded on the rail in front, backs straight, eyes on the teacher—is to realize something of the iron code of authority which was in many schools a seemingly inseparable concomitant of the system, particularly where, as was frequently the case, from 70 to 120 children had to be controlled by a single teacher, or even sometimes a pupil teacher, for the allotted five and a half hours. The amount of punishment which was inflicted in the five-day week must in many cases have far exceeded that now inflicted in five months or even five years in most modern schools. In boys' schools every sum wrong, every spelling mistake, every blot, every question which could not be answered as the fateful day of examination drew near, was liable to be visited by a stroke of the cane. 'I never remember seeing my headmaster in school when he had not a cane hanging by the crook over his left wrist. Every assistant master had a cane and so had the pupil teachers, but pupil teachers were not allowed to have a crook so that if any question arose they were only pointers. There were no backs to the desks and backs of boys were straightened by means of a stroke of the cane.' So wrote one of the best-known headmasters in London, who was a pupil teacher from 1889–93.

In girls' schools the punishments, if less sharp, admitted of greater refinement. Miss Ethel Mannin has somewhere told a story of how she was made to kneel, with her arms stretched out, on the floor of the empty hall while the school were receiving religious instruction. Such experiences may afford some clue to the much-lamented paganism of many women of her generation.

The Inspectors who had all, as well-nourished school-boys of 14–18, been flogged at their public schools did not apparently see anything very reprehensible in applying such methods to children who were often under-nourished and all under-age.

'In one school I found a young pupil teacher of about 15 or 16 years sitting up with a long cane in his hand. When I asked him if he used it much he replied "Yes, when it is wanted." I reported it to my colleague the inspector of that district who I believe checked the youthful Busby.'[1]

This is no doubt the dark side of the picture, and it must be remembered, lest it be construed as a criticism of the teachers, that every year there were many bruised shins and even broken limbs caused by rough boys kicking young women teachers. 'A scholar in the above school', wrote a perplexed clergyman to their Lordships in 1878, 'some days ago brought small apples into school and threw some at the girls during the sewing lesson; he was of course told to desist but persisted in repeating the offence. Summoned to the desk for corporal punishment he threw himself on the floor and said aloud "Damn you, I'll mark your shins if you come any nearer." ' Modern teaching methods might have been applied by a teacher of genius here and there even to such boys as these, but it is permissible to doubt whether they would have survived in most schools for a single week!

'I once saw a boy', wrote James Runciman in 1887, 'draw a nine-inch knife, and dash it into the back of another. The blade ran along a rib, slipped in, and barely missed the base of a lung. What does the sentimentalist say to a youth of that kind?'

It is interesting to note that the Government of the U.S.S.R., having tried for eighteen years to work a system of free discipline without examinations in their schools, were forced in their educational laws of the 1930s to institute annual examinations and to apply 'drastic' measures to cope with all forms of hooliganism and anti-social conduct among children.

Fortunately there was a bright side too.

Undoubtedly the exhortation in the Code of 1875 'to bring up the children in habits of punctuality; of good manners and language; of cleanliness and neatness; and also to impress upon them the importance of cheerful obedience to duty, of consideration and respect for others,

[1] *R.E.D.*, 1894, Mr Brodie.

of honour and truthfulness in word and act' was, so far as conditions permitted, faithfully observed by both teachers and managers. Indeed the direct inculcation of civilized behaviour was by no means neglected in many of the poorer schools and, however quaintly the rules of the so-styled 'Manners Guilds' may read today, there is no doubt that they did a good job.

'Object. To promote manly courtesy, cleanliness and honour.'

'Manners. Yes sir. Please. Thank you. Salute. Polite and pleasant to superiors, inferiors *and equals*. Special consideration for aged persons, cripples, blind and weak intellect women.'

That there was much that was cruel and unimaginative in the system there can be no doubt. That it was almost valueless from the point of view of the development of the individual child's self-reliance cannot be denied. But with every generation that passed through its rigours there was some gain in civilization. It is therefore difficult to disagree with the dictum of Mr Sharpe, H.M.I. for London, that 'if it were not for her 500 elementary schools London would be overrun by a horde of young savages', or with the Inspector who, summing up its results in his general report for 1895, the year in which it was finally modified, used the following words: 'Anyone who can compare the demeanour of our young people at the present day with what it was five and twenty years ago must notice how roughness of manner has been smoothed away, how readily and intelligently they can answer a question, how the half hostile suspicion with which they regarded a stranger has disappeared; in fact how they have become civilized.'[1]

The substitution in the Code of 1895 (S. 84(6)) of 'visits without notice' by H.M.I. in the case of approved schools for the previous annual visits was recognized on all sides to mark the end of an evolutionary era, and to constitute an invitation to the best schools to begin a new period of freedom; freedom, that is, to experiment, freedom to initiate less rigid classification, and freedom in the preparation of experimental syllabuses.

But although their lordships made haste to report in 1896 rather sententiously—'We have now the satisfaction of reporting that the change has so far been justified by its results, and that it appears to have given more freedom to the life of the schools without impairing their technical efficiency'— the system lingered on here and there for many years. This is shown clearly by Mr Edmond Holmes in *What is and What might be*. It will be remembered that so late as 1911 it was his attempt (couched, it must be admitted, in unforgivable language even for a document designed for private circulation) to protect the schools against control by Secretaries for Education trained in the old methods,

[1] *R.E.D.*, 1895, Mr King, p. 103.

which led to the loss to education of Sir Robert Morant, one of the greatest of its public servants.[1]

[1] The fullest account published of the Holmes-Morant circular appears in Dr B. M. Allen's *Life of Sir Robert Morant*, 1934. It is doubtful whether the full circumstances will ever be made known. If they were I cannot help thinking that a great many hasty conclusions arrived at in the heat of the controversy would have to be revised.

CHAPTER II

THE STATE OF PUBLIC ELEMENTARY EDUCATION IN 1895

The number, quality, pay, and pensions of the teaching staff.—Their difficulties.—The pupil teacher.—A school place at last for every child requiring one.—The difficulty of enforcing attendance.—Half-time attendance and release for domestic employment.—The first 'Black List'.—Cookery instruction.—Introduction of handwork.—Drawing.—Physical Training.—Reading.—The object lesson.—Buildings and furniture.—Out of school activities.—The improvement of the infant schools.—The increase of 'night schools'.—The blind, deaf, and defective.—The general educational result.

H A V I N G described the system which had for thirty-three years formed the background of public education, let us proceed with our stock-taking.

The number and quality of the teaching staff—always the first index of the health of any educational system—had been rising steadily, though not sensationally in the case of male teachers, since 1876. Out of 53,000 certified teachers, however, only just over half (29,000) had received two years' training in training colleges, the remainder having passed the Acting Teachers' Certificate Examination. Thus in 1895 exactly one certificated teacher was employed to every 100 children on the roll. Dilution by 28,000 assistant teachers and 31,400 pupil teachers (aged 14–18) reduced the overall average to 47·1 children to every certificated, assistant, or pupil teacher in service.[1]

Salaries too had risen. The average salary of certificated masters was £122. 6s. 7d., of certificated mistresses £81. 3s. 3d. Throughout the whole country only 400 headmasters, but no headmistresses, received a salary over £300 per annum. One fortunate assistant master received £300 or more and 7 women assistants between £150 and £200.[2]

The output from training colleges was just beginning to overtake

---

[1] *R.E.D.*, 1895, p. xxiii *seq.*

[2] One would need about £700 in the post-devaluation England of 1968 to give the same purchasing power as £100 in 1895. This must, however, be regarded as giving only a very broad indication of the change in the internal purchasing power of money owing to changes in the spending habits of the people and the need to link different price indices together.

the wastage (6 per cent). No national scales of course existed to protect the country districts from the 'cornering' of the best teachers by the wealthier towns. London, where the average salary of headmasters was £290 in board schools and £154 in voluntary schools, and Manchester, which had almost doubled her trained teachers in three years, had already taken full advantage of this fact.

Pensions were inadequate in number, fitful, fortuitous, and beggarly. As one H.M.I. reported in 1895:

> The great relief afforded by the more generous distribution of pensions to many well deserving teachers deserves mention. In this district several teachers have been enabled to retire from a painful struggle for existence into comparative ease and comfort. One case is very touching.
>
> A schoolmistress had contrived to live for many years on £40 a year and a house, and to bring up part of a sister's family who were thrown on the world. At length when age began to tell she found the schoolwork too difficult, and to add to her misfortunes a warning of inefficiency was issued. One of the family whom she had maintained was a pupil teacher in a large town school and completed his engagement soon after his aunt's misfortune occurred. He came to her and taught the school vigorously, and it is needless to say with what great pleasure the inspector was enabled to cancel the warning which he had issued. Now the schoolmistress has been pensioned, the youth obtained employment at once, and we may hope that they may both continue their happy exercise of affection and duty until the final separation comes.[1]

Despite these unpropitious prospects for those who in the language of the day essayed to 'ply the irksome task of public instruction', little difficulty appears to have been experienced in obtaining teachers for urban schools. The real difficulty lay with the rural areas. By 1935, although few teachers as yet owned cars, good roads, frequent omnibus services, and rural telephones already linked the country teacher with the market town, its cinema, and her friends. Wireless programmes, and in many cases women's institutes and county libraries, had begun to offer the prospect of evening recreation. It was therefore becoming increasingly difficult to picture the isolation and barrenness of the rural teacher's life in the last decade of the nineteenth century. She did not readily fit into any of the strata into which the village communities of the day were divided. The cottage folk were, as always, friendly, but often ill at ease in the presence of 'book learning', the shopkeepers and large farmers superior, the county families and parsons inclined to be aloof. A comfortable home would have been an alleviation, but her salary was a pittance often as low as £40 and when a house was provided there was not the wherewithal to furnish it. The attempt to drill single-handed perhaps sixty or seventy children in the minutias

---

[1] Mr King, H.M.I. *R.E.D.*, 1895, p. 108.

The old donkey shed opened by Dr. Barnardo as a school in 1865.
It had an earth floor and was attended by 100 children

Inside an early charity school on the day of the Manager's visit,
circa 1870

'They were a wild lot.' Children of the 1870s.

of the standards—in the knowledge that her salary might depend upon the result—made the schoolwork needlessly arduous. The managers —or rather manager, for the greatest difficulty was often experienced in finding two persons other than the reverend correspondent to sign official documents—were often difficult to please. Capricious dismissals and extraneous duties were common, nor did they by any means stop at the 'organ on Sundays'. They might even extend in the case of some unfortunate bachelors to marriage with the 'elderly ugly daughter' of one of the managers. Occasionally rank injustice was perpetuated, as, for example, when a teacher's salary was cut by the amount he had earned by conducting evening continuation classes. This actually occurred in 1895, but the persecution to which the teachers of an earlier day were sometimes subjected can only be judged by readers of such works as *Schools and Scholars*. One illustration must suffice.

The head teacher of an early London board school was being attacked (about 1878) by a section of his managers because he refused to go beyond the syllabus of religious instruction laid down by the school board.

The teacher was reading for a science degree and left on his desk during the lunch hour a work on physiology by a Dr Michael Foster.

A woman manager, described in the language of the day as 'a strong-minded person who contrives to combine the advocacy of purity with the investigation of indecency', discovered the book. A violent correspondence was thereupon engineered in the local paper under such pseudonyms as 'an Indignant Parent'.

The following are excerpts from the letters which appeared:

'Are we to be taxed in order that the faith for which Ridley and Latimer suffered may be crushed? Let us expel this cockatrice from our midst, Sir, and let the flag of Britain wave unsullied in the breeze.'

'Sir, We were informed that our poor children were to be taught reading, writing and arithmetic only. Now this schoolmaster teaches them the contents of their own insides and thus adds to the rudeness which is innate in the lower orders. If the Author of the Universe had meant us to know what our livers are like he would not have hidden them away in security.'

The picture can be enlarged indefinitely. The results, as is only to be expected, were patchy. But the good undoubtedly predominated. Witness the following extracts from the General Reports of H.M.I.s:

'There is no doubt that the great body of teachers do their work if not always in absolutely the best way still with honesty of purpose, great diligence, steady and increasing success.'

'Forlorn indeed is the lot of the young mistress in some of these outlying rural nooks. It is not surprising that many of them become mere birds of passage: that the country teacher is dying out and being replaced by the failures of the towns. The marvel and the honour is that not a few of them do so well and bravely against wind and tide.'

'England owes a debt of gratitude to the teachers who treat a drunken mother and her neglected child with a patient courtesy deserving of high praise. Indeed, they seldom find occasion to pursue with any severity and endeavour to win the child by firm and constant gentleness.'[1]

No survey of the state of the public system of education in the closing years of the nineteenth century would be complete without some special mention of the pupil teachers.[2]

Their lot by present standards was hard. The less fortunate majority left home at 8 a.m. to walk to school (a good bicycle in those days would cost upwards of £15). They controlled a class of as many as sixty or seventy children for five hours, arriving home about 5.30 p.m. In the evenings they studied from 6.15 to 10 p.m. unless they attended a 'voluntary' evening class for pupil teachers. Saturday mornings from 8 a.m. till 1.30 p.m. would be spent at a pupil teacher centre and the best part of their Saturday afternoons preparing for next week's classes. Thus with the exception of a few hours on Saturday and the late Victorian Sunday their whole week was fully occupied by school work. The more fortunate minority were treated—as in London—as half-timers. They attended the school, as teachers, for half the day and the pupil teacher centre, as taught, for the other half. Experience as to the value of this system of centres was accumulating gradually. But to recall that there were forty-seven scholars on the books for every pupil teacher is to realize the difficulty which overworked head teachers must have experienced in releasing them to go to the pupil teacher centre or in regarding them when in school as students in the art of teaching placed in the schools for the benefit of the future generation. It was no doubt easy enough—with the 'Madras' system still a living memory—to defend this form of apprenticeship on the ground that early familiarity with children was to the apprentices' advantage. But one suspects that a great deal was learnt at the expense of the children and that, judging by modern conceptions of industrial psychology, a great deal more might have been learnt had the hours been shorter. It is true that long hours, often without holidays, were general in those days. Even their lordships of the Treasury were known to observe that they could not see the force of a demand for longer holidays on the part of the Civil Service since they already enjoyed a fortnight's leave 'and 52 Sundays' every year! But the more one learns of the frequent inadequacy of the supervision, the long hours at a time when, as little

---

[1] *R.E.D.*, 1894, pp. 21 and 62; 1895, p. 148.
[2] For the lot of the pupil teacher, see *R.E.D.*, 1894, pp. 23, 38, 85 and 86; *R.E.D.*, 1895, p. 51 and p. 83.

more than children (14 –17), they should have been enjoying some of the pleasant times now regarded as the right of youth, the more one is inclined to take off one's hat to that splendid body of headmasters and headmistresses who retired from the profession in the 1930s and who in their youth endured so much with so little hope of public recognition or reward.

It is curious to anyone who has made a study of the figures to find how prevalent is the belief that, almost immediately after Parliament had passed the Education Act of 1870 (and Matthew Arnold had talked hopefully of 'sweetness and light'), every child in England and Wales trooped gladly into school.

In reality, as we have seen, this happy state of affairs was not reached for twenty-five years, although in certain areas something was done to get children into temporary school accommodation.

The first School Board for London, appalled by the shortage of places revealed by the method of calculation advocated by the Education Department, rather disingenuously invented a new method of their own, thus proving to their immediate satisfaction but subsequent undoing that they had some tens of thousands less places to provide than in fact proved to be the case. For the Education Department's method of calculation unfortunately turned out to be correct.

It should be remembered that despite annual death-rates up to ten times as high as those today (1968) the school population was increasing rapidly between 1870 and 1895 owing to the astonishing birth-rates of the late Victorian era.

By 1895, however, that remarkable piece of national organization to which reference has been made had almost succeeded in providing a school place for every child entitled to one. In the south, the eastern counties,[1] Wales, and the Midlands, this result had been achieved mainly through the energy of the School Boards: in the more individual north and north-west by manufacturers and coal-owners who rated themselves to provide schools rather than submit to rating by a School Board.

It is true that most of the schools were uncomfortably full, owing to the steady rise in the school population, and that the floor area allowed per child was still less than a square yard. This meagre allowance led to special difficulties where the rooms were small, for as an Inspector once remarked, 'Unfortunately the size of the teacher does not vary with the size of her class.' One hopes that the aphorism was intentional, but candour compels one to admit that he was probably thinking of the

---

[1] It should, however, be recalled that owing to the disasters to British agriculture so clearly described by Mr R. C. K. Ensor in his *Oxford History of England 1870–1914* (pp. 115–18) nearly a million agricultural labourers emigrated in the 1880s, the greater number from the eastern counties.

space occupied by the teacher's desk, blackboard, etc. Moreover the abolition of fees, the increasing appreciation of education by the parents, and the greater attractiveness of the teaching which became possible under the Codes of 1891 and 1895 were continually adding to the pressure by bringing children into school earlier and inclining them to stay longer. In the new 'dormitory' areas such as West Ham and in the rapidly growing Welsh coalfields school supply still struggled to catch up with the demand.

Passing, too, were the difficulties, which must have seemed almost insuperable ten years earlier, of securing regular attendance or even any attendance at all. Here again the removal of fees had helped, the attendance leaping by 7 per cent to 10 per cent at once in certain areas and prosecution becoming easier.[1]

The law was still very weak, the magistrates hostile, vacillating or tender-hearted. One might still read of parents convicted for the twentieth, thirtieth, fortieth, and even the sixty-first time and of admission being sought by large numbers of children between 6 and 10 who had never attended school before. Facts such as these seem shocking enough today, but it should not be forgotten that wages were often extremely low and that no system of unemployment insurance stood between the worker and the selling up of his home. The following letter is typical of thousands which used to reach the Education Department and the offices of the School Boards from parents who were able to express their feelings on paper.

I now write a few lines to you to ask you if my daughters can leave school because we cannot finde them in clothes and food and keep a home for them any longer without there help there Father his 60 years of age and he goes 4 miles every morning and four miles back that makes 8 miles a day and then if it is fine all the week so he can work on the farm he gets 14s. but if it his wet he cannot work on the farm he his paid for the days he does work so his earning never amounts to more than 10s. a week and very often under 10s. in the winter months so what can we do if there should be any illness not a farthing to help ourselves with . . . 4s. rent for the house 4 children to keep in food and clothes to provide for in illness fireing and everything it really cannot be it his impossible . . . no wonder the farmers do not prosper when they oppress the labourers has they do and this cruel cruel law of a school board it his too bad we cannot cannot do it because the climate his not warme enuff for them to go without clothes.

On the other hand experience was proving two things: first, that where it was distinctly understood that the law would be enforced the difficulty was not insuperable; second, that the influence of a good teacher and of an attractive school was the best attendance officer. The civilizing influence of the schools, too, had played its part. One reads

[1] R.E.D., 1894, p. 31.

less of the spirit of open defiance by parents, which appears in such a lurid light in the evidence tendered to the Cross Commission by the superintendents of school visitors eight years previously.[1]

The country districts were as usual behind the towns. Potato picking in the autumn, turnip singling and potato dropping in spring, pea picking and the hay harvest in early summer gave far too many farmer members of School Boards a direct interest in irregularity of attendance, and supplied far too many parents with the wherewithal to pay any small fine which might be imposed. Epidemics, too, tended to neutralize the efforts of the school attendance staff. Measles, whooping cough, and scarlatina, spread by nature's provision for the cleaning of slates (spit and coat-sleeve!), were regarded and treated as trifles. Correspondingly they took a far heavier toll of a school population, the vitality of which was generally lower—largely owing to the absence of licensing hours—than in later generations brought up in the principles of healthy living. Thus the predictions of those doctors who had opposed Mr Forster's Education Act of 1870 on the ground that universal popular education would be the means of spreading every kind of infectious disease were to some extent justified. For another decade had to pass before the school medical service was born.

Where a real drive to secure a high average attendance was made —by school banners, prizes, medals, etc.—astonishing results could be achieved. Those who point to such results today, however, should be on their guard in comparing them with present-day figures. No one today would tolerate the idea of really ill children being carried to school in blankets in order that they might earn their medal.

In one respect at least the public system of education had by 1895 taken a marked turn for the better. Since the Elementary Education (School Attendance) Act of 1893, which had raised the school age for both total and partial exemption from 10 to 11, the numbers of half-time scholars had fallen by 20,000 a year.

The system was still widespread in Lancashire where despite death-rates in the first year of life amounting to 250 per 1000 (and 40 deaths in every 100 of all ages being those of children under five in some towns) children were still plentiful but unprized. Yorkshire, Cheshire, and, in a much smaller degree, Staffordshire and Leicester contributed the balance of the 125,000 half-timers. It was argued by the mill-owners that the supple young fingers of children made them specially valuable as 'doffers' and 'piecers'; and by the parents that they could not afford to go without their contribution to the family income. For the morning 'turn' from 6 a.m. to 12.30 p.m. on six days a week they would receive 2s. to 3s. 3d. per week (39 hours); for the afternoon turn from 1.15

[1] See particularly the evidence of Mr Williams, superintendent of school visitors for Lambeth.

p.m. to 5.45 p.m. (27 hours) the wage was 1s. or 1s. 6d. to 2s. 6d. a week. Even multiplying these rates by seven to give 1968 values, one stands amazed at the number of people who still refer to the good old times. As one Inspector put it, 'The most inflexible Draco amongst us would hesitate to punish a poor woman who keeps a child at home occasionally "to mind the baby or look after the home while she is at work".' The observation of one of his colleagues that 'Domestic half-time is much worse than the factory and "necessary and beneficial" employment is construed with great laxity'[1] should render the modern generation of teachers and educational administrators thankful that the Education Act of 1936 which sought to reintroduce these pernicious principles was nipped in the bud by the events of September 1939.

It remains to be added that a great many minor improvements had been effected in the premises of schools since the issue in 1892–3 of the Education Department's first 'Black List' (Circular 321). The willingness with which H.M.I.s' criticisms had been met by managers had been a welcome sign of the times, for as one Inspector remarked, 'This great work affords an exemplary instance of true public spirit. The man hardly builds to fame who adds a cloakroom to a school; he merely benefits his neighbour in an effective and unobtrusive way.'

It is necessary, however, to add that the Inspector of those days was not inhibited, as in later times, by an undue fear of restraint from Whitehall. He knew what he wanted and how to secure it. One recalls such gems from the past as 'The premises of this school consist of a third-class station waiting room and a jam cupboard'; or the sting in the tail of the report of another Inspector who discovered a class of scantily draped ladies pirouetting to music in the central hall of a Nottinghamshire School, the surrounding mezzanine windows of which were lined with collier faces whose owners should have been attending evening classes in the building. 'The limbs did not justify their display.' One courageous individual chanced to visit the school owned by Mr Gladstone at Hawarden at the time when special trains used to be run from the northern towns and halted at the station to allow their passengers a sight of the G.O.M. chopping wood. Finding that the school still had a stone floor, he commented severely upon the fact in his report, adding, 'It is not as though it is not common knowledge that plenty of wood is cut on this estate.' Tradition has it that the G.O.M. demanded his dismissal in a missive in his own hand on the paper of 10 Downing Street; that the Inspector concerned, secure in his knowledge that he held his appointment from the Queen and not from the political state, minuted on the letter 'Another example of backstairs influence'. He was hastily transferred to another district!

The officials of the Education Department, too, could on occasions

[1] *R.E.D.*, 1895, pp. 95 and 13.

exercise a freedom unheard of today. On one occasion when the correspondent of a school had written protesting his complete inability to comprehend their lordships' letter, the reply began: 'Their Lordships note the Correspondent's statement that he is completely unable to understand their Lordships' point of view. That, if they may say so, does not appear to their Lordships to be a matter which calls for any observations on their part.' It is, of course, possible that such a *jeu d'esprit* as this would become memorable essentially because the minutiae and routine of life in a government office in those days was in general so compassed about by formalities. For example formality decreed that every letter which issued from the Education Department of the Privy Council should begin 'I have laid your letter before their Lordships who direct me to say'. If, however, the writer was a member of the Upper House the formula ran 'I made haste to lay your Lordship's letter before their Lordships who desire me to reply'. A distinguished member of the administrative staff still recalled on his retirement in the 1920s how on his first day in the office he was given a file to read about the death of a schoolboy from a cuff on the head by a teacher and asked to recommend suitable action, which he did at some length. 'Quite wrong,' said his official superior, 'our first action must be to inquire whether a punishment book is kept at this school.'

To trace through the Codes of the Education Department the development of the curriculum of the public elementary schools would require a separate volume. The background formed hitherto by the 'payment by results' system has been described. Since this is a study rather of the expansion of the public system and of the various elements which contributed to that expansion, it only remains to point to a few of the newer tendencies observable as the century drew to a close, and to utter a caution against the acceptance of the statistics of particular forms of instruction as representing their modern equivalents.

For example, to read that cookery instruction had spread to nearly one department in ten is to conjure up a vision of the 122,000 girls, who earned the 4s. grant,[1] at work in caps and aprons in centres or travelling vans of the type so well known in later years, and engaged under trained cookery teachers on a graduated course of two or three years' duration.

The real picture is very different. At one extreme the inquirer would find a slovenly classroom, as often as not unswept, filled with

---

[1] This grant was not available to all schools. Mr Chuter Ede, who played such an important part when Parliamentary Secretary of the Board of Education in securing the passage of the Education Act 1944, has recalled how he attended cookery classes from his higher grade elementary school in order that his sister, who was not allowed to attend (because her school was not higher grade), might benefit from the notes he took!

the fumes of uncovered gas rings. Disposed about the various desks he would discover groups of girls, from four to six in number, under their ordinary class teachers, interfering with each other's efforts to make beef tea, rock cakes, and pancakes, or to re-cook cold meat cooked by the previous class. At the other extreme he would encounter large classes of girls drafted to cookery centres fitted with elaborate stoves and appliances of a type which they could never hope to see in their own humble homes, and by sheer weight of numbers compelling their harassed teachers to set them to endless rubbing of flour through sieves and the picking of every single stalk from every single currant. That there cannot have been very many centres of the latter type may, however, be inferred from the opinion expressed by one Inspector that £12 to £15 should be an ample allowance to provide the whole equipment required for cookery classes.

In one case an Inspector reported (1896) to their lordships in some perplexity that 'owing to all the Managers of the School being strict Vegetarians no meat dishes were allowed to be taught in the school. The children were only being taught to make pastry and cakes and such light and fancy foods.' The managers retorted with some heat that 'our syllabus shows bread, Yorkshire Pudding, Savoury Omelettes (not the French one but a real substantial dish). Further we urge that it is an article of religion in the Church to which these Schools belong to abstain from fish flesh or fowl and consequently it is a matter of conscience with us that we could not possibly surrender.'

On the other hand, however makeshift appliances and methods might be, encouraging signs were not wanting. First there was observable an awakening interest in the principle of 'learning by doing', an importation from German experience. Centres for woodwork and metalwork were springing up in London. The first had been started by the schoolkeeper, an ex-carpenter, at Beethoven Street School in 1885. The auditor surcharged the expenditure, but the City and Guilds paid for the class until it could legally be provided. Earlier centres had been started in Manchester and elsewhere. The first class ever started was in a non-provided school, which was struck off the roll by the Education Department for its audacity. Clay modelling, brushwork, paper folding, cutting, and pasting were making their appearance, and if their evident popularity with the children was making some schools even more uncomfortably full than before, it was also contributing to the lengthening of school life—or at least checking the tendency so noticeable eight years before for school life to shorten. Of even greater importance perhaps was the fact that the rapid spread of 'night schools' was teaching the staff the value of preparing syllabuses and that they were carrying this experience into the day schools.

Drawing, which at the time of the Cross Commission, seven years earlier, had hardly been taught at all[1]—although already well taught on the Continent—was becoming more general. Unfortunately, however, the inquirer who is not content to be impressed by mere figures will find that it amounted to little more for Standards I and II than the ruling of interminable squares with their diagonals at the top of the slate and the laborious copying of the resultant figure in freehand below. Rectangular models, prisms, and cones, with paper on which to draw them, as yet only made their appearance in Standards III to VII.

A new spirit was abroad, too, in the world of physical training. It is true that military drill, first recognized by the Code of 1871, still held sway in 1343 schools. It was a convenient method of managing masses of children in a small compass in those thousands of schools, for example, which possessed no playground. It might even show sporadic signs of new vitality around the military and naval centres, or under the stimulus of an active school manager retired from one of the services. 'At Torquay an enthusiastic school manager has provided the school with 100 dummy rifles, 100 solid leather belts with bayonets and leather sheaths complete; as preliminaries, however, only to a more real gun drill with actual carbines procured from the Horse Guards for the elder boys.'[2] But its death-knell had in reality been sounded by the work of such pioneers as Madame Bergman Osterberg, who, as organizing teacher in London, had imported the Swedish system and demonstrated its advantages in substituting harmonious development of every muscle at once for the biceps over-developed by dumb-bells and the 'pouter pigeon' chest, which contributed to the heavy mortality from pneumonia among the gallant sergeants of those days. In 1894 schools had been notified that the higher grant for discipline would not be paid after 31 August 1895 to a school not providing for the teaching of the Swedish system. Although we read that 'teachers are easily fluttered and the new requirements have somewhat alarmed many of them', we are reassured by the statement that 'the more thoughtful have already considered matters attentively and are beginning to see their way'.[3] Thus after the Boer War the army awoke to find that many of its potential recruits had been trained (where school playgrounds had been large enough to allow of more than 'wrist and arm' drill[4]) in a new system—the importation of a very remarkable woman.

The ground had been cut from under their feet, and a syllabus in the preparation of which the War Office had been too obviously interested was in 1901 subjected to severe parliamentary criticism. The Swedish

---

[1] *C.C.R.*, Sir Philip Magnus' evidence.
[2] *R.E.D.*, 1894, p. 15.
[3] *R.E.D.*, 1894, p. 11.
[4] Within a mile radius of Charing Cross there were 30,000 children in schools without a square yard of playground.

system was adopted willy-nilly and the millions of 1914–18 were spared both dumb-bells and pneumonia.

'Reading' appears to have varied greatly from school to school. In the country districts the mumbled monotone, which would change electrically to a shrill sing-song on the teacher's exhortation to 'shout it out', was dying hard. The child who ever opened a book at home shone at H.M.I.s' visits like a good deed in a naughty world.

In the town schools, on the other hand, as evidence that a new spirit was abroad, we find H.M.I.s stressing the fact that children, 'not necessarily the better for being good writers, cipherers, grammarians, or embryo scientific scholars', 'save for habits of attention and industry which mastery of any useful branch of knowledge implies', could be trained morally by the influence of good reading lessons blended with poetry and history. The great difficulty then, and indeed for many years later, was the absence of good reading matter specially designed for school use. As late as 1911 a team of L.C.C. Inspectors of schools, after visiting a large number of the poorest schools in London, reported: 'We consider that there is need for a simpler type of book than is often found. Many of the standard authors are quite outside the range of the poor child both as regards difficulty of the language and the ideas contained in them. We think it unwise, for example, to put such books as "The Mill on the Floss", "Esmond" and "The Talisman" into the hands of these children for class reading. Poems like "Comus" and "Samson Agonistes" which we found in a very poor girls' school are clearly unsuitable. Some teachers, recognizing the poverty of the children's vocabulary, have sought to increase their stock of words by giving more time to formal exercises in word building and by teaching Latin and Greek roots. We cannot report that these methods were in any way successful.' No good child's history of England as yet existed, but magazines and newspapers were beginning to make their appearance in the schools. A few schools too had libraries ranging from 60 to 1,000 volumes. At the same time the idea that older children might sometimes profitably be allowed to learn for themselves from a textbook was still regarded as somewhat revolutionary, and individual notebooks for science lessons had so far only made their appearance in Sheffield.

This is perhaps not so surprising as it may seem, for elementary science as a school subject was as yet in its infancy. As noted earlier, it traces its origin to the 'object lesson'. These object lessons were strongly advocated by their lordships, and from 1895 onwards a miscellany of objects of truly alarming variety began to find their way into the schools' museum cupboards. In the case of urban schools or the remoter rural schools a bird's nest full of assorted eggs was usually the *pièce de résistance*, but stuffed dogs and even alligators were not unknown. It is perhaps difficult for the science teacher of today surrounded by the electrical apparatus made in the boys' department, or the charts and specimens prepared by the girls' department to illustrate the life cycle of the frog or genetic experiments with rabbits, to restrain a smile at these quaint beginnings. Probably, however, few developments in education during the last decade of the nineteenth century exercised a greater influence in changing the attitude of children to their work. The interest excited might, in fact, prove quite embarrassing, as the following extract from a report upon a school by H.M.I. in 1906 clearly shows. 'The premises have a very neglected appearance. The offices are inadequate and dirty. A dead stoat and other litter was in the boys' offices and had apparently been there for some time.'

These strictures elicited the following spirited reply: 'The mistress, following the directions and suggestions of the officials of the Board of Education, collects specimens of natural objects and encourages the children to collect them themselves. Thus the stoat came. After being used for the purpose of teaching it was buried, but the boys further interested themselves after school hours and dug it up more than once. The dirt and litter referred to consisted of the substances which had become associated with the stoat in the course of re-interments and re-exhumations. There was no order from the Home Office for these proceedings, but boys will be boys and curiosity when excited often leads to a desire for further examination.'

Buildings and furniture which had been acceptable when education was optional were beginning to be called in question now that it had been compulsory for fifteen years. The cheerful atmosphere of so many modern classrooms with their bright pictures was, it is true, a thing of the future, but such amenities as cloakrooms were appearing in country schools, where coats had hitherto been hung in the crowded school-rooms or thrown promiscuously into baskets. The blackboard was replacing the reading cards or letter sheets hitherto almost universal. For the era of 'chalk and talk' had to intervene before the era of text-books. Wall maps were becoming more plentiful, although we read of a pupil teacher who was found industriously illustrating a reading lesson on the geography of the British Isles from a wall map of Africa! Dual desks—frequently made to do service for three children—were replac-ing the backless forms in London. They seem in the opinion of some Inspectors to have been replacing them almost wantonly at times, for we read that 'the tendency is very strong to resolve all school buildings into nests of classrooms all furnished with desks. A babies' room with 35 little dual desks covering all the floor may be looked on as the *reductio ad absurdum* of this system.' Another Inspector was, however, less critical, for he had made the discovery that these nests of classrooms actually permitted 'silent' lessons to proceed at the same time as 'noisy' lessons. Moreover, the dual desks for infants' rooms led eventually to an appreciation of the advantages of a level floor. In other schools the high galleries, often thrown together by the village carpenter, continued for many years to confine the infants to their weary seats. Free activity was almost unheard of for the simple reason that it was not usually feasible. It is recorded as a phenomenon that one school in the country was so much in advance of its time (Huddersfield Higher Grade Boys) that it was lit by incandescent electric lamps, but Huddersfield of course had a reputation for enlightenment to keep up, for had it not been the first town to run electric trams in 1884?

Out-of-school activities and corporate life still lay largely in the future, except in London where pioneers among the teaching staff had already begun to organize cricket and football clubs. Swimming, too, was beginning to be taught—rarely to girls—although the general inability to swim even among boys who lived in the seaside towns was a matter of frequent comment. One enterprising school had already built its own bath in the playground. That this too was a phenomenon is illustrated by the comment passed by another Inspector on the contention of well-meaning reformers like Margaret McMillan (who had persuaded Bradford to give a lead in this direction) that a bath ought to be provided at every school and children should compulsorily be made to wash at least once a week: 'How School Boards and voluntary school managers would receive the suggestion we may leave to the imagination!' Finally school savings banks were springing up like mushrooms since the abolition of fees, a development which was to exercise a remarkable influence on the saving habits of the people in time to come.

To anyone who knows our schools today, and even to those who knew them in the late thirties when some nineteenth-century features had still not been erased, the picture presented so far must seem a dark one: a picture of ragged bodies matched by ragged minds, of frail forms sustained by slender resources, of unshod feet little prepared at 11 for the roughness of life's highway. Yet in reading the general reports of Inspectors for these years two encouraging features stand out clearly: the tendency of the infant schools to become the most distinctive contribution to educational science which this country had yet made, and the renaissance of the evening continuation schools.

In a sense both owed this distinction to the same circumstance. The infant schools had never known the full rigours of the 'payment by results' system, the evening continuation schools had been released from those rigours in 1893. Indeed it seems likely that the expansion which followed this release had much to do with the framing of the new conditions for day schools in the Code of 1895.

Inspector after Inspector bears witness to the contrast which the infant schools presented to many of those for older scholars.[1] Here the cynic might observe that the Inspector must have approached the infant school with the pleasurable anticipation of a morning's 'inspection' rather than a morning's 'examination'. That this would be unjust seems to be borne out by the weight of evidence as to improvements in methods. 'Revolution is the only word which will convey to the mind the contrast between what I found 25 years ago and what obtains at the present moment. Instead of being huddled together on low forms in a corner of the principal, or rather the only, schoolroom, the infants have now almost everywhere a classroom of their own.' 'All the good teachers have more or less adopted the Kindergarten method.' 'There is a visible and decided advance in the teaching and bad styles are disappearing, such as counting on the fingers and unnatural sing-song. The old-time formal methods, abstract and verbal, have been discarded and superseded by the real, practical, vivid, and concrete.'

The girl pupil teachers must have been more at home among the infants too, for their youth would supply that need for cheerfulness, brightness, and a constant supply of animal spirits which so readily replaces the infection of dullness by the contagion of brightness. 'Even Thule is gained at last', writes an Inspector. 'The high tide of infant instruction is gradually reaching even the remoter classes in country schools.' With their musical drills, hand occupations, kindergarten work, games, and fairy, maypole and other dances the infant schools seem to have impressed the preponderantly male inspectorate of those days as 'almost as good as any imperfect human institution can be'.

It remains to be added that (as graphs A (p. 32), B (p. 33) and C (p. 34) show) the number of infants of four, three and even two years of age attending the schools of 1895 was many times as great as today, a testimony to the improvement in working-class homes during the intervening years.

The evening continuation schools were in like case.[2] The substitution of inspection for examination, by the Evening School Code of 1893, and the action taken by the Technical Education Committees of the county councils (established under the Technical Instruction Act of 1889) to encourage the formation of classes and guarantee them financial support out of the 'Whiskey Money' (see p. 40) had already begun to exercise a remarkable effect upon the attendance, which was to multiply sixfold between 1892 and 1900. By 1895 the numbers of scholars on the registers had risen to the respectable total of 270,285, taking Inspectors by surprise and causing more than one of them to wonder whether the new popularity 'of the night school' was more than a 'flash in the pan'.

[1] R.E.D., 1894, pp. 7, 10, 60; 1895, p. 48.
[2] R.E.D., 1894, pp. 43, 57; 1895, pp. 108, 137, and 138.

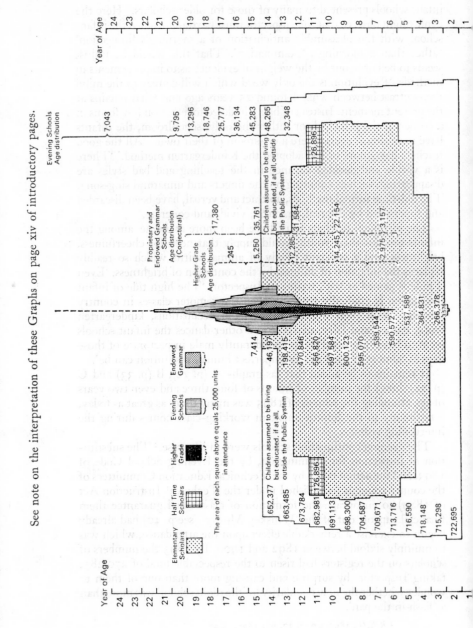

Graph A (1895)

See note on the interpretation of these Graphs on page xiv of introductory pages.

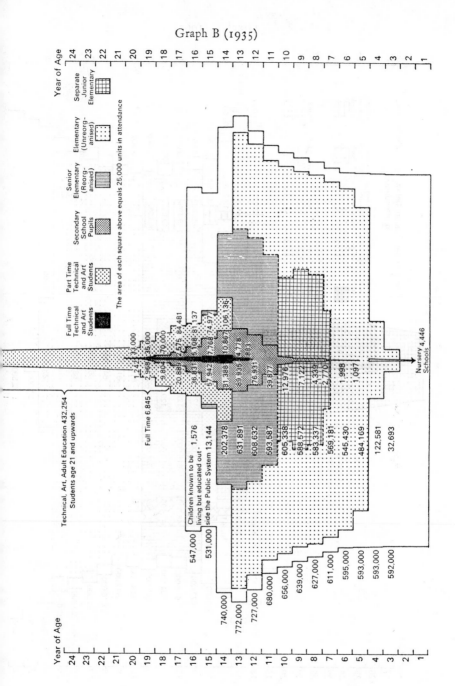

Graph B (1935)

Graph C (1965)

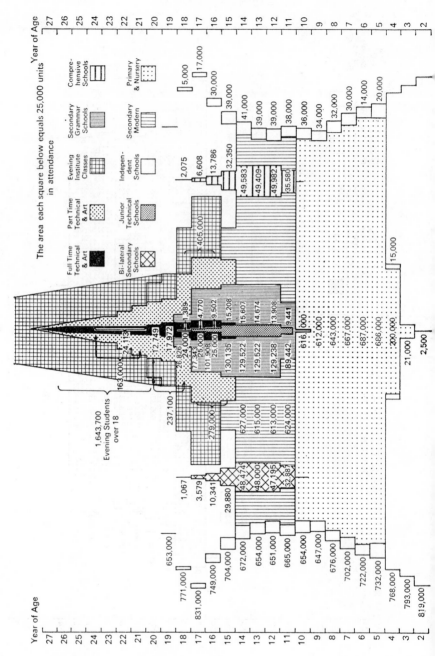

The area each square below equals 25,000 units in attendance

Year of Age

| Comprehensive Schools | Secondary Grammar Schools | Evening Institute Classes | Part Time Technical & Art | Full Time Technical & Art |
| Primary & Nursery | Secondary Modern | Independent Schools | Junior Technical Schools | Bi-lateral Secondary Schools |

1,643,700 Evening Students over 18

The truth was, as some of the more intelligent Inspectors were quick to appreciate, that (as in the case of Italy in the 1960s) a very large body of men and women had experienced in their own minds the fugitive qualities of the instruction they had received in the day schools. But they were sensitive, afraid of their own voices, afraid in particular of displaying their ignorance in public. The annual examination before 1893 had called those who braved the night schools sharply to account for their work, and had stood them up to be made ridiculous in the sight of their neighbours. This annual examination once removed, they flooded into the evening continuation schools. Moreover, what many of the schools lost, in the sense that they ceased to be properly continuative of the work of the day schools, they gained by the accession of older men and women who came meaning business and prepared to suppress the sportive tendencies of their more youthful companions, 'to demand wholesome and nutritious food in place of the confectionery plum'. 'It is a well-known fact,' wrote one such student, 'that if a boy leave school, and in the course of about two years he be asked a few questions, it is surprising what he has forgot' . . . 'a few nights at the evening school, however, and it soon comes back.'

Thus, as is to be expected, the elementary subjects, reading, writing, and arithmetic, attracted the largest numbers, followed by geography (32,469), needlework (29,290), shorthand (26,222), vocal music (20,087), and mensuration (18,648), then *longo intervallo* by domestic economy, 'the life and duties of a citizen' (politically suspect though it was in certain areas), French, German, 'the science of common things', English, elementary physics and chemistry, human physiology, chemistry, algebra, agriculture, magnetism and electricity, and elementary physiography.

Sometimes grandfather and grandson would be found side by side. More frequently the father or mother would appreciate their own deficiencies from observation of the progress of their own children at school.

'At a night school for adults a middle-aged man was found struggling manfully with a sum in compound long division. The pounds he could divide, but the treatment of the "remainder" was a mystery that defied solution. The Inspector tried to explain the puzzle, eventually with some success; and then the man opened his heart—"I have a boy", he said, "in the 5th Standard, and he can do all these things, and he thinks I can, but I can't, and I shouldn't like him to know it".'

Thus although the same difficulties existed which still existed up to the Second World War—the long hours in shops, overtime at Christmas, the attractions of the streets and music halls to those newly emancipated from the standards, the tendency for numbers to fall off in the spring, the deterrent of fees (usually 3*d.* paid three-monthly in advance)—the evening schools were at last alive. Moreover, in those days they did not have to contend with such home attractions as wireless and television programmes. The teachers rose to meet the needs of the new type of student admirably. They were 'free and easy', no standing on dignity, no tripping up of blunderers. Attention and courtesy were given to any question or remark made, however inconvenient. 'A rural policeman complained that his occupation was almost gone since the night school opened.' 'I believe parents and farmers would prefer compulsion by night to compulsion by day,' one Inspector records.

Our stocktaking so far as elementary education is concerned would still be incomplete without some brief reference to the lot of the blind, deaf, and the physically and mentally defective.

That humanitarian determination to afford help to those least able to help themselves which has built up the English educational system from the bottom—thus avoiding so many social pitfalls—had already achieved something for the blind and deaf. The elementary Education (Blind and Deaf Children) Act of 1893 had enabled those special schools which had been established for the blind and deaf to escape from confinement by the strait-waistcoat of the Elementary Code. The application of the Code had sometimes led to ridiculous results in their case, for it had prevented the school earning any substantial grant for no other reason than that the blind scholars could not do what sighted children could. New schools, mainly residential in the case of blind scholars, were being provided, and the number certified by the Department had risen from 78 in 1894 to 87 in 1895, with accommodation for 1,460 blind children and nearly 3,000 deaf. Nevertheless the cold shadow of charity still hung over too many of these schools. Stone floors, inadequate equipment, and absence of toys and games too often rendered barren indeed that part of the day which was not filled with 'healthy work and recreation'. The dietary, too, if plentiful, was often unimaginative, a conspicuous defect being the complete absence of green vegetables.

A tendency was, however, observable among parents of blind children to send them to school earlier. The Act of 1893 had wisely recognized the need for two further years' education to the age of 16 to compensate these children for their defects. They had need of all the help the schools could give them, for the earnings of a capable blind worker were not as yet supplanted by the local authority, and in those days were not more than 2s. a day for a man and 1s. a day for a woman.

In the deaf schools instruction usually proceeded for the first year or two by 'silent' methods, and oral instruction through lip-reading gradually supervened.

The case of the mentally defective was hard indeed. Apparently only

London and Leicester were making any attempt to discover them and segregate them in special classes. In the rest of the country they generally remained in the lower standards and hindered the work of the other scholars, adding considerably to the burdens of the pupil teachers. Sometimes, no doubt, school attendance officers were advised not to be too zealous in discovering them.

If the home was respectable they might be 'treated as a disgrace or encumbrance to the family and be hidden away, in some obscure corner, not allowed to play, and in one case, which was brought to an Inspector's notice, "forbidden even to walk" '.

If the home cared even less for them they often drifted into the hands of the guardians. The extreme number in England and Wales stated to show signs of mental weakness was thought at the time to be 80,000, and this may go some way to explain, though it cannot palliate, the remarkable gap between the total number of children of each age-group known to exist and the number known to be attending school.

Of the physically defective no record appears at all. It is to be presumed that those who could hobble to school, on crutches or otherwise, did so and that the rest spent their schooldays either at home or in hospital.

What, one may well ask, was the total educational result of the public provision for elementary education as disclosed by this stock-taking?

If the picture I have attempted to draw is a fair one it will be realized that, despite much roughness among 'the great horde of street loafers who infest every large town',[1] the majority of the children left school disciplined and well grounded in reading, writing, and arithmetic. But they left far too young; just at a time, in fact, when what they had learnt was most easily lost and ought to have been carried on and made a part of them; just at a time when proper religious and moral training might have done the most for them in the formation of habits and character; just at a time when they could not be expected to follow up what they had learnt by a profitable use of their leisure and the intelligent reading of good books. It will be realized, too, that in far too many cases their physique had been impaired by preventable illness, and that if they had the misfortune to be crippled or mentally defective life could not hold much in store for them.

At the same time the importance of affording their children a longer school life was being brought home to a few at least of the parents, whose self-appreciated deficiencies were sending them back in increasing numbers to the evening schools. Half-time was decreasing, the

---

[1] This, it must regretfully be noted, embraced the unemployed—whose lot was in those days seldom a matter which called forth sympathy. See Halvéy, *History of the English People, 1895–1905*, particularly pp. 367–8.

number and variety of subjects taught increasing. Both teaching methods and the more glaringly insanitary schools were being improved; and equipment was becoming a little more plentiful.

The real task of the time was the twofold one of prolonging school life and linking elementary education with secondary education, and the training of the teachers with the universities.

In London and the great cities Manchester, Birmingham, Sheffield, and Leeds, the initial difficulties created by the conscription of 1876 had been overcome with greater success than in the smaller towns and in the country districts.

I can hardly conclude [wrote Mr Sharpe, Senior Chief Inspector, referring to London in 1895] without testifying to the immeasurable benefit which the School Board has conferred upon the East End of London. Clergymen have told me that they hardly knew their own parishes, so great has been the change for the better. The Board has covered the ground with schools and the schools are filled with children. This however is but the first step. The schools are all on a level each competing against the others. We may look forward to a time, may it not be far distant, when the Board will organize their great aggregation of schools, grading them according to the different needs of the people and bringing them into connection with the higher schools so as to form the whole into one system capable of giving suitable education to every class of the vast population of London.

Of one thing I am quite sure, that so far as their teaching goes it is thoroughly intelligent and practical, but it rests with the generation of 10 or 15 years hence to pronounce how far it has been successful in training English men and women for their lives' work.

One wonders if he lived to see the triumphant vindication of his London elementary schools by the London battalions in the withering machine-gun fire at Gommecourt, in the desperate resistance at Cambrai and Gavrelle, on the sun-scorched plain at Gaza and in the mud of Glencorse Wood.

CHAPTER III

THE PLIGHT OF SECONDARY EDUCATION IN 1895

Absence of data to determine number of schools and scholars of secondary type.—The ancient grammar schools jeopardized by the revival of the public schools.—'Whiskey Money' to the rescue.—Numbers in attendance in 1895 probably about 75,000.—Parental indifference towards secondary education.—The upthrust of the older age groups in the elementary schools leads to formation of higher grade schools.—Summing up.

To the modern investigator of the educational system as it existed at the close of the nineteenth century no feature presents more baffling problems than the extent of the provision for education above the elementary stage. Despite the nine volumes of the Report of the Royal Commission on Secondary Education and the annual output of the Charity Commission, the Science and Art Department and the Education Department, the figures either do not exist at all or have to be extracted from lists of schools running into many hundreds of pages. Moreover, no attempt ever appears to have been made either in the Board of Education or elsewhere to clarify the position. The only existing evidence of such an attempt is contained in a chapter[1] in the Board's annual report for 1911–12. This hazards a guess that there were probably about 800 schools, endowed and proprietary, which ultimately became recognized secondary schools.

It only remains therefore to set out the evidence available and to draw from it such conjectural inferences as are possible.

Outside and remote from any contact with the rising public system of education stood the so-called public schools, then, as now, mainly attended by boarders whose parents could afford to pay a substantial fee. They had been saved and made respectable earlier in the century by a galaxy of strong headmasters and rendered accessible by the development of the railways. Their success in attracting the sons of those whose fortunes had been made at a time when England was still 'The Workshop of the World' had ruined some and jeopardized many of the ancient grammar schools, and had called into existence many proprietary schools which sought to imitate their example in the matter of high fees and social exclusiveness. It is impossible to calculate the numbers

[1] § 20, p. 7, and § 24, p. 9.

in attendance, but it seems unlikely that more than 30,000 to 40,000 pupils were receiving within their walls what would today be regarded as a good secondary education. The ancient grammar schools with their endowments totalling nearly three-quarters of a million, and a handful of higher-grade schools to be referred to later, provided what was virtually the sole avenue by which the brilliant child of poor parents might attain higher education.

It appears to be a fairly common supposition among modern students of the history of education that these ancient grammar schools continued to languish, in every stage of financial and educational inefficiency, until they were rescued by the generous subventions made to them by the Local Education Authorities for Higher Education first established by the Education Act of 1902. This view appears to be only partially true. The process of rescue had in fact begun much earlier, with the work of the Endowed Schools Commission whose activities and fate have been briefly mentioned on page 4. It continued with the diversion to some at least of the schools of a substantial amount of the 'Whiskey Money' which became available under the Local Taxation (Customs and Excise) Act of 1890. This windfall amounted to nearly three-quarters of a million pounds annually[1]—or slightly more than the total annual income received by all the schools from their endowments. It was intended originally to compensate publicans whose licences had not been renewed. But Mr (later Lord) Goschen, who from his German associations was a strong believer in technical education, was at the time Chancellor of the Exchequer, and was persuaded, perhaps by Mr (later Sir) H. Llewellyn Smith, to devote it to the promotion of technical education. Thus it came about that, by one of those illogical twists of the late Victorian conscience which sometimes set on foot such remarkable social movements, it was made payable to county borough councils and to the recently formed county councils. In fact—as a witty member of the House remarked—these newly created organs of local government were told 'to distil wisdom out of whiskey, genius out of gin, and capacity for business out of beer'. At the same time one feels that this parliamentary wag missed his full opportunity. For to be comprehensive he ought to have added 'and pensions for Robert Peelers out of rum punch'. Apart from this first charge for policeman's pensions it was earmarked, although with no guarantee of permanence,[2] to be expended on technical education or in relief of the rates. As we have seen, some part of it found its way into the evening continuation schools, which offered perhaps the nearest approach to technical education in most parts of the country in those days. Another part was devoted by parsimonious areas to the relief of the rates, another less legitimately by certain county boroughs

[1] *B.C.R.*, Vol. 1, pp. 442–5.   [2] *B.C.R.*, Vol. 3, 6238.

(whose accounts were not then subject to the scrutiny of the government auditor) to a variety of purposes ranging from the cost of a cricket and football ground to the expenses of a deputation visiting London. Fortunately for the renaissance of secondary education in England—the Welsh Intermediate Education Act of 1889 had already set a similar renaissance on foot in Wales—by far the most substantial part was from an early date given to the local grammar schools. Rarely of course was it given on any considered plan. Sometimes the gift took a non-recurrent form—as for example a contribution to build science laboratories to earn the grants available from South Kensington; sometimes the form of an annual subvention in return for the offer of scholarships.[1] Moreover, the schools which profited varied greatly in standing. Usually they had already established a firm local reputation for sound work, but occasionally they exercised a less legitimate 'pull'[2] through the interest of a local representative on the new county council. In 1895 the counties made such grants to 198 schools containing about 23,000 scholars, and county boroughs to 20 further schools containing about 5400 scholars.[3]

What proportion of the total did these 218 schools represent?

On this point the nine volumes of the Bryce Report preserve a discreet silence. Indeed it must seem almost inconceivable to anyone conversant with the thoroughness of Royal Commissions today that a commission specifically charged 'to consider what are the best methods of establishing a well-organized system of secondary education in England, taking into account existing deficiencies', should not have made it their first object to find out how many schools offering education of secondary type already existed, how they were distributed and what were the numbers in attendance.

The explanation probably lies in a change in the attitude of governments to Royal Commissions. The tendency today is for a Royal Commission appointed by the Government to be regarded as a convenient delaying device. The publicity attendant on its appointment gives the appearance of a keen interest at Downing Street in some national question, but in reality the existence of the commission enables the Government to parry awkward questions until they have dealt with other planks in their platform. The Bryce Commission, on the other hand, appears to have been appointed, by Lord Rosebery's Government on its accession to power, with a view to early action. It originated in a conference held in the Examination Schools at Oxford, and the chairman may have been told privately to report as soon as possible. Cer-

---

[1] B.C.R., Vol. 1, pp. 378–99.   [2] B.C.R., Vol. 3, 6236.

[3] I have arrived at this figure by tracing the number in each school from all the available reports of the Science and Art Department, the Education Department, and the Bryce Committee.

tainly the statistical volume, the ninth produced in less than two years, bears every mark of hurried compilation, and by its inaccuracies, both clerical and mathematical, goes some way to explain the Treasury's greater friendliness towards secondary than towards elementary education. For the Government and local government services of those days must have found it a difficult matter to recruit an adequate supply of efficient clerks. This difficulty was clearly in Lord Lingen's mind when he gave evidence to the Cross Commission some years previously, and it is also mentioned in an early report of the Board of Education (1904, p. 45).

Thus all it is possible to say is that if the average size of the endowed schools in six of the seven counties which the commission found time to investigate was reproduced in the country as a whole, and that if those counties were representative, the number of scholars attending the 621 endowed schools of secondary type shown in the 'Roby' return cannot well have been less than 75,000.[1]

It is true that the commission may have chosen counties for investigation—as they undoubtedly chose Bedfordshire—because they suspected that they were better supplied with endowed schools than other counties. It is true too that their report described the provision for secondary education as unevenly distributed. But since they had apparently neither a map nor figures for thirty-six of the county areas their conclusion on this point is perhaps open to question.

If in fact the attendance by 1895 had reached 75,000 and that at the proprietary schools not conducted for profit 34,000, certain interesting deductions ensue. For, looking back to an estimate of 15,000 compiled twenty-seven years earlier by Matthew Arnold in his report on 'Higher Schools and Colleges in Germany', it becomes clear that the real founders of what an Eton master (Mr C. H. K. Marten) some years ago described in The Times as 'that wonderful system of Secondary Schools now scattered all over the country' were the Endowed Schools Commissioners, Lord Lyttleton, Mr Roby, and Mr Griffith Boscawen.[2] Again, looking forward from 1895, it becomes evident that the growth of our modern system of secondary education does not date from the Act of 1902, although that Act provided the means by which forces already at work could find expression.

Of the thoroughness, or otherwise, of the education provided by the endowed and proprietary schools of those days and of the parental attitude towards secondary education, all that can justly be said is that

---

[1] For the 'Roby' return, see B.C.R., Vol. 9, pp. 7–175.

[2] Mr Roby (well remembered as the author of a Latin grammar) was Secretary to the commission from 1864 to 1868 and a commissioner up to 1874. He subsequently became M.P. for a Manchester division, and was a governor of the Manchester Grammar School and Hulme Grammar School.

both exhibited the widest variations between school and school, district and district, parent and parent.

It should be remembered that the idea of secondary education as a second stage in education following upon a primary stage was at this time virtually unknown in England. The grammar schools were generally regarded as schools which catered for a different social order from that attending the elementary schools, although a few scholars from the elementary schools might, it was thought, profitably spend a couple of years at a grammar school after leaving the elementary school at 13 and before becoming apprenticed.

The established schools such as Manchester and Bradford Grammar Schools were already supplying an education which, if cramped as judged by modern standards, was at least threatening the prerogative of the 'public schools' in the production of sound scholarship, and the capture of the prizes offered by the universities. The tendency to attempt to force all scholars into an antique mould instead of endeavouring to find the mould to fit the individual scholar was of course still strong. But it was giving way gradually under the material inducement of the Science and Art Department grants.

Of some of the smaller and remoter schools perhaps the less said the better. As the Rev. M. G. Glazebrook told the Bryce Commission:[1]

The [Manchester] Grammar School is an efficient first-grade school numbering about 800 boys; the Hulme School is a successful second-grade school on a smaller scale. That would be a poor provision for Manchester and Salford alone with their population of 600,000. But not more than two-thirds of the boys come from Manchester and Salford.

The rest come in by train from Oldham, Bolton, Rochdale and Bury and a score of outlying towns. I have even known boys come daily from Fleetwood (40 miles) and Huddersfield (35 miles). The reason is that in those towns there are no efficient schools. In some like Oldham there has hitherto been no secondary school at all. In others, there are small grammar schools, which produce such miserable results, that all parents who desire solid teaching are obliged to send their boys into Manchester. Out of a population of five or six millions, that is, some 1200 boys are enjoying an efficient secondary education. If that were a district in Germany there would be at least one good school for every 100,000 inhabitants.

Moreover, for every parent who was prepared to send his boy eighty miles daily for secondary education there were no doubt many at the opposite extreme. Their attitude may perhaps best be summed up in the words of the Devonshire farmer reported by the Bryce Commission to have said: 'My boys want to go in for bicycling and athletics and these 'ologies, but I say to them—A man consists of three parts, back, belly, and brains. Now this technical education may work the brains but it won't fill the belly; but if you work the back you can fill the belly and so get on.'

No system of inspection, of course, existed to ensure either that those who benefited by endowments, worth three-quarters of a million, were in any sense capable of profiting by secondary education, or that those who gave it kept up their educational qualifications. It is to be feared that there must have existed many quiet backwaters where the staff would have echoed the retort of an endowed school headmaster to an official of the Charity Commission: 'My dear Sir, ambition and I have long been strangers.'

The tendency, already noted, for children to stay longer at school than the strict letter of the law enjoined was, however, presenting a new problem to the more active School Boards. By 1895 there were nearly half a million children over 12 and 250,000 over 13 in the elementary schools, and obviously the conception of a militia training supplemented by a small professional army in the ancient grammar schools was breaking down. For every year an increasing number of children worked through the seven standards and was found to be capable, where the necessary equipment existed, of earning for the school the grants made available by the Science and Art Department. Now to give such children an adequate training not only special equipment but specially trained staff were desirable. Moreover, the principle of concentration already applied to pupil teachers by certain School Boards, with such gratifying results in the form of Queen's Scholarship Examination successes, had already been well understood for the past ten years.[1] Sir Philip Magnus, an educational reformer forty years ahead of his time, who lived to see many of his dreams realized, had as early as 1887 given the following exposition of a substantial part of what would later be called the 'Hadow' policy: 'Among the advantages of the grading of schools and of the establishment of higher elementary schools may be mentioned the fact that by collecting together the élite from a large number of different schools better instruction can be provided than if the instruction is given to a few pupils in a large number of different schools. I think this is a strong reason for the establishment of higher elementary schools. For in these schools scientific instruction might be given in laboratories provided with suitable appliances, and drawing might be taught in rooms furnished with the necessary models, and handicraft instruction might be given in workshops provided with the requisite tools. Great economy, I believe, would be effected by the collection of the best children from the ordinary elementary schools into graded schools thus furnished.'[2]

The solution to which Sir Philip Magnus pointed, namely, the higher grade, central or higher elementary schools, was in fact widely

[1] *C.C. Final Report*, pp. 90 and 271.   [2] *C.C.R.*, Vol. 2, 28,616.

adopted, and to modern educational thought the rapid growth of these schools in the 1890s, so cruelly cut back by the 'Cockerton' judgement of 1899, must always appear one of the 'might have beens' of English educational history. For had not Sir Robert Morant, in his midnight reading, found just one answer out of 60,000 given to the Cross Commission[1] which threw doubts on their legality, and had he not communicated that doubt to his friend Dr Garnett, the Hadow reorganization might have become possible a decade or more before 1926. Moreover, England might have developed, parallel to the secondary school system, a complete system of schools providing alternative forms of secondary education, of a highly practical type, akin to the German Realschulen and to what were later known as junior technical and commercial schools.

By 1895 the growth of these schools had not, it is true, proceeded very far. A detailed investigation of the 300-page list of schools aided by parliamentary grants discloses no more than 67 schools specifically termed higher grade, containing 24,584 scholars, while the Association of Headmasters of higher grade-schools had as yet under fifty members. Moreover, the term 'higher grade', like the later term 'central', did not mean the same thing from area to area. The majority undoubtedly 'creamed off' those scholars who had passed Standard VII from the whole district, seeking to carry their education beyond the elementary stage and to give them a practical education fitted to their future occupation. But there were others where the permission to continue to charge fees—and higher fees at that because the education cost more—conferred a social rather than an educational *cachet*. Lastly there were so-called higher-grade schools which combined both 'social' and 'selective' features and had in addition a full range of younger children.

Their greatest stronghold was in Lancashire and the north, and the evidence of the Rev. M. G. Glazebrook quoted above no doubt supplies the reason. The Bryce Commission found fourteen higher-grade schools in Lancashire containing 7,664 scholars and twelve in the West Riding containing 8,263 scholars.

A number of the secondary and higher-grade schools were recognized as 'organized science schools'. In theory an organized science school could be a separate entity sustained by the grants paid on results by the Science and Art Department at South Kensington. In fact, in the first ten years after their creation only one school (Nottingham High Pavement) existed. In the next ten years (up to 1895) ninety-two more schools were recognized. Only after 1895, when capitation grants replaced payment by results and modifications[2] were introduced in the 'Directory' to allow schools to be recognized in spite of the taint

[1] Answer, 35,481.   [2] *B.C.R.*, Vol. 2, 1243-96.

of humanism, did the number increase with any rapidity. On the other hand, a number of schools contained separately organized science and art classes, the total, including evening classes, amounting to 3,011.

To sum up. The revival in the numbers attending the endowed schools had evidently proceeded steadily since the Endowed Schools Commission had imparted the first impetus to it. But, apart from those pupils in attendance at certain of the specially favoured schools, usually those in large towns, probably not more than 30,000 out of a total attendance of 75,000 were as yet receiving an education which would be recognized either in point of quality or length of school life as a sound secondary education today. That is, few of the schools were yet able to 'offer to each of their scholars a general education of a wider scope and higher grade than that of an elementary school, given through a complete progressive course of instruction continuing up to and beyond the age of 16', and 'in a group of subjects so selected as to ensure due breadth and solidity in the education given'. The salaries of the staff were lamentably inadequate, even lower than those of favoured elementary school teachers. Finally, many of the grammar schools were beginning to feel the competition of the higher-grade schools with their lower fees and more practical education, a competition which was to reduce seriously the numbers in the London endowed secondary schools before 1902.

CHAPTER IV

THE LAST DAYS OF THE SCHOOL BOARDS

The Education Act of 1902.—Its interest and what it achieved.—Its place in the history of English education.—The part played by Mr Morant.—The chaos in the central control of public education.—Gradual rejection of *laissez-faire* by local government opinion.—The Local Government Act of 1888 completes the system of local government.— Sir Francis Sandford's attempt to bring education into the main stream of local government.—Its failure.—The views of the Bryce Commission.—The unpopularity of the smaller School Boards.—Their parochialism.—The new County councils ready to take charge of all forms of education.—The difficulty, rate aid for the voluntary schools.— The Duke of Devonshire versus Sir John Gorst.—The higher-grade schools a final obstacle.—Their dramatic destruction by the Cockerton judgement.

I T is an axiom of political thought, that, however desirable it may seem to translate the views of the time into an Act of Parliament, it is not sufficient for those views to be felt keenly by a few of the population for all of the time and by a larger proportion for some of the time. If the Act is to be worked it must receive the assent of the majority for all of the time. Public opinion, in fact, may be moulded but it cannot be driven.

Thus to the social historian the real interest of an Act of Parliament is often not so much its precise terms, and the interplay of parliamentary forces by which they were fixed, as, first, the slowly moving currents of public opinion which, converging naturally or by human design, produced it; secondly, the results which flowed from it.

From both these points of view the Education Act of 1902 is one of the most interesting, in the sphere of social legislation, which has ever found its way on to the Statute Book. For, in the first place, although its main outlines had been on paper since 1888, it is at least doubtful whether they could have obtained a sufficient measure of parliamentary assent at any time within the fourteen-year interval, despite Lord Rosebery's anxiety at the time of appointing the Bryce Commission in 1894 to undertake some such comprehensive legislation. Two earlier attempts, that of 1896 to be referred to later and an end of session attempt in 1899, had in fact already failed. The knowledge that the Government could not afford to fail a third time probably had a good deal to do with Mr A. J. Balfour's decision to take charge of the

Bill himself—although he was First Lord of the Treasury and became Prime Minister during its passage. In the second place, even when the Act had reached the Statute Book, after one of the most bitterly contested passages in history, it was in certain respects so far in advance of public opinion that it gave rise to a substantial passive resistance movement involving 70,000 prosecutions for non-payment of rates, and took some years to gain acceptance in Wales.

Lastly, as the first Act to deal with education in England and Wales as an integrated whole, it achieved three remarkable results at once. The first of these results was the extinction of no less than 2,568 School Boards, and the abolition of the direct access to Whitehall, with no intermediary, hitherto enjoyed by 14,238 bodies of voluntary school managers. By the substitution of 328 Local Education Authorities for this multiplicity of small or independent bodies education was for the first time brought into the main stream of central and local finance. Remembering that the School Boards had in most cases enjoyed a clear run of thirty or more years in which to establish vested interests, this achievement would have been sufficiently remarkable standing alone. But it was excelled by the second achievement, the conferring of rate aid upon the hard-pressed voluntary schools which had hitherto subsisted on 'grants, endowments, ping-pong tournaments, whist drives and jumble sales'. This achievement, by securing that the salaries of teachers, whether serving in board or voluntary schools, were all paid from a common initial source—the rates—set in train that movement which ultimately led to the Burnham salary scales. Thirdly, the Act unobtrusively, and probably to the surprise of its authors,[1] launched a great system of higher education, accompanied by an astonishing expansion of the facilities for passage from the elementary grade of education to the secondary.

With the Act of 1899, which established the Board of Education, the Education Act of 1902 remained the bedrock of the educational system of England and Wales until 1944.

To appreciate the genesis of these two Acts and to form some estimate of the forces which might have brought them to shipwreck, it is necessary to go back to the evidence of witnesses before the Cross Commission fifteen years before, and the Bryce Commission seven years before; for anyone familiar with this evidence will be able to detect every point made in the introductory speeches of Mr A. J. Balfour and Sir Robert Finlay (who spoke for the Government in the absence on first reading of Sir John Gorst).

---

[1] See Mr A. J. Balfour's admissions quoted by Halévy in his *History of the English People, 1895–1905*, p. 207. Also footnote on p. 201. An even more interesting clue to Mr Balfour's subsequent concern at the cost of the machine he had set in motion will be found in a speech he delivered on 1 March 1907, *H*, Vol. 107, Col. 428.

Undoubtedly, too, the most interesting way in which to study the Acts is to survey the educational scene, not as described in the last chapter when seen through modern eyes, but as it must have presented itself to an educational administrator lately returned from abroad, namely, Mr (later Sir Robert) Morant. For he it was upon whose broad shoulders largely fell the burden of the initial administrative synthesis; the assessment of the forces at work; the calculation of the probable balance between the general desire of the Liberal opposition for a move forward and their reluctance to pay the Unionist price by bringing the church schools on the rates; and finally the measures necessary to fit together elementary and higher education into an articulated whole. Moreover, as we can now appreciate, he must all the time have had to disguise his fear that if the Bill failed, the forces of tradition and the vested interests of the School Boards would probably combine to prevent its resurrection, and to disguise even more completely (owing to the cost of the South African War[1]) his almost passionate conviction that education in this country could never hope to enjoy the financial resources it would require unless it was brought into the main stream of central and local finance. This realization and the superhuman efforts which he put out in organizing the Board of Education, lobbying in favour of the Bill, and advising Mr Balfour simultaneously, constitute Sir Robert Morant's greatest contribution to English education.

Morant had hitherto imagined that his career lay in the East where, as tutor to the Crown Prince of Siam and later educational adviser to the Court, he had earned the title of 'the uncrowned king of Siam'. He returned to this country in 1894, having as he imagined seen 'the things he gave his life to broken'. How must he have regarded the educational scene? Probably the first thing which would strike him as an administrator would be the muddle at the centre, which was to be dealt with by the creation in 1899 of the Board of Education to co-ordinate and supervise the development of all forms of education.

Mr (later Lord) Goschen, when President of the Local Government Board in the seventies, looking at the local government scene of the day, had told Parliament: 'There is chaos as regards authorities, a chaos as regards rates and a worse chaos than all as regards areas of taxation.'

Something of this chaos still persisted in the multiplicity of authorities which divided among them the control of education in Whitehall.

From the office of the Privy Council in Downing Street the Education Department wove its web of annual Codes for the uniform regulation of the elementary schools, assessing the grant annually on every individual school in the country and endeavouring to correspond directly with the 2,568 School Boards and the correspondents of the 14,238

[1] See particularly Dr B. M. Allen's *Life of Sir Robert Morant*, 1934, p. 168.

schools which were independent of School Board control. That the Department's endeavours to do so expeditiously were not always crowned with success is evident from the complaint made to the Cross Commission by the chairman of the Manchester School Board that they had been waiting ten months for a reply to an important letter!

From Gwydyr House on the opposite side of Whitehall the Charity Commission made new schemes for such of the endowed schools as desired them, priding themselves on their advanced outlook in the matter of making concessions to the upstart claims of science to a place alongside the time-honoured 'classical studies'.

At South Kensington the Science and Art Department—whose grants were also paid on results until 1895, but whose 'Code' was known as the 'Directory'—lost no opportunity to extend its sphere of influence impartially among the higher-grade schools, the secondary schools, and the evening continuation schools. If all was fish which fell into its net, it is to be feared that before 1895 the curriculum of many of the schools which were enmeshed tended to become sadly warped by the undue insistence on a preponderantly scientific training. In that year new rules, requiring a sound course of literary instruction with one modern language, began to adjust the balance between literary and purely scientific instruction.[1]

Finally, yet another of the Whitehall Departments—the Board of Agriculture—made grants to universities and to one county council in aid of agricultural education.

In all, ten members of the Cabinet controlled educational institutions supported out of the rates and taxes.

It is not perhaps fair to suggest that no liaison whatever existed between the three Departments principally concerned, for a joint departmental committee was appointed before the Bryce Commission came into being 'to consider generally the question of a properly organized system of secondary education for England and Wales, and particularly the relation to one another of the three Departments represented on the Committee'. The Bryce Committee's appointment terminated the first but not the second of this committee's terms of reference, and we are told that the committee afforded a valuable organization to avoid contradictory or inconsistent action. On the other hand, the avoidance of contradictory or inconsistent action is a very different thing from the harmonious working of a single great Department of State free from those inter-departmental jealousies which must have complicated the labours of Mr Bryce and his colleagues, and which complicated still more the early days of Sir Robert Morant when he became Permanent Secretary. Members of the staff transferred from the Charity Commission to the Board of Education

[1] *B.C.R.*, Vol. 3, 11,972; Vol. 4, 17,309.

The picture in H.M.I. Dr. Sharp's mind when he wrote 'The schools are filled with children'. School interior, 1894

Infants in a gallery class in 1906

'The real difficulty lay with the rural areas.' A rural school of the 1890s

Penny dinners were organized by the teachers in some of the poorest schools, circa 1880

to deal with secondary schools used to recall the saying in pre-Board of Education days that 'the secondary schools are administered by gentlemen for gentlemen, the elementary schools by men for men, but the technical schools by cads for cads!' The jealousies of the Departments of course obtrude themselves on the notice of anyone who reads between the lines of the witnesses' evidence to the Bryce Commission. The Charity Commission perhaps took a proselytizing interest in the Education Department, but the Science and Art Department as 'poachers' were anathema to both.

In the provinces, on the other hand, the shape of things to come could already be dimly discerned.

Fawcett's *Political Economy*, first published in 1863, was still widely read by those interested in local government—even by Cardinal Archbishops.[1] But it no longer, by its appeal to the good Victorian principles of individualism and 'self-help', ruled administrative thought so exclusively as it had a generation earlier. For the achievements of the Birmingham 'Radical' school of Liberalism were beginning to overshadow those of the Manchester schools. Those Birmingham Liberals who had even dared to say 'Let us acquire the gas undertaking and run it for the benefit of the town' were making men wonder if there might not after all be some fallacy in Fawcett's uncompromising dictum that 'the conclusion above all others which we desire to enforce is that any scheme, however well-intentioned it may be, will indefinitely increase every evil it seeks to alleviate if it lessens individual responsibility by encouraging the people to rely less upon themselves and more upon the State'. The assertion of one M.P. in the First Reading debate on the Bill that 'the tendency and the spirit of the age are in favour of municipal socialism' must of course seem an exaggeration to modern notions. On the other hand the Fabian Society—many of whose leading members Morant would meet at Toynbee Hall—and other thinkers were continually widening the circle of those inclined to inquire whether in fact the best, fairest, and cheapest way to secure the services they wanted was not by co-operation through the rates; nor is it probable that an observer returning from abroad could fail to notice how the whole tendency of the times seemed to be for Parliament to devolve upon the local authorities new schemes for social amelioration calling into existence new rates.[2]

Most important of all, the desire to straighten out the overlapping

[1] See Cardinal Manning, question to Lord Lingen in final volume of evidence to Cross Commission.

[2] Fawcett quotes ten cases: the Burial Board Rate, the Public Library and Museum Rate, the General District Rate, the Sewerage Rate, the Parish Improvement Rate, the Animals' Contagious Diseases Rate, the Borough Lunatic Asylum Rate, the Borough Baths and Washhouses Rate, the Borough Improvement Rate, and the Borough Burial Board Rate.

and financial chaos to which this tendency had given rise had led at last to the completion of the system of local government by the creation of the county councils in 1888. At last a stock had been provided upon which an articulated system of education could be grafted.

Against these imponderable tendencies Mr Morant would no doubt balance others.

If the Local Government Act of 1888 had provided a stock, the first attempt to graft education on to that stock had proved abortive. It had been made by Sir Francis Sandford, a former Secretary to the Education Department, when serving as a member of the Cross Commission. Just before the Local Government Act was published he had presented to the commission a memorandum showing how the county councils, proposed in the new Local Government Bill, could take over the work of the School Boards and assume the responsibility for aiding the voluntary schools.[1]

A study of the text suggests that he had at least shown the draft to Lord Lingen and Mr Patrick Cumin, his predecessor and successor respectively, at the Education Department. Probably the three had worked out the plan together. For Mr Cumin had told the commission that to establish areas wider than those of the rural school boards would present undoubted administrative advantages.

No doubt he was thinking of the county boards recommended by the Newcastle Commission twenty years before and also by the Royal Commission on Technical Education, 1884, who had reported (Vol. I, p. 517): 'It is to be desired that in the proposed reorganization of local government, power should be given to important local bodies like the proposed County Boards and the municipal corporations, to originate and support secondary and technical schools in conformity with the public opinion, for the time being, of their constituents.' County boards, he explained, would get rid of an immense number of elections and perpetual expense—the last School Board elections had cost £50,000. A very superior class of person, including ladies who would not face a School Board election,[2] would be attracted to serve on education committees; jealousies between school and school might be expected to decline; finally, county authorities would have far less difficulty than voluntary managers in raising money for necessary improvements and would be able to employ skilled supervisors of handicraft, cookery, physical training, and needlework.

Lord Lingen's mind too had been shown by his evidence to be moving in the same direction, and Lord Lingen's mind may be taken for all practical purposes to have represented the mind of the Treasury,

[1] *C.C. Final Report*, pp. 204 and 233.

[2] The election of Margaret McMillan to the School Board of Bradford in 1894 had the widest repercussions both locally and nationally.

from the secretaryship of which he had recently retired. It was not of course the case that their lordships' solicitude for elementary education was such that they were anxious to spend more upon it, although the time was one of unparalleled budgetary prosperity.[1] Quite the reverse. Lord Lingen had in fact seen the Education Department as a colander. The more money their lordships poured into it the more holes it found through which to escape and the less could the demand for the next year be calculated. To Lord Lingen devolution to county boards was attractive because it would enable a scheme of block grants to be instituted as a barrier against parliamentary pressure and the importunities and inventiveness of the Education Department. The Treasury policy towards education was at least consistent for the next seventy years, although their experience of block grants under the Local Government Act of 1929—which was followed by such sharp changes in the values of money—may have done something to modify for a time at least their old beliefs.

The majority of the commission—Mr Morant would no doubt observe—had been impressed by the evidence of these two witnesses. But like other commissions after them they had shrunk from the consequences of their own logic. 'We recommend', they had said, 'that the school boards might in time, if not at once, be merged in the local authorities charged with the general civil administration.' 'Sir Francis Sandford has prepared a scheme; without expressing any opinion upon it we think it worthy of consideration.' 'But in the present uncertainty as to the form which county government may hereafter take it would be premature to make any definite recommendations as to the nature and the powers of the local educational authorities which it may be necessary to constitute.'[2]

Those who signed the minority report, on the other hand, angered by the readiness of the majority to contemplate rate aid for the voluntary schools, had been frankly caustic.

Lord Lingen brings the vigilant economy of an ex-Secretary of the Treasury to bear against the tendency to increase the burden on the Exchequer. Mr Cumin brings the grievances of an overworked secretary to the Education Department to bear, from other motives in the same direction, the decentralization of our educational machinery and the throwing [sic] more responsibility and more power on local authorities. ... We are of opinion that the

---

[1] I have used the word 'budgetary' advisedly because although there was usually a substantial annual surplus about this time and our invisible imports in the way of interest on capital invested abroad (producing 100 millions annually) were buoyant, there was a good deal of anxiety about our industries and commercial position vis-à-vis Germany and the U.S.A., whose exports were rising whereas ours were stationary or decreasing. (See Halévy, op. cit. Chapter I.)

[2] C.C. Final Report, pp. 204 and 222.

large changes opened up by the evidence of Lord Lingen and Mr Cumin, of which aid from the rates to denominational teaching forms only a small part, would not be acceptable to the mass of voluntary managers who value highly their present direct relations with the Education Department, and, while we dissent from their views, we think that the consideration of so extensive a revolution must be consequent on any new scheme of local government that may pass into Law.[1]

If the scheme put forward by so able and authoritative a team as Sir Francis Sandford, Lord Lingen, and Mr Cumin had proved stillborn so recently as 1888, were the chances of reviving that scheme any brighter now seven years had passed? On the whole they must certainly have seemed to Mr Morant to be distinctly brighter. For a great deal of water had flowed under Westminster Bridge in the interval.

In the first place the Bryce Commission (1895), with seven years' experience of the working of the Welsh Intermediate Education Act, and the distribution of the 'Whiskey Money' by county councils to guide them, had begun their consideration of the chaos at the centre and the problem in the provinces where the Cross Commission left off. Where the Cross Commissioners had groped in the dark the Bryce Commissioners—as it were—emerged on a fully lighted stage. Where the Cross Commission were divided they were unanimous. 'Some central authority is required, not in order to control, but rather to supervise the Secondary Education of this country': 'it ought to consist of a Department of the Executive Government, presided over by a Minister responsible to Parliament, who would obviously be the same Minister as the one to whom the charge of elementary education is entrusted'. He should be served by 'a permanent secretary with a general oversight of the various branches' 'and qualified Secondary Inspectors'. The Minister should be advised by an Educational Council (Consultative Committee). Further, 'There should be created Local Authorities for Secondary Education in every county and in every county borough; that is to say speaking generally boroughs with a population exceeding 50,000.' Moreover, 'it should be the duty of the Central Office to require from the various local authorities a statement of the provision existing or proposed to be by them created for Secondary Education in their respective areas and to consider these statements for the purpose of ascertaining whether that provision is or will be sufficient in quantity and quality, due regard being had to the character and wants of the population of each area'.

So much for the future organization of secondary education for which Matthew Arnold had pleaded so eloquently and for so many years. He had died before the Bryce Commission reported, but their

[1] *C.C. Final Report*, p. 356.

references to him and quotations from his works show the influence he had exercised upon them.

'But', Mr Morant must have wondered, 'can the School Boards be expected to assent to their extinction, and the handing over of their powers to the county and county borough councils, without a severe struggle? Do the county and county borough councils want those powers? And if so, which can be expected to secure the greater sympathy from Members of Parliament, the sitting tenants or their would-be dispossessors?

On this point he may have felt more at ease. For the smaller School Boards had probably made themselves fairly unpopular; the number of Members of Parliament who regarded 'looking after roads and bridges' as the proper business of the new county councils was decreasing, and the number of county councils which expected to be given the control of all forms of education was increasing; and finally a large number of those who served as members of the better School Boards had also gained seats in their town and county councils.

The unpopularity of many of the smaller School Boards appears to have gone deeper than that normally to be expected by bodies sufficiently small for their members to be known personally to many of those whom they are called upon to regulate. It should, moreover, be remembered that only 1,189 out of the 2,527 had been brought into existence by popular demand. The remaining 1,355 had been formed compulsorily or of necessity to replace closed schools. Moreover, if the enforcement of school attendance had made them unpopular with the rank and file of the parents, they had become unpopular too with the intelligentsia of the day, among whom Mr Morant moved. On this point the contemporary reports of H.M.I.s leave no possible doubt. A single example will suffice:

On the bombardment of the vicar of one of these parishes—by the vicar of the other—who (by help of the village blacksmith's battering ram) smashed through the door of this same school and captured the meeting (going on inside) under the chairmanship of the above-mentioned vicar (the former)— the management has fallen into the hands of a committee. This though not a School Board, too faithfully represents the faults of small rural Boards.

A neighbouring similar Board Chairman asked me if I could find them a mistress over 40 as (he whispered) one of the members of the Board is dead on any woman under 40. This very chairman who signs this letter was dragged drunken out of a public house by women who literally tore out his whiskers so that he was seriously ill for a time. . . . When I had occasion to complain of the schoolmaster's visits to the alehouse, they alleged their incapacity to interfere as they met him there!

To me, it is astonishing that the wider areas so long pronounced advisable by good authorities still lag behind. I wish the heads of the Department could be asked to read this, as it is in their power to shape coming legislation.

Well might Mr Sidney Webb remark that the smaller School Boards had made themselves hated, and even the sober Mr Asquith admit that 'The School Board system has not been a success!'

Mr Forster had indeed proposed in the original draft of his Bill in 1870 to make the electoral body for the school boards the town councils, and in counties the select vestries, or failing that the vestries.

It was perhaps natural that they should have belied their first promise. Men of the stamp of Huxley who were attracted to School Board membership immediately after the Act of 1870 could not perhaps be expected to face for long the turmoil and expense of repeated elections—especially since the expenses of a single election in a large town might amount to as much as £700. All too often the Huxleys were replaced by those who sought election from less disinterested motives; the status it would give them in their local community or the power of patronage. Dark stories began to be told and no doubt exaggerated in the telling; of teachers, for example, who had been given to understand that the reversion of a coveted headship would be brought distinctly nearer by a subscription to a School Board member's organ fund. Thus one witness after another before the Cross Commission expressed dissatisfaction with the increasingly parochial outlook, the lack of education, or the greed for 'cheap labour' of those who had begun to secure election, particularly to the rural boards, after the initial supply of enthusiasts had dropped out.

One reads of the cab stall proprietor whose knowledge of education was nil but who was elected to the local School Board by the cumulative vote of the local cabbies because he sold good coffee; of farmers who put up the fees to children as soon as they reached the age of exemption in order to force them out into the fields; of the candidate who was disallowed election expenses of £60 spent on 'oyster patties'; and, strangest of all to modern notions, of the notice posted in a school to the effect that double fees would be charged in future in respect of any children whose parents had joined the labourers' union!

These were no doubt extreme cases, but they serve to illustrate the weaknesses to which small 'ad hoc' authorities were prone in the 1880s, the criticisms to which they were subjected, and the stories which Mr Morant would hear—with embellishments—in the clubs. Indeed the evidence shows that they were being told in the lobbies of the House of Commons itself. How stories such as these must have reinforced Mr Morant's longing to sweep away an outworn system and bring it into the main current of local government! How the administrator in him must have despaired at the sight of education in the hands of 'ad hoc' bodies so small that the addition of a single teacher to their schools would often involve a penny on the rates! In Northamptonshire, for instance, there were forty boards, twenty-three exercising jurisdiction over a population of less than 1,000, one over a population of less than 250. Moreover, by 1902 only about half as many voters went to the poll to vote at School Board elections as at county council elections.

As to the willingness of the majority of the county and county borough councils to add education to their growing powers and duties there could be little doubt. The fundamental of crowd psychology, that every crowd likes to increase its number and sense of its own importance, could be trusted to operate. Moreover, the success of the county committees established by the Welsh Intermediate Education Act, under which at least fifteen new secondary schools had been opened by 1895, had been impressive; the English county councils too had acquired a taste for dealing with education through the Technical Instruction Acts and the Whiskey Money; and this had made them inquire 'If secondary and technical education why not elementary?' As Mr Haldane remarked, 'Local Government begins to show signs of getting uninteresting.'

In the First Reading debate on the Bill of 1902 Sir John Dorington announced that his county (Gloucester) had been looking forward to a Bill of this kind for many years, and that he was strongly of opinion that the county councils would be found quite capable of undertaking and willing to undertake the work. One can almost picture Mr Morant settling more comfortably into the uncomfortable seats of the officials' gallery to the right of the Speaker's chair!

One question remained. How far had public opinion progressed in a tolerance of the notion of bringing the church schools on to the rates?

This was the crux of the whole matter, for no advance could be made towards a national system of secondary and technical education except on the basis of a more efficient system of elementary education. There could be no profit in attempting to teach a boy engineering if he had first to attend a preparatory class to learn over again what he should have learnt in the elementary school.

How far could the voluntary schools, with their devoted £40 teachers, offer this efficient preparatory teaching? They numbered over 14,000 and contained more than half the school population. In at least 8,500 districts, too, the parent had no choice at all. The law compelled him to send his child to the denominational school—and there were no omnibus services. The most he could do was to make himself and his child conspicuous by exercising his right to have the child withdrawn from religious instruction.

The answer was clear. However devoted the teachers, the voluntary schools could very rarely offer anything comparable to the strictly educational advantages of the rate-fed board schools. Their premises and equipment were inferior, their teaching staff less well qualified,[1]

[1] *H*, Vol. 107, Col. 905—In the board schools 51 per cent of the teachers were

and their income from subscriptions, although double that raised in 1870,[1] was only equivalent to 6s. 5d. a child plus a special aid grant of 5s. as compared with the 25s. 6d. per board school child contributed by the rates.

Yet the child in the voluntary school was just as much a citizen of tomorrow as the child in the board school. It was clear that the voluntary schools must either be ended or mended. If Mr Morant and others saw this clearly,[2] and the Vice-President of the Council (Sir John Gorst) 'saw no difficulties', why did the Lord President (the Duke of Devonshire) 'see nothing else'?[3]

Historical perspective favours the judgment of the Duke who, as nominal leader of the Liberal Unionists, was of course in a difficult position.

In the first place the last parliamentary election which had been in any real sense indicative of the balance of forces likely to be encountered on a question of domestic policy—as distinct from foreign relations, imperial development, and the Boer War—had been a very near thing. The Unionists (340) and Liberal Unionists (71) had, as it appeared, secured in 1895 a comfortable majority of 152 over their Liberal (177) and Irish Nationalists (82) opponents. But it was in reality a majority with feet of clay. In fact it rested on nothing more substantial than a 76 per cent poll and, more ominous still, a margin of a bare 31,000 votes. Clearly despite the 'khaki' election of 1900 Liberalism was not dead. Rather it was disrupted, disunited, or dormant. At any time it might be galvanized into life by an issue of home politics upon which all shades of Liberal opinion could be induced to feel sufficiently strongly.

Nor could the available religious statistics have afforded the Duke much ground for confidence. For a number of religious censuses made about this time all told the same story. The six leading Nonconformist denominations provided seats in their places of worship for 9,610,000; the Church of England for no more than 6,718,000. How many of these seats were occupied was of course more doubtful. George Cadbury's religious census of Birmingham in 1892 had shown that the seating accommodation in Anglican, Catholic, and Nonconformist

---

fully certificated; in the voluntary schools 38 per cent. In the board schools there were 76 children to each certificated teacher; in the voluntary schools, 103. In the board schools the cost of teaching staff was 45s. 2d. a child; in the voluntary schools, 35s. 2d.

[1] H, Vol. 107, Col. 904—1870: 8,281 schools, 1,693,000 children, income, £418,000; 1902: 14,319 schools, 3,056,000 children, income, £863,000.

[2] See letter from Dr Garnett to Mr Morant quoted on p. 113 of Memoir of William Garnett by Dr B. M. Allen.

[3] Sir Almeric Fitzroy, Memoirs, Vol. I, p. 62.

places of worship in that city could barely hold a quarter of the population, and not 1 million in the 5 million in London, it was supposed, ever visited church or chapel.

The rolls of the Nonconformist Sunday schools contained 3,103,285 names; those of the Church of England 2,329,813. Again it was stated that 1,000,000 children, or nearly half the total number in the Anglican voluntary day schools, were Nonconformists.[1] Next—the Duke must have wondered—would the rural voter welcome higher rates as readily as his county council was likely to welcome the control of the voluntary schools, a control which would be bound to raise those rates? For the rural voter was then, as now, the mainstay of the Duke's adopted allies the Tories, and then, as now, he paid his taxes in sorrow but his rates in anger.[2]

To put the whole of the children in the voluntary schools on the rates, at the 15s. a child required to bring the expenditure per head up to that of the board schools, would cost several millions. Some of the county councils had spent the Whiskey Money readily enough, but not all. Gloucestershire was in 1902 still only giving a moiety, Hereford half. Even London had applied £1,100,000 to relief of rates in ten years. That, however, was other people's money. Would they spend their constituents'? No county council had as yet dared to raise a rate over its area as a whole to supplement the Whiskey Money.[3] When they were suddenly faced with the necessity to demand 4d., 5d., or 6d. more in rates from those in whose power it was to express their indignation at the polls, would they face the outcry? Might they not rather seek to level down the board school expenditure in order to balance the new charges for the voluntary schools? Or might they not demand that the Exchequer should foot the bill? The Royal Commission on Local Taxation had recently been incautious enough to refer to education as a 'national service'. Worse still, the First Lord of the Treasury himself (Mr A. J. Balfour) had included in his election address in 1895 'Poor Law and School Board rates to be charged on the Imperial Exchequer' —although he had since repudiated such an alarming intention.[4]

Lastly, the Duke must often have had cause to exclaim, like many politicians both before and after him, 'Oh Lord, save us from our adopted friends.' The churches might justly remind him that they had provided and largely sustained what education there was before 1870. They might with equal justice claim that the parsons had often come to

[1] H, Vol. 107, Col. 1102.
[2] See letter from one of the Duke's chief supporters quoted by Dr B. M. Allen, *Life of Sir Robert Morant*, p. 164.
[3] *Fabian Tract*, 106, p. 5. In 1899–1900 22 county boroughs added £44,960 to their Whiskey Money. A few counties levied a rate on part of their areas.
[4] H, Vol. 107, Col. 905.

control the schools for the simple reason that they were usually the only people in the neighbourhood who took any real interest in education. Nevertheless some of those parsons had behaved very badly and some very incautiously. 'Our syllabus is arranged so as to give distinctive denominational instruction.' Canon Pennington, a diocesan inspector of schools for twenty years, had written in *The Guardian* on 4 August 1897, 'I always saw it was given, and always asked the children, *chiefly the children of the Nonconformists*, questions bearing upon it. Thus in fact we trained the children of the Nonconformists to be children of the Church.'

Poor Duke! He was probably a much shrewder man of affairs than later educational critics have supposed. But as a survivor from an earlier 'patrician' era in political life he must have found it a difficult matter to adjust himself to the new ideas stirring beneath the surface. For example, his contemporaries were not slow to attach to him the story told by Mr Winston Churchill of his father, Lord Randolph, that, confronted with the decimal points in his estimates, he had complained wearily that he could never understand those damned dots! With what a delicious sense of a painful duty to be tactfully performed he must have put his head round Sir John Gorst's door on his return from the Cabinet meeting which had decided to abandon the Bill of 1896. And yet the only words of comfort which rose to his lips were 'Gorst, your damned Bill's dead!'

This Bill, after passing its second reading by a big majority, made no progress after eleven days in committee owing to the revolt of the smaller boroughs whose School Boards were to be extinguished, and the joint objections of the teachers and the Nonconformists to 'right of entry'. This the teachers had always resisted, and the Nonconformists had not sufficient clergy to implement.

But if the Bill of 1896 was dead, Sir John Gorst was still very much alive. So were the Church of England authorities who had already seen the writing on the wall in the Liberal Welsh Disestablishment Bill of 1894. Both set out to learn what lessons their failure had to offer. The Church must close her ranks. The Vice-President must recognize that, the School Boards being radical strongholds, he could not hope to hand over all education to the county and county borough authorities. He must allow boroughs with a population over 10,000 and 'urban districts' with a population over 20,000 to retain powers over elementary education. Moreover, a way must be found to enable the Anglican school teachers to be better paid, without 'right of entry' for the clergymen of any denomination.

The Church of England, therefore, led by the Bishops of Rochester and Winchester, redoubled its efforts to prevent collapse, and set out its claims clearly in a lengthy statement by Convocation. Sir John Gorst on his part did much by administrative measures and minor legislation which appeared 'innocent' to bring about a position in which it could be represented that a final settlement did not change the existing order too drastically. Thus by a series of additional grants he set out to undermine the understanding which had formed the basis of the Act of 1870. That understanding had been that the cost of the denominational schools should be borne in equal thirds by fees, subscriptions, and exchequer grants. By 1902 it had been so radically altered that the exchequer was bearing 77 per cent of the cost, subscriptions 14 per cent, and other sources of revenue the remaining 9 per cent. The cost of public education, in fact, was doubled between 1895 and 1902.

More important still, the school-leaving age was twice raised; first in 1899 to 12 without exemption, achieved by the Vice-President's precipitate and hearty support, without Cabinet authority, of a private member's Bill,[1] secondly by a government measure passed in 1900 under which School Boards were permitted to make bye-laws raising the age in their area to 14.

The year 1899 also saw the first Act to deal with defective and epileptic children; and a system of annuities for teachers was instituted in 1898.

Clearly some new force was beginning to stir in the field of popular education, but one obstacle stood firmly in the way of comprehensive legislation—the system of higher-grade schools. As we have seen, every year saw more and more of these schools coming into existence to meet the upward thrust of the hundreds of thousands of children now desiring to remain at school beyond the statutory leaving age, and to provide a substitute for secondary schools. There was therefore no time to be lost. For once a School Board established such a school it soon began to take more pride in it than in any other aspect of its work. From this it followed that the greater the increase in the number of such schools, the greater would be the difficulty in getting the School Boards to relinquish their powers to the county and county borough councils; the greater, too, the difficulty in establishing, against their competition, a system of secondary schools which could fulfil Mr Morant's dream of rendering the pupil teacher system obsolete by providing an alternative stream of recruits to the teaching profession, every one the product of at least a partial course of secondary education.

Obviously the higher-grade schools could not be killed outright. But could they somehow be absorbed into the secondary system as the Bryce Commission had appeared to desire? Could it, for example, be proved that they were really not elementary schools at all and that the School Boards had no business to conduct them? If some such thoughts as these were passing through the mind of Mr Morant they were not, it is clear,

[1] Elementary Education (School Attendance) Act, 1893. Amendment Act, 1899.

shared by his official chief, Sir George Kekewich. Sir George, in fact, was making missionary journeys to tell the School Boards that 'these advanced schools have now become not a mere luxury but an absolute necessity.'[1] Mr Morant was still a very junior official. What was he to do? Was he submissively to watch his Permanent Secretary building the obstacle higher? Or was he to burn his boats and throw in his lot with those who, like Mr Sharpe, the Senior Chief Inspector, had conceived a prejudice against higher-grade schools and had told the Bryce Commission that they would be dangerous competitors if it were desired to set up a state system of secondary schools?[2] We know now the choice he made and the part he played in hatching a plot against them. As suggested earlier, it seems probable that his reading of the evidence before the Cross Commission gave him the first clue. This he followed up by tracking down two decisions by Mr Cumin, throwing doubts on their legality. Next he published his discovery to the world in—of all things—a report on Swiss Education. Finally he made quite sure that his friend Dr Garnett, secretary of the London Technical Education Committee, appreciated the importance of this discovery, and used it in a case he was preparing against the School Board for London.[3] Dr Garnett brought in Sir John Gorst, and the Cockerton judgement, followed by that of the Queen's Bench and Court of Appeal which ensued, probably did as much to clear the ground for the Act of 1902 and to render its passage inevitable as all the preliminary activities of the Church and Sir John Gorst put together.

The Court of Queen's Bench ruled that the London School Board could not, out of the School Board rate, conduct classes for the examinations and grants of the Science and Art Department, or go beyond the Code of the Education Department, or give instruction of any kind to adults, whether in day or evening schools. This ruling would still have left the School Board free to conduct such classes if they could render them self-supporting by fees and the use of endowments. The Court of Appeal, however, endorsed the more radical view of Mr Cockerton himself, that the School Board did not possess the right to apply to a form of education which came under the control of the Science and Art Department any portion of the school fund, that is to say, any portion of the funds to which the School Board was entitled under the provisions of the Act. Thus they held the power to be non-existent even if the schools could be made self-supporting.[4]

Mr Morant's strategy had been learnt in Siam, and looked at from the point of view of strategy alone this ruthless and apparently pre-

---

[1] *H*, Vol. 107, Col. 1199.
[2] *B.C.R.*, Vol. I, 1501–17, also *R.E.D.*, 1895, p. 123.
[3] Dr B. M. Allen, *Sir R. Morant*, pp. 121 and 129.
[4] *The Times*, 31 May 1901.

meditated indiscretion was a masterstroke, purchased at a price which it has taken educational opinion many years to appreciate, and in some senses to regret. Looked at from the point of view of modern Civil Service ethics, it is better to admit frankly that in the light of the campaign of his official chief it seems to have been an astonishing step for an official, however clearly destined for high promotion, to have taken.

CHAPTER V

THE BALFOUR–MORANT EDUCATION ACT
OF 1902

The proposals in the Bill as presented.—An historic debate.—The optional clause.—The religious difficulty.—The clash of conviction.—The party machine takes control.—The Government's resolute use of the closure.—The influence of the Boer War, and of foreign trade competition.

THE Government produced their final and definitive solution in the late spring of 1902. Any county or county borough council, any borough council with a population over 10,000, and any urban district with a population of over 20,000 would have power by resolution to take over the work of the School Boards in their area, so becoming the 'Local Education Authority'.

The county and county borough councils (but not the borough and urban district councils) were, in addition, charged to consider the education needs of their areas and take such steps as might seem to them desirable, after consultation with the Board of Education, to supply or aid the supply of education other than elementary and to promote the general co-ordination of all forms of education; over and above the 'Whiskey Money' they might expend a 2*d.* rate upon such higher education.

The new Local Education Authorities (L.E.A.s) so created were to have the control of all secular education in the schools hitherto provided, or to be provided in future, by the denominations. Thus the aid of the rates was for the first time to be brought to the 'non-provided' schools, but—significantly—although the ratepayer was to find the cost of maintenance as distinct from the provision and upkeep of the fabric, four foundation managers might be appointed by the denomination compared to two by the local authorities.

The appointment of teachers was vested in the managers subject to a veto on educational grounds by the L.E.A. Assistant and pupil teachers—as distinct from the principal teacher—might be appointed if thought fit without reference to creed or denomination.

'I think we have reached a point', Mr Asquith remarked, during the fourth day of debate, 'at which it would be impossible for the wit of man to contribute a new idea to this discussion.' The historian faced by the imposing pile of *Hansards* which contain the debate may perhaps be pardoned if he is tempted to echo such a time-saving sentiment. Yet if he would understand the profound influence which this debate, and those which ensued upon the attempt to repeal the Bill in 1906, were to exercise upon the future growth of the public educational system, he cannot afford to leave the pile unread. Better still, he should try to imagine himself an impartial spectator in one of the galleries or sitting next to Mr Morant in the officials' gallery to the right of the Speaker's chair.

It now seems clear that had the Bill been confined to the twofold task of creating L.E.A.s and endowing them with power to establish and maintain secondary and technical schools, and training colleges for teachers, there would have been little opposition to it. For the mind of the House was clearly set upon these reforms, and a great deal of favour was shown to the Bill even by those who felt obliged to announce their intention of voting against it.

Indeed, one leader of the parliamentary opposition, Mr Haldane,[1] actually refused to vote against the second reading. In what must surely be one of the half-dozen greatest speeches upon education to which the House has ever listened, he had the courage to tell them that they were discussing a question far beyond sects and priests, whether of conformity or nonconformity, a question vitally affecting the whole national life; a question in fact which, with the rise of the industrial competition of Germany and the U.S.A., had become one of vital national urgency. The Bill was a step forward to the creation of an enlightened public opinion which would demand improvements such as had not been seen for twenty-five years.[2]

A curious feature of the debate is that few members actually spoke directly against the School Boards, despite the general agreement that they must be abolished. Many in fact paid graceful tributes to their work. This would in any case have been natural, for Parliament knows intuitively how many tears to shed in the performance of a painful duty. More important, perhaps, Mr Joseph Chamberlain, the real leader of the Liberal Unionists—arbiter of the Cabinet and of the Bill—was known to be a supporter of the School Boards, and to favour the optional clause which would have allowed any School Board to remain in existence unless the appropriate county or county borough council passed a resolution in favour of taking over its functions.

But as the third day of debate was running its course the fate of the optional clause was virtually sealed outside the House at the Westminster Central Hall, where a meeting of the County Councils'

---

[1] Mr Haldane was of course a great friend of the Webbs, who had done so much to set out the case for comprehensive legislation in Fabian Pamphlet No. 106: 'The Education Muddle and the Way out'. See *Sidney and Beatrice Webb*, by Mary A. Hamilton, p. 128.   [2] *H*, Vol. 107, Cols. 703–16.

Association resolved by thirty votes to seven 'That without expressing any opinion on the controversial questions raised by the Education Bill, the proposals contained in that Bill to place the control of all education in administrative counties under local education authorities, meet with the general approval of this Association; and that as regards the administrative counties, the County Councils, acting through Committees as the educational authorities, are well qualified and prepared if so requested by Parliament, to undertake the powers and duties imposed upon these authorities by the Bill.'

In the face of this resolution, it must have become clear that there could be little further justification for the concession to Liberal Unionist sentiment contained in the clause, which would have left certain School Boards 'with a noose round their necks liable to be tightened with fatal consequences by any casual majority at a town council election'.

The clause was accordingly dropped in committee, a hansom cab accident to Mr Joseph Chamberlain, which kept him away from the House, facilitating its demise.

'I would ask anyone whether, if the educational objections to the Bill had been the only objections present, there would have been a division on the Second Reading,' said Mr A. J. Balfour at the close of the fifth day of debate, and Mr Dillon for the Irish Nationalists was equally emphatic. 'If you could eliminate the religious difficulty, your Education Bill would pass the Second Reading in a single night and the Committee stage would not take a week.'

In what then did this historic religious difficulty consist? What currents carried it forward to become for two decades the bane of politicians, whatever their party, and the nightmare of all progressive administrators; to fill the single school areas with little mushroom undenominational schools; to inhibit the natural growth of the elementary school system until the 'Hadow' Report of 1926 came like a clean wind to blow away some of the cobwebs which obstructed administrative thought? Was it sustained merely by prejudices and grievances, long since remedied, or did it rest upon deep spiritual convictions touching the very springs of national life?

The historian who would attempt a simple answer has not read his sources. Deep spiritual conviction was certainly present, but it was not confined to those who, like Dr Clifford, opposed the Bill as a flagrant encroachment upon the Englishman's inalienable right to liberty of conscience and religious equality. It was equally shared by the Catholics[1] who, placing dogma and authority over the right of individual judgment and holding no subject secular in the sense that all, to their minds, should be permeated by their distinctive beliefs, welcomed the

[1] *H*, Vol. 107, Cols. 991–1000.

Bill wholeheartedly. The Catholic school problem was, however, a comparatively small one and principally confined to the urban areas, where a choice of school existed. Theirs was a standpoint for which the Nonconformists could make allowances. Was it deep spiritual conviction which enlisted the support of the Anglican clergy, or did the Bill merely seem to them a just reward of patience held out to them by their Unionist friends to relieve them of an 'intolerable strain'? No one can read Lord Hugh Cecil's Second Reading speech without realizing that here too was deep religious conviction; the belief that, however readily a churchman might agree that the minutiae of dogma were an unsuitable pabulum for infants, the church schools would fail in their purpose if they did not teach a religious habit of mind and religious customs; if they did not in fact seek to implant in the minds of those who attended them the idea of membership and the desire to attach themselves to a denomination.

A moment's contemplation of this clash of conviction is sufficient to explain why few Bills have ever offered more material for the skilled debater—or, let it be added, been debated in the initial stages with a loftier earnestness.

But as the debate proceeded, and as the Nonconformist press and pulpit campaign grew in intensity, making the proceedings in the House seem tame by comparison with the 'froth and frenzy' outside, less lofty if more practical minds were quick to see in it an irresistible opportunity to restore the breach in the Liberal party caused by the Liberal Unionist secession.[1] Here surely was an issue of home politics upon which that great party could be united once more. Split by the eleventh-hour conversion to Home Rule of the aged Gladstone, by the conflict between the *laisse-faire* policy of the Manchester school and the radicalism of the Birmingham group, shaken by the difficulty of obtaining for the 1895 election candidates who were wealthy as well as suitable, further divided into Liberal Imperialists and 'Little Englanders' by the Boer War, disturbed by the emergence of Socialism in the Trade Union Movement upon which they had relied, they must have welcomed this Unionist Bill as a shipwrecked boat's crew would welcome the sight of land. The strong impression made upon one who has attempted to regard the debate in impartial historical perspective—after himself spending many weary and a few edifying hours in the gallery to the right of the Chair, endeavouring to assess the trend of debates upon later education Bills—may be summarized quite briefly. From the moment when Mr Lloyd George rose at 2.40 p.m. on the fourth day the whole trend of the debate changed, and it began to have less and less to do with education, more and more

[1] For the standpoint of a leading Liberal Unionist outside Parliament, see *H*, Vol. 107, Cols. 728–9.

to do with the movement which led finally to the Liberal triumph of 1906. Mr Lloyd George's speech was, in fact, as it later proved, the first in a four years' successful election campaign.

For the Nonconformists, more united than for many years owing to the efforts, conceived with very different motives, of Mr George Cadbury the Quaker, could produce perfectly genuine grievances which at the time must have seemed unanswerable to the ordinary voter—although, let it be repeated, they have all, or nearly all, long since been remedied.

They could, for example, claim that in 12,000 out of 14,000 denominational schools conducted by and in the interests of a single denomination, 8,000 to 9,500 of them being the only schools available in the district, 700,000 Methodist and perhaps 300,000 other Nonconformist children were either being compelled to make themselves conspicuous by withdrawal from religious instruction or to run the risk of petty proselytization. They could add that so far from seeking to end this injustice the Government were proposing to perpetuate it by compelling the parents to support it out of the rates, thus incidentally relieving the squire, the parson, and the richer inhabitants of the parish from the burden of its support. Moreover, they could show that although the Government could not produce a single precedent where ratepayers had not a controlling voice in the management of a fund derived from the rates, the proposals in the Bill would ensure that the two representative managers appointed by the local authority would be in a permanent minority. Worse still, in every one of these 14,000 schools no head teacher could be a Nonconformist, and few Nonconformist children could hope to become pupil teachers without accepting Anglican Baptism.

Even where a Nonconformist pupil teacher passed high in the King's Scholarship examination for entry to a training college, he must, it was claimed, be prepared to see those he had beaten in the examination obtain places before him. For nearly all the colleges were Church of England colleges and the few Nonconformist colleges, being expressly undenominational, were filled as to a quarter to a third of their number by Anglican students. Much capital was made out of the case of an Anglican student who was No. 2681 in order of merit on the examination list and was at once received into a Church training college, while No. 237, a Nonconformist, had to wait a year.

Yet—it was asserted—the total cost of the staff of the Church schools was only £3,400,000 as against grants from the State totalling £3,600,000, and the 'intolerable strain' represented no more than a farthing a week per head for every adherent of the Church of England.[1]

---

[1] For these and other Nonconformist arguments see *H*, Vol. 107, Cols. 909, 982, 1000, 1102–9, 1139, 1140, 1174, 1194.

We have seen the system under which a large part of the electorate of that day had been educated and the attitude of hostility too often engendered towards the teachers and parson, as representatives of the system, by the discipline and drudgery of payment by results.

If such electors could not appreciate the subtleties of the religious debate, grievances of this latter type—as one or two by-elections showed—were both genuine and readily intelligible. They were in fact the very ammunition with which to batter down the crumbling defences of a Party Government—although not, as the Liberals were to discover in 1906, ammunition sufficiently durable to effect the repeal of a four-year-old Act.

It is easy for the historian in the light of his later knowledge to regret the slowing down of progress which resulted in the field of elementary education. But once he realizes the gradual supersession of those in whose minds religious principle was uppermost by the more practical and purposeful party machine, much in the debate which would otherwise be obscure becomes plain: why, for instance, the Methodist Conference overruled their Education Committee, which in its annual report had appeared to give a modified support to what were understood to be the intentions of the Bill;[1] why the Nonconformists turned a deaf ear to repeated appeals to them—one backed by the offer of the whole Irish Nationalist vote—to get together and propose a concordat on the Irish or Scottish model or that which had in Liverpool anticipated the later 'Anson Byelaw'.

Looking at the debate today in the light of the educational achievements of this century, it is difficult not to sympathize with the far-sighted remark of the member for Peterborough, Mr Purvis: 'It is a fictitious agitation got up by disappointed politicians in search of a cry, and the truth, when revealed by experience under the working of the Bill, will be rightly appreciated by the country.'[2]

The Government, who at the start of the debate had felt secure in their own majority, reinforced by the Liberal Unionists and Irish Nationalists, found themselves faced by a difficult situation. They met it courageously. Realizing in time that no legislation 'goes bad' so quickly as legislation which can be represented as touching matters of conscience, they forced the Bill through as quickly as possible by the use of the newly invented machinery of the 'closure'.[3]

[1] *H*, Vol. 107, Cols. 1004 and 1191.

[2] Contemporary evidence for the view that political influences were taking hold of the Free Churches will be found in *H*, Vol. 107, Cols. 847, 849, 914, 1001, 1125, 1189, 1190, 1211.

[3] It is just possible that had the Labour Government in 1930 adopted similar tactics, the school-leaving age might have been raised to 15, for the House of Lords was undoubtedly encouraged to veto the Bill by the back bench and Catholic revolt which led to the 'Scurr' amendment. The same Labour Government a few

Was it then solely by the use of their 'big battalions' and the closure that the Government finally placed this Act on the Statute Book?

Although it seems doubtful whether a simple referendum on the principle of bringing the Church schools on to the rates would have secured a majority in the country, there is much evidence to suggest that final success was in reality ensured by two factors which have barely been noticed by any of those who have written about the Bill. The first was the genuine and widespread uneasiness in industrial and commercial as well as educational circles over this country's educational resources compared with those of her competitors; the second factor, equally widespread, was that the new spirit, which as we have noticed was stirring in educational affairs, was sustained by a genuine popular interest in education; an interest heightened no doubt by psychological factors arising out of the Boer War, the commencement of a new century, and the fact that the children of the first generation to receive compulsory education were by this time in the schools.

It would be an interesting study to trace how often in the course of the history of western Europe warfare, whether actual or economic, has stimulated interest in education. Indeed there seem to be substantial grounds for the assertion that an unsuccessful campaign has usually stimulated interest in secondary education, lack of success in the economic field interest in technical education, and successful war interest in elementary education.

No doubt an unsuccessful campaign is usually attributed by a western government to defective educational equipment in its officer and official classes. 'We must make up intellectually what we have lost nationally', said a Minister to his Sovereign after Jena, and upon that sentence was built the Prussian system of education.[1] Similarly, lack of success, supposed or real, in the economic field has directed men's minds to the nation's technical equipment—as is evidenced all through later nineteenth-century British history. Even at the very time when Victorian complacency probably reached its zenith with the opening of the Great Exhibition of 1851, it is interesting to read in the panegyric of *The Times* leader upon 'that stupendous act of homage to industry and the peaceful arts' such sentences as the following: 'The great attention which the industrial communities of Europe bestow on matters of artistic design and ornamental manufacture enabled them to decorate their divisions of the nave in a manner more

---

months later suddenly decided to leave the Sunday Cinemas Bill to a free vote of the House.

[1] Cf. also the Danish high school movement whose organizers felt, after their first school had been driven out of North Slesvig by the annexation of 1864, that 'What Denmark has lost in outward power she must strive to gain in inner strength.'

effective than we, with our utilitarian tendencies, could hope to achieve.' Or again, following a paragraph in which lavish praise is bestowed upon the sculptures from Italy, a reference to 'several objects of art in our own division which we could have wished removed to some quiet and retired coal cellar, among them especially a very lachrymose group called "The Mourners" at which foreigners will be much amused'.

Just as that exhibition produced the Department of Practical Arts, placed at first under the Board of Trade, so the Paris Exhibition twenty-five years later led to the appointment of the Royal Commission on Technical Education, and the trade difficulties of 1921–6 to the renaissance of interest in technical and art education in which Lord Eustace Percy took such a leading part. The severe economic difficulties after the Second World War once again provided the stimulus for the far-reaching extension of all kinds of further education which we have witnessed since the 1950s (see Chapters XVIII and XIX).

Why a successful war should stimulate an interest in elementary education it is more difficult to say. Is it some deep biological reaction concerned with the preservation of the race, such as that which sends up the number of male births after a war or renders girls only half as prone to street accidents as boys? Or is it wholly answered by the simpler explanation that national consciousness is roused to a higher pitch, and a keener public appreciation is fostered of the debt which the country owes for its preservation to the ordinary man in the street?

> For it's 'thank you, Mister Atkins,'
> When the band begins to play.

Whatever the ultimate reason, government spokesmen are sensitive to the importance of the phenomenon. In fact they are usually among the first to proclaim that 'a land fit for heroes' must be created by schemes of social amelioration for those who return.

The Boer War ended on the day that the debate on the 1902 Bill began. It had cost £270,000,000, just ten times the capital sum which Mr Balfour estimated would have been required to replace the whole of the voluntary schools at the building costs then current. But only one member had the audacity—with income tax at 1s. 3d.—to suggest such a daring solution. The conclusion of the war found not one but all these psychological factors at work. For the wiser heads in the services were far from happy about the educational equipment of the officer class, a wave of interest in elementary education was apparently sweeping over a people not hitherto remarkably sensitive to its claims, and everywhere business men were regretting that the city offices were forced to employ so many thousands of well-grounded and industrious German clerks for want of a home-grown substitute.

The uneasiness of the city had found expression in Prince George's 'Wake up England' speech at the Guildhall. In Whitehall and parliamentary circles it was focused upon our educational deficiencies as compared with those of 'the solid, laborious German, the eager, nimble-witted American' by the arresting series of Special Reports on educational subjects edited by Mr (later Sir Michael) Sadler, who had been appointed by the Education Department to direct such inquiries in 1895.

The contrast between this country's leisurely progress in educational affairs hitherto and that achieved by America and Germany was indeed an alarming one. Men compared the 150 day students at the Manchester College of Technology with the thousands gathered at Charlottenburg, increasing on an ordered and organized plan since Germany—already it was thought sixty years ahead of this country—had realized that it was impossible for a modern nation to progress without the training of experts. They contrasted Germany's 22 universities for a population of 50 millions, and the 484 men's and 162 women's colleges and 48 schools of technology valued at £57 millions in the U.S.A., with our own humble provision of 7 universities for a population of 31 millions. The attendance at public, primary, and high schools in the United States was put at 16,000,000. The number in the 5,000 high schools and 2,000 private schools there had, it was stated, risen from 280,000 to 480,000 between 1890 and 1896. Here was common ground upon which members of all parties could meet, whatever their differences upon the religious clauses of the Bill.

The Imperialist seized upon Mr Sadler's phrase, 'The very existence of the Empire depends upon sea power and school power.' His 'Little Englander' opponent echoed the same sentiment but with a different twist: 'Education after all forms the basis of a nation's greatness far more than fleets and armies, and the country is at last beginning to find out that this question is more important than imperialism.' The sober Liberal in Mr Asquith spoke to the same effect: 'The relative ignorance of our people menaces our very national existence as well as our industrial supremacy'; and the Radical Mr Charles Trevelyan added: 'This Bill has not originated in the complaints and clamour of convocation. It is demanded by the people from a sense of shame in our possessing the worst instructed peasantry in the West of Europe, a fear on the part of our industrial population that we shall not be able to meet commercial competition, and the belief that the time has come when equality of opportunity should be really given to all men.'

The popular interest, too, which the Bill provoked cannot have centred wholly on the religious issue. It is true that any political meeting was probably better attended in those days than today. The cinema did not yet afford to the citizen a weekly chance of satisfying his herd instinct without undue mental exertion, or the wireless and television networks absolve him from quitting his fireside for the gas-lit hall, where he could hear his local Member on the problems of the day. Even so, Members seem to have been taken by surprise by the interest aroused by the Bill. Audiences of 5,000 were apparently common, and one Member went so far as to say that in Manchester no subject, the South African war excepted, exercised such an appeal upon his audiences as education. The inspired oratory of Margaret Mc-Millan would attract audiences of 4,000, many of whom walked five or even seven miles into Bradford to hear her speak in St Georges Hall.

After the deletion of the 'optional' clause, the extraction of three concessions from the Exchequer to still the forebodings of those who feared too abrupt an increase in rates, and the passage of the Kenyon Slaney clause,[1] the Bill received the Royal Assent on 1 December. At last the Mother of Parliaments, after a difficult labour, had produced an Act destined profoundly to affect the social life of England and Wales for many decades. If Sir Francis Sandford was the real father of the Bill, it had been brought into the world by the forensic skill of Mr A. J. Balfour with Mr Sadler as consultant,[2] under the watchful eye and assisted by the tireless ministrations of Mr Morant, who was to continue to nurse it for the first nine years of its existence.

Sir John Lowndes Gorst, the faithful servant, was dismissed for his uncertainties of temper[3] at a critical stage.

Mr Sidney Webb hastened to announce the birth in the *Daily Mail*.[4] 'For the first time', he wrote, 'the Bill definitely includes as a public function education as education, not primary education only, or technical education only, but anything and everything that is education

[1] This clause provided that religious instruction in a non-provided school must be in accordance with the terms of the original trust deed of the founder. It was, of course, designed to meet the apprehensions of Nonconformist parents, having children in attendance at a Church school, lest a change of incumbent might lead to the introduction of ritualistic practices in the school.

[2] Mr Sadler's reports on the educational system of other countries had clearly been studied by almost every Member who spoke. Mr Balfour himself did not, to his discredit, consult him personally.

[3] He had offended the Government's supporters in the rural districts by such injudicious utterances as the following: 'The School Boards in country districts have . . . represented the worst kind of local authority that could be devised and have in many cases very greatly neglected the duties which Parliament put upon them.' We know today that he was right, and the more one reads of his speeches the more one comes to think of him as a man born in advance of his time.

[4] 17 Oct. 1902. Mr Webb's contribution had been no mean one. His Fabian Pamphlet No. 106—but in its first form before he himself rewrote it—had been circulated as a 'Cabinet paper' by Sir John Gorst. Moreover, the Webbs strongly supported the Bill throughout. Sidney Webb had seen the working of the secular

from the Kindergarten to the University. This renders the Bill of 1902 epoch-making in the history of English education.'

It only remains to be added that the School Board for London, granted the boon granted by Polyphemus to Ulysses—that of being swallowed last—was duly consumed in the following year by a separate Act. Its work was handed over to the L.C.C. after various vicissitudes. These, although they engendered considerably more heat than light, did at least give rise to one of the most charming mixed metaphors to which the House of Commons has ever listened: 'The Government has thrown down an apple of discord which has burst into flames and flooded the country.'

---

solution in the United States and in Victoria (Western Australia) and it offended his sense of fairness in the treatment of minorities. Moreover, he wanted to preserve variety in methods of teaching, variety in subjects taught, and variety in atmosphere. See *Sidney and Beatrice Webb*, by Mary A. Hamilton, p. 127.

PART II

The Building of the System of Public
Education

RETROSPECT AND PROSPECT

WE have seen how during the quarter of a century which followed the Act of 1870 the central problem of public education had been the housing of a huge army of infant and junior children. It has further been shown how during the next seven years (1895–1902) the focus shifted; how with the upthrust of the older age-groups a new problem had arisen, namely, how to provide a second stage of education for those older children who were remaining at school. The promoters of the Act of 1902 no doubt believed that they could find the answer to this question by the expansion of the small professional army in the grammar schools. But long before that Act had outlived its usefulness they were to find themselves called upon to provide post-primary education for a whole conscripted nation of adolescents.

In the chapters which follow, an attempt must accordingly be made to trace, first, the growth of the system of public secondary education for which the Act had prepared the way; secondly, the progressive enlivenment of the elementary schools (as 'payment by results' fell astern), leading up to the 'new prospect' initiated in 1926 by the 'Hadow' Report on the education of the adolescent; thirdly, the emergence of our modern system—or rather systems—of technical and further education drawing their strength both from the secondary and (since 1926) the Hadow senior schools.

Before taking our leave of the Act of 1902, however, it should be noted that on its passage England found herself for the first time in possession of the three essential ingredients of a democratic system of education; first, a Department of the central Government responsible for the general supervision of all forms of education (but not empowered to order what should be taught at the political whim of the Minister of the day); second, Local Education Authorities each responsible for the detailed control of education in their several areas and largely composed of members answerable to the local government electorate; third, bodies of local residents to serve as the governors or managers of the actual schools, enjoying certain defined powers and duties with regard to the school or schools under their control, but obliged to admit to their number an admixture of representatives appointed by the local authority in return for the privilege of rate assistance.

Two-thirds of a century had passed in the building of this tripartite partnership. The remaining third was to see it change the whole face of English education.

CHAPTER VI

THE EXPANSION OF SECONDARY EDUCATION
1902–1935

THE growth of secondary education in England and Wales between 1902 and 1935 has been compared to a rising tide. The simile is not inappropriate provided it is remembered that the rate of flow varied considerably from year to year and that the phenomenon was by no means confined to these islands or even to the countries of the northern hemisphere.

Readers of certain books on secondary education, which appeared before the Hadow Report 1926 and were written with an avowedly political flavour, may well ask whether in fact it justified the appellation 'phenomenon' at all so far as these islands are concerned. They might raise their eyebrows in surprise to discover such a disinterested and acute observer as Professor Halévy writing in 1923 of the rapid growth of numbers in the secondary schools from 1902 to that date and describing it as 'a social revolution of the first magnitude'.[1]

After 1926, however, a clearer and more widespread conception developed of the task which lay before any nation that would claim to have found a solution to the problem of the proper educational treatment of the adolescent. The realization that in 1926 more than half a

---

[1] *History of the English People*, 1895–1905, p. 205. *Secondary Education for All. A Policy for Labour*, edited for the Education Advisory Committee of the Labour Party by R. H. Tawney, did not of course fall into the error of minimizing what had been achieved between 1902 and 1922. 'The number both of pupils and school places in 1922 is, as we shall show below, all too small. But, inadequate as they are, they represent something like an educational revolution, compared with the almost complete absence of public provision which existed prior to 1902,' p. 20. This book, written about 1923, advocated the wider interpretation of secondary education later adopted by the Hadow Report.

million children were still leaving elementary schools for employment every year at the age of 14 made those interested in public education chary of laying too much emphasis on the fact that 102,000 were by then passing on every year to secondary or other full-time schools.[1]

But, if there had been a slump in superlatives, no one could study a diagram showing the growth which had actually taken place without realizing that something very important had certainly been happening in the field of secondary education since 1902. He might with the figures at his elbow be tempted to describe it as quite remarkable. But with the figures of the corresponding growth in the United States at his other elbow he would hardly dare to call it sensational. This may be all to the good. For the English never like to espouse a new cause too wholeheartedly before they are quite sure that they are not abandoning some 'old good'. The assets accumulated by older traditions must be carried forward to each new page of the balance sheet. England had not absorbed her efficient public and proprietary schools[2] at the same pace as the United States. Moreover, the pace had not been too hot to consolidate the ground won; to secure a steady numerical expansion concurrently with the lengthening of school life; to preserve that 'variety set in a national framework' which was the envy of our more thoughtful friends abroad.[3] At the opposite extreme the United States had at times seen the rising tide become a tidal wave, to the considerable concern of many of those most jealous for the good name of secondary education.[4]

Whatever may be the ultimate verdict of the social historian of the future upon the efforts made by successive British Governments, in co-operation with the local authorities, to repair in three decades the neglect of three centuries, this much is certain, that their efforts quite outstripped the capacity of the man in the street to keep abreast of what had been happening. Much politico-social writing of the 1930s

[1] *B.E.R.*, 1934, Table 7, p. 114.

[2] In 1935 these probably contained another 30,000 pupils, perhaps 50,000 to 70,000 carrying their education to a high standard, see *E.P.* No. 94, p. 21 (H.M.S.O.).

[3] I. L. Kandel, *History of Secondary Education*, 1931, p. 383.

[4] For the increase in numbers in the U.S. secondary schools see I. L. Kandel, *History of Secondary Education*, 1931, p. 449. Number of pupils, all secondary schools—1889–90, 297,894; 1899–1900, 630,048; 1909–10, 1,032,461; 1919–20, 2,041,308; 1927–8, 4,486,562.

For the results and dangers see I. L. Kandel, *History of Secondary Education*, 1931, p. 449; also *The Quality of the Educational Process in the United States and in Europe*, 1927, by Dr W. S. Learned, pp. 4–7 and 42–8; also the report by Dr A. Flexner, *Universities: English, German, and American*, 1930. On the other hand, it was claimed by Professor Charles H. Judd in *The School Review* (University of Chicago, February 1928) that Europe was in fact following America about a generation behind.

was accordingly vitiated by the tendency to demand social revolution without first pausing to discover how far and how fast the silent social revolution effected by educational changes had proceeded.

The social historian who seeks to do justice to the advance of English education must avoid several pitfalls. For he might be tempted to look rather at the number of new secondary schools built, or old schools restored, each year rather than at the actual numbers in attendance and the lengthening of school life. Worse still, he might neglect what is even more difficult to recapture, namely, the rising standards of improvement in teaching power from year to year. In that case he might even be tempted to believe that no great movement had taken place at all. For he would find that England possessed one grammar school for every 8,300 of her population in the year 1546, one grammar school for every 23,750 in 1867, one grammar school for every 46,700 in 1895, and one secondary school for every 29,145 in 1934.

To look at the matter in this way would of course be to overlook a number of crucial facts. That the grammar schools of 1546 were often, if not invariably, the only schools of any type which existed; that even by the standards of the day some of the 830 grammar schools of 1867 'were very elementary and some decrepit'; that it seems at least doubtful whether more than 30,000 pupils were receiving in the grammar schools of 1895 anything which would be recognized as secondary education at all; but that the 1,381 secondary schools on the Board of Education's grant list in 1934 contained nearly 450,000 full-time pupils enjoying an average school life of nearly five years after the age of 11.

Thus if the total of those receiving an efficient secondary education in the endowed schools in 1895 may be put at 30,000, the number had increased fifteenfold in a bare forty years. Reckoning purely on the basis of numbers without regard to efficiency, there may of course have been as many as 75,000 attending the endowed schools and another 35,000 in the proprietary schools, and some of these latter schools subsequently became grant-aided secondary schools although in 1895 they were completely outside the *public* system. This would make the number 4 in 1935 for every 1 in 1895, irrespective of any question of length of school life or efficiency of instruction.

The comparison is equally remarkable if it is made on the basis of the facilities which had come into existence for children to enter secondary schools from homes which forty years before would have had no choice but the elementary school, or the private school of more than doubtful efficiency.

For in 1895 probably not more than from 3 to 6 out of every 1,000 children leaving the elementary schools can have passed on to one of the endowed grammar schools: by 1934 the proportion had increased to 119 per 1,000.

Again the slender thread, beaded with scholarships of short duration and doubtful value, which joined the elementary to the secondary school in 1894, had become, if not a broad collar of costly pearls, at least a respectable necklace. For the total number of pupils then holding county and county borough council scholarships (usually of strictly limited duration) at schools of secondary type was 2,424[1] as compared with the 224,981 totally and 23,188 partially exempt from the payment of fees in the grant-aided secondary schools of 1934.

To put the matter in another way, the odds against a child in an English elementary school gaining a scholarship to a secondary school in 1894 were 270 to 1: the odds against a child in a public elementary school (England and Wales) gaining a special place had, forty years later, been reduced to 11 to 1. By 1934 the scholarship link between the secondary schools and the universities was of course stronger than was the link between the elementary and the endowed grammar schools in 1894. The average number passing immediately from the grant-aided secondary schools to universities over the four years 1930–4 was 4,318, and probably a further 1,000 entered the universities each year after an interval spent at work or abroad. Of those who entered universities in July 1934, 1,983 of the men and 831 of the women had commenced their education in elementary schools; 2,209 paid no fees; 54 paid partial fees.

In contemplating these figures it is interesting to recall the reply given in 1888 to the Cross Commission by a 'father of three' described as 'Mr T. Smyth, a representative of the working classes'. He appears to have tried the patience of some of the Commissioners by the expression of sentiments which today would barely be challenged at a meeting of a society for the preservation of the prerogatives of the landed gentry. One of the commissioners asked him sharply if he was not aware that children from public elementary schools sometimes reached the universities. 'It would be next to expecting a boy out of the London Board Schools to take wings', he replied, 'as to expect him to advance by his own efforts to the university.'[2] He was right. The odds against such an event were at this time almost astronomical. One would suspect that the commissioner had been reading his *Joseph Vance* too assiduously overnight if that remarkable book had not, although written, been lying unpublished in a bedroom cupboard.

Finally, a marked change took place over the same period, if not in

---

[1] *B.C.R.*, Table in Vol. I, p. 405. The length of tenure must have been very short, for the total number elected to scholarships by county and county borough councils had been: 1892, 635; 1893, 1,442; 1894, 2,207.

[2] *C.C.R.*, 52,653–5.

the devotion of the secondary school teacher to his work, at least in his attitude towards his subject and his training to expound it.

Before the twentieth century opened, apart from the limited opportunities afforded for the interchange of professional experience by the meetings of the associations of head and assistant masters and mistresses, hardly a single association of teachers had been called into existence with the professed object of studying teaching techniques and pooling new experience in the teaching of the various subjects.[1] The proportion of graduate teachers, too, in secondary schools increased from 62·7 per cent in 1905 to 85·5 per cent in 1934 in the case of men and from 41·7 per cent to 68·1 per cent in the case of women. Moreover, although the alteration in the cost of living makes a full comparison difficult, the attractiveness of the profession to the best product of the universities was, by 1935, probably about three times as great financially as at the commencement of the century, when the remuneration of secondary school teachers was even lower than that of their colleagues in the elementary schools.[2]

To anyone studying the growth of the public system of education in this country it is of greater interest to inquire why, rather than to ask how, this progress was achieved.

In the mechanical sciences the development of the machine is the point of interest; the motive power is usually simple or reducible to a formula. In the world of education it is the political, economic, and social forces which have provided the motive power that are interesting to the student of social history. But before passing to an attempt to trace these currents, social, political, and economic, which have carried the movement forward, some brief review of the successive stages in the development of the machine must be undertaken.

Five main periods are discernible, although they overlap, merge into each other, or are difficult to distinguish when a laboratory study is made of a single area.

(1) The period of survey by the new L.E.A.s for higher education during which the elected members had themselves to be educated to an appreciation of the claims of secondary education.

This period had, as we have seen, begun before 1902. For practical purposes it may be said to have ended with the commencement of the free place system in 1907.

---

[1] Mathematical Association, 1871 (an association for the improvement of Geometrical Teaching); Geographical Association, 1893; Science Masters Association, 1900; Classical Association, 1903; Historical Association, 1906; English Association, 1907; Music Teachers Association, 1908; Modern Humanities Research Association, 1918.

[2] For the salaries payable see the evidence tendered to the Bryce Commission by the teachers' associations and the reports of Sir Michael Sadler on the counties and county boroughs which he surveyed by invitation: Essex, Hants, Liverpool, etc.

'Feet little prepared for the roughness of life's highway.' A school group of 1894.

'The teacher of originality found herself free for cautious experiment.' A pets competition in 1906

By contrast a young farmers' club thirty years later

(2) The period of steady expansion, 1907 to 1914–15.

(3) The period of rapid expansion due to the improvement in the economic condition of the wage-earning classes during the war and immediate post-war period 1914–15 to 1920–1.

(4) The period of consolidation in the face of economic difficulties.

In this period the interest aroused by the publication by L.E.A.s of schemes of educational development required by Mr Fisher's Education Act of 1918 prevented a setback, in spite of the trade difficulties of this country. Moreover, those very difficulties called forth a livelier appreciation of the importance of education for economic success in the international competition for markets; and, if they gave rise to industrial upheavals, they turned the minds of those in authority to the part education should play as a factor in social progress and the appeasement of class consciousness (1920–1 to 1929).

(5) The period of readjustment of function as between the secondary schools proper and the alternative forms of secondary education arising out of the educational reorganization set on foot by the 'Hadow' Report. During this period the lengthening of school life became as important a factor in growth as the increase in the annual entry (1929 to 1935).

(1) *The period of survey and self-education by the new L.E.A.s.*

As we have seen, the local authorities, led by the county councils created by the Local Government Act of 1888, had already moved some way before 1902. They had used the Whiskey Money and, in a few cases, had applied a local rate to make some inroads upon the vested interests and popular inertia which had brought the Endowed Schools Commission to an inglorious end. Already by 1895 the county and county borough councils separately or in combination had seventeen secondary schools newly completed or 'on the stocks' to match the fifteen provided in Wales[1] under the Welsh Intermediate Education Act of 1889. In 1902 it was claimed by Sir John Gorst in the House of Commons that between 1889 and 1901 the English county councils had established 391 new schools of secondary type and extended, or modified and adapted, 282 more, making a total of 673. This claim should be treated with great reserve. I suspect that the clerk concerned must have counted all the pre-Cockerton judgment higher-grade schools and added up all the secondary and proprietary schools to which a county or county borough had ever given a grant. With three separate departments issuing lists of schools, organized science schools, endowed schools, and higher-grade schools, it must have been very difficult in 1902 to avoid counting the same school twice. What is at least clear is that the number of schools

[1] *B.C.R.*, Vol. I, p. 358.

recognized by the Board of Education, including endowed schools and those provided by the local authorities, had reached 272, with 31,716 pupils taking the approved course.

Despite these efforts, real or parliamentary, wide areas of England were still living at the commencement of the twentieth century in the social atmosphere of the eighteenth. The 'pale-fence' tradition of a landed aristocracy of 'county' families and their dependants, so brilliantly described by Mr H. G. Wells in *Tono Bungay*, still pervaded many of the shires.

This landed class was well represented on the county councils. Its members might agree with the Bryce Commissioners that a few more scholarships would enable children of scanty means and exceptional ability to prolong their education. But they could easily be led astray by specious arguments and appeals to their sporting instincts—or prejudices. They reared pheasants. Would it not be 'bad form' to trespass upon the preserves of the private schools? And might not scholarships, if too liberal, draw promising boys from the less wealthy schools in much the same way as they suspected their neighbour's keeper of enticing their birds into his coverts?

The newly created Board of Education too was suspect in some quarters. A central department had long been suspect in principle, and the Board was regarded in much the same light as a new and very young arrival to the staff of a public school. It spoke with the mild accents of Winchester and New College and might be sparing of chastisement, but it had yet to prove its genuine eagerness to lead rather than to drive and its capacity to grow up with its charges.

It is no longer possible to trace by what diplomatic channel it was first suggested to various county and county borough councils that to get an independent report by an expert might prove the best way to carry out the 'survey of the needs of their areas' required by the Act of 1902. Probably some authorities were influenced by the example of London, where the zeal of Mr Sidney Webb and the resource of Dr Garnett had already worked wonders following a comprehensive report upon facilities for higher education in the metropolis prepared in 1893–4 by Mr (later Sir Hubert) Llewellyn Smith. Others no doubt listened to the suggestions of Whitehall or the advice of the local Inspector of schools. It is sufficient to record that within a few years of the passage of the Act Mr Michael Sadler (who as Director of Special Inquiries and Reports had played such an important part in educating parliamentary opinion to the necessity for action, but who was now free from the restraints of Whitehall)[1] had been commissioned to report upon areas covering a ninth of the population.

[1] He had been disgracefully treated by Whitehall, but like others after him achieved far greater distinction by quitting the Civil Service than by remaining.

Still other areas invited the good offices of His Majesty's Inspectors.

Mr Sadler's reports were written in 1905, but fortunately no expense seems to have been spared on their printing and binding. To the teacher they must still present a rich storehouse of arguments in favour of a liberal education. To the administrator they are an object-lesson in the art of arousing the popularly elected representative by an appeal to his sense of civic responsibility, by interesting him in the past achievements of his area, and by providing him with just the right arguments with which to still the murmurings or rebut the arguments of his constituents. A brief analysis of one report must suffice. The county councillors of Essex were told how for many generations during the middle ages there were public secondary schools supported by town guilds and corporations as at Colchester, and reminded of the fine tradition of taste and craftsmanship in their country churches. Their existing provision for secondary education was compared with that of corresponding areas in the United States and Germany. A tactful reference was made to the 'good human ore' in their rural districts, and by the contrasted example of semi-feudal Russia and democratic Hungary they were warned of the social dangers of neglecting rural education. In parenthesis it was mentioned how the Danish butter trade rested at bottom on the co-operative spirit and the scientific intelligence generated by an appropriate and elevating kind of popular education. Coming nearer home, it was explained how necessary it was for the market gardener to know how to organize, to use intelligent scientific methods, to combine and co-operate in putting produce on the market in convenient and attractive forms. Examples were quoted of sons of Essex grammar schools whose names were household words, and of the more modern successes of the winners of the six major and twenty minor county scholarships which in those days represented the counties' effort to provide an avenue to higher education. All this and more, but always embodied with it and surrounding it a mass of graphs, statistics and thorough, pertinent, and sound advice about the proper payment of teachers, the number of pupil teachers who ought to be trained annually, the need for more scholarships, the way in which private schools could be brought into the county system, and the contribution which the Exchequer ought to make but was not yet making.

So too with the other reports. All were equally detailed—for in those days the modern administrative maxim 'stop the mouth of inquisitiveness with the sugar plum of apparent information' had not gained currency. All displayed the same lucidity. All were written in a style which could not but compel the admiration of the county councillors for the product of a liberal education. All showed too that same understanding of the probable reaction of the critics which filled several pages of the report upon Hampshire—always a county rich in expensive private schools—with a trenchant analysis of the reasons why private schools could not meet the real needs of the day. Many years later the author of these reports was to refer to Ruskin's definition of a liberal education in *The Crown of Wild Olive*: 'Not teaching the youth of England the shapes of letters and the tricks of numbers; and then leaving them to turn their arithmetic to roguery and their literature to lust; but on the contrary training them to the perfect exercise and knightly continence of their bodies and souls.' His comment speaks for itself: 'These remarks, if made to the members of a City Education Committee assembled at a meeting with the usual agenda, would not be persuasive!'[1]

Although Mr Sadler's surveys probably did as much as any other agency to diffuse a widespread interest in secondary education as rapidly as possible—for they were read outside the counties for which they were written—the Board of Education too played a notable part. They did so first by requiring that pupil teachers should in future (from 1 August 1905) be educated full-time up to the age of 16, where possible in a secondary school. In the second place, they urged a more liberal provision of scholarships not only for intending teachers but 'open to the cleverest pupils from all the schools in the area without distinction', and incidentally themselves set a good example by increasing the local science and art scholarships to 7,110. Thirdly, they secured the services of a strong team of Inspectors of secondary schools. The reports of this team could not, it is true, be tuned to such a persuasive key as those of Mr Sadler, but they evidently pricked the foursquare civic pride of the individualist north. To quote a typical account: 'At the request of the local authority the secondary schools of the city were inspected by the Board of Education in the Autumn of 1905. From the report it was evident that the provision for secondary education was inadequate and unevenly distributed, whilst some of the schools were insufficiently staffed and badly equipped.'[2] By 1906 the number of schools on the grant list had risen to 689, with 81,370 scholars taking the approved four-year course; 25,269 scholars (in 600 of the schools) were paying no fees and had entered from public elementary schools. The odds against an elementary school child obtaining a free secondary education had thus fallen appreciably although the materials for a calculation are not available.

(2) *The period of steady expansion, 1907–14.*

With the election of 1906 politics entered the field. To quote once more our 'father of three', Mr T. Smyth, a representative of the work-

[1] *The Outlook in Secondary Education*, p. 43.
[2] *Education in Leeds. A Backward Glance and a Present View*, 1926.

ing classes: 'We say that the State should defray the whole cost and absorb to itself for such purposes all funds and endowments left for educational purposes, not otherwise specified, giving large control to local school boards in the management with strict national supervision under a Minister responsible to Parliament.' 'At present I believe most of the higher education, at least there is a tradition amongst us that all the higher education, is practically free to the upper classes. The State provides it largely, but (for) the universities and grammar schools, and all sorts of places to which the poor have no access. The universities possess lands and endowments, and that being, I say, national property, the upper classes are receiving education freely.'[1]

The State was still nearly as far as it had been in 1888 from defraying the whole cost of secondary education, since the grant payable for each scholar taking the approved course merely amounted to two or three pounds according to the scholar's age. It had certainly absorbed to itself funds and endowments left for educational purposes, the value of which by the year 1888 would have made Mr Smyth incoherent with anger had modern scholarship by that date disinterred this ancient wrong. I refer of course to the action taken under the Chantries Act of Edward VI (1547). In brief the State absorbed the lands and merely continued to pay out of the proceeds the amount bequeathed by the pious founder to be paid to the schoolmaster—often a matter of a few pounds a year since money had possessed a wholly different value when the bequest was made.[2] Judging by the present-day value of the lands of a few schools which were wise enough to purchase back their lands after confiscation, the Commissioners of Crown Lands should have been able to pay for a substantial part of the State system of secondary education as it existed in 1934.

On the other hand, 'large control' had at last been given to local School Boards with strict national supervision under a Minister responsible to Parliament. Clearly working-class opinion had done much between 1888 and 1906 to make itself felt!

The time now seemed ripe to strike another blow at privilege as represented by the endowed schools. Accordingly in the spring of 1907 new regulations for secondary schools were promulgated by the new Liberal President of the Board of Education. These raised the grant to £5 on each pupil between the ages of 12 and 18 in secondary schools which satisfied certain conditions 'in respect of freedom from denominational restrictions or requirements, representative local control and accessibility to all classes of the people'.

The third of these conditions heralded the 'free place' requirement under which schools accepting grant at the higher rate were ordinarily

[1] C.C.R., 52,313, 52,321, 53,332.
[2] See English Monks and the Suppression of the Monasteries, 1937.

required to open a proportion of school places, equal to 25 per cent of the total admissions of the previous year, to scholars from public elementary schools who passed an approved entrance test of attainments. It is interesting to note that the free places were originally intended to be gained by a mere qualifying test. The growth of demand for secondary education soon made that test a highly competitive one. The idea of making grants conditional upon the acceptance of scholarship winners by the school was not a new one. It was originated by Mr Webb and Dr Garnett in London in 1894.

Hitherto some of the schools[1] and most of the parents of fee-paying scholars had enjoyed the benefit of both grants and endowments without giving any serious thought to the social implications of what they were doing. The alarm and misgivings aroused by the new regulation were therefore considerable.

A few of those governing bodies who felt themselves to belong to the socially superior order of 'armigerous gentlemen' hastened to shelter behind the school's coat of arms. Some indeed successfully resisted the acceptance of free place scholars for several decades to come.

The 'pale-fences' in the shires rattled with indignation or apprehension. Headmasters of the most expensive private schools spoke gravely to their boys of the increased competition they would have to face—when their 'public' schools and universities had done their best for them—from these new secondary schools where the boys did such an unfair amount of work.[2]

Ingenious arguments were not wanting to prove that the new requirement would empty the schools, weaken their quality, and shorten the average period of school life. Secondary school masters and mistresses serving at the time later remembered that the sole question they were asked at the visit of one of their governors was 'How many girls in your class have nits in their hair?' or 'How many of your boys have skin disease?' As a matter of sober history the greater readiness of the parents of scholarship holders, as compared with those of fee-paying pupils, to encourage their children to enjoy what they had won for as long as they could, assisted the schools to continue their numerical growth as steadily as ever, lengthening rather than shortening school life. Thus instead of the quality of the work being lowered, sixth-form work began to be developed. Finally the payment of the more liberal grant at a lower age tended to stabilize the age of entry at 11. This last achievement was to have valuable repercussions on the elementary

[1] Not all; for in the schools as a whole 24 per cent of the pupils were already paying no fees and 54 per cent had entered from the elementary schools.

[2] Although I was only ten at the time I can clearly remember one such talk and the impression it made on my mind. I recall the incident not in any spirit of criticism but merely as showing how far class-consciousness has since been sublimated by the social forces at work—education among the first of them.

school system; and it prepared the way for the embodiment in Mr Fisher's Act of 1918 of the dictum that brains and character are qualities which cannot be bound by any social distinctions or limitations, and the final acceptance of the principle of secondary education for all in the Education Act of 1944.

The truth is, of course, that widening social and educational opportunity operates as a sedative upon class-consciousness. The social or educational innovation of today unobtrusively broadens down into the accepted commonplace of tomorrow.

Moreover, the peculiarly English tradition that no pains should be spared to obtain the best possible man or woman to put in charge of a school, and that the candidate finally chosen should then confidently be left alone, was gradually providing the schools, now that the prospects seemed better, with an appreciable constellation—if not a galaxy—of first-class heads. This tradition is very old. In founding St Paul's school in 1510 'nothing gave Colet so much anxiety', wrote his friend Erasmus, 'as the question to whom he should entrust the management of the school. . . . And so he appointed as master of his school a married man with a large family.' These new heads were quick to appreciate the value, both intellectual and—it should be admitted—material, of drawing into their schools the most intelligent scholars from the elementary schools and accepting the increased grants.

By the outbreak of the 1914–18 war the grant-aided schools had increased in number to over 1,000, the numbers in attendance to 187,000. The odds against a child from a public elementary school obtaining a free secondary education at the age of 11 had been reduced to 40 to 1, and 56 elementary school children in every 1,000 of the 10–11 age-group were finding their way to the secondary schools.

(3) *The period of rapid expansion, 1914–15 to 1920–1.*

During this period the rate of growth of the schools more than doubled. Unfortunately no materials exist for its study except those contained in a few admirably condensed pages in the report of the Board of Education for the year 1923–4. The publication of the annual reports and statistics of the Board ceased during the war. By 1934 statistics, which in earlier days employed fifty clerks and took eighteen months to produce, were turned out by electrically operated tabulating machines and a few typists in three months. From 1914 to 1918 the fifty clerks were otherwise engaged and, even if the statistics had been compiled, paper upon which to print them was too valuable to be devoted to such a purpose.

The curtain which closes over the schools was not lifted till 1920. It rose upon a very different scene. Obviously the diffusion of the national wealth among new classes of the population in the form of so-called 'war wages' had made it considerably easier for wage-earning parents to pay fees. One read a great deal in those days of the luxury spending of war profiteers, of the miner who bought a piano and then bought a second piano to keep it company on the other side of the fireplace. The unprecedented demand for places in secondary schools and the mounting sales of War Savings Certificates represented the other side of the picture, less romantic in 'news value' but perhaps a truer index of the national character.

The writer of the chapter in the report of the Board of Education for 1924, whose anonymity does not conceal either his obvious experience or his great capacity to form conclusions, based on an intimate knowledge of the schools as a whole, saw other factors also at work. 'The changes that had been going on in the previous twenty years— the multiplication and the increasing accessibility of schools, the growth of appreciation among parents, the example of others—had been working silently and unsuspected beneath the surface to create a new desire for education.' Obviously the same leaven which we have seen at work at the time of the South African war and the 1902 Act was again stirring the inertia of large sections of the population.

Moreover, the flower of the pre-war secondary schools for boys had been swept away, and the places of those who would never return had to be filled when the war came to an end. It was not yet realized how heavy a proportion of the casualties was suffered by those age-groups which had passed through the secondary schools immediately before 1914. The number of names of those killed appearing on the 1914–18 'Roll of Honour' of most secondary schools will usually be found to approximate to the total number in the school at the beginning of the war. That it was a 'subaltern's war' is indicated by the fact that whereas 720 old members of one school were killed, a count of the sons they had left for the school to educate in the future revealed a bare 80 names. Old boys of the pre-1914 'public' or secondary schools felt with good reason that they were the survivors of a lost generation.

William of Wykeham, contemplating the dearth of 'a due supply of men fitted to serve their country in Church and State' caused by the ravages of the Black Death, founded his college at Winchester. His successors in a modern age, the L.E.A.s, contemplating the ravages of the Great War, set about modernizing and adding to the number of their grammar and county schools.

The 'outburst of demand' led to much overcrowding of premises built before the war and even to the exclusion at the beginning of 1919–20 of 10,000 applicants for admission as fee-paying scholars, and of a further 10,000 who would have been qualified for admission as free-place scholars. Some of those qualified for free places ultimately, however, secured admission as fee-payers.

By the year 1920–1 the number of schools on the grant list had risen to 1,205, the numbers in attendance to 337,000. The odds against a child from a public elementary school obtaining a free secondary education at the age of 11 had been reduced to 21 to 1, and 97 elementary school children in every 1,000 of the 10–11 age-group were finding their way to a secondary school.

(4) *The period of consolidation, 1920–9.*

Despite the inevitable 'time lag' in providing adequate premises to house nearly twice the number of pupils for whom it had been necessary to provide before the war, the rapid increase of numbers brought strength to the schools in a variety of ways. Moreover, surprisingly enough, expansion did not suffer any marked setback when the industrial activity of the war years gave way to the economic difficulties of 1921. Probably this may to some extent be accounted for by the publicity afforded by the L.E.A.s, at Mr Fisher's suggestion, to the 'Schemes' for the development of all forms of education in their areas required by his Education Act of 1918. The continued demand, in the face of a falling index of national prosperity, provided a welcome indication that secondary education in England had at last come into its own.

With the greatly increased attendance and larger average size of the schools consolidation was able to take a variety of forms.

For example, the occupation of school places by young children in preparatory departments could no longer be justified when older children were unable to obtain admission. Correspondingly parents could be expected to sign agreements to keep their children at school for a full course to avoid vacant places in the higher forms which might have been filled by older pupils. Thus in the junior stages of the school course the tendency to stabilize the age of entry about the age of 11, already fostered by the higher grants obtainable after that age, was increased, and the larger numbers of seniors remaining at school enabled 'advanced courses' and sixth-form work to be developed.

Again, order was in 1917 brought into the dense jungle of unco-ordinated and unstandardized examining bodies which up to that year had been able to compete for the custom of the schools.

Superimposed upon the structure of examinations qualifying candidates for entrance to the universities were examinations devised by professional bodies, competitive examinations for the Civil Services and the Army, and various special examinations in science. The effect upon the coherence of secondary education was undoubtedly serious. Enough separate examining bodies existed to give half the pupils in every form a new objective for every year of their course.

Each examining body could require those pupils seeking to enter for its examinations to follow a separate syllabus giving effect to its particular theory of the proper content of a secondary education. Each could refuse to accept examinations already passed as equivalent in value to its own.[1]

This chaos was resolved so far as the schools (though not the universities) were concerned by the institution of the 'first' and 'second' school examinations conducted by eight recognized examining bodies. A national currency was assured for the two School Certificates, lest bad coinage should drive out the good, by the institution of the Secondary Schools Examinations Council, which investigated every few years the whole machinery of each of the eight bodies with a view to the maintenance of a correlated standard.

The institution of the School Certificate undoubtedly contributed to the growth of secondary education by altering the attitude of middle school boys and girls to their work, requiring the development of habits of personal effort and providing their future employers with a readily understood criterion by which to assess their quality and persistence. The tendency of industry and commerce to regard the possession of the certificate as a *sine qua non* for all recruits to their businesses was often a potent factor in causing parents to demand the provision of a local secondary school. Unfortunately the very success of the system in the course of years led to a considerable volume of dissatisfaction among parents and educationalists alike. Briefly, the parent saw in the three years' strenuous preparation for the examinations a potent source of overstrain, particularly in the case of girls. As the report of the Consultative Committee on 'Differentiation of Curricula between the Sexes' pointed out, if a girl is given too much homework she will often break down. A boy on the other hand will not do it. Similarly those jealous to ensure that the secondary schools should give a liberal education (as distinct from a largely disciplinary education with an academic bias to conform with the requirements of universities to which a great majority of the pupils did not pass forward) feared the re-enactment in the secondary schools of many of the educational dangers from which the elementary schools escaped when 'payment by results' came to an end.

Fortunately that care in the selection of candidates for headships, and that freedom accorded to heads after appointment, which has been mentioned above, seemed by 1935 likely to come to the rescue. English educational history abounds in instances where heads, refusing to take the line of least resistance, have—to adapt Pitt's words—saved

[1] E.g. in 1934 the University of London refused to accept a candidate for entrance to a degree course who had obtained an open scholarship at both Oxford and Cambridge and taken fourth place in the examination for the Home and Indian Civil Service, on the grounds that these were not equivalent to 'London Matric'.

their schools by their own efforts and English education by their example. Already by 1935 some of the universities had announced their readiness to free their School Certificates to develop along the lines originally laid down, by devising a new and separate passport for those who desired to enter upon university courses on leaving the secondary schools. Already, too, some headmasters and headmistresses had worked out, with the co-operation of the university examination boards,[1] alternative courses of study adapted to the circumstances of their individual schools but still leading to an examination which would confer the certificate. Possibly but for the Second World War the School Certificate examination as conducted in 1934 would have become a thing of the past and would have been replaced by a 'modified internal' examination still possessing a national currency, on the model set by the National Certificate Examinations in mechanical and electrical engineering, building, chemistry, naval architecture, and commerce.

Before passing from the period under review (1920–9) two further developments remain to be noted. First that the whole conception of the term secondary education was to be altered by the 'Hadow' Report on the Education of the Adolescent (1926). That report in fact so widened the conception of post-primary education that the grammar and county schools began increasingly to be regarded as constituting one only among the many roads which must in future lead to higher education. The fundamental reorganization of the whole educational system which that report initiated set in train the revolution under which the secondary school no longer catered rather indiscriminately for those whose parents could pay the fees demanded and for a leavening of scholarship winners from the elementary schools. Progressively they came to be restricted to that intellectual élite who, irrespective of their home circumstances, are required by a modern democracy to recruit its universities, its professions, and its municipal and civil services.

Again, during the closing year of this period a considerable quickening of conservative thought in regard to higher education was observable. Largely through the brilliant advocacy of Lord Eustace Percy[2] it was led first to an appreciation of the fact that a nation situated, as Great Britain is, in a competitive modern world can only hope to maintain and improve the standard of living of its crowded population by a continual increase in the volume, value, appeal, and design of its exports, in fact that the struggle for existence, like the battle for civilization itself, must be fought with the weapons of science; secondly, it was led to a truer understanding of the place of secondary

[1] See the article on 'The New History Examination' in *The Times Educational Supplement* of 23 May 1936.
[2] President of the Board of Education, 1925–9.

education and a liberal scholarship scheme as factors in the promotion of social unity.

Thus the long-drawn industrial unrest of the post-war years which reached its climax in the General Strike of 1926 was followed by Mr Baldwin's appeal for co-operation, unity, and appeasement. In this, secondary education had a special part to play. 'One of the strongest bonds of union between men', Mr Baldwin wrote in a letter addressed to the teaching profession in 1929, 'is a common education, and England has been the poorer that in her national system of schooling she has not in the past fostered this fellowship of the mind.'

'The classification of our schools has been on the lines of social rather than educational distinction; a youth's school badge has been his social label. The interests of social unity demand the removal of this source of class prejudice and the drastic remodelling of the national structure to form a coherent whole.'

At the close of this period (1929) the number of schools on the grant list stood at 1,341 and the total number of scholars in attendance at 386,993. Of this total 169,254 were paying no fees and had entered from public elementary schools. The odds against an elementary school child obtaining a free secondary education had been reduced to 13 to 1, and 113 per 1,000 children of the 10–11 elementary school age-group were passing on to secondary schools. For purposes of comparison it may be noted that a reply in the Chamber of Deputies on 1 August 1928 gave the numbers attending secondary schools in France in 1927–8 as follows:

(a) Public Lycées and Colleges ...	...	167,781
(b) Private	...	...	...	...	118,909
				286,690

(5) 1929–35

The years between 1929 and 1935 may be described as a period of readjustment of function as between the grammar and county secondary schools and other full-time schools providing parallel educational courses for the adolescent.

During this period, the first preoccupation of the central and local authorities was to increase their provision for such alternative forms of secondary education as those provided in the junior technical schools and to ensure a proper 'place in the sun' for the new senior schools created by the spread of 'Hadow' reorganization. The grammar and county secondary schools therefore tended to take their rightful place as one among a variety of roads along which children might travel to a higher education. Moreover, a feeling began to spread in Whitehall and parliamentary circles and among the local authorities themselves

that the country probably had for the present enough accommodation
in secondary schools (which should look to the university) to satisfy the
specific needs for which such schools should cater in a modern community. Several counties indeed, surveying their provision for secondary education and contemplating the extent of the problem of reorganization which lay before them, came to a definite decision to call
a halt in the provision of new schools. These two tendencies checked
the building of additional schools, but the numbers in attendance continued to rise by 7,000 to 10,000 a year. The schools were slowly
reaching a position of equilibrium in exactly the same way as the
population of the country was in those years remaining constant despite a decline in births. In the one case pupils were remaining longer at
school, in the other the population was living longer.

Another important feature of the period was the final acceptance
by conservative thought (as embodied in a National Government) of
the theory that ultimately the secondary schools must be thrown open
completely, and on no other basis than talent, to those most fitted to
receive a secondary education in whatever stratum of the population
they might be found.

This came about in a curious way.

When the century opened, as we have seen, the idea was deeply
rooted that elementary and secondary education represented not successive stages of education, but alternative kinds of education meant for
different social classes. When the free place system was instituted no
test of parental income appeared necessary. The fact that the parent
had allowed his son to be educated for two years previously in an
elementary school was thought to provide a sufficient guarantee without further scrutiny of his income that he could not afford to send him
to a secondary or private school as a fee-payer. The 'scouring away of
old class barriers' and the ever-increasing attractiveness of the elementary school achieved by thirty years' progress appeared to the Committee on National Expenditure (the May Committee, 1931) to call for
the imposition of such an income test upon the parents of the greatly
increased number of scholarship winners of 1931. The Board of
Education sought to give effect to this principle by the substitution for
'free places' of 'special places' carrying a value related to the income
of the parent. The Board's circular to L.E.A.s on the matter (Circular 1421) aroused a controversy so considerable as to cause the
Government to consider anew the logical principles upon which
accessibility to the secondary schools should ultimately rest. In a
matter of a few weeks 1,600 resolutions from meetings of protest were
received at the offices of the Board, besides a heavy volume of correspondence from individuals and Members of Parliament. The result of
the Government's second thoughts was stated by Lord Irwin in the

House of Lords as follows:[1] 'It seems to me that there are two principles upon which a reformer of our secondary education system might think it proper scientifically to proceed. He might say that his idea was that secondary education should be made entirely free for all pupils, quite irrespective of parents' means, and parents would be invited to make no contribution; or he might say "let us build up a system under which we will charge full fees, reduced fees, or no fees, according to the circumstances of the parents of all the children in the school, and not confine this remission or graduation of fees only to the parents of children who secure a fixed and limited proportion of special places"; that is to say, admit all your children by a competitive examination and, when they are there, decide what their parents are to pay towards the cost of their education.'

Either system, he continued, would be logical, and in particular the first might well be kept before the country as an educational ideal, although in the existing circumstances the country could not afford it.

To this ideal the Government returned after the restoration of the reductions made in educational expenditure in the circumstances of 1931. In their statement of policy before the general election of October 1935 appeared the following words: 'Brains are the prerogative of no single class. They are as likely to be found in the poorest as in the richest homes, and wherever they are found it is essential in the interest of the State, as well as of the individual, that they should be given every opportunity of development.' . . . 'The National Government intend to remove altogether the existing restrictions on the discretion of authorities in regard to the proportion of children who may be admitted to secondary schools either free or at reduced fees.'

For the future the chief administrative problems in the field of secondary education seemed by 1935 to be three in number:

(a) To perfect the machinery in each locality to ensure that no child whose ability and bent of mind fitted it for a full secondary course failed to obtain that course because its parents could not afford to send it or keep it there. This, would clearly involve the award of much greater sums than hitherto in maintenance allowances on top of remission of tuition fees.

(b) To prolong the period of attendance at secondary schools so that there were no empty places in the top forms where the real benefit of a secondary education is felt.

In 1935 far too many children were still leaving at 14, 15, and 16. A general extension of school life to 17 would have increased the numbers in the schools to well over half a million.

[1] H, Lords, Vol. 85, Col. 910.

(c) To find a satisfactory way out of the burden and over-pressure along a narrow channel caused by the School Certificate and Matriculation examinations. As noted above there were by 1934 hopeful signs that this might be achieved by action on the part of the universities and the schools themselves.

This brief sketch of the advance of secondary education in England from 1902 to 1935 exhibits a typically British adaptation to meet the pressure of social, economic, and political forces. Yet the task of isolating and evaluating those forces is a difficult one. It is now perhaps possible to view those earlier currents which led up to the Act of 1902 in a perspective which may not appear unduly distorted to the future historian. The streams which combine to make a river at its source can be traced on a map. But in the broader river of more recent times, the complex social, political, and economic currents are more difficult to separate. In 1935, an observer on education might still have had many doubts and questionings.

Had the demand for secondary education on the part of parents in reality increased? Would there in fact have been so many times the number of children receiving it as forty years before if the provision of special places and maintenance grants by the local authorities had not been so liberal? Was it not perhaps the case that the very provision of facilities for secondary education had bred a demand for it? Such questions might in fact very properly have been asked by a foreign observer confronted for the first time by the number of 'special places' then held, the amount spent on maintenance allowances annually and the number of fee-paying scholars in the total number.[1] But they betray serious understandings. The truth of the matter was never more clearly stated than by the Schools Inquiry Commission nearly seventy years before.[2] 'It is vain to expect to educate the people of this country except by gradually inducing them to educate themselves. Those who have studied the subject may supply the best guidance, and Parliament may be persuaded to make laws in accordance with their advice. But the real force whereby the work is to be done must come from the people.

'The people perhaps cannot give guidance but they can give life, which is even more valuable than guidance. With the people what we may do may be imperfect, without them we shall probably do little or nothing.'

If the first impulse towards our national system of elementary

---

[1] Total number in the schools, 1934, 448,421; total number of free scholars, 1934, 216,255; partially free, 15,152; Aid to students, £2,329,625. This figure, however, includes aid to students in training colleges.

[2] R.C.E., 1868, p. 658.

education arose out of the humanitarian conscience of the more fortunate elements in the community, the national system of secondary
education was built principally upon the aspirations of the wage-earning classes, and the determination of those in receipt of small salaries
themselves to equip their children to earn larger ones. It is an interesting study, for example, to compare a graph showing the rise in the
attendance at secondary schools with one showing the rise in the
membership of trade unions.

England, it has been remarked, is primarily a social democracy,
using the word 'social' in the sense that the logical conception of a
career open to talents finds far less ready acceptance than, for example,
in France. It is replaced by a much less rationally based solicitude on
the part of the English parent to afford his particular child a better
chance in life than he himself enjoyed. In this reason and self-interest
normally play a lesser part than sentiment and the feeling that the
commencement of wage-earning is not of itself a desirable thing if circumstances permit it to be postponed, and if, by such postponement, a
start can be made in a job carrying or leading to greater social prestige.

On the other hand England had not yet, in 1935, whole-heartedly
accepted, as a democratic ideal, the principle of affording secondary
education to all who showed any desire to receive it, which had filled
the secondary schools of the United States. Her conservative habits of
thought and the equally conservative financial traditions of her central
and local government, accentuated by the financial strain of the 1914–
18 war, had been brought at last to accept the theory, first enunciated
by Comenius three hundred years before, that there must eventually
be equality of educational opportunity where there is equality of
capacity to profit by it: but they had never conceived it to be possible
to entertain the much more expensive theory, first put forward by
Robert Owen in the 1830s, that 'all inequality of educational and
social condition must cease' and the secondary schools be thrown open
to all who demand admission to them.

The public attitude towards secondary education in England thus
seemed to occupy by 1935 a middle position between that of France
and Germany on the one hand and that found in the United States and
in certain parts of Wales on the other. For it is interesting to note that
in Wales 223 children per 1,000 of the elementary age group were
already passing forward to secondary schools as compared with 119 in
England.

While the 'gentlemanly amateur' was still setting the tone in
England, France and Germany had long been concerned to recruit a
substantial officer and official class, to advance the national welfare by
intellectual achievement, and to secure that the corpus of human
knowledge painfully acquired over the past centuries should be

handed forward to the safe keeping of a sufficient intelligentsia in the next generation.

Yet the army of pupils receiving secondary education, which had grown up in England in less than a third of a century, was respectable even by continental standards. What is more, it had grown up without such adventitious aids as 'military privileges' to induce parents to seek secondary education for their boys; without the prospect of compulsory military service at 18 to check premature withdrawal; without even any clearly expressed philosophy of secondary education in the mind either of State or parent beyond a vague belief that it might lead to better opportunities in life, such as a wider circle of friends or a happier marriage, to greater competitive efficiency in securing a job or to increased chances of rendering service to society. Characteristically, too, the schools avoided what the English parent might regard as the rather rigid erudition fostered by the German secondary school or the too purely intellectual tone of the French lycée.

Instead there had grown up a loosely knit complex of schools exhibiting the widest possible variety in their methods and curricula, but all endeavouring, according to their several conceptions, to achieve a final product which would respect scholarship without neglecting the claims of games and outdoor activities, cultivate adaptability whilst guarding against superficiality, and know how to achieve a balanced personal standpoint whilst recognizing that there are two sides to almost every question. The 'gentlemanly amateur' was in fact becoming sublimated into the 'all rounder', conscious of his obligations to a social order in transition.

Was a parent who perceived these qualities in his neighbour's son or daughter (although he was probably very far from clothing them in words), and desired that his own child should possess them too, guilty of nothing more than a mild form of snobbery? Or was he to be held up to moral obloquy as a relic of Victorian subservience to the wearer of a black coat? Those who accepted the latter view of the matter would call up in their support the undoubted fact that the success of the managing and proprietary classes, in the days when England was a country of small private concerns with few industrial competitors, was often attributed by their workmen to the possession of a 'public school' education. Education, however ill adapted it may in reality have been to the management of a business, seemed to spell power. Their sons, they argued, might become managers too if they could only afford them a better education. They would call up too the many individual cases which had undoubtedly occurred where the social advantage conferred by the right to wear the same old scholar's tie as the son of the foreman or the manager had been known to influence promotion.

A widespread popular desire for those better opportunities in life to which higher education was—often erroneously—supposed to be the gateway had admittedly played a substantial part in the growth of the schools. But it was not mere snobbery. The decline of the small private business, its replacement by huge and correspondingly impersonal amalgamations, the demand for new aptitudes and the reorientation of others, and finally the steady levelling pressure of death duties—which all continued apace after the Second World War—had already begun. This new appetite for secondary education was on the whole a perfectly legitimate and praiseworthy attempt on the part of the sensible citizen to endow his child with a good education as the best, perhaps the only, capital asset which he could hope to pass on to him.

Other influences, too, of a social nature had been exercising a steadily increasing effect upon the growth of the schools.

In the first place, more than 1,000 schools had now been in existence long enough for hundreds of thousands of pupils who had passed through them to have married and become the fathers and mothers of a new generation. A parent who has himself enjoyed the advantages of a secondary education is usually among the first to make whatever sacrifices may be called for to afford it to his own son or daughter. The degree of sacrifice required, too, probably tended to diminish with the spread of birth-control and the consequent diminution in the size of families.

Just as compulsory elementary education appeared to display a new strength when it had entered upon its second generation, the secondary schools were now forming a similar self-perpetuating tradition.

Secondly, the schools were now continually being reinforced by the upthrust of new strata of the population. Arrangements were already being made by nearly all the L.E.A.s for higher education to submit to a general examination, at about the age of 11, all children in the elementary schools who appeared likely to be capable of benefiting by a secondary school course. Many L.E.A.s had of course gone further, and were spending considerable sums annually to bring to the notice of parents by advertisement, open days, education weeks, exhibitions, and literature, the chances and choices offered to their children by higher education. The L.C.C., for example, had begun to issue a simply written pamphlet, 'Now you are 10', to all children in its schools on attaining that age, in the hope that the parents would read it also. This served to call the attention of parents to their children's promise and, if it resulted in many disappointed hopes of a 'special place', it ensured a steady stream of fee-paying entrants from homes which might not otherwise have thought of sending their children to a secondary school. Those curt refusals to accept the offer of a free place, often scrawled on the back of a sugar bag or an envelope, which used to be so common in the L.E.A.s' postbags in earlier days, were much more rare.

Other agencies too had been at work in the same direction. The University Extension movement and the spread of county libraries had been steadily widening the circle of those who preferred to follow the uphill path of seasoned knowledge to the distractions and rewards of more directly specific or remunerative information. Some interesting evidence as to the determination on the part of those who attended University Extension courses to secure secondary education for their children was made available in *Learn and Live*, compiled by Messrs Williams & Heath for the Institute of Adult Education. The great variety of newspapers, reviews, magazines, and technical periodicals sustained by a population compulsorily educated for sixty years was continually pointing to new fields of interest. A demand had thus been created for the educational equipment necessary for their more thorough exploration and intelligent assimilation. The broad cultural influence of the films and of broadcasting had already begun to add their contribution to the same end. The Women's Institutes and numberless societies such as the British Drama League were enlarging the opportunities for the profitable use of leisure by the young, and in doing so contributing to the realization by their elders that a liberal education had come to rank among the chief goods of life.

There was a day not long before the twentieth century opened when it was necessary to plead for the higher education of women on the ground that the community, by denying it to them, was depriving itself of the trained contribution which it might expect to receive from more than half its membership. By 1895 this battle had been won, at any rate so far as the educated classes of the day were concerned, although the shortage of secondary schools for girls was still serious when the Bryce Commission reported. A great deal was evidently done to make good this shortage between 1895 and 1910. After that the disparity between the places available for the sexes ceased to be serious nationally, whatever may have been the case in individual localities.

If woman was able to unlock the door to the secondary schools before the First World War, she had of course by 1935 come to enjoy the full freedom of the latchkey to practically every learned profession[1] and even to the older universities. Victorian fathers were often inclined to spend their substance on the education of their sons and to be content to provide each daughter with a single accomplishment. In reparation they usually expected the sons to fend for themselves and left what savings they had accumulated to those daughters who had

---

[1] The Customs Preventive Service and the Consular Service were still exceptions, but for special reasons. Readers of *Women's Work in Modern England*, 1928, by Miss Vera Brittain, will of course know that the problem of finding suitable and remunerative work for well-educated girls was still, however, a serious one.

failed to find husbands. The next generation, in an age of universal woman's suffrage and growing equality of opportunity, were changing their views. The prospect of his daughter's marriage began to seem to her father rather as an argument for affording her a liberal education than as a reason for withholding it. With the experience of the 1914–18 war behind him and before him a future which often appeared dark and always uncertain, he remembered the widows of his friends too often existing on small means because they had neither a business career to which to return nor the training to take one up.

Finally, although figures are difficult to obtain,[1] there is no doubt that the first third of the century had witnessed a great expansion of the older professions and the creation of a remarkable number of new ones. There was an ever-increasing call for new types of professional service to minister to social and domestic needs, leisure, and even entertainment. Human society, like the biological species, was moving from the unspecialized to the specialized. The annual recruitment to professional careers, in which the secondary schools played the most important part, was already many times as great as it was when the century opened.

Of the *economic* factors which played a part something has already been said in the historical survey. A healthy reaction was already setting in among those whom the larger-scale organization of industry had brought to positions of management, against the 'gentlemanly amateur's' aversion to discuss anything but cricket and golf. It was no longer 'bad form' to discuss and give thought to the recruitment policy of one's works or business. This in itself was in part no doubt to be placed to the credit of a more broadminded education. The employer who did think about these matters very soon came to realize that to live by exports (in a world in which economic nationalism, expressing itself in customs barriers and trade restrictions, had become a moving force in every land) this country must utilize every atom of trained ability she could produce. To go on repeating that the British workman was the best in the world would be vain unless the goods he made could surmount tariff barriers because they were better designed, more skilfully advertised, more durable, more reliable, and more up to date

---

[1] Those interested should consult *The Social Structure of England and Wales*, by Professor Carr Saunders and Mr Caradog Jones, particularly Chapters V and VI. The following figures are also illuminating:

	Census 1891	Census 1931
Professional occupations and their subordinate services	507,870	746,085
General or Local Government	144,300	293,108
Commercial occupations	416,365	2,071,420

The number of persons professionally engaged in entertainment and sport rose from 82,794 to 114,023 between 1921 and 1931.

than those with which they competed. England in fact must for ever be seeking to anticipate the market or produce goods requiring a degree of scientific precision unattainable, at similar cost, elsewhere. *The Times* has seldom done a greater service to the nation than it did during the First World War in calling public attention to the lack of an intelligent respect for science, which had hitherto been too common, and the need for scientific method and a scientific habit of mind as vital to the continued existence of this country as a great power. For it was out of this correspondence that the reports of the Prime Minister's Committee on Science in the Secondary Curriculum arose, and those reports led to a marked development of science in the schools.

Again, although a modern democracy must ultimately move forward on the brains of its men of genius, it continues to exist because countless myriads of trained workers with hand and brain, whose names never appear in the newspapers, are doing the thing near at hand and doing it as well as possible. This economic fact was still, however, too often overlooked by leaders of industry and leaders of national life alike. Many of them did not begin to understand, let alone assimilate, the immense number of complicated sources of wealth which go to make up the national income and the balance of trade.[1]

Finally, the growth of secondary education owed much to the development of motor transport and the cheapening of the humble bicycle—two economic assets which have often been overlooked. While, paradoxically enough, the development of the railway network in Victorian times nearly killed the ancient grammar schools, the bicycle and motor-bus often became a means to their resuscitation. The railways made it possible for the manufacturing classes in the heyday of industrial prosperity to send their sons to the public and private boarding schools, made respectable by the work of Arnold and others, instead of to the local endowed school. It is an interesting reflection that much of the life of Matthew Arnold was devoted to a passionate crusade to restore the schools thus jeopardized by his father's success. A few local endowed schools, such as Blundell's and Manchester Grammar School (see p. 43), profited, but the majority were adversely affected.

Some of the *political* movements which contributed to the advance of secondary education in England have been indicated in the historical survey. We have seen (p. 65) how all shades of political opinion supported the higher education sections of the Act of 1902. Each con-

---

[1] The absence of knowledge of economics in political leaders of the day was often astonishing. The Treasury had to import an economist with a flair for simple explanation of economic facts, Mr Hartley Withers, author of *The Meaning of Money*, in order to instruct Mr Lloyd George in simple economic trends.

tinued to make its distinctive contribution. In matters affecting the homes and life of the people all parties are liberal at heart. The Act which made it possible stands to the credit of a Conservative Government with Liberal Unionist support. The working-class demand for the restoration to the 'poor scholar' of endowments left for his benefit was interpreted by the free-place requirements of a Liberal Government. It was reinforced by much activity in re-scheming the endowments of old foundations and concurrent measures to import a greater control by popularly elected representatives. The Labour party consistently supported the efforts of such agencies as the Workers' Educational Association to arouse a greater appreciation of the advantages of higher education. It also constantly kept before the country the need for a new basis of social equality, an equality of social opportunity, and was never slow to call attention to potential ability allowed to run to waste for want of additional scholarships and maintenance allowances.[1]

Thus working-class aspirations and the new scientific outlook were both moving towards the same point, the inadmissibility of class and caste distinctions in a new social order. They were reinforced by the recognition by conservative opinion, first, that modern industry and commerce required an élite no less than the administration of central and local government, the professions, and the ministry of the Church; secondly, that enlarged social opportunity was the safety-valve of class feeling.

In sharp distinction to the practice of many other countries, however, the direct interest of the State in promoting a vigorous and well-balanced system of secondary education as a factor in competitive efficiency at home and national prestige and colonial development abroad, in England took the form of silent pressure rather than noisy nationalistic stimulation. This pressure was exerted through official circulars; prefatory memoranda to grant regulations—backed by the potent inducement of ever-increasing grants; full inspections of schools by H.M.I.s, followed by conferences between the governing bodies and the reporting Inspectors; conversations between Inspectors and the executive officers of the local authorities; and speeches by the leaders of local or national life at the opening of new or rebuilt schools, prize days and education weeks. By these means pride in the local schools was substituted for nationalism, a sense of civic responsibility for centrally directed government propaganda. As the late Dr James Graham remarked in the handbook he provided for the Leeds Education week in 1926, 'An efficient system of secondary schools is an

---

[1] See particularly *Secondary Education for All*, edited by Prof. R. H. Tawney (1922); Mr Kenneth Lindsay's *Social Progress and Educational Waste* (1926); and the report on 'The Secondary School' by the Bradford I.L.P., 1928–31.

essential for any progressive community.' This local pride and sense of civic responsibility was of course greatly stimulated by the profound stirring in all phases of national thought and activity due to the 1914–1918 war.

When the twentieth century opened England seemed in the sphere of secondary education to be sixty years behind her neighbours. Blindly perhaps, or at least without any very conscious directive purpose, but impelled rather by a confused medley of interacting, social, political, and economic tendencies, she covered herself in some thirty years with a reputable network of secondary grammar schools.

As inheritors of ideals handed down by the older educational foundations of the past they paid service to the English respect for tradition. But by virtue of their modern equipment, their broad-based democratic clientèle, the academic distinction of their staffs, they were able without misgiving to make their peculiar contribution to the realization of the bold words of Comenius: 'I aim at securing for all human beings training in all that is proper for their common humanity.'

CHAPTER VII

THE EMANCIPATION OF THE ELEMENTARY SCHOOL

The change in the public attitude towards the elementary school since 1895.—The objectives of elementary education as seen by educationists of the 1890s.—Sir Robert Morant's manifesto of 1904.—Difficulties which hindered its realization.—The proper educational treatment of the adolescent, an ever-growing problem.—The 'Hadow' Report.—Its implications.—The conception of the function of the elementary school in the 1930s.

WE have seen how the Local Government Act of 1888 and the Education Act of 1902 provided a stock upon which a national system of education could be grafted. In the preceding chapter we have traced the growth of the first branch grafted on to that stock, secondary grammar education, and seen it blossom and begin to bear fruit. Before examining the second branch, technical and further education, it will be well to follow out some of the changes which the Acts initiated in the sphere of elementary education—by enabling the maintenance of all schools whether board or voluntary to be put on a common financial footing and thus preparing the way for the Burnham Salary Scales, Mr Fisher's Education Act of 1918, and the Hadow Report on the Education of the Adolescent. For technical and further education could only in exceptional cases begin before the point at which the elementary schools, and in many instances the secondary schools, had done their work. It must in fact be sustained by an educated entry. This chapter will not therefore be concerned to follow the numerical growth of the elementary school system, which reached a high-water mark in 1904 at 6,070,296 on the registers and would have reached 6½ millions if attendance had then been compulsory till 14. Its purpose is rather to show the gradual emancipation of the elementary school from nineteenth-century ideas and practice after the arctic winter of payment by results, and to study the consequent change—slow as it was—in the public attitude towards the elementary system. How great this change was could only perhaps be appreciated by the older members of H.M. Inspectorate and by teachers who began their career as pupil teachers in the 1890s and were retiring from the profession during the 1930s. Perhaps few even of these could recall with any clarity the full extent of the change. How many of us could, for example, recollect in precise detail the aspect of the street in which we were born and the changes which have taken place in its outline and in the manners, customs, and bearing of its inhabitants?

One of the great difficulties which confronts anyone who tries to review a period of forty or fifty years in balanced historical perspective is to strike the mean between the attitude of those whose actions or practice were definitely in advance of public opinion and those whose ideas were as definitely in its wake. Progress in education, as in many other departments of national life, is achieved by the illumination of genius, fertilized by the imitative power of the enthusiast in contact with genius, and disseminated by the missionary effort of inspectors, administrators, and the educational press. But the work of a genius here and there must never be mistaken for the common level. Take the simple, if painful, case of corporal punishment. Even so early as Dr Johnson's day, it will be remembered, he was proudly informed that schoolboys were being thrashed less and learning more Greek (he is said to have replied, 'That shows, sir, that what they are losing at one end they are gaining at the other'). No doubt there have always been teachers who have been ready to write to their sons 'If you have to cane a boy you must consider that you have failed'.[1] But to suppose that these represented the average of their day would be to fly in the face of history and the recollection—in this instance often only too vivid—of many whose education took place at a much later date.

It has been remarked (p. 4) that the common denominator in the public attitude towards the elementary school in the period from 1870 to 1900 was the general belief that its purpose was to give the vast mass of the children of the nation, who could not aspire to be anything but labourers, artisans, domestic servants, and laundry girls, the minimum mental equipment necessary to launch them upon life.

Stalwart social reformers like Mrs Burgwin might tell the Cross Commissioners that their aim was 'not merely to turn out an educated but a good and happy woman'. Others again might express their conviction that the payment by results system was 'turning out children well principled and conscientious'. But the general attitude was perhaps more nearly expressed by the Rev. D. J. Stewart, M.A., one of the Senior Inspectors of Schools: 'What has always struck me as being the thing to do for boys and girls who have to live by any form of

[1] This was actually written by the grandfather of a head teacher of the 1930s to her father. By 1902 the Instructions to Inspectors contained the following sentiment: 'If discipline were perfect, punishment would be unknown, for the result of efficient discipline is to engender the good habits which render punishment unnecessary. This happy consummation can hardly be realized but should be the teacher's ideal.' One finds it difficult to read this pious thought without imagining its author translating it into polished Latin verse!

labour, is to give them a thorough knowledge of a very few things—to teach them to read with ease, to write a good legible hand, to spell correctly, and to know the first four rules of arithmetic simple and compound, so as to be able to use them for the ordinary little problems of daily life as they grow older.' 'Does not education consist in the complete formation of a man?' one witness was asked. 'Do you think that it is the function of a day school completely to form the whole life and character of a child?' 'If it is the function,' he replied, 'it certainly will not succeed in doing it. It is certainly not the function of a day school to teach the scholars a trade to earn their living, but it can so direct their energies that they can earn their bread and butter more easily.'

The truth is that, however remarkable the results achieved by teachers of genius here and there, at least 50 per cent of the work of most of the ordinary elementary schools was, during the whole of the first generation of compulsory education, social and disciplinary. There were plenty of remarkable teachers, but it is more than doubtful if they could have applied modern teaching methods to the great majority of the children of that day.

It could hardly be otherwise when a sufficiency of trained teaching staff did not exist; when the whole pressure of payment by results was in the direction of intellectual rigidity, of cram, and worse still of regarding children as counters in a money-making machine; and finally, when a proportion of the parents had hardly as yet been touched by any civilizing influence. 'The children are fairly intelligent,' resignedly remarked one witness, who during the past sixteen years had visited nearly every Catholic school in the country, 'but coming from very poor homes with wretched surroundings the present race cannot be immensely raised in intelligence.' 'Country children are quite capable of receiving a higher education,' remarked another, 'but it is not necessary for them.'[1]

So far as *education* was concerned the questions at issue were simpler and more practical. The preoccupation of the Cross Commissioners was not with whether 'the children of the classes that frequent those schools' were receiving something which might start them on the road to a liberal education, but rather whether the schools were keeping a proper balance between fitting them for trade or artisan life and fitting them for clerical jobs. Elementary instruction was a gift from the State to the child. It was not a first stage in an educational process admitting of several stages. Care must be taken lest in attempting to raise too much the standard of education the country might defeat the object for which education was given, namely, that manual labour in which so many children must be occupied afterwards.

[1] *C.C.R.*, 17,310; 3357; 48,950–4; 20,107–13; 26,744–5.

We have seen how with the modification of payment by results in 1895 this static conception of the place of the elementary school began to give way; how the teacher of originality found himself free for cautious experiment. Thus H.M.I.s reported in 1896 (*R.E.D.*, p. viii): 'There is ample evidence of greater originality, of more freedom and elasticity and consequently of more effective teaching.' 'Sympathy, gently lifting over difficulties and stimulating to self-help, which is the essence of true teaching, has its full weight now, and not the mere result, however achieved, at whatever cost to future health, to sound thoughtfulness, and to real abiding taste for intellectual pursuits.' We have seen also how as soon as compulsory education had entered its second generation a current of new interest seemed to carry the schools forward. This current was probably assisted by good resolutions made at the opening of a new century and indirectly by the Boer War. For the educational deficiencies of recruits to the army attracted some notice, and the sufferings of the Boer children in the concentration camps stirred the public conscience in regard to the seemingly more favoured children at home.

No Code of Regulations for public elementary schools before 1903 had dared to give expression to the State's conception of the purpose of the elementary school. The 1902 Code was content to define an elementary school as 'a school or department of a school at which elementary education is the principal part of the education there given, and does not include any school or department of a school at which the ordinary payments in respect of instruction from each scholar exceed ninepence a week'. But in the year 1903 a new and significant note appeared. 'It should be understood', wrote Sir Robert Morant, who had now become Permanent Secretary of the Board of Education, 'that the following Code is provisional in character. It is issued to cover a period which is transitional, a period during which some elementary schools will, as heretofore, be maintained and conducted by School Boards, or by voluntary managers, while others will be passing, at various dates in various localities,[1] under the control of the new statutory Educational Authorities. Early in next year, the Board intend to replace this provisional Code by a Code better adapted to meet the changed conditions which will have been created by the new Act.' The introduction to the new Code, that for 1904, which these words heralded, was in fact a manifesto. The final synthesis is usually attributed to Sir Robert Morant's own pen—and indeed, as has been pointed out, it opens with a paraphrase of the 'Manners makyth man' of his old school—although it was probably based on many contributory

---

[1] The passive resistance movement and Nonconformist hostility, particularly in Wales, delayed the absorption of the School Boards for some years in various localities.

drafts by H.M.I.s. No such complete attempt on the part of the State to set out the purpose of the elementary school has ever been made in any other country:

The purpose of the Public Elementary School is to form and strengthen the character and to develop the intelligence of the children entrusted to it, and to make the best use of the school years available, in assisting both girls and boys, according to their different needs, to fit themselves, practically as well as intellectually, for the work of life.

With this purpose in view it will be the aim of the School to train the children carefully in habits of observation and clear reasoning, so that they may gain an intelligent acquaintance with some of the facts and laws of nature; to arouse in them a living interest in the ideals and achievements of mankind, and to bring them to some familiarity with the literature and history of their own country; to give them some power over language as an instrument of thought and expression, and, while making them conscious of the limitations of their knowledge, to develop in them such a taste for good reading and thoughtful study as will enable them to increase that knowledge in after years by their own efforts.

The School must at the same time encourage to the utmost the children's natural activities of hand and eye by suitable forms of practical work, and manual instruction; and afford them every opportunity for the healthy development of their bodies, not only by training them in appropriate physical exercises and encouraging them in organized games, but also by instructing them in the working of some of the simpler laws of health.

It will be an important though subsidiary object of the School to discover individual children who show promise of exceptional capacity, and to develop their special gifts (so far as this can be done without sacrificing the interests of the majority of the children), so that they may be qualified to pass at the proper age into Secondary Schools, and be able to derive the maximum of benefit from the education there offered them.

And, though their opportunities are but brief, the teachers can yet do much to lay the foundations of conduct. They can endeavour, by example and influence, aided by the sense of discipline which should pervade the School, to implant in the children habits of industry, self-control, and courageous perseverance in the face of difficulties; they can teach them to reverence what is noble, to be ready for self-sacrifice, and to strive their utmost after purity and truth; they can foster a strong respect for duty, and that consideration and respect for others which must be the foundation of unselfishness and the true basis of all good manners; while the corporate life of the School, especially in the playground, should develop that instinct for fair-play and for loyalty to one another which is the germ of a wider sense of honour in later life.

In all these endeavours the School should enlist, as far as possible, the interest and co-operation of the parents and the home in a united effort to enable the children not merely to reach their full development as individuals, but also to become upright and useful members of the community in which they live, and worthy sons and daughters of the country to which they belong.

If this at the time it was penned was a manifesto, stating an ideal rather than describing the average school, it was also a challenge. For a prefatory memorandum added that the Act of 1902 had placed elementary education under improved financial conditions, which had made it possible to look for a higher degree of efficiency than was possible in some areas in the past. The Board, having instituted a normal grant at a single rate, reserved power to reduce the grant, in case of defects, by a somewhat greater amount than was possible under former Codes. Simultaneously the Instructions to Inspectors were replaced by a 'Handbook of suggestions for Teachers and others concerned in the work of Public Instruction'. How far some schools fell short of the ideal set out in this manifesto may be inferred by readers of *What is and What might be*, written on his retirement, in 1911, by Mr E. G. A. Holmes, Senior Chief Inspector; or by those who read between the lines of such sentences in the Board's annual reports as the following: 'Not only are we confronted at every step by questions which are still the subject of public controversy, but we are also bound to recognize that in many directions the full effects of the forces which were set in motion by that Act have not yet manifested themselves, that the adjustment of men and methods to new conditions is still incomplete . . . that in fact we are still in a period of transition.'[1]

It is difficult for the modern educational administrator or teacher to realize to what an extent the controversies which attended the passage of the Education Act of 1902 and the Liberal Government's attempt to repeal it in 1906 inhibited educational advance between 1902 and 1926. Reference has already been made on p. 16 to the loss to education suffered through the transfer to the Insurance Commission of Sir Robert Morant, following the Holmes–Morant circular to Inspectors of 1911. This accentuated the tendency for cautious administration, in which sedative draughtsmanship became almost the sole virtue and of which the new Permanent Secretary, Sir Amherst Selby-Bigge, a product of the Charity Commission, was a leading exponent. Although he never put pen to paper without improving the draft before him, as an administrator he was caution personified; and Morant had exalted the office to such Olympian heights that when the leader of a north country deputation (who was hard of hearing) addressed him as Sir Amorous Selby-Bigge no one present dared even to smile![2]

---

[1] *B.E.R.*, 1908–9.

[2] One of the author's most amusing memories (alarming as it was at the time) was a summons in 1921 to the Establishment Officer to discuss a report which his official superior had made upon him at the end of his two years' probation. 'There are in this report things which are good. Oh yes I will say distinctly good! But there are things which are shall I say "bad". No I will not say bad but shall we say not so good? For example there is this. "Mr Lowndes has always shown himself very ready and willing to take responsibility." Now that is a very serious thing to be said of a young officer!'

The important thing to remember, however, is that the manifesto and its influence on those who read it remained unaltered in all subsequent editions of the Code until 1926. In that year in consonance with the new prospect opened up by the Hadow Report, and with the desire of the Board to free L.E.A.s and their teaching staffs from everything but the irreducible minimum of regulations demanded by Statute, the Code itself shrank from the seventy-six page document of 1902 to a mere paper of ten pages, which many teachers, in all probability, never saw.

While the purpose which should inform the conduct of the elementary schools might be enshrined in these six glowing paragraphs, it was a very different matter to give full effect to that purpose. In the face of the steadily increasing upthrust of the older age-groups, as more and more authorities between 1902 and 1914 made bye-laws raising the age for exemption to 14 and restricting the issue of labour certificates, achievement was seen as steadily to be falling short of aspiration.

Already by 1895 Inspectors had begun to note the tendency for children to be kept 'marking time' in their last year at school.[1] In his report upon secondary education in Essex (1906), Mr Sadler had pleaded for the collection of the older children from the village schools by horse-drawn vans into aggregated schools resembling those which were springing up in the United States and Canada and had added prophetically: 'It is impossible at present to say what may be feasible by means of motor communication in a few years' time.' London and the bigger L.E.A.s were commencing to 'cream off' the abler children from their elementary schools into central schools, as some of the ill-fated higher-grade schools had done before the Cockerton judgment. *The Times* was pleading for a junior secondary school policy—or heresy as it was described by some. Mr Duckworth at Carlisle was reorganizing the schools of that city.

The Board's reports were advocating the same policy on financial grounds. 'If a school in one parish', they wrote in their Report for 1908, 'would agree to take the infants or the older scholars from a neighbouring school in another parish, the problem of making the supply of school premises adequate and satisfactory would in many

---

One hopes that the treatment of their young administrative staff by other government Departments was less rigid. Sir Amherst had waged a bitter struggle to be allowed to continue appointment by selection instead of from the Home and Indian Civil Service examinations. For some years he used to refer to my generation as 'The Bassinette Contingent' although it included at least one Fellow of All Souls and a future headmaster of Winchester and Bishop of Peterborough.

[1] The account of the principal currents leading up to the Hadow Report which follows is, of course, a very condensed one. The whole subject is brilliantly and exhaustively dealt with in the introductory chapter (by Dr R. F. Young) to the report itself. I have confined myself to noting some material not hitherto recorded.

areas be simplified.' In fact the educational arguments in its favour went back to the pupil teacher centres started by the large towns in the 1870s and 1880s,[1] and were, as we have seen (p. 44), well understood by educationists like Sir Philip Magnus. Mr Fisher's Education Act of 1918, by abolishing all exemptions from school attendance before the end of the term in which the age of 14 was reached and requiring the provision of practical and advanced instructions for the older scholars, still further accentuated the problem. Although the continuation school provisions of the Act excited greater interest at the time, these two sections are now generally recognized to have been among the greatest benefits which it conferred. To a great extent it was a problem of school organization and as such might have been solved slowly and not, in all probability, without friction by circulars and pressure from the Board of Education. The Board did in fact urge authorities, in a circular (No. 1350) issued in January 1925, to organize all new schools and wherever possible all existing schools in such a way as to secure separate departments for all the senior children.

But if this problem of the proper educational treatment of the adolescent, which had been slowly accumulating ever since the passage of the Act of 1902, was to be tackled with the resolution and resources which it would clearly demand, something more than an official circular was clearly necessary. Morant's manifesto of 1904 must give way to a new one. Its conception of the purpose of the elementary school must be recast. The steady growth of the facilities for passage from the elementary schools to the secondary and technical schools was seen to demand something more than a pious aspiration that, as a subsidiary object of the elementary school, it should seek 'to discover individual children who show promise of exceptional capacity and are qualified to pass forward'.

Cynics could remark, and in fact were remarking, although not very audibly, that if a child was able, the State would lavish money upon his education in a secondary school; if he was naughty, the State would not scruple to segregate him expensively in a reformatory school; if he was mentally deficient or epileptic he could again be sure of an expensive education; but that if he belonged to that worthy 75 per cent of the school population which was just ordinary, the all-age elementary school and subsequent evening classes must suffice for him.

It was this paradoxical state of affairs which the framers of the Hadow Report on the Education of the Adolescent set out to remedy. Administrative change would be worthless unless behind it there existed a real conviction and a new outlook. Elementary education could no longer be treated as a thing separate in itself. It must be treated henceforward as one only of two or three stages in education.

[1] Liverpool in 1876, London in 1882; *C.C.R.*, Part III, Chapter V

It must be the primary stage to end at 11 and to be followed by a 'post-primary' stage where all children—not a few selected children—would be able to follow a variety of types of secondary education suited to their capacities and bent of mind. They must be able to do so by entry to the secondary schools looking to the universities; by promotion to senior schools looking to the continuative education at last available in the commercial, literary, and evening institutes; or by further promotion from both secondary and senior schools to the junior technical schools offering an alternative form of secondary training for those hoping to enter skilled careers, a training to be followed up by national certificate courses.

Finally legislation should be passed to compel, and not merely permit, all children to remain at school up to the age of 15 as from 1932.

Like Morant's manifesto of 1904, the Hadow Report was, in many parts of the country, in advance of its time. The 'real conviction and the new outlook' had to be painfully built up, against the misgivings of parents and the rigidities of school buildings planned to take children of all ages.

The full implications of this 'Piers Plowman's charter' staking out the claims of every inhabitant of the 'fayre field full of folke' to a minimum of four years post-primary education are still working themselves out today. But like Morant's manifesto it was also a challenge. Public education in this country has been fortunate since 1904 in having two such manifestos towards which to work after the arteriosclerosis induced by 'payment by results'. The L.E.A.s had already by 1934 taken up the challenge to such purpose that more than half the pupils over 11 were in reorganized departments. The progress of reorganization was shown with great clarity on Chart 7 of the publication *Educational Administration in England and Wales*.[1] The number of pupils over 11 in reorganized departments in 1934 was 1,089,000 as compared with 959,000 in unreorganized departments. In the Greater London area reorganization had been 80 per cent achieved.

What then was the conception of the purpose of the elementary school in the 1930s? It will not be found in any code of regulations, or in any official publication, except in so far as it may be inferred from the Board's *Handbook of Suggestions for Teachers*. Much of Morant's conception of 1904 still stood, and deserved to stand for all time. From time to time too a departmental committee viewing the elementary school from their own angle would add a new contribution. The following is a good example:

A quasi scientific theory has long been accepted that the process of education is the performance of compulsory hard labour . . . a gritting of the teeth

[1] Educational Pamphlet No. 105 (1936).

Elementary education comes to life. A debate in a rural school in 1935

Physical education had been transformed by 1935

upon hard substances with the primary object not of acquiring a particular form of skill or knowledge, but of giving the mind a general training and strengthening. This theory has now been critically examined and declared to be of less wide application than was thought. Its abandonment would make it possible to secure for the child a living interest and a sense of purpose in his work, and it would replace the old wasteful system of compulsion and mere obedience by a community of interest between pupil and teacher. This community of interest would be felt instinctively and immediately by the pupil, and if rightly conceived by the teacher should lead not to the storing of compartments of the mind, but the development and training of faculties already existing. It proceeds not by the presentation of lifeless facts but by teaching the student to follow the different lines on which life may be explored and proficiency in living may be obtained. It is, in a word, guidance in the acquiring of experience.[1]

In the next chapter an attempt will be made to show how far the elementary schools had proceeded by 1935 in securing for the child a living interest and a sense of purpose in his work; but first an attempt must be made to set out the conception of the purpose of the elementary school in the mid-thirties for comparison with that of forty or fifty years before. My account is based on the reading during 1919–35 of many thousands of reports on schools of all kinds in every part of the country.

In the nursery school or class, where one existed, the child entering at the age of two would learn before he passed into the infant school to act, and to act often with considerable self-possession, as a member of a social community.

In the infant school all children should have been formed into membership of such social communities, and where some of the entrants had the nursery school behind them they would at once form nuclei of order around which the other infants would tend to gravitate. Not all infants by any means entered the infants' school 'trailing clouds of glory'. Many of them in fact were already rather spoilt or self-centred though none the less charming little individuals. Monsieur Piaget in his *Judgment and Reasoning in the Child* concluded that up to 7 the average child has little or no idea of physical or logical necessity, that he is in fact egocentric and finds it difficult to see things from another's point of view. But few infants would enter from a nursery school without trailing something of far greater practical utility, an aura of self-reliant obedience and good social habits.

In the infant and junior schools the children learnt at least an elementary and sometimes even a fairly advanced familiarity with the simple printed word, the simple spoken word, and the simpler concepts of number. They came to realize that other persons might see things

---

[1] *The Teaching of English in England*, 1921, Introduction, pp. 7 and 8.

differently and to feel the desire to prove that they were right on occasion. While they were usually content to argue by analogy, they were beginning to understand the use of words like 'because' and 'although'.

In the senior schools the children were becoming increasingly able to draw conclusions from the facts learnt in the junior school and to carry out mental experiments on the plane of pure hypothesis. In the three or at most four years which remained they had, therefore, to be taught to get the fullest use out of those first tools of education which they had acquired in the junior school; to be encouraged to take the maximum of intelligent interest in the world about them; and finally, if possible, to be passed out into life with a desire to utilize their leisure and enrich their lives by the intelligent reading of good books and the independent exercise of the senses which the school had endeavoured to develop in them. Educational thought was at last generally alive to the importance of the senior school and the difficulties which had to be faced in giving it a 'place in the sun'. It was already becoming evident that it was upon the purpose or want of purpose of these schools that the best educational thought of the nation must be concentrated in the next twenty years, if the ideal set before English education by the Hadow Report was to be completely realized. Moreover, the difficulties needed to be resolutely faced. The competition for entry to the secondary schools and to a lesser extent the central schools, where they existed, had become so keen in many towns that it was almost impossible for parents, or even for the junior school teachers, to refrain from spurring the junior child to greater effort by the warning that if he did not work harder he would not get a place in the secondary or central school. Thus if he failed in the examination he might tend to take the road to the senior school with a sense of discouragement or to draw an unfavourable contrast between the secondary and the senior school, a contrast which, however much it might still be supported by older and more cramped buildings in the senior schools and less generous provision of amenities, would have been emphatically repudiated by the framers of the Hadow Report. Moreover, if the free place examination did its work properly, the senior schools would be receiving annually batches of children of all grades of ability ranging from perhaps 20 per cent possessing intelligence above the normal to perhaps 40 per cent who would in the former undifferentiated school have remained in a class with children one, two, or more years younger than themselves.

To arouse the interest of these children, to restore or strengthen their confidence in themselves, to provide them with a new environment of craft work, organized games, and realistic studies where, starting level with their new class-mates, they could regain their opinion of themselves, should, it was realized, be the purpose of the senior school. It must never let the children it received accept the verdict of the free place examination as the modern equivalent of the old dunce's cap, or they would very soon fatalistically conform to it. Moreover, it would have been looked upon as a disaster in those days if senior schools were ever to set before themselves the object of becoming anaemic reflections of the secondary grammar schools, or if they were to yield to outside pressure for the taking of leaving examinations. Where these objects were being successfully achieved (and the number of schools achieving success was increasing rapidly every year) 'marking time' became a thing of the past, and the most unlikely children were found capable not only of hard work but of successful work. Despite the real renaissance in the 1925–35 decade in rural education there were still, of course, too many children who left unreorganized 'all age' schools unable to take the intelligent interest in the conditions of life in their neighbourhood, or to play that part in their own environment which a critical public was beginning to expect. But equally there were hundreds of thousands leaving reorganized senior schools (and even unreorganized rural schools) who had acquired some understanding of their country's past, of its social, economic, and industrial life and relationships, of how things worked and how they were made, of the lore of the countryside; who could read the newspapers, visit a play or film or listen to the wireless with more than a bare understanding; who might have come near experiencing perfection in the music of their school—for music is probably the only subject in which a child of 14 can attain perfection; who had learnt to read good books intelligently and to find them in the public library; who had a sufficient idea of the geography of human knowledge to prevent them looking on the mountain tops[1] when they ought to have been looking in the valleys for the piece of information they needed; who would find the farmyard not only an interesting place but one which called for the exercise of intellectual processes; who expected to find in a museum not 'a last resting place of travellers' mementoes and of fossils that have undeservedly survived from ages long ago',[2] still less a repository of two-headed calves and curios to make the people laugh, but something which would feed their curiosity and set them to expand their knowledge; who could even assemble their ideas with sufficient self-reliance to take an intelligent part in a conversation or debate.

If this brief survey of the changing attitude towards the public elementary school in the fifty years between 1885 and 1935 is a fair one, it will be seen that before the twentieth century opened the elementary school was regarded (except by those in advance of their

[1] The phrase is Lord Eustace Percy's. It occurs in that remarkable book *Education at the Cross Roads*.   [2] *E.P.* No. 87.

time) as a kind of waiting-room for life. The Victorian railway network had spread itself to the remotest hamlet, carrying with it the
division of the population into first-, second-, and third-class compartments. The elementary school inevitably therefore became a third-
class waiting-room for life, the private schools and the ancient grammar schools second-class waiting-rooms, and only the 'public' schools
travelled first-class. 'The premises of this school', reported one H.M.I.
in the 1890s, 'consist of a third-class waiting-room and a jam cupboard.' One suspects that he might have applied the simile to the social
atmosphere, and not merely the premises of this and many other
elementary schools of that period.

In the intervening years the second-class had been absorbed both on
the railways and in the educational system. Here the analogy ends, for
the elementary school had not developed into a 'general waiting-room'.
On the contrary, under the impulse of the Hadow Report it was
changing its nature and becoming an anteroom, a place not so much of
preparation for life as a place of rehearsal of life itself, a place in fact
where every child should spend not the least happy and memorable
ten years of its three-score years and ten. Moreover, from being a
place seeking to implant the minimum necessary knowledge to launch
a child upon life, it had become rather a place where the desire for
further knowledge should be awakened and where the child should be
put in the way of acquiring that further knowledge for himself. This is
well illustrated by the growth of the reading habit. It was remarked in
Chapter II that the rural child of 1895 who ever opened a book at
home shone like a good deed in a naughty world. By 1935 the L.C.C.
were finding it necessary to open nightly in the winter 250 warmed and
lighted class-rooms in the poorer districts where children could come to
read or do their homework. The county libraries served a population of
13,352,000 in England and Wales and were issuing 50 million books
a year to 2,164,000 borrowers. More encouraging still in the opinion
of those who investigated the matter, there had been a continuous
improvement in the quantity and quality of the reading matter. The
extension of the electricity grid to rural villages had no doubt been a
contributory factor. There were still, of course, thousands of cottages
with one small downstairs room and a single lamp sharing the table
with father's supper and mother's laundry. And yet some children did
now manage to read in such conditions. In the towns the public libraries
served another $7\frac{1}{2}$ million borrowers who in 1934 read 190 million
books. Before 1920 many rural villages even of considerable size had
no second postal delivery and the London newspapers were usually a
day late. By 1935 both daily and weekly newspapers appeared in the
great majority of homes. Those who were interested in education[1] and

[1] One of the most astonishing features of the years between, say, 1935 and 1965 has

realized what it had done for the population were always puzzled by the liability of the local press to attack the schools. It seemed like biting the hand that sustained it.

---

been the growth in the number of people interested in education and the amount of space devoted to the subject in the press. It was quite unusual for a book on education—unless it became a textbook—to sell more than 500 copies in 1935.

CHAPTER VIII

ELEMENTARY EDUCATION COMES TO LIFE

A growing public interest in the elementary schools.—Developments which improved the teachers' lot.—Increased numbers of teachers and improved professional qualifications.—Reduction in the size of classes.—Improved salary scales.—Superannuation rights.—The segregation of the defective.—Improvement of amenities in the schools.—Developments which improved the lot of the elementary school child.—More realistic studies.—Educational visits.—Growth of specialized teaching, practical work, corporate activities, school journeys, more interesting physical training and games.—Less rigid discipline.—The growth of parental interest in the elementary schools.—Open days. Exhibitions. School magazines.—Parents' associations.—The case for an effective raising of the school leaving age to 15 as seen by educational reformers in the 1930s.

I n previous chapters some attempt has been made to trace those social, economic, and political currents which had been at work in the field of public education from 1902 to 1935. Those currents had not merely carried forward the secondary schools. They had also played their part in stirring parental interest in the elementary schools. This interest had in its turn begun to find expression through the sensitivity of popularly elected representatives, and signs were not wanting that it was steadily becoming a weightier factor with each local election. In some areas the vivification of elementary education had proceeded much more rapidly than in others, but everywhere it had been brought about by a variety of interwoven factors—one leading out of or supporting another so inextricably that it is impossible to describe them in any connected or logical order. Each of these factors again had a literature of its own, often so extensive that within the limits of a single chapter it is impossible to do more than give a bare outline of the principal tendencies.

This outline may for convenience be grouped under three general though arbitrary headings:

(1) Those developments which tended to make more attractive, more fruitful, and on the whole less arduous the lot of those whom we saw in Chapter II 'plying the irksome task of public instruction', and to improve the amenities of the schools themselves.

(2) Those developments which made the scholar's life fuller, more varied, and more interesting.

(3) Those developments which in addition to changes described in (1) and (2) contributed to a deeper parental and public interest in the schools.

(1) *Developments which improved the teachers' lot.*

First in importance of those factors which tended to yield an increasing educational return for the money expended upon the public system by the rate and taxpayer was, of course, the strengthening of teaching power.

Since the abolition after the 1914–18 war of the 'acting teacher's certificate examination' college-trained teachers had been steadily substituted for the untrained and for those who formerly obtained their certificate by evening study. During the first three decades after the passage of the Act of 1902 the day training colleges in connection with the universities and the university training departments, offering third-year or fourth-year post-graduate courses, in the main catered for the expanding needs of the secondary grammar schools. But as soon as secondary grammar education began to reach a state of equilibrium graduate teachers found their way in increasing numbers into the elementary school service. The English genius for the organization of short 'refresher' courses, which had been displayed so remarkably behind the Flanders front during the 1914–18 war, also played a notable part in providing opportunities for the ordinary class teacher to revive his interest in his subject and to learn new and more lively methods of presenting it.

The building up of what Robert Lowe described in 1862 as a 'respectable army' of teachers must (as for example the U.S.S.R. found) always be the first object of national concern to any country embarking upon the education of its whole people. Remarkable progress was made during the years 1895–1935 in converting a very small professional army of trained and certificated teachers, backed by a levy of badly equipped (though vaccinated[1]) assistants and juveniles. Taking as a convenient starting-point the fact that in 1895 there were exactly 100 children on the books for every certificated teacher in service and 47 for every certificated, assistant, vaccinated, and pupil teacher, it is interesting to note that by 1934 there were 43·1 for every certificated teacher, and 32·1 for every teacher in service, and that pupil teachers, student teachers, and other or occasional teachers no longer counted. Again it is interesting to notice that whereas in 1909–10 the Board of Education calculated that something like 20,000 additional certificated

---

[1] At one time proof of successful vaccination appears to have been the only qualification demanded!

teachers would be required to bring the staffing of all areas of each type (county, county borough, borough, and urban district) up to the standard maintained by the most progressive authority of that type, there were by 1934 actually 43,232 more in employment.[1]

Educational statistics, it may be argued, are at best lifeless things, and teaching power cannot be assessed by mere numbers without regard to the teaching capacity of the flesh-and-blood individuals comprised in those numbers. It may therefore be illuminating to look at the teachers' task under the conditions obtaining in 1895 as viewed by a contemporary Inspector:

'I spent an afternoon in a village school. The number present was 44; 35 of these were spread over the first five standards, and 9 infants were in two groups. Thus the master, a man of 60 years, had seven classes to teach. And he had no help whatever, except for the needlework. I sat in the school and watched him with deep interest. Seven classes were to be kept going. How would it be done? First, the two groups of infants were set to copy some letters that had been put on the blackboard; then Standard I was set to transcription; IV and V worked sums from their arithmetics; and the master gave the object lesson for the day to II and III combined. This lesson was remarkable; it was broken in so many pieces. A boy would stand up in IV or V and say 'Please, sir!' The master would turn from his class, ask the interrupter for his difficulty, give him a hint, or step to his side, and quickly returning, pick up the thread of the broken lesson as best he might, or with a side glance he would observe a boy or girl apparently stuck in a sum; and 'Are you fast? Tell me if you are fast' was thrown encouragingly again and again to the group at Arithmetic. Two or three excursions to the infants, a hasty inspection, from his place, of the Standard I transcription, an order to clean slates[2] and refill them; such breaks were constantly recurring; yet on through it all went the object lesson. But

(1) What an impossible task.
(2) What a strain upon the teacher.
(3) What a waste of the children's time.

The efforts of the master to meet the demands upon him were pathetic. A school so staffed wastes much of the children's time, and makes a slave of the teacher.'

The lesson to be drawn from such a report as this is not that there was any substantial ground for complacency in 1935, but that the nation was getting a very inadequate return for its money forty years

---

[1] *B.E.R.*, 1909–10, p. 25. No. of C.T.s, 1909, 97,422; 1934, 130,654, but for an average attendance about 100,000 higher.

[2] Slates remained in use in many areas until the end of the first decade of the century. Chalk boards were beginning to be used by some schools by about 1906. Architects and builders demolishing old schools are sometimes puzzled by the blocks of hardstone fitted into the brickwork of entrances and playground walls. These were, of course, placed there for the scholars to sharpen their slate pencils.

earlier. Teachers and Inspectors hailed the end of 'payment by results' as introducing a new heaven, for as one of them wrote, 'under the new system a change has taken place inside the schools as if some dark shadow had passed away, and sunshine poured in with cheering rays'. So too the 1926–39 generation were inclined to hail the new prospect opened up by the Hadow Report. But it should never be forgotten that the two chief stumbling-blocks in the way of educational advance have always been the over-academic and the over-parsimonious. The former could turn the new search for realism to dust just as the latter soon found that when inspection of methods was substituted for evaluation of results, the greater security of income enjoyed enabled school managers to employ, without detection, a much higher proportion of untrained staff.[1] The Board of Education played a big part in securing an improvement of teaching power, but they preferred to use an elaborate 'yardstick' to the other type of stick placed in their hands by the power to fine backward areas. The Annual Codes up to 1926 laid it down that in no case would the staff of a school be considered sufficient if it was not at least equivalent for the average attendance measured by a scale on which the head teacher counted for so many, each assistant teacher (certificated) for so many, each uncertificated assistant for so many, etc. The values assigned to certificated teachers were increased and those assigned to untrained teachers gradually reduced as the years went by. But in due course even this yardstick disappeared from the Code, to be replaced by a complicated and unpublished staffing formula. This enabled the Treasury to persuade timid Presidents of the Board of Education in the later inter-war years to place artificial restrictions on the volume of teacher training in the supposed interests of economy. The output of the secondary grammar schools was increasing, the school population generally falling, and the demand for the product of the secondary grammar schools from industry, the commercial world, agriculture, and the civil and local government services far less keen than it has since become. If ever there was a time when the shortage of teachers could have been remedied it was the 1930s. The opportunity was deliberately jettisoned.

Concurrently with this improvement in teaching power the years between 1902 and 1934 witnessed the gradual reduction in the size of classes in the schools, the Burnham salary scales, the Teachers' Superannuation Acts of 1918 and 1925, the segregation of the more seriously abnormal children into special schools and classes, and some improvement in the amenities of the school buildings themselves. The first undoubtedly tended to give the country a better return for its money; the second to raise the position of the teacher in the eyes of a public still far too prone to evaluate service on a cash basis; the third

[1] *B.E.R.*, 1909–10, p. 8.

to enable him to retire after the age of sixty instead of trying to carry on until he could do so no longer; the fourth to free him from the impossible task of giving a 'full share of conscientious attention' to those for whom that attention should be afforded by different methods or at a slower pace; the fifth to make service in an elementary school more attractive and to improve working conditions. Obviously a small volume could be devoted to each of these points, and within the limits of a single chapter no attempt will be made to indicate more than the salient points of contrast between the position reached by 1935 and that forty years before, and the more important milestones.

(a) *The reduction of the size of classes.* As we saw in Chapter II, the increasing popularity of the schools when payment by results came to an end aggravated the overcrowding in many schools, and combined with the shortage of trained teachers to force up the size of classes to 70 or 80 or more. When a teacher fell ill the school was either closed, often for a month on end, or the children were distributed over the remaining staff.

Under such conditions mass instruction must have been the rule rather than the exception and continuity of syllabus was often out of the question. Indeed every photograph of school activities at this period displays enormous classes in which all the children are doing precisely the same thing at the same time. By 1909, however, the increasing supply of teachers available was enabling the more progressive authorities to organize a service of 'supply' teachers to replace temporary casualties. The Board of Education too, turning aside from their preoccupation with the building up of the secondary grammar school system, found it possible to shorten their yardstick. The 'value' of supplementary and student teachers was reduced to 20 children in average attendance, uncertificated teachers to 35, head teachers to 35, while certificated assistants continued to count for 60. An investigation into the staffing of London schools disclosed 1,982 (out of 15,168) classes with over 60 scholars on the books, and the L.C.C. was fined £10,000 'pour encourager les autres'.

This action on the part of the Board was followed in 1912 by the initiation by the L.C.C. of the well-known '40 and 48' scheme, to limit classes of infants to 48 and those containing older scholars to 40. This set a standard for emulation by progressive authorities elsewhere. Unfortunately at this point the war brought reaction. Twenty thousand teachers joined the new armies, schools were often requisitioned for the billeting of troops, and many children were released from school attendance to serve on the land.[1]

Similarly the new era of hope introduced by Mr Fisher's Education

[1] C. Birchenough, *History of Elementary Education in England and Wales from 1800 to the Present Day,* pp. 208–210.

Act of 1918 was rudely shattered in 1921 by the fall of the 'Geddes Axe'. Where H.M.Is had been charged before to call immediate attention to the failure of a school to comply with the staffing yardstick set out in the Code, the formula 'as soon as financial circumstances permit' crept in to supply a ready excuse for inaction.

The return to power in 1924 of the first Labour Government 'reversed the engines', and except for a brief check following the second economy campaign of 1931, the reduction of numbers in classes to a size where mass methods can give way to education has since that date been one of the first objects of every Government. Whereas, for example, there were in 1922 28,000 classes in England and Wales containing between 50 and 60 children and 5,000 with over 60, the numbers had by 1934 come down to 6,138 with between 50 and 60 and a bare 56[1] with over 60. The centrifugal tendency of the population of the larger towns as a result of the rehousing of their populations in housing estates enabled many L.E.A.s to carry this progressive reduction to considerable lengths. In London, for example, which contained about 10 per cent of the children of the country, all council schools were organized on the '40 and 48' basis. Infants' classes had been restricted to a maximum roll of 46 in 85 per cent of the council's schools and 81 per cent of the non-provided schools, and all classes mainly composed of children under five years had been reduced to 40 except where, owing to special circumstances, pressure on accommodation existed.

Thus the country had made a beginning, although it had still some way to go before it attained the ideal set before the Cross Commission nearly fifty years before by the Rev. T. W. Sharpe (afterwards Senior Chief Inspector). For Mr Sharpe was so far in advance of his time as to hold that 'the number of a class should never exceed 40, and for the highest class in the school and the lowest class for infants you ought not to have more than 25 to one teacher'. Matthew Arnold was more complaisant, since in his view, with a sound system of elementary teaching, a competent teacher might have a class of 50 scholars on the roll. This would be equal, he explained, to not quite 45 in average attendance.[2]

(b) *The Burnham Salary Agreements.* Little need be said here. The tendency noted in Chapter II for the wealthier areas to make a 'corner' in the best teachers by the payment of higher rates of salary than their poorer neighbours had by 1920 produced several severe crises and inequality between the educational opportunities afforded to

---

[1] *B.E.R.*, 1934, p. 108. The 56 classes with over 60 were probably cases where, owing to the absence of a teacher on 31 March 1934, two classes were combined for the day.

[2] *C.C.R.*, 4229 and 5297–8.

children in adjacent areas, as glaring as it was unjustifiable. This inequality had made a great impression on Mr Fisher, and indeed it was accentuated by the rapid rise in the cost of living which followed the 1914–18 war. The country too was in a generous mood and inclined to think in millions after spending 8 millions a day for some years on the prosecution of the war. Accordingly Mr Fisher's endorsement of the action of the associations of L.E.A.s and teachers in coming together to seek an orderly and progressive solution of the salary problem met with widespread approval. If Mr Fisher was not, as is sometimes supposed, the father of the Burnham Scales, he was certainly their godfather, for he had to sponsor them in a Cabinet of imported business men whose views on public education were often pre-twentieth-century.

The observer of today who makes an unbiased comparative evaluation, from the standpoint of service to the community, of the rewards offered by a teaching career and those obtainable in other professions in the 1930s is not likely to regard them as unduly generous. For example, the maximum salary obtainable by the headmaster of the biggest school in the most highly paid area could not then, apart from special allowances, exceed £606 per annum. The average for the country as a whole was of course much lower. It was about £420 for men head teachers and £327 for women head teachers. On the other hand, whatever criticisms may be levelled against them, the Burnham Scales had raised the average salary of all certificated men teachers from the £94 of 1870 or the £122 of the 1890s to £311 in 1935, and of all certificated women teachers from £57 in 1870 and £80 in 1895 to £242 in 1935,[1] although the cost of living too had changed considerably in the interval. (Salaries in the United States were in certain States nominally higher, but the extent to which insecurity robbed them of this nominal advantage may be gauged by readers of an article in *The Times Educational Supplement* for 31 August 1935.)

(c) Moreover salaries had been reinforced by a *superannuation scheme*[2]—at first non-contributory, after 1925 contributory—more generous in some respects than that afforded to the Civil Service. No Government would today dare to speak as one did in 1848 of its 'determination as an indispensable means to improve the condition of the poor, to elevate the position of the schoolmaster by qualifying him to occupy a higher station and by rewarding his more efficient services by superior emoluments'; no Government would now tell H.M.I.s to remind intending teachers that 'the present low standard of the

---

[1] For average salaries at various dates see *H*, 26 July 1933, Questions and Answers.

[2] For a comprehensive account of the history and provisions of the Teachers' Superannuation Acts see Sir W. R. Barker, *The Superannuation of Teachers in England and Wales*, 1926.

salaries of schoolmasters and their equivocal if not mean position in Society are the consequences of the humble estimate of attainments and skill which have been adopted with respect to them, and that it is impossible to raise them to a position of dignity or comfort unless the dispositions of the Government in these respects are seconded by their own efforts to qualify themselves to obtain these rewards'.

But the effect of the Burnham scales was undoubtedly to raise the status of the profession in the eyes of a predominantly industrial and commercial community, to relieve it of its more pressing embarrassments, and to enable many women teachers and some at least of the men to enlarge their horizon by holidays farther afield.

Perhaps the future historian may see in the work of Lord Burnham and his colleagues something more important still, namely, the first break by any country in the strongly rooted tradition that in education bricks and mortar count for more than men. Mr Fisher by his endorsement of the original Burnham agreement endorsed more than a series of complicated scales arrived at by a process of give and take. He endorsed the doctrine so sedulously preached by Sir Michael Sadler in his reports of 1903 to 1907, that 'the most gorgeous buildings are useless if the salaries paid to the staff who work in them are such as to unsettle the young, dispirit altogether the old, discourage the skilled and make inevitable the unskilled'.

(d) *The segregation into special schools and classes of the mentally and physically defective, the deaf and the ineducable,* to say nothing of the provision of spectacles for the short-sighted, had done much to relieve the difficulties endured by teachers of an earlier day. It had freed them, too, to give their attention to normal children classified according to their normal abilities. This point was already by 1935 in danger of passing into oblivion as the number of teachers who remembered the problems presented by such children in the elementary schools of forty years before diminished with the years. Mrs Burgwin, for example, who had already been teaching for twenty-one years when she appeared in 1886 as a witness before the Cross Commission, claimed that much more discretion should be given to teachers in withholding children from the annual inspection for 'results'. Her evidence[1] shows that in a single standard during the previous year she had two children paralysed, one child an idiot unable to walk but kept at school in order to enable an elder sister to attend, one obviously 'dull', and eight so delicate that they were in constant attendance at a hospital. In Standard I in that year (1887) she had fifteen girls unable to see the blackboard from the back row of their class.

There are still of course many people who are silently apprehensive about the amount of money required to provide special education for

[1] *C.C.R.,* 17,097; 17,370; 17,257; 17,167; 17,169.

such children, as compared to the cost of educating the normal child, but this apprehension is seldom shared by those who know best the success which had attended the efforts of the special schools to turn them into self-supporting members of the community. The work of the late Dr Alfred Eichholz, C.B.E., who was appointed H.M.I. before the close of the century, is already fittingly commemorated in London. Moreover, although it is an argument which never finds its way into official reports, their segregation has contributed very materially to the changing attitude of middle-class parents to the elementary school, and to their greater readiness to send their children to receive an efficient education in the local elementary school instead of a possibly less efficient one at a private school. A comparison of graphs A (p. 32) and B (p. 33) will at once reveal what a remarkable growth took place in forty years in the use made by parents of the elementary schools as compared with private schools. Although the decline of numbers in the private schools between 1895 and 1935 is difficult to estimate, it had clearly been substantial. Whitaker stated that there were 18,000 private schools in 1895, but would not answer letters asking for their authority for the statement. The number in attendance was put at 750,000 by witnesses before the Bryce Commission. The number in 1935 was probably about 300,000 in about 10,000 schools.

(e) Finally, *the rehousing of large sections of the school population* in modern school buildings on the new housing estates, the progressive reduction in the rolls of the schools serving the central areas of towns owing to the centrifugal tendency of the population, the decline in numbers in most of the rural schools, and the migration of whole populations, for example, to the South Yorkshire coalfield,[1] all combined to give the schools more elbow-room and enabled many minor amenities such as staff rooms to be provided. The work of the School Medical Service, too, in controlling epidemics and eliminating ringworm and pediculosis, and the spread of civilization among the parents made teaching a healthier and more attractive occupation even if it brought with it more routine clerical work.[2] Although probably at least £50 million of capital had by 1935 been expended upon school buildings since the 1914–18 war, the large proportion of them which still dated from the first two decades of compulsory education gave

---

[1] Much of the South Yorkshire coalfield was practically non-existent in the 1890s. The influx of collier populations with a fertility as high as 33 per 1,000 probably necessitated the building or enlargement of 150 new schools by the West Riding County Council after the 1914–18 war.

[2] The amount of clerical work imposed by payment by results was, however, very heavy indeed. In 1886 every teacher in the London schools had 171 forms to fill up annually.

grounds for concern.[1] There were in fact many competent judges who believed that nothing short of a national loan would succeed in bringing school plant up to date within a reasonable term of years.

(2) *The improvement in the children's lot.*

We saw in Chapter II how one of the most serious results of the pre–1895 system was its tendency to make children hate their school-days, and that the inclination noted by the Cross Commission for children to leave school on the day upon which they could pass the necessary standard was only checked by the increasing parental interest when compulsory education entered upon its second generation.

The charge that boys and girls left school unable to use their brains and unaware of the activities of the intellectual world that bears upon their life, in short with an attitude towards learning which might almost be described as barbarian, was of course still a familiar one. (Indeed it is still being levelled today.)

On the other hand, where reorganization and the more realistic curriculum which it brought with it had made the greatest progress, there had been a change in the children's attitude towards school so marked that it was already having a beneficial reaction not only upon the length of school life but upon the attitude of the parents. The work of the School Attendance Staff in controlling truancy had been immensely lightened, and in those areas where reorganization had reached 100 per cent it had almost become a prize-day platitude to contrast Shakespeare's schoolboy 'creeping like snail unwillingly to school' with his eager modern counterpart. Moreover, although the formal request by the distinguished visitor for a special holiday might still win an immediate cheer, most teachers know that the enjoyment of the actual holiday itself would not seem half so wonderful to the children as a full day's release from school would have seemed to their predecessors of a generation before. This new attitude was well illustrated by the case of a party of schoolgirls from a school in the home counties who in 1930 were taken to the Zoo for their local Girl Guide outing. The school had specialized in the spinning, dyeing, and weaving of wool. They had carried out every process from the collection of their raw material on the hedges, in the orchards and at shearing time, to the production of patterned material coloured with the traditional dyes of the countryside (lichen leaves, heather, onion skins, elderberries, hips, etc., not omitting alder twigs, which, they had noticed, stained the road after being run over by a car). At the Zoo, instead of

---

[1] £50 million at the building costs current between the wars would of course be equivalent to £250–£300 million today (1968).

waiting their turn for an elephant ride, they searched out independently in the insect house the cochineal insect in order to see it in its natural habitat! Yet the formal work of such schools, so far from being cramped by the pursuit of such an absorbing practical interest as this school had evidently found in the spinning, dyeing, and weaving of wool, would generally be found to have improved because all the other subjects had been made to radiate out from it. In the scripture lesson Joseph's coat of many colours had taken on a new significance, the art and geography work had become more real, social history from the Bayeux tapestry to the coal-tar products of today had come to life, and the literature of the countryside was finding a new understanding.

To what was this change in attitude attributable? No one at the time who had studied the slowness of change in other human affairs —the resurgence, for example, of the Old Adam in international relations despite the war-weariness of 1919 and the existence of the League of Nations—would have been bold enough to attribute it to some subtle psychological change in the children themselves. They had, it is true, become more civilized—home influences in particular had usually changed remarkably for the better—but they could not in a mere forty years have become more psychologically amenable to school life except in so far as their schools had learnt to enlist their interest, to preserve and build upon that sense of wonder which is childhood's fairest possession. Their reaction to the methods of instruction of forty years before would probably have been much the same as that of their prototypes. The change was in fact one of outlook. It had been achieved by teachers who had been able to bring in rare instances genius, in many instances aptitude backed by skilled training, but in far the greatest number of cases enthusiasm and a new attitude of mind, to bear upon the problems affecting the children attending their schools, having regard to their probable future occupations. Their enthusiasm had infected their immediate circle, but their originality of method had been disseminated by H.M.I.s and 'Organizing Teachers' at short courses and had often been made available to a wider circle by articles in the educational press.

The silent revolution in teaching methods which had taken place in the course of a century, even in the formal subjects of instruction, is easily traceable by anyone who studies textbooks or examination papers of particular dates.

Less than a century earlier the idea of extending education to the 'lower orders' was still so novel, and experience so limited, that men could genuinely believe such maxims as 'open a school and you will close a prison'. Accordingly it was fashionable to believe that the attainment of this desirable consummation could be accelerated by inviting the child to swallow the pill of instruction with a liberal covering of sugared moral precept. The length to which this belief was carried is almost unbelievable. The arithmetic books were full of such problems as the following: 'The children of Israel were sadly given to idolatry, notwithstanding all they knew of God. Moses had to put three thousand men to death for this grievous sin. How would you express this number in digits?' This example comes from an early National Society textbook, but the length of time that textbooks where they existed were made to do service was often remarkable. An entry in a log book of 1900 of a school which it would be unfair to name reads as follows: 'Found the children learning the prayer for the Restoration of the Monarchy. Stopped this practice as the prayer is now quite out of date.' We may stand in astonishment before the sampler produced by 'Mary Anne Jones aged 11 years 1847'. We may be tempted to compare with modern examples of the work of children of 11 the meticulous stitchery which produced the woebegone expressions on the faces of Adam and Eve, the serenity of the angels with their flaming swords, and the self-satisfied serpent twined around the tree covered with the rosiest of apples. But we may rightly wonder what was the effect on poor little Anne's eyesight or what moral lesson she can possibly have derived from the painfully executed lettering:

> Blessed with the joy of innocence
> Adam our Father stood
> Till he debased his soul to sense
> And ate the unlawful food.

By the middle of the century it is clear that doubts as to the efficacy of this type of instruction had begun to assail those in authority. In a letter dated 28 July 1847, to H.M.I. of Schools on the subject of the meagreness of the supply of books of general instruction in elementary schools, we find the Education Department complaining that 'The Holy Scriptures and books of a purely religious character, when used as a means of Instruction in an almost mechanical art, cease to be regarded with due reverence by the scholars. To learn the art of reading from the Bible is not only not to teach religion, but to degrade the Bible to the level of a Horn-book.' Such teaching fails 'to operate as a rule of life'.[1]

Unfortunately the gradual abandonment of the era of moral precept seems to have ushered in an era which can only be described as one of arid verbosity. Probably the general absence of good children's books, and indeed of the resources to buy them had they existed, forced teachers to employ almost automatically the rococo phraseology of

[1] *R.E.D.*, 1847–8, Vol. I, pp. xvi and xviii to xlvi.

their own libraries. Thus a witness before the Cross Commission gave a list of questions set on paper to boys ranging between 11 and 12 in Standard V which contained such gems as the following:

'Compressibility is due to the approach of the molecules. It is a proof of porosity. Explain the words underlined.'

We may compare with this the description in *What is and What might be* (p. 94, footnote) of a lesson in religious instruction to ninety-four children on 'Prayer', of which there were apparently five varieties: 1, Invocation; 2, Deprecation; 3, Obsecration; 4, Intercession; 5, Supplication. The almost unbelievable aridity of the training college courses endured by many of the older teachers probably accounts for some of this phraseology. As late as 1880 young men and women were expected to 'paraphrase' Shakespeare's 'Full fathom five' as follows, at one of the best-known training colleges: 'Your male parent is deposited at a depth of thirty feet and his bones are converted into coral. All the soluble tissues of his body are altered by the chemical action of the salt water into interesting and valuable objects.'

This epoch, sometimes known as the era of 'chalk and talk' from the predilection which some of the older members of the staffs of schools showed for reinforcing verbosity by the use of the blackboard, gave place gradually to one in which attempts were increasingly made to impart interest to the hard subjects upon which the scholars were expected to 'grit their teeth' by relating them, at first in rather a formal and utilitarian way, to life. The examination papers of 1910–1919 are full of such questions as:

'A workman earns 10½*d*. an hour. If he works 51 hours a week and has two weeks' holiday in the year, how much does he earn during the year?'

'The dairy bill for a family was £2. 0*s*. 8*d*. for a month. This included seven pounds of butter at 1*s*. 4*d*. a pound. The rest was for milk at 2*d*. a pint. How many quarts of milk were bought?'

But once the idea of 'interest' became firmly established the transition to a more modern conception of 'realistic studies' was half achieved. Where a child in 1920 might write a make-believe letter to a child of his own age in France, fifteen years later he would probably write an actual one to a living child in that country. Where he learnt in his geography that a ship would take so many days to carry coal from South Wales to the Argentine and to bring a return cargo of grain, he was now beginning to learn the details from actual correspondence with the captain and crew of the tramp steamer which his school had adopted. The principle was the same but the interest had become a personal and living one. The search for greater realism was of course in itself producing many changes in school organization, all of which were tending to make school life less formal and therefore more attractive to the child.

Visits to the local park, the museums, the farmyard, the ancient manor or castle, the factory, and the docks had of course for many years been occupying an increasingly important place in the curriculum of most schools. The small girl who before the First War might have regarded 'drains' as a topic of doubtful validity now looked forward for weeks to a visit to the local sewage farm as an essential ingredient in her civics course. But whereas the object used to be to bring back from such visits enough nature material, or new ideas for arithmetic work, to keep the children busy at their desks for a week, there was now a growing tendency to make the park or farmyard an extension of the classroom in the true sense, in that much of the work previously done at the desk was now actually done out of doors away from the classroom atmosphere. There was the zest of both novelty and accomplishment in learning one's arithmetic by practical work with a home-made theodolite, U level and Gunter's chain in the local park, or in working out the weight of water passing down a river if a seat on the river bank took the place of a chair in the classroom. Here the rural school seemed to be at a definite advantage over the school in the large town, for it had the resources of the countryside at its gates. To a school in search of realistic material a few square miles of country are better than thousands of pounds' worth of potential teaching material locked in the glass cases of a museum. There was, however, a new movement to use the museums more effectively, and the L.C.C. had appointed an Organizer of Museum Activities to act as a liaison officer between the museums and the schools. What the schools still needed of course was a children's room in every museum like that already provided at the Science Museum in London, and a circulatory collection of material which they could actually handle.

If work outside the classroom had increased, the classroom itself had in many instances been transformed by the growth of specialization in the teaching staffs of the senior schools, often accompanied by the allocation of particular rooms to particular subjects. There would be, for example, a history room surrounded by time charts and ship models or postcards (and even humble cigarette cards) illustrating the development throughout history of subjects ranging from transport to dress. In such a room there was little place for what have been aptly described as the 'woebegone portraits of royalty and conjectural caterpillars conceived by amateur tacticians' which used to fill the old-type history books.

It was probably owing to this growing belief in the value of learning by active participation rather than by passive reception that this country was slower in making extensive use of the cinema and the wireless than the United States and Russia. By 1935 probably about 800 schools were equipped for the use of the film, and a somewhat larger number, probably about 5,000, made intermittent use of the broadcast lessons. But until there were as many good educational films as there were good children's books, in general it seemed likely that they would be employed by wise teachers to illustrate, vivify, and supplement lessons previously learnt, to put the coping-stone on courses already fully worked out in schools rather than as substitutes for class teaching or individual work. The great difficulty hitherto had been the inadequacy of the supply of non-inflammable films suitable for 16 mm projectors, the limited bookings that they could anticipate, and the heavy cost of production. Moreover, the projector still failed to admit of being stopped and repeated at will. Tests had been carried out to determine the relative value of a talking film as compared with the same film shown silently and expounded by the teacher who knew the children's background of knowledge and preparation. The teacher had always won! The day when the film would come to form a valuable adjunct to the illustration of technical processes and an aid to the art student was still in the future, despite its already wide cultural and emotional influence on the public at large.

In assessing the relative importance of those developments which had made the children's school days more varied and more interesting, a high place must also be given to the attention increasingly paid to craftwork and handwork in the junior schools leading to the numerous forms of practical instruction in evidence in the senior schools.

Any attempt to illustrate the growth of the practical subjects by statistical comparison of the position in 1902 and that achieved by 1935 must to a large extent be vitiated by the corresponding growth which had occurred in the width of the syllabus, the length of time devoted to the courses, and the range of tools and equipment provided. It is, however, interesting to note in passing that an attempt to encourage practical subjects had been a feature of elementary education in this country almost since the Act of 1870. Domestic Economy was required in the Code of 1876 as the first specific subject to be taken by girls. This raised the number taking it from 3,307 in 1876 to 59,812 in 1882 when the first grants became payable for it. Laundry-work started about 1890, Manual Instruction in 1890, the number of schools taking it rising from 145 in 1891 to 949 in 1895. At the time of the passage of the Act of 1902 special grants were given to encourage Cookery, Laundrywork, Dairywork, Household Management, Manual Instruction, Cottage Gardening, and Cookery for boys in seaport towns. In the intervening years the number of departments taking gardening had increased sixteenfold, the number taking manual instruction sixfold, and the number taking the domestic subjects had increased from 4,700 to 11,062.

1,080 departments were by 1935 taking other subjects virtually unknown in 1902, and the number of departments containing senior children in which no practical subjects were taken had been reduced to 2,551 as compared with 15,045 taking one or more.[1]

Although Cookery, Housewifery, and Laundrywork were first in the field, as briefly indicated in Chapter II (p. 25), accommodation and equipment left much to be desired. It must have been far from easy for the most imaginative girl to have assembled into the picture of her future home the type of cookery room then normally in use and the overworked 'specimen' pieces of linoleum, carpet, and upholstery materials upon which she was instructed, often in a vacant classroom. The passage of the years brought revolutionary changes. The first centres, usually expensively divided into three separate compartments each in charge of a different teacher, began to appear in London and the larger towns about 1906. Just before the 1914–18 war these water-tight compartments in turn began to be abandoned in favour of combined domestic subjects centres.

Reorganization introduced the demand for domestic subjects rooms forming an actual part of the senior schools themselves, and about a quarter of the schools taking domestic subjects were already so equipped. By 1934 too the most up-to-date housewifery flats were at length able to attain the first objects of all domestic subjects instruction, namely, to cause girls who attended them to 'realize the value of the Home as a social and national asset, to provide a model which will stimulate the desire for improved conditions in their own homes; to help them to appreciate the importance of domestic and personal hygiene, well-balanced economical meals and labour-saving methods in home organization'.[2]

---

[1] The figures which will be found in the statistical volumes of the Board of Education for 1903 and 1934 are as follows:

1902			Debts.	1934			Depts.
Cookery	..	..	3,744		Domestic Subjects	..	..	11,062
Laundry	..	..	783					
Household Manage-				4,700	Handicraft (wood and metal-			
ment	..	..	173		work)	..	..	10,695
Manual Instruction	..	..	1,816	Gardening	..	..	..	5,506
Cottage Gardening	..	..	379	Other practical subjects	..	1,080
Other subjects	..	..	9					

The 2,551 departments containing senior children but not taking practical subjects were probably in the main small 'all age' departments in remote places or non-provided schools in poor parishes in the north.

[2] I am indebted to Miss C. A. Bright, Inspector of Domestic Subjects for London, for this admirable statement of modern aims.

A similar revolution to that which had taken place in the domestic subjects work for girls had also overtaken the boys' handicraft work. Earlier conceptions of manual instruction as a disciplinary exercise designed to train hand and eye to accuracy and due appreciation of form were giving way. The painstaking construction of set models of little or no artistic value in wood and metal was departing. One marvels today at the misguided ingenuity expended in thinking out models so utterly incapable of any possible utility as many of them were! The aim by 1935 was to encourage the boy to acquire facility in the use of the simpler tools and materials as quickly as possible, in order that he might pass on to expression work in which he would be expected to work more and more alone. The finished standard of work produced in many departments was already an enduring cause of astonishment to the mere uninitiated adult, and even to those who were in daily contact with the life of the schools. Much interesting experimental work was being carried out in the installation of time-saving power machinery and in the establishment of schemes for circulating photographs of well-designed furniture and metalwork, with a view to helping boys to an appreciation of character and good design in everyday things. That realism was pervading this branch of instruction also was evidenced by the joint achievement of a school for senior boys and girls who built a small house and furnished and equipped it throughout—the girls providing the soft furnishings.[1]

Reorganization was of course bringing a new freedom to the junior and infants' schools to develop along their appropriate lines, and their handwork, though simpler, was often a surprisingly effective means of developing self-expression. The most tongue-tied little boy readily found his voice if he had to take the part in a play written for the puppet which he had constructed out of monkey nuts (and his twin sister had dressed). Needless to say, the part would have been written by the children themselves, who would have constructed it out of some well-known nursery rhyme or story as part of their English expression work.

As with the handicraft and domestic subjects so with the science work, the art (including pottery, bookbinding, illumination and even heraldry!) and the rural studies. One school would select the study of books, their construction, binding and illumination, as the focal point from which the whole of its activities were made to radiate; another the making of pottery, often with the goodwill of a local brickworks; a third some dying but traditional craft of the neighbourhood, such as the construction of wattled 'handles'; others the scientific rearing of poultry and the making of all the impedimenta of the experimental poultry farm; another the arts of the seaside village; others again the

[1] See *Teacher's World*, 10 June 1936.

canning of surplus fruit to save the buying of imported fruit in the winter. The help afforded by the schools during the 1930s in the completion of the rural survey of England is well known.

Finally, the whole life of the schools was being enriched by the development of a new corporate life sustained by that tradition of co-operation by the teaching staff in the out-of-school activities which had been handed down from the older educational foundations. The amount of contact outside the classroom between the English teacher and his scholars and the extent of his knowledge of their homes was usually at once the envy and the admiration of the thousands of foreign and Commonwealth observers who already visited our schools every year. Societies and clubs of every kind, ranging from 'young farmers' clubs' to stamp societies, had begun to stimulate the imagination and cultivate the hobbies of the children. Boys from slum schools had been known to walk cheerfully as far as eight miles to find some coveted botanical specimen. School magazines too were beginning to cultivate both self-expression and artistic gifts. More important perhaps, they circulated in the homes to be read by the parents.

Another development, namely educational visits, which were first authorized in the Code of 1902, had been the means of opening windows in many narrow lives, for previously it had seldom been appreciated how 'local' children were in their movement, especially in the big towns where it was impossible to reach the country. There must have been many thousands out of London's half a million children in 1935 who had never seen the River Thames. Seventeen girls from the top class of a school in a poor district saw the sea for the first time on a school journey in 1928. Five of them saw a live cow for the first time. The educational visit grew out of the school ramble; the school journey in its turn grew out of the educational visit. The first two school journeys were undertaken in 1896, a party from a London school going for a week to Malvern and another from a Liverpool school for a fortnight to the Isle of Man. In the intervening years the movement grew to such proportions that by 1935 probably more than 1,000 schools were conducting journeys annually[1]—in addition to those which utilized camps and youth hostels for short periods in the middle of the week. The English school journey aims at transporting the children with their teachers to a new region where a prepared programme of educational work can be carried out under new conditions and in an atmosphere which cannot be obtained in the classroom. It is probably freer than its German counterpart, which is usually of a more definitely pedagogic character and is often spent in a permanent school camp. It was already hoped that the movement

---

[1] In 1928 London schools organized 480 journeys, provincial schools 200, and in addition there were 200 journeys abroad.

would develop to a point where every child from big cities would have undertaken at least one school journey before leaving school, for other countries, notably Denmark with her Copenhagen Country Holiday Scheme, were in many cases considerably in advance of us in this respect. Country children too might well, it was thought, visit the towns more than they were doing in those days. There was scope here for the return of the pious founder to present and endow school journey hostels like the Lady St Helier Hostel in the Isle of Wight.

Those who followed the growth of physical training, organized games, dancing, and swimming, both in and out of school hours, from the wrist and arm exercises of the cramped nineties to the playing-field policy of the 1930s knew that, while much remained to be done, the Board of Education made no idle boast when they claimed: 'The scope and quality of physical education have in general been transformed during the last thirty years from a narrow system of school drill into a balanced scheme for the physical development of children throughout their school life.' Less obvious to the public at large was the amount of voluntary time and effort expended by the teaching staff in organizing swimming galas and sports days or in ensuring, for example, to take a single town, that 22,000 London boys should get a weekly cricket match in the summer and 900 football, hockey, and lacrosse teams should play regularly throughout the winter on pitches in the parks.[1]

If the formal subjects treated with a new realism were coming to life; if this new vitality was being stimulated by the attention increasingly being paid to the practical subjects; if school societies, visits, journeys, and games were enlivening the social and corporate side of the work of the schools, what could be claimed to be the immediate results? It is fair to say that the schools had taken their greatest stride forward in the ten years since the Hadow Report. The 'time lag' before good work makes itself felt in the community at large is a distressingly long one, probably a generation. If one looks at the educational opportunities which existed at the end of the nineteenth century, one marvels at the way in which the country had met post-war adversity. We seemed to be moving towards at least a moderate return of prosperity—too soon, alas, to suffer the setback of the second World War.

Some reference has already been made (p. 118) to the growth of the reading habit and the apparently greater ability of children who had passed through the reorganized senior schools to take an intelligent interest in the world about them, whether it was the life of the London streets or that of the countryside. For example 80 per cent of school leavers in Halifax were taking up leavers' tickets, which gave access to

[1] *Times Educational Supplement*, 16 May 1936.

the public libraries, although in other towns the contact was sometimes broken for a few years after the child left school, to be resumed later. Again, if one was brought up in the countryside, it came as something of a surprise to see an entirely new bird in a lane on a Westmorland hillside and to be charmingly informed by a child under 10 that it was a pied flycatcher! Undoubtedly too the work in practical subjects was having a marked influence on thousands of homes, gardens, orchards, and poultry farms. There were cases on record where boys had made as many as seven upholstered ottoman seats out of packing-cases for various relations and friends. (It took rather longer for the demand for quality and good appearance in articles and materials in everyday use to improve, when a new generation of purchasers appeared who had learnt that design is an essential part of construction and not an extraneous decoration superimposed as a concession to the business man's notion of art.)

In the schools themselves, or at large assemblies of children, such as the assembly of 70,000 on Constitution Hill and in the Mall on 11 May 1935, to greet His Majesty King George V and Queen Mary on one of their Jubilee drives, and the assembly of 37,000 on Coronation Day, 1937, the features which struck observers, comparing past and present, were, first the greater alertness; secondly, the much more self-reliant and less 'drilled' discipline; thirdly, the orderliness and absence of noise. The 70,000 children did not leave a piece of paper the size of a stamp in the two miles of roadway and stands. The park cleaners of the Office of Works found the park cleaner after the children had gone than it had been in the morning.[1] As regards the absence of noise, it is interesting to recall Joseph Lancaster's dictum, in his observations for masters penned 100 years before: 'The less a master's voice is heard among his scholars, the more he will be obeyed. The noise of a school is generally in proportion to the noise a master makes in it himself. The punishment of the scholars, and the fatigue of the master, is nearly in like proportion.' This self-reliant discipline, which was accompanied by a charming reluctance to 'take advantage' next day, or presume upon the relaxation of restraints which took place, for example, at school Christmas parties, was no doubt due to the extension of the 'house system'. Where a child is working, playing, or just going about his ordinary school jobs for the honour of his house, the bad-conduct mark counts for far more than sharper punishment. What is more important, he is learning one of the first requisites of democracy, the capacity to live and work with one's fellows for a common object.

[1] These two assemblies were, within the next two years, to form the precedent which enabled the Government Evacuation Scheme to be organized with such confidence (see Chapter XII).

Whether some of the old mechanical accuracy had gone it is difficult, in the absence of comparative examples of work, to say. It must be admitted that investigations into the attainments of children of given age in arithmetic sometimes yielded rather surprising results.

On this matter there have always been, and probably always will be, two schools of thought. The one school affirms that one should no more absolve a child for inaccuracy on the ground that he knew how to tackle the sum than one would absolve one's partner at golf for missing his tee shot—on the ground that his swing was perfect. The other school of thought is well illustrated by the letter sent to Archbishop Temple by the Duke of Devonshire. 'My advisers admit that you are correct in your belief that (since the withdrawal of payment by results) the children are getting less sums right, but they tell me that they are doing the sums more intelligently.' To this it is said the Duke added a postscript, 'I'm afraid I don't follow what they mean.'

Where comparison was made of composition exercises or manual work with scripts and specimens that had survived from forty years before, the improvement was not in doubt.

(3) *The growth of parental interest in the schools.*

The growth of the scholarship system, the segregation of abnormal children, the slow but persistent attrition of class barriers, and the liberal education of the 1914–18 war generation by the widening of their horizons had all combined to create a far keener sense among parents of their obligation to the public educational system. The old hostility was giving way to interest, sometimes to appreciation where that interest was fanned by open days, exhibitions, flower shows, and propaganda. There were even occasions when the help of the police had to be called in to control the crowd seeking entry to an exhibition of school work. Farmers would ask the local school to make them an accurate plan of their fields. Mothers would proudly display their child's contribution to the school magazine, or the latest present from the handicraft centre. Fathers, who in their service days always returned to their old schools when on leave from the front, would now come back for advice about brooding hens and incubators, or to find the price of a sealing machine for canning fruit. Here and there parents' associations were coming into being to establish closer ties and greater confidence between school, staff, and parents. The activities of such associations, as diverse as they were beneficent, ranged from the supervision of out-of-school play to the organization of entertainments for other schools in poorer districts, from lectures on child psychology to the passing on of outgrown overcoats and mackintoshes at 1d. each to the less fortunate.

Statistics are cold things but one of the most encouraging pieces of evidence of the increasing regard for child life in the past seventy years can be found in the reduction which has taken place in the number of children killed in accidents. For example the annual toll, as a result of accidents of all kinds, in the early years of the century was around 5,700 of which a large proportion were traffic casualties. By 1933 the total had fallen to 3,076 of which only 1,474 were due to traffic despite the fact that the number of vehicles on the roads had gone up to $2\frac{1}{4}$ million. Of these 1,474 probably over 200 were among children under five or children who were passengers in vehicles. By 1967 the number had fallen to 885 of whom 113 were passengers and 310 were under five, although the number of vehicles on the roads had increased to over 14 million. Teachers, parents, police, the Highway and Hospital Authorities, school traffic patrols and by no means least the Royal Society for the Prevention of Accidents can all congratulate themselves on such a success story.

No chapter on the 'coming to life' of elementary education between 1902 and 1935 would be complete which made no mention of the steps which had been taken to implement, or frustrate, the most controversial and, as some thought, the most important of the recommendations of the Hadow Report, namely, that the school-leaving age should be raised compulsorily for all children as from 1932.

Seemingly insuperable obstacles hampered the Bills promoted by Sir Charles Trevelyan in 1930 and 1931. The third of those Bills was finally rejected by the House of Lords after having been impaired in the Commons by the misgivings of the Catholic community over the religious concordat proposed, by a momentary failure in party discipline, and by some irresolution in Government circles.

Another attempt to give partial effect to the Hadow recommendation was made by a Conservative Government in 1936. The Education Act passed in that year would have raised the school-leaving age to 15 from September 1939, but with exemption for children who at 14 secured satisfactory jobs or could produce evidence that their presence at home was similarly necessary and beneficial. Had this Act not proved stillborn, as a result of the outbreak of Hitler's war on the day it was due to come into operation, it would have placed the L.E.A.s in much the same position as that created by Sir John Gorst's acceptance of a Private Member's Bill in 1899 (p. 61) but with the age of 15 substituted for 14. But they would have found themselves supported, or goaded, by a much greater public interest in the schools. The sudden surge of interest in education which was witnessed by the last years of the nineteenth century might, by the end of the 'realistic thirties', have given way, if the Hadow senior schools could have been developed as they should have been, to a solid backing of public opinion. Unfortunately, although school building programmes were moving into top gear from 1935 to 1939, the menace of Nazism and the financial claims of rearmament tended to divert men's minds from the developing social services.

Some attempt may be made to assess in historical perspective the attitude towards the raising of the school age as seen through the eyes of what one may call the ordinary intelligent man of goodwill about 1935. He might have expressed himself somewhat as follows:

'I admit that no two children are born with an equal endowment, but no ordering of society is really going to satisfy me which does not, so far as human ingenuity can order it, seek to provide every child born into this world with the greatest possible measure of equality in that equipment for life and livelihood which will make for his or her happiness and usefulness in the sphere of life to which he or she attains. Education in its widest sense, which includes spiritual as well as intellectual equipment for life, is surely with, or possibly after, good health the greatest factor making for happiness. Remembering the opposition to the abolition of child labour in Victorian times and the consistent way in which the gloomy forebodings of the opponents of the extension of educational opportunity have been falsified for the past sixty years, I am not impressed by the purely negative argument that the country cannot afford to go forward. I am not even sure that a competent economist could not prove that every extension of educational opportunity in this country has been followed by an increase in the national wealth.

'Moreover, as I see it, the whole sweep of industry and commerce in modern times is towards larger and therefore more impersonal amalgamations, with the corollary that the worker must become more interested in the world about him and spiritually self-contained, in order that he may be able to resist the deadening effects of a machine age and better able to employ his leisure. What I hear, too, of the efforts which our industrial competitors abroad are making in the educational sphere sometimes leads me to wonder, not whether we can afford to improve our education in this country, but whether we can afford not to do so.

'I am not at all convinced that modern industry and commerce, as I know it, is a fit place for the modern child of 14, who has probably led a more sheltered life than his prototype of sixty years ago. Certainly I should not send my own child into an office or workshop at 14 if I could afford to keep him at school. In fact, if those responsible can really satisfy me that the children will not have to "mark time" for another year but will in truth be able to put, as it were, a coping-stone on to the work they have done in the schools, and acquire that attitude towards self-education which will make them want to pursue it after the doors of the school close behind them, I should have no hesitation in voting for the introduction of the extra year at the earliest possible date.'

To this those primarily interested, namely, the educational administrator, the social worker, the parent, and the teacher, would now have found themselves, perhaps for the first time since the 1914–18 war, able to give the following unequivocal reply:

'We are,' they could say, 'at last able to give you an emphatic and, we believe, convincing answer to your questions. We can show you that over large areas of the country we can offer your child not merely an extra twelve months at school, but something worth infinitely more than he has received in any previous twelve months of his school career; we can prove to you that whereas to have raised the school leaving age five years ago might have meant the provision of an enormous amount of new classroom accommodation and equipment and the training of a small army of additional teachers, for whom it would have been difficult to find continued employment after 1936, we can now effect the change with the minimum of such extra provision and consequently at the minimum of extra cost; we can do more, we can actually offer you at a critical time, when the number of the younger unemployed is bound in the nature of things to increase to an alarming extent unless the present improvement in employment is sustained for ten years, the withdrawal from an overstocked labour market of a whole age-group of children, with the certainty that many of the places which they would have taken in industry and commerce will be filled by their elders. It would naturally follow that the need for the provision of juvenile instruction centres and classes as a stop-gap method of salvage for those juveniles who have fallen out of employment will be greatly diminished.

'We do not want to bore you by the recital of volumes of figures. We would only implore you to believe that we are faced with a wholly new situation which so far only a few far-sighted individuals have really had the vision to grasp. As a speaker in the House of Commons recently put it: "One of the chief difficulties of democracy is the difficulty of inducing people to discuss an old subject from a new angle. We continually seem to be locked in debate on the old lines, entirely ignoring the actual situation with which we have to deal."

'Let us look at our three assertions in this light:

'In the first place, we claim that the extra year from 14 to 15 would be worth far more than twelve months' extra schooling at any other age. Why? The answer requires some understanding of the child's process of mental development. Up to the age of 11 the main concern of education is with the acquirement by the child of quite general powers, such as the arts of speech, reading, and writing, and with such fundamental ideas as those of magnitude and number. From the age of 11, on the other hand, the child progressively emerges from that stage of his education which has been exclusively devoted to general preparation for life and begins to become more and more conscious that he has embarked upon specific preparation for a particular kind of life. To quote the Hadow Report on the "Education of the Adolescent", "there is a tide which begins to rise in the veins of youth at the age of eleven or twelve. It is called by the name of adolescence. If that tide can be taken at the flood and a new voyage begun in the strength and along the flow of its current, we think that it will 'move on to fortune'." This great report therefore proposed that about the age of 11 every child should be transferred to a post-primary school, secondary, central or senior, catering for his or her particular bent at least for a full four-year course up to the age of 15. At that age, but not, be it marked, before, the pupils will have had time to form that real personal interest in their special bent which will lead them, in the great majority of cases, to pursue their interests voluntarily and of their own free will until they attain the status of an independent and self-reliant citizen.

'It is precisely to this end that a scarcely realized but nevertheless fundamental reorganization of our school system has been proceeding since 1926. In many areas every child over 11 is now receiving a three-year course from 11 to 14 in a separately organized senior school. In London 88 per cent of the schools are reorganized, and in the country as a whole, even counting rural districts, more than 50 per cent of the schools have been reorganized. Obviously, therefore, the time has come to complete the reorganization and to make the Hadow Report fully effective.

'In the second place, we claim that the present time is quite exceptionally favourable for the change, far more favourable than five years ago. Why is this? Because, for good or ill, the schools have recently lost the abnormal numbers of children who were born in the years which followed the 1914–18 war. These post-war age-groups have been working their way up through the schools and have now worked out at the top, to be succeeded by age-groups of normal dimensions, or rather less than normal dimensions, owing to the progressive fall in the birth-rate. Had the school-leaving age been raised in 1932, new school accommodation would have been needed for these swollen age-groups, and new teachers would have had to be trained to deal with them in their senior years, whereas by the time that the raising of the school-leaving age could now be put into force there will be something like half a million fewer pupils in the schools, and the new age-groups can be added with a very small increase in accommodation and teaching staff.

'Thirdly, we claim that unless the school-leaving age is raised now there may eventually be a calamitous increase in unemployment, owing to the emergence of these same age-groups on to an already over-stocked labour market, but that if the school-leaving age is raised, the withholding of a whole age-group must have the effect of reserving for the pupils of 15, 16, 17, and 18 many of the jobs which would have been given to the 14-year-olds. The number of additional boys and girls over and above the 1933 figure available for employment during the year which ended on 31 March 1934, was 55,000. During the year 1934–5 it was 115,000; during the year 1935–6 it will be 306,000; and during the year 1936–7 no less than 443,000. How can anyone contemplate these numbers with equanimity when he knows that, with hardly any additional buildings, with hardly any additional teachers, and with hardly any additional cost, the schools can retain the 14-to-15-year-old age-group and virtually solve the problem?'

Some of these arguments were valid indeed, but the assumptions based on past and present birth-rates, looked at in the light of the changes which have taken place in the past thirty years, provide a good illustration of the danger of forecasting population trends from current educational statistics.

The trend of population in these islands up to 1935 had been such that whereas in 1935 there were about 10 million children below the age of 15 it seemed as though in 1971 (when the survivors of that 10 million would be 45 to 60 years of age) there might be barely 4 millions. The alteration of the balance in the age stratification of the population to which these figures seemed to point was not, unfortunately, likely to lead to an improved standard of life for everyone. On the contrary, it was thought that the child of 1935 might have to face in his later life and his old age economic difficulties far greater than the lot of his parents in the years 1930 to 1940.[1]

1 Such forecasts as this were widely canvassed around 1935, when the number of live births annually was stationary or falling (average 1930–8, 612,000). They were of course falsified by the great increase in births which followed the Second World War (average 1944–58, 714,000); full employment and later retirement; a substantial increase in the expectation of life; and immigration. Projections by the Government Actuary suggest that the per centage of dependants (children and pensioners) will increase from the 1965 figure of 38·2 per cent to a peak of 42 per cent about 1980 but will then tend to fall. (*The Times*, 8 August 1966, p. 10.)

CHAPTER IX

THE EXPANSION OF TECHNICAL AND FURTHER EDUCATION 1902–1935

Wide range of subject.—Some comparisons between 1902 and 1935.—
Public opinion ripe for advance in technical education at close of nineteenth century.—Rapid increase in provision of new polytechnics between 1833 and 1902.—Sixfold increase in evening class enrolments
between 1892 and 1899.—Public interest in technical education sidetracked to develop secondary education, 1902–18.—The reasons.—
Revival of interest owing to post-war difficulties of industry and commerce.—A spate of blue books followed by a new determination to
advance.—The four main types of student who seek technical and
further education.—Is technical education true education?—The
answer.—The growth of co-operation between the business man and
the schools.

I T is always an interesting experience to observe the reactions of those
whose education has followed the normal liberal and academic lines
during their first visit to a great modern polytechnic. If they do not
come away with a deeper respect for the range and complexity of the
avocations of their fellow-men, one of two things is certain—they have
either failed to take in what they have seen or they have lost their
sense of wonder!

For, as the Adult Education Committee of the Board of Education
early pointed out, adult education alone covers a range of courses from
Greek Dancing to Greek Literature, from Home Carpentry to
Astronomy, from Boxing to Metaphysics, and that range is growing
every year. A picture which appeared in *Punch* summed the matter
up even more trenchantly. The picture showed a father inquiring
whether his son could obtain an evening course in lion-taming and
being assured gravely by an official that if he could find the necessary
number to form a class the matter would receive consideration! Turning to technical education proper, the inquirer will find in one and the
same institution young men who have travelled half way across Europe
to study the mysteries of advanced rubber technology and women who
are seeking to qualify themselves to be cooks in roadhouses! The number of separate occupations in a community so highly industrialized
as England and Wales was already by the 1930s over 2,000.

A full account of those industries and occupations which employed the largest number of workers had appeared in a series of painstaking pamphlets prepared by H.M.I.s. But a consideration in detail of either technical education proper or that wide range of courses for the cultivation of interests of every kind, affecting every side of life, which are loosely termed adult education, is an absorbing study for the specialist but a labyrinth full of pitfalls for the layman. If anyone therefore asks himself 'What happened in the sphere of technical and further education in England in the thirty years after the Act of 1902?' there is only one way in which he can set about finding the answer.

First he must try to see in perspective the gradual emergence of four or five main streams of students each seeking different types of course to satisfy separate and distinct needs. Next he must try, still from the same distance, to trace the steadily gathering recognition by industry and commerce of the importance of technical and further education as a factor in industrial and commercial efficiency, and the consequent growth of co-operation, local and national, between the business world and the schools.

If he adopts this plan he will probably find three things. In the first place, he will find that when the Act of 1902 was passed the country possessed the nucleus of what are now the older city universities (in those days amounting, with a few brilliant exceptions such as Owen's College, Manchester, to little more than congeries of technical and literary classes); a small number of polytechnics with a few full-time staff, mainly in London; a rather larger number of organized science schools and evening science and art classes; and a large body of night schools mainly attended by those who were seeking to supplement or recapture what they had learnt in the old-style elementary school. He will, in the second place, note how the growth of secondary education, the enlivenment of the elementary school, the increasing interest of employers, and above all the growing appetite for education among all classes of the community particularly after the 1914–18 war, had in the intervening years up to 1935 converted the rather sparse provision of 1902 into a loosely knit complex of full- and part-time day and evening classes containing rather over twice as many students as they enrolled when the twentieth century opened.[1] But thirdly, he will probably experience a sense of disappointment, a feeling that the close of the nineteenth century was full of promise for technical education, but that that promise was belied by performance in the first three decades of the twentieth.

[1] Number of students at evening schools in respect of whom grants were paid by the Government in 1902–3, 440,718. Number of full-time and part-time students attending courses recognized under the Board of Education's regulations for Further Education (977,000) and the Adult Education Regulations (47,283) in 1934, 1,025,000.

He will, for example, observe the heart-searchings in regard to this country's declining prestige in the world of discovery, invention and design which followed each international exhibition from 1851 onwards.[1] He will trace the rise of the machinery of technological and art examinations, associated first with the Society of Arts and later with the City and Guilds of London Institute.[2] He will follow the propagandist course of the Royal Commission on Technical Education (1883). He will see that propaganda beginning to bear fruit in the foundation—or refoundation and endowment with the aid of the £50,000 a year made available for the advancement of further education in the Metropolis by the City Parochial Charities Act (1883)—of many of the great London polytechnics, the Regent Street Polytechnic, Birkbeck College, the City of London College, the Goldsmiths' Institute, the People's Palace, the Borough and Battersea Polytechnics, the South-Western and Northern Polytechnics, and the Northampton Polytechnic. He will notice the multiplication without state aid of the institutions which were to become city 'redbrick' universities,[3] and the use between 1889 and 1902 of the 'Whiskey Money' to provide 12 more polytechnics or technical institutions in London, 13 in the provinces, and more than 100 organized science schools.

Next he will watch the enrolments at the evening classes conducted by the School Boards increasing sixfold between the years 1892–3 and 1899. He will note the reiterated demand by Members of all parties, during the debate upon the Act of 1902, for technical education to bring this country to the level of her industrial competitors; and he will see the first step taken towards the satisfaction of their demands by the conversion at a single stroke of all the elementary evening continuation schools into institutions of higher education. Anyone who reads Lord Haldane's speech in the Second Reading debate on the Education Act of 1902 will find it interesting to speculate how technical education might have developed before the 1914–18 war if he had not been compelled to accept the War Office at £5,000 instead of the Presidency of the Board of Education at £2,000.

[1] The best description of this is contained in Halévy's *History of the English People, 1895–1905*, pp. 157–63, but echoes of it will be found in almost everything written about technical education during this period, from the Great Exhibition to Sir Philip Magnus' article under the heading 'Technical Education' in the 9th edition of the *Encyclopaedia Brittanica*.

[2] The City and Guilds of London Institute was brought into being by the City Livery Companies first as a teaching establishment but later—owing to lack of funds—as an examining body. It took over the Society of Arts technological examinations in 1878.

[3] Liverpool, Manchester, Leeds, Birmingham, Sheffield, Newcastle, Bristol, and Nottingham.

And yet, despite all this promise, he will find that the number of first-class technical schools built between 1902 and 1918 can almost be counted on the fingers of his two hands.[1] He will lose sight of the organized science schools and find most of them re-emerging (after a decent interval of classification as 'Secondary Schools Group A') as institutions almost indistinguishable from the revived grammar schools. He will discover that, in the light of developments in Germany and Switzerland, the Consultative Committee of the Board of Education reported as early as 1909 in favour of the introduction of compulsory day continuation schools to be brought into being by local option.[2] He will follow the fortunes of this report and find that no Government had the resolution to face the issue before the war, and that when it was finally faced by Mr Fisher in 1918 irresolution, the Geddes Committee, and the opposition of parents and employers combined to render this portion of the Act abortive.

In his search for reasons for this apparent starvation of technical education the conclusion at which he will probably arrive will be this: the Board of Education could not persuade the Exchequer to allow them the necessary funds to do more than one thing well. They therefore elected to put all the funds they could get into secondary grammar education. They did so primarily to meet the clamant demand for the supersession of the pupil teacher system and the production for the elementary schools of hundreds of thousands of teachers who could have behind them the liberal education afforded by a full secondary school course. Moreover, the Board justified their policy on another ground, that no sound system of technical training could be built up except on the basis of a sound system of secondary education.[3] They were, in short, obsessed by the danger of the 'formula mind'.[4]

But if the pre-occupation of the Board of Education before 1926 with the training of teachers and the building of the national system

[1] For particulars see *Survey of Technical and Further Education in England and Wales*, p. 25. (H.M.S.O., 1926.)

[2] Report of the Consultative Committee on Attendance Compulsory or otherwise at Continuation Schools, 1909, p. 224.

[3] The Regulations for Technical Schools

(1) made no provision before 1918 for grants towards the capital cost of new buildings;

(2) before 1905 refused grant to any classes held in the day-time if they were below the standard appropriate to pupils who had attended a secondary school for at least three years.

Moreover, even as late as 1913 it was stated in a prefatory memorandum to the first regulations for junior technical schools that 'These new Regulations are not intended to promote the establishment of courses planned to furnish a preparation for the professions, the universities, *or higher full-time technical work.*'

[4] For an assessment of the responsibility of Sir Robert Morant and his successors in the light of papers now available see p. 322.

of secondary schools may be selected as the principal cause of this apparent neglect of technical education, it is not necessary to look very far below the surface to find that other causes too were at work. A country so predominantly industrial and commercial as England and Wales, and, be it added, one so comparatively untrammelled by rigid prejudice against promotion from the ranks, must surely have woken up to her deficiencies if there had not been political and social reasons to make inaction seem more prudent than activity. Such reasons unfortunately too often did exist.

In the first place, the great majority of small employers were entirely apathetic before the 1914–18 war in their attitude towards technical education. Moreover, those few who were ready to encourage their young employees to attend courses had to walk warily. For there unfortunately existed many older workpeople who were only too ready to suspect that the management might be trying to train up young men who might oust them from skilled employment.

Next, parents, if not apathetic, were often confused. The secondary grammar schools seemed more respectable than attendance at the elementary school till 14, followed by day or evening classes. The need for the expansion of secondary grammar education, by a broadening scholarship system, seemed to be the goal of all who understood education. Ought they not therefore to try to send their boys and girls to a grammar school if they wanted to afford them the best start in life? And might not the technical school in fact be no more than an inferior substitute for secondary education?

Thirdly, the idea of schools to replace apprenticeship for skilled workers was late to appear in England. In Germany and France the transition from home industry and apprenticeship to large-scale factory production and the sub-division of labour followed or accompanied rather than preceded the creation of a public system of education. Thus the immediate problem of providing elementary school accommodation was solved earlier, and there was money to spare to supply 'écoles d'apprentissages' and 'Fachschulen' *pari passu* with the decline of the old-style apprenticeship. In England industrialization was nearly complete and apprenticeship in rapid decline before a place in an elementary school had been found for every child. Had Kay Shuttleworth had his way, trade schools would probably have developed much earlier in England, but the institution of 'payment by results' (1862) discouraged practical work, and the day schools of industry started under the Code of 1846 were transferred in 1860 to the Home Office to become, before long, industrial schools associated in the public mind with early disgrace and penal discipline.

In the face of these difficulties and hesitations, and remembering the deeply rooted north country tradition of early wage-earning to support the family, perhaps it would have needed more than courage for a pre-war Liberal Government to have faced the issue of compulsory continuation schools. For as one witness remarked to the Consultative Committee in 1909: 'If the hours of labour are not reduced the pupil objects. If the hours of labour are reduced, but not the wages, the employer objects. If the hours of labour and also the wages are reduced the parent objects!'

The lean years (1902–18) did not at once give way to years of plenty. On the contrary, they were followed by what may be described as 'the years of inquiry'.

The difficulties of British industry and commerce which followed the First World War increasingly directed men's minds to the need for an overhaul of commercial and industrial processes, for a better understanding of the principal factors in industrial and commercial efficiency—education among them.

The word 'rationalization', borrowed from the United States, was upon everybody's lips, and no prize-giving ceremony at a technical college was complete without its reference to the need for education and industry to get closer together.

Thus in the decade which followed the 1914–18 war the presses of His Majesty's Stationery Office poured forth a spate of reports concerned with technical and commercial education. Reference has already been made to the reports by H.M.I.s upon particular aspects of technical and commercial education. Many of these and most of the more general reports appeared between 1926 and 1929, having been initiated during the Presidency of Lord Eustace Percy—probably the first President of the Board who really grasped the full implications of technical education.

It is a common belief that no one in England reads blue books, or that at best they perform the limited function of preaching to the already converted. While it must be admitted that these reports probably did not reach a very wide circle directly, there is some evidence that their message—or some part of it—was much more widely disseminated among business men than the actual sales would suggest. Probably the questionnaires sent out by the various committees served the useful purpose of making many firms, which had not hitherto given much thought to their recruitment policy, commence to do so. For, as we shall see later in this chapter, the growth of local co-operation between the business man and the schools did accelerate to a remarkable degree in the 1925–35 decade. Moreover, there is some evidence that whereas before 1930 the impulse towards technical education came principally from the ambition of the individual student, it was after 1930 increasingly reinforced by a tendency among employers to put pressure upon their younger workers to improve their qualifications. Between 1935 and the outbreak of the Second World War (which brought all developments to an abrupt stop) there were signs that at last the country was perhaps on the threshold of an advance in technical and commercial education which might have had important consequences for British industry and commerce and the balance of trade in the next fifty years. The Board of Education's Circular 1444 (issued 1 January 1936) might have initiated a new era of expansion comparable to that which in the case of secondary education began in 1902. Hitler and the vacillations of post-1946 Governments virtually suspended any advance in the technical education sector until twenty years later.

In the light of this brief sketch of the factors which tended to promote or hamper the development of technical education after the Act of 1902, let us endeavour to distinguish the general characteristics of the main streams of demand. By 1935 they were dividing themselves naturally into four principal categories:

(1) The demand for vocational or professional training which arose from those who were ambitious to rise to better-paid, more secure, or more congenial positions; from parents who were sufficiently ambitious for their children's future to forego one or two years of the relief which an extra wage-earner could afford in the home in order to launch them into a skilled career through a junior technical, domestic, nautical, or art school; from employers who appreciated the advantages to their business of encouraging their young employees to improve their educational equipment either by attendance at part-time day courses or evening classes.

(2) The demand for further education as something of value in itself without immediate reference to employment or as a tonic to brace the system to stand either the strain or the lack of stimulus in modern life and industrial, professional, and commercial employment.

(3) The demand for practical courses in the main based on the home, which would enable a higher standard of life to be enjoyed on a limited income.

(4) The need for continuative education in a 'clublike' atmosphere to attract and awaken wider interests in the unskilled, and to combat deterioration among those sections of the youthful population where no desire for further formal education was normally present.

(1) The first type of demand, that of which *ambition* was the primary motive force, in the 1930s probably sustained a greater number of courses, both day and evening, than any of the other types. It expressed itself at one end of the scale in a great number of courses devoted to such minor professional occupations as pharmacy, shorthand, bookkeeping, and typewriting, at the other in the three to five

years' continuous and intensive study with concurrent workshop experience or office training designed to lead to the National Certificates and Diplomas awarded jointly by the Board of Education and the Institutes of Mechanical Engineers, Electrical Engineers, Chemistry, Builders, and Naval Architects. National Certificates in Textiles and Commerce were also obtainable, although no professional institute as yet existed to endorse the latter. A certificate of a slightly different type was similarly obtainable in Gas Engineering.

When the former night schools conducted by the School Boards were converted by the Act of 1902 into institutions of higher education, it soon became apparent that in so far as they were designed to prepare young men and women for their vocation, they were gravely in need of systematization. In other words, it was impossible for a boy entering an evening class in a technological subject—say cotton spinning—to proceed very far with it unless his knowledge of mathematics, science, and drawing proceeded *pari passu*.

Thus systematization had to be achieved by requiring students to take 'grouped' courses of related subjects on three or more nights a week and putting difficulties in the way of those who endeavoured to take a single subject. Lancashire and Yorkshire led the way,[1] owing no doubt first to their simplified industrial structure based on the predominant industries of cotton, wool, and coal, and secondly, to their strong evening school tradition. (What inhabitant of Burnley does not proudly recall that Lord Snowden (Labour's first Chancellor of the Exchequer) once attended an evening class in the town?).[2]

The success of the grouped course system in securing greater regularity of attendance, improving the quality of class work and homework, and facilitating the organization of evening schools was both immediate and impressive. How great a need existed for some such reorganization is shown by the fact that out of a total of 250,000 students in London it was estimated that in one year 43,000 failed to make 14 hours of attendance. By 1906-7 the percentage of evening scholars to day scholars in Bolton (32·5), Burnley (32), Blackburn (31·7), Halifax (31·6), Manchester (30·2), and Bury (29·5) had outstripped that in London (29·3) despite the 'flying start' afforded by

---

[1] In the interests of strict accuracy it should be noted that organized courses were in operation in the Sanitary Engineering Department of the Manchester Technical School in 1890 and spread in 1898 to the Technological Department. Shipley followed suit about the same year. The first town to adopt the course system throughout its evening continuation schools was Halifax in 1902. For an account of the beginning of the system see *The Course System in Evening Schools*, H.M.S.O., 1910.

[2] He was living at the time in Todmorden, and as Bradshaw's Railway Guide for the period does not show that he could have got to Burnley by train, he probably had to cycle. The cycle accident which crippled him occurred after he entered the Civil Service.

the City Parochial Charities' assistance in creating the network of polytechnics.

By one of his greatest triumphs of organization Sir Robert Blair, Education Officer to the L.C.C., thereupon introduced the course system simultaneously into all the London Evening Institutes in the year 1913.

The next step could not be taken until after the 1914–18 war. Systematization was not enough. Few robust and ambitious young men, compelled from force of necessity to enter industry at 14, can have felt at peace with their conscience on finding themselves associated at the bench or in the office with young men of their own age who had acquired that indefinable status conferred by attendance, for example, at a secondary grammar school. Deep-seated psychological cravings of this kind, widely diffused throughout the community and at the same time repressed for want of a means of expression, were a fruitful source of unrest. Could the evening class system offer any way out? Could some qualification to be obtained by examination be devised, for example, which would give these young men a sense of status, based on achievement, comparable to that enjoyed by the possessor of a university degree? Obviously the examination must be one of some severity, of a uniform standard from year to year, and only attainable by at least three, or better still five, years' hard work in a progressive evening course. But could concurrent workshop experience and application as evidenced by homework and terminal reports somehow be brought into the final assessment? Could the boys' own teachers in some way be associated with the external assessors? Finally, could the certificate awarded receive the endorsement of the Institute which represented the apex of the profession on the one hand, and of the Board of Education which represented the apex of the public educational system on the other?

It must have been with some such thoughts as these in his mind that one of His Majesty's Inspectors approached the Institute of Mechanical Engineers in 1921. The scheme for the National Certificates and Diplomas in Mechanical Engineering, which eventuated in 1922 and was followed in subsequent years by the other National Certificates already mentioned, achieved all these desiderata. From the initiation of the scheme up to 1934 the total number of certificates and diplomas awarded was 25,000[1] and the demand as evidenced by entries was

[1] Distributed as follows:

Mechanical Engineering examinations since 1923	...	...	...	13,454
Chemistry	,,	,,	1923 ...	...	...	1,584
Electrical Engineering	,,	,,	1924 ...	...	...	7,688
Naval Architects	,,	,,	1927 ...	...	...	106
Building	,,	,,	1931 ...	...	...	2,202

The Textile and Commerce Examinations had not yet commenced.

rising every year. Moreover, evidence was accumulating that those selected students who had had the persistence to win through to these certificates by five years' devoted study in evening classes were now tending to make their way to positions of leadership at least as soon as, if not before, their more happily circumstanced neighbours who were able to proceed by way of the secondary grammar school and university degree courses. I was particularly interested to hear during 1935 in a crowded railway carriage the following remark by one business man to another: 'Well of course the National Certificate is just as good as the B.Sc. though less academic perhaps.'

Thus whether they were looked at from the sociological point of view, or merely as England's most distinctive contribution to the science of examination, the National Certificates were already coming to be recognized by foreign—and particularly Dominion—observers as one of the most interesting developments in English education.

Of the other forms of training for the ambitious little need be said. The first trade (or junior technical) schools normally for boys and girls of 13–16 arose from the ashes of the higher-grade and organized science schools, in response to a well-founded anxiety about 'blind alley' employment, in 1905. Their development was initially limited by the determination of principals to make certain that a good opening in a skilled career should be found for every leaver. In 1934 they numbered 194 with an attendance of 22,158 and an annual output of nearly 10,000. In effect, therefore, they were as yet numerically of no greater importance than the 'public schools'.

The growth of part-time day classes for employees can be better considered in the later stages of this chapter.

(2) *The demand for further education as something of value in itself without immediate reference to employment, or as a tonic.*

Before the 1914–18 war the principal impulse to seek further education, after the elementary or secondary stage, was a professional or vocational impulse. The word vocational should of course be understood to include the vocation of wife and mother. The following quotation from the Consultative Committee's Report of 1909 (pp. 82 and 84) is in point: 'Nearly half a million students over 17 years of age entered Evening Classes in 1906–7. . . . The majority of these classes are technical in character. They are attended by those who desire to increase their skill in the work by which they earn their living or (especially in the case of women) in those practical home arts, dexterity in which increases the comfort of life and enables more advantageous use to be made of personal income. . . . The weaker side of these adult Evening Classes is the non-technical. Instruction in history, literature, and citizenship has hitherto failed to evoke widespread interest among the masses of the people.'

But in the intervening years something very interesting had been happening. 'The main centre of interest of the worker's life', wrote Sir Hubert Llewellyn Smith in the final volume of the *New Social Survey of London*, 'is being shifted more and more from his daily work to his daily leisure, whether that leisure be the time available for rest and recreation after the day's work is done or the compulsory leisure imposed by the total or partial failure of his means of livelihood.'

That profound stirring in every department of national life caused by the 1914–18 war, which we witnessed (p. 90) at work in the sphere of secondary education, had combined with this readjustment of focus as between work and leisure noticed by the compilers of the survey to set on foot a highly significant expansion in the demand for new forms of further education, sociological, cultural, practical, and recreative. The self-perpetuating tendency of all educational systems was also at work, directly in that the broadening of the avenue to the secondary grammar schools and enlivenment of the elementary schools stimulated enrolment at evening schools; indirectly in that the successful pursuit of technical education by increasing numbers of workers usually brought them greater security of employment and with that greater security a desire for cultural self-improvement.

Thus the tutorial class movement, which can be said to have begun with the foundation of the Workers' Educational Association in 1903 and consolidated itself in the work of the joint committee of Oxford University and working-class representatives in 1908, had by 1919–20 doubled the number of its classes as compared with 1913–14 and had by 1935 trebled the 1919–20 number, besides expanding in many new directions such as one-year and terminal classes.

To trace the development of this movement would be outside the scope of an inquiry concerned solely with the public system of education. It is sufficient to record that it 'set before itself the great conception of bringing together the scholar and the working man in the common enterprise of education': that 'its success in widening the circle of those who prefer to follow the uphill path of seasoned knowledge, in search of the discernment which such knowledge brings, to the distractions and rewards of more directly usable education is one of the most remarkable features of recent years':[1] that it was actuated not so much by a scientific or aesthetic interest as by a desire to arrive at some more satisfactory philosophy of life: and that it proceeded by way of the patient study of some well-defined branch of knowledge or thought continued through three years of systematic, continuous, and disciplined tutorial teaching, writing, and discussion of a university

[1] I cannot trace this quotation, but I believe it appeared in a message from Lord Eustace Percy to university tutorial class students.

honours standard. It therefore stood at the apex of the inter-war movement towards education for leisure.

Below this movement, although of far greater importance so far as numbers are concerned, were the wide range of courses concerned with the appreciation or study of literature, music and the drama, and with such subjects as history, economics, and sociology. Sometimes these were concentrated in self-contained buildings as in the London Literary Institutes.[1] More often they shared with vocational work accommodation in the local technical college. The impulse which brought them into being was in general the same. In every large community a considerable number of men and women were now found, as a result of the educational advance since 1902, who, having received a good elementary, often followed by secondary, commercial, or sometimes a university education, were not content to feel that they might be

> Travelling unprofitably towards the grave
> Like a false steward who hath received much
> And renders nothing back.

Some might have retired from active work, but in the main they would be found to be engaged during the day in professional work, the civil or municipal services, the banks, the insurance offices, financial and shipping houses, or the offices of lawyers and publishers. Perhaps they might have cherished literary, artistic, or musical aspirations in the past but found themselves becoming less and less ready to continue to keep themselves abreast of modern thought, and more and more prone to slip away from the cultural standards they used to set before themselves into listless scanning of the pages of the society paper and the detective story. Perhaps they used to dream boldly for their future but now found themselves discouraged. Or again, there were those who were seeking escape from the nervous tension of their professional life; escape, that is, into an atmosphere in which, in association for a few hours with a great number of other people whose mental energies were all concentrated in the same direction, they could forget the petty realities of workaday life in trying, in a dramatic class, for example, to present the greater realities of life as it ideally should be. It is surprising how many individuals may be helped by dramatic work to overcome personal difficulties: the self-conscious, to whom it will bring confidence; the over-confident, to whom it will bring a better appreciation

---

[1] The first of the London Literary Institutes came into being experimentally in 1913. Their success was astonishing. 9 Institutes were re-established in 1919, and by 1935 there were 12 with an enrolment of 12,300. For details see 'The Literary Institutes of London: A Phase in Adult Education', L.C.C. publication; 'Pioneer Work in Adult Education', p. 19, H.M.S.O.; 'The Scope and Practice of Adult Education', p. 62, H.M.S.O.; 'Adult Education and the L.E.A.', p. 61, H.M.S.O.

of their gifts relatively to those of others; the self-centred, whom it will teach to sink their personalities in the team for the sake of the play; the shallow, to whom it may bring the love of plays and play-reading for their own sake, and by a natural transition the ability to discern and like what is good.

In short they came to the literary institutes because they found themselves in need of an educational tonic in a social atmosphere, and they discovered there the secret that the best relaxation is often a complete change of mental activity.

(3) *The demand for practical courses based primarily on the home and resting upon the desire to enable a higher standard of life to be enjoyed on a limited income.*

'There has been an enormous advance in the last ten years', wrote Mrs Arnold Glover in her evidence to the Adult Education Committee in 1922.[1] 'The working girl of today is full of capacity; indeed it is almost an Elizabethan period. . . . Girls are realizing their own talent.'

The girls of 1922 were the women and mothers of 1935, and what the spread of domestic subjects in the elementary schools had done for them the spread of gardening, manual work, and metalwork had done for the men they married.

Thus in the afternoons and evenings when the housework was done but the children were at school or in bed, an increasing number of women would be found ready to return not to 'school' or even to a 'class' but to an 'institute' or 'club'. They came to learn how to provide their husbands with better meals when they returned from work; how to make the family income and their dress allowance go further by making their own dresses, gloves, and millinery, or the children's clothes. Their husbands, with the same object, took courses in household tasks, painting and decorating, papering, home carpentry, gardening and bee-keeping.

Amongst the most distinctive features of England between the wars were probably the redistribution of the national wealth[2] and the development of housing estates for the £200–£300 a year family. It was from these families that the demand for practical courses based on the home increasingly came. They were already determined to have a house and garden which should stand comparison with any in the neighbourhood, and determined too, if possible, to maintain a car. The wife in particular was anxious to dress herself and her children neatly, and yet to find time to belong to a lending library and to keep herself abreast of what was going on in the world and on the screen.

[1] 'The Development of Adult Education for Women', 1922, p. 35, H.M.S.O.
[2] See *The Social Structure of England and Wales*, Carr Saunders and Caradog Jones, p. 115, Table 11.

Again, the remarkable strides which had been made in the public health services and surgery during the three previous decades, and the falling birth-rate, made it appear that in the future the young would have to do more to support the old. In 1911 the expectation of life of a man was about 47 years and of a woman about 55. In 1931 it had already risen to about 58 in the case of a man and to 65 in the case of a woman. The total population was expected to fall in the next 40 years from 45 to 33 millions, and the number of children under 15 to fall in the same period from 10 to 4 millions. Thus the country seemed to be reaching a position in which the national income would have to be shared among a greater number of family units, their tastes increased by a more practical education, and their willingness to accept a lower standard of life proportionately diminished. It was therefore to the technical colleges and the day and evening institutes that they increasingly turned to discover the best way to make a reduced family income go further.[1]

(4) Lastly, further education was just beginning to attract the broadest stream of all—and by no means the least worthy—the stream composed of those who had left the elementary school for unskilled or semi-skilled work with little ambition or desire for further education in any formal sense.[2] Hitherto the problems of attracting this stream had hardly been faced except in London, in a few northern and midland towns, and in the countryside through the Women's Institutes. Those who composed it, the dock and general labourers, the taxi and van drivers, the porters, packers, lightermen and fish curers, the errand and van boys, the girls in cardboard box factories, were not to be attracted by an atmosphere which appealed to the studious or in which they felt constrained or 'out of their depth'. It is interesting to recall that the failure of many of the earliest of the Mechanics' Institutes was due to their tendency to attract the types who in these days would enter the technological courses proper. The earliest attempt to deal with this special problem through the Recreative Evening Schools Association came to an end in 1895 when the work of the Association was taken over by the School Boards, and its special aims were lost in the reorganization of evening continuative education which followed the Act of 1902. Thus the work of the association falls outside the period

[1] As we now know these prognostications of the 1930s were not realized for the reasons given in the footnote to page 145.

[2] Various inquiries into the first appointments received by children leaving elementary schools in the 1930s suggested that the proportion entering skilled, semi-skilled, and unskilled occupations might be put at roughly a third to each (see *Social Structure of England and Wales*, p. 140). It was from the first two classes that technological education drew the bulk of its recruits. Nearly 75 per cent of boys leaving secondary schools in some areas were already entering upon technological courses.

covered by this book, but the Cross Commission were impressed by its value (the Rev. J. B. Paton, D.D., of Nottingham, who gave evidence, was its spokesman) and the following passage in their report was nearly as true in 1935 as when it was written: 'There will be for many years the great mass of the ordinary boys and girls who leave school without having obtained the full benefit of a good elementary education, and for them a humble evening school is needed, which will aim, not so much at building up a higher edifice of knowledge, as at preserving the perishable and scanty accumulation from being swept away by the inroads of continuous and especially of unskilled labour.' Those aims re-emerged in 1920 with the opening of the first five 'Men's Institutes' in Battersea, Bethnal Green, Deptford, Southwark, and Stepney. The methods followed in these institutes, though varying in detail, were in essence the same: to enlist the interest and win the confidence of those living in some of the least favourable surroundings of modern urban life by an appeal to them to cultivate their 'hobbies' in a club atmosphere; to lead them through their hobby to pride of achievement and so to a greater self-respect; to build upon these foundations a realization of new powers and a desire to use leisure to better advantage; and, after wider interests had been awakened and unobtrusive training in self-government had done its work, to establish the institute on these sure foundations as the centre of social life for the whole neighbourhood.

What the men's and women's institutes were doing for the adult members of this section of the community, the 'Junior Men's Evening Institutes' and the corresponding institutes for girls were doing for the youthful sections. Here the methods were similar, but there existed the further object of giving a training and discipline which would combat the deterioration which too often set in after the doors of the elementary school closed behind the youngster of 14. The elementary school may have failed to awaken a vocational outlook in these boys, but it had given them strong practical interests; it may have failed to awaken in the girls a desire to read good books, but the needlework and domestic subjects rooms had opened windows on a life which they might not find in their cramped homes. It was the purpose of the institutes, by offering them such pursuits as physical training, games, boxing, home carpentry, inexpensive hobbies, boot and clothes repairing, music, and popular science, to preserve the benefits of the elementary school by substituting enlarging interests for the circumscribed life of tenement and street.

No account of the lines upon which technical and further education had been developing between 1902 and 1935 and no attempt to classify the separate sources of demand can be complete without some estimate of the economic and social importance of what had been happening. Few economists would now deny that 'an increasing stock of practical ability in a nation enlarges the range of its economic activities and rapidly adds, through all gradations of directive responsibility, to the number of well-remunerated posts which could never have existed if men had not been forthcoming to fill them.'[1]

The social worker inevitably found more attractions in the non-vocational work, in particular perhaps that of the men's and women's institutes and the literary institutes. Slowly but inevitably as each successive generation of students left its mark upon them he saw them developing, as older places of learning had before them, a tradition and an atmosphere; an atmosphere of fellowship united by common devotion to worthy activities; a tradition as the local centres of the peculiar cultural influences for which each institute in time came to stand.

Moreover, 'by establishing contact between men and women of the most widely varying callings and promoting a free interchange of the experience which each can contribute to the common pool, the institutes are doing a unifying work of the highest social value. It is a work which must have been the means of bringing better understanding, a keener appreciation of the good qualities to be found in every walk of life, and greater neighbourliness to thousands of homes.'[2]

Lastly, how far could our provision for technical and further education up to 1935 in reality claim to be *education*, in the commonly accepted sense of the term, at all? The answer must of course depend upon the individual questioner's view as to what precisely constitutes education. The uncompromising point of view of those educated in the older academic tradition was well exemplified by Cardinal Newman in *The Scope and Nature of University Education* (1859): 'Call things by their right names and do not confuse together things which are essentially different. A thorough knowledge of one science, and a superficial acquaintance with many, are not the same thing; a smattering of a hundred things, or a memory for detail, is not a philosophical or comprehensive view. Recreations are not education; accomplishments are not education. Do not say the people must be educated when after all you only mean amused, refreshed, soothed, put into good spirits and good humour, or kept from vicious excesses. I do not say that such amusements are not a great gain, but they are not education. Education is a high word; it is the preparation for knowledge, and it is the imparting of knowledge in proportion to that preparation.'

Cardinal Newman, writing in 1859, could not of course foresee the

---

[1] *R.C.C.*, 1909, pp. 47 and 48.
[2] From a message contributed by Mrs Lowe, Chairman of the L.C.C. Education Committee, to the souvenir handbook issued in connection with the 21st anniversary celebration of the reorganized institutes.

strides which would be made during the next eighty years in the
preparation for knowledge of a democracy more than twice as populous; nor could he possibly have foreseen the success achieved by
grouped courses in imparting knowledge in proportion to the preparation of the students to receive it. But there still existed, particularly
among those educated in a similar tradition, a widespread misunderstanding both as to the purpose and content of technical and further
education and as to its influence upon the recipient. Such critics were
usually ready to admit the high cultural value of the tutorial classes.
Some might go further and be ready to agree that much of the work
done by the evening institutes, whether of the literary type or the more
social and practical type, fell within the definition of a liberal education put forward in the Report on the Teaching of English in England
(see p. 115). For it was obvious that the work proceeded, 'not by
presentation of lifeless facts, but by teaching the student to follow the
different lines upon which life may be explored and proficiency in
living may be obtained'. On the other hand, far too many people still
failed to appreciate the cultural significance of technical and vocational
education proper. The most enthusiastic exponent of the success
achieved by 'realistic studies' in the elementary school in illuminating
and interpreting to the children the life of the world around them
would sometimes fail altogether to appreciate that this was precisely what the evening class in technology could do for the boy or girl
whose working life was spent at the bench or in the workshop. Yet
it is impossible to explain in any other way the success of those who
followed national certificate courses. By six or seven hours' work
each week for the five years of the course they had proved themselves
able, despite the fatigue of their daily workshop round, to keep pace
with, and often later surpass, students in the same subject who had
remained at secondary schools and were taking a full-time university
course. The explanation was admirably expressed in a speech on 'The
cultural possibilities of Vocational Education' delivered in February
1932, at the annual meeting of the Association of Principals of Technical Institutions by Mr J. W. Bispham, then Principal of the Borough
Polytechnic: 'In more academic forms of education we take considerable pains to present to students artificial problems akin to those of real
life, in order that the principles we teach may appear to mean something. We adopt all kinds of devices to "motivate" our teaching. The
university student gets an over-rich diet of general principles—that is
to say, of abstract facts as we have thought of them. They come to him
as a burden to be borne by his memory, for they simplify nothing that
was complex; whereas to the evening student who is at work during
the day they come as simple links holding the complex facts together
and relieving the memory. To the academic student they come

arbitrarily; to the evening student they are sweet reasonableness itself.'

Anyone who reads the literature concerned with the development of technical education during the first three decades of the century will make one interesting discovery. Employers who had given a fair trial to the release of their young workers for part-time continuative education were at last beginning to find out for themselves exactly what the Consultative Committee, so long ago as 1909, had predicted that they would discover.[1] They were, in fact, becoming increasingly ready to admit that they secured a fuller loyalty and a greater content-ment among their employees, and that the firm had gained financially in that accidents were fewer in number, scrapped work less in quan-tity, and misunderstandings between departments of less frequent occurrence.

Such a revolution in outlook could never have come about had the schools remained content to go their own way and had they not deli-berately set out to discover the needs of the business world. For when the Act of 1902 was passed the great mass of employers were very far from appreciating that what was nightly going on in thousands of class-rooms might be of direct consequence to the whole future of their works or office. On the contrary, all but a few of the more far-sighted were inclined to regard the local technical and evening school provision as affording at best an opportunity for ambitious young men in their works to follow stereotyped academic courses confined to the scientific principles underlying their vocation and completely divorced from local requirements.

By 1909 the Consultative Committee, although admitting that 'the great majority of employers are still indifferent', noticed signs of an awakening interest among those concerns employing the largest number of skilled workers. Fourteen out of the sixteen railway com-panies were granting facilities for their employees to attend technical classes, seven out of the fourteen encouraging day classes.

The example of Messrs Mather and Platt, who had maintained their own technical school from 1873 to 1905, and of Messrs Brunner Mond, who had encouraged the technical education of their employees since 1884, was being followed by other large firms.

On the other hand, such forms of local co-operation as did exist— and the committee mentioned eight as being in actual operation—all proceeded from the assumption that the contribution of the manage-ment began and ended with the encouragement of selected employees to improve their educational qualifications by the payment of their fees or the offer of such inducements as 'time off', prizes, scholarships, extra wages, or promotion. All these forms of assistance were still of course

[1] *C.C.R.*, 1909, pp. 121–4 and 128–30.

continuing. Indeed for every firm employing one or other method in 1909 there must by 1935 have been many doing so, for where any considerable proportion of the larger firms in a given area had found that it paid them to use the educational facilities provided for them by the rate and taxpayer, the smaller employers soon found that they could not afford to stand out indefinitely. It was unfortunately still the case, however, that the lead almost invariably came from the big firms. There were those who regretted that when industry was relieved of a substantial proportion of its rates by the Local Government Act of 1929, the opportunity was not taken to institute some contribution in aid of technical education as was done in France by the *Loi Astier*.

The most important development in the intervening years must, however, be sought elsewhere. Up to 1935 it lay in the success which had attended the efforts of the schools themselves to enlist the active co-operation as 'honorary consultants' or as members of 'advisory committees' of the leaders of local industry[1] in person. It could be found in the much greater readiness of the business man to visit the technical institute to discover its potentialities for himself, and sometimes even to return bringing some technical problem of his own for solution. It had found expression in the growth of happier relations and a clearer understanding of the scope and aims of technical education among the all-important foremen, upon whose goodwill the release of the young worker so often depended, and in the increasing friendliness of organized labour.

The growth of advisory committees was first noticed officially in an educational pamphlet of 1928.[2] After that year it accelerated considerably. It not only brought industry and commerce into a more direct partnership with the technical school system; it provided the teaching staffs with the liaison and intelligence service which they needed if they were to adjust their organization to meet the continually changing types of demand created by the kaleidoscope of industry. In many parts of the country improved conditions of transport had tended since the 1914–18 war to convert the more localized technical institutes of pre-war days into the recognized centres of higher education for widely diversified industrial regions. I can recall a case where 18 students travelled an average distance per student of 650 miles during a single session to attend a particular class. Some of them lived 40 miles away and used to come by car to the class. It followed that the principal and his heads of department must be constantly on the alert to detect not only changes in established local industries but the rise of new forms or subdivisions of industry in the 'catchment area' of the college, and that

---

[1] In the term 'leaders of local industry' I include of course representatives of organized labour as well as of the management.

[2] *E.P.*, 64.

any one of these might occasion a demand for the establishment of wholly new types of class. In this effort to watch and provide for a changing demand, advisory committees connected with each department served both as eyes and ears. To attempt to enumerate, however briefly, a comprehensive list of the methods of co-operation already existing between industry and the schools by 1935 would require a separate chapter. On the other hand, some of the more general methods may suitably be illustrated by an attempt to answer the question which might well be asked by an interested foreign observer: 'In what ways might one have expected to find a progressive and favourably situated business on a large scale making the maximum use of the local provision for technical and further education?'

In the first place, it must be assumed that such a firm would have decided upon its policy of recruitment and promotion as a whole.

It might, for example, have come to the conclusion that it would take a certain number of young workers from the senior elementary schools annually, a smaller stream from the junior technical schools and secondary grammar schools at about the age of 16 or 17, to fill vacancies for skilled workers on the production and the office side of the business respectively, and a still smaller number from the universities to be trained for the higher posts. The first group would be engaged direct from the senior elementary schools on the recommendation of their head teachers. If their employment was to be, initially at least, of a routine nature, the firm would be concerned to counteract the monotony of the day's work by encouraging them to continue those activities which had made the greatest appeal to them at school. It might achieve this object by causing them to attend a day continuation school either provided out of its own funds or by the local education authority.[1] Alternatively, it might encourage them to attend evening institutes of cultural or recreative and social type according to the advice of the former head teacher in consultation with the welfare staff of the firm. To encourage attendance the firm would probably pay the initial registration fee, if any, or return it to the young employee on evidence of satisfactory attendance and conduct.

Every facility would be granted for the advertisement of evening school facilities in the works and for talks to new entrants by the heads of the evening institutes concerned. The firm would also make it known that permission would be granted to all those attending evening classes to leave work in good time to enable them either to get a cheap

---

[1] Of 53 day continuation schools in existence in England and Wales in 1935, 46 were controlled by local education authorities and 7 had been provided by private firms. An interesting account of the activities of some of these schools is contained in *The Entrance to Industry*, 1935, published by P.E.P., 16 Queen Anne's Gate, S.W.1.

meal at the works canteen or to return home for a meal and change of clothing before the classes commenced. Occasional half-holidays would be granted at slack periods to employees upon whose work and attendance the firm had received good reports. It might also be made known that such good reports would lead to increments of wages and, other things being equal, would confer some measure of preferential treatment where promotion was in question. For those young workers who had shown exceptional capacity at the elementary school, release might be granted on two half-days a week to attend part-time day classes in technological subjects.[1]

The next group of entrants, those coming from the junior technical[2] and secondary grammar schools at 16 or 17, would be encouraged to enter at once upon the senior courses, lasting for three years and often leading to a further two or three years in advanced courses, at the local technical institute. Similar inducements as regards return of fees, 'time off' and preference in promotion would be offered to this group also. The sessional examinations marking the termination of each year of the course would qualify those obtaining the best results for prizes. These would be awarded out of a common prize fund administered by the institute but paid for out of the pooled contributions of all the firms in the area whose employees were making use of the college.[3] They might take any one of a variety of forms, for example, book allowances, the payment of the next session's fees, tools (an arrangement commoner in Belgium than in this country), or perhaps, where the student had passed out of the third year senior course into the advanced course, a scholarship, carrying a subsistence allowance to compensate for loss of wages, admitting to a full-time course of study or a period of residence in another town to visit works and study industrial organization.

During their progress through the senior courses the students would be afforded opportunities by the firm, and by others similarly well disposed, to visit not only the works and offices in which they themselves were employed but those of other concerns. At these visits machinery would be kept working after hours for their benefit, and members of the staff of the firm would be available to explain methods of production and such matters as accounting machinery and filing systems. Occasionally actual class sessions were held in works, and they had even taken place at the bottom of a coal mine! The third group of

---

[1] The number of boys and girls so released in 1934 was probably between 20,000 and 30,000. They would be found among the 28,000 pupils attending technical day classes and the 15,000 attending day continuation schools.

[2] Certain firms, particularly those in the rubber industries around Manchester, engaged their employees from the elementary schools but required them to take a full junior technical school course before commencing work.

[3] The pooling of money given for prizes was a comparatively recent innovation. The first case I can recollect was at Stockport about 1933.

entrants to the works, those recruited at a later age from the university, would similarly be encouraged to take courses in business administration, accountancy, commercial law, and works management.

The management of any firm which had developed co-operation to such a degree as this would no doubt be represented on the various advisory committees of the technical college or institute. Alternatively, selected members of the directing staff would have accepted appointment as 'honorary consultants'. Thus in addition to encouraging the attendance of their younger workers at the various courses, they would simultaneously be in a position to advise as to special equipment, the appointment of teaching staff, the circularization of trade organizations, the securing of supplies of consumable material and equipment for use by the students, and the placing of students in employment.

It was generally through the good offices of members of advisory committees and the contacts that they were able to establish that the schools received a steady stream of gifts ranging from the heaviest machinery to books for the library, from consumable material such as the supply of lead and copper tubing to offers to undertake the repair of apparatus or to finish students' work up to sale standard in the local factory. The total value of the gifts received annually had by 1935 become quite substantial. The total value of those made to 92 schools in the three years ending March 1925 was placed at £120,000.

In return the schools organized open days and exhibitions to demonstrate their potentialities to employers and foremen, the staff contributed articles to works publications and in some cases carried out tests on behalf of co-operating firms in their laboratories, and local scientific and professional societies were encouraged (particularly in Lancashire) to hold their meetings at the college.

This new interest of local industry and commerce in technical and further education, which found expression in the invention of so many novel means of co-operation with the local technical institutes, had its counterpart on the national plane. Here in general it took the form of an increasing concern on the part of the professional associations, old and new, the federations of manufacturers, the joint industrial councils, and the research associations to formulate the educational requirements of different grades of workers in the various industries; to translate these requirements into schemes of training for the guidance of their members in local industries; and to devise, in co-operation with examining bodies, such as the City and Guilds of London Institute, examination passports which would have a national currency.

The development of technical and further education was already seen by the far-sighted to be the main task which lay before this country in the sphere of higher education, just as the development of

the senior elementary school was seen to be the main task in the sphere
of elementary education.

The technical colleges were already attracting half their students
from the secondary schools, and in some areas three out of four boys
who left secondary schools entered upon evening courses almost immediately. In many towns, however, the man in the street could still
only recall with difficulty where the technical college was situated. To
rebuild these colleges in a manner worthy of the place they should fill
as the centres of vocational and cultural education for the region which
they served, to develop their corporate life, and to remove all restrictions upon their availability to students living outside the boundaries of
the local authorities actually providing them, would—as we shall see in
later chapters—be tasks sufficient to tax the best administrative ability
of the nation for the next three decades.

CHAPTER X

THE SPECIAL SERVICES OF EDUCATION

School medical inspection.—What the doctors found in 1908.—What they would find in 1935.—Why was not medical inspection instituted earlier?—How did the service develop so rapidly?—The school doctor's contribution to the education of the people.—The 'special schools'.—Provision of meals.

WHILE the growth of a system of higher education and the enlivenment of the elementary school had changed the face of English education, the school medical service had been changing in a literal sense the faces of the school population. This may seem a bold assertion, but if anyone doubts it let him study side by side photographs of school classes of the 1890s and the corresponding classes in the same schools in 1935.[1] Even making a liberal discount for externals such as the changes in dress and the tendency of schoolgirls to wear their hair short, he could not fail to come to the conclusion that the school child of 1935 looked younger, fresher, better-tempered and less ethereal than his or her prototype of thirty years before.

The explanation is simple enough to anyone to whom comparative statistics are not a dull compilation of figures but a living record of progress, or to anyone who has followed the educational work which the school medical service carried out among parents and teachers.

Perhaps the easiest way by which the layman can comprehend the achievement of the school medical service[2] is to ask himself the question, 'What would a doctor examining a school of 1,000 children in a poor quarter, hitherto untouched by the school doctor or nurse, have expected to find before 1908, and what changes would he find by 1935?'

The most obvious external sign of improvement would be that which had taken place in cleanliness of body and head. In the early days of the school medical service from 700 to 970 of the 1,000 children would have been dirty in varying degrees ranging from 100

[1] For such photographs see *The Special Services of Education in London*, pp. 14–15 and 18–19.

[2] It was in the Usher Street School in Bradford, where the first medical inspection on record took place in 1894, that 100 out of 400 children examined were found not to have had their clothes off for up to nine months.

who were described as 'very dirty', 600 as dirty, 260 as somewhat dirty, to 30 describable as 'clean'. If the winter was approaching a proportion of the children might have been found to have been actually sewn into their clothing and sometimes padded in addition with cotton wool.[1] The presence of vermin in the clothing and hair, besides lowering the self-respect of the children, led to constant fidgeting and worse still to disturbed or sleepless nights. Among 1,000 girls in a county area as many as 600 might be found with 'nits' or pediculi present in the hair,[2] while in a town school the number would be about 500. Most doctors who were engaged in medical inspection at the commencement of the school medical service will recall cases where the whole head appeared to be slowly moving with vermin. The boys, having shorter hair, were less affected, but the parents of perhaps 50 or more out of a sample 1,000 would have had to be approached.

The next obvious outward sign that medical inspection was overdue would be afforded by the number of little faces puckered by the continuous attempt to see the blackboard or to do fine needlework in spite of defective eyesight. In a number of cases (about 20 per 1,000) obvious signs such as squint and inflamed eyelids would point to something amiss, but further examination would disclose from 100 to 200 out of the 1,000 children with vision so seriously defective as to require the immediate provision of spectacles, and a further 100 with lesser degrees of defect.[3] Anyone who calculates what this must have meant in headaches, lassitude, overstrain, or, worse still, early blindness will understand the remark of a noble lord who, speaking on the clause in Mr Birrell's Bill which sought to establish a system of medical inspection in 1906, expressed the view that the results of defective vision alone must be responsible for more suffering every year than a war.

When the doctor had picked out 10 to 20 children out of the 1,000 suffering from ringworm,[4] and perhaps 40 with a record of discharging ears, due to middle ear disease, he would proceed to a more thorough clinical examination. This would reveal in our school of 1,000 children from 700 to 800 cases of dental decay, probably more than half of them with four or more decayed teeth,[5] from 150 to 180 suffering from diseases of the nose and throat, from 100 to 130 showing definite signs of malnutrition, 26 to 80 suffering from diseases of the heart and circulation, and from 10 to 30 having diseases of the lungs.

[1] Medical inspection was imposed upon local authorities as a duty in 1907, but it took some years for the system to become comprehensive. In general, I shall compare the position in 1908 with that in 1934.

[2] C.M.O., 1909, p. 29.

[3] C.M.O., 1908, p. 60; 1909, pp. 51–60.

[4] C.M.O., 1909, pp. 34–42. The LCC had to start a special school for children suffering from Flavus, a particularly revolting form of ringworm unknown today.

[5] C.M.O., 1908, pp. 54–57 and C.M.O., 1917, p. 171.

Since these children were born in the first decade of the twentieth century and since the expectation of life of a man born in 1901 was only 45½ and that of a woman only 48½, one wonders if any of those exhibiting the worse forms of illness are still alive. One wonders how many might have been alive had the school medical service been in existence before the century opened, and had not parliamentary and local fears of 'pauperizing' the parents and encroaching upon the preserves of the private practitioner delayed any universal provision of schemes of treatment for an appreciable number of years after medical inspection had become general.

What, in contrast, would the doctor have found in inspecting the same school in 1935?

The improvement in cleanliness, which was always the most immediate gain experienced when the first school doctors and nurses were appointed, was remarkable. Out of a total of over 16 million examinations of individual children carried out in 1934 less than 27 per 1,000 were found to be unclean, and only about a third of this number had to be cleansed under arrangements made by the L.E.A.[1]

Although the treatment of all children's eyes at birth to eliminate ophthalmia neonatorum had produced a welcome decline in preventable visual defect, about 78 children in every 1,000 inspected would have still been found to be suffering from visual defects. Only 5 new cases of blindness were ascertained in London in 1934 as compared with some hundreds in earlier days, but other factors had no doubt operated in London, e.g. the centrifugal tendency of the population and the decline of immigration and with it of trachoma, a disease of Central Europe. Ophthalmia neonatorum accounted for about 36·8 per cent of the children in London schools for the blind in 1904. Congenital venereal disease probably accounted for another 30 per cent. Before the days of the school medical service the teacher who found a child could not see clearly had usually only one remedy—to bring him nearer the blackboard. Dr Macnamara was honest enough to confess to the House of Commons that by adopting this expedient he had once ruined the eyesight of a boy who ought to have been sent farther away,[2] and such cases must have been only too common. By 1934 there were few children who did not secure glasses either immediately or within a short period after they had been seen by one of the ophthalmic surgeons employed by every authority but one. Where our doctor of 1908 might find from ten to twenty cases of ringworm among his 1,000 children, the doctor of 1934 would probably have been surprised to find more than one. Thus, what was once a bane of the child population had become a rarity. With its virtual disappearance had

[1] *C.M.O.*, 1934, p. 138.
[2] *H.*, Vol. 160, Col. 1384.

gone one of the last valid objections of the middle-class parent to sending his child to the public elementary school.

Otorrhoea (middle ear disease) had declined steadily[1] to 4·7 cases per 1,000 inspections, although of course it tended to vary with the incidence of epidemic diseases. These could now be predicted with some accuracy and preparations made to meet them. Moreover, now that the slate had vanished from the schools (pp. 23 & 122) they were usually kept under remarkably efficient control by the school nursing staff. In 1891-5 some 8,000 children under 15 died annually of measles alone. In 1933 the figure was 1,918 and in 1934 (a bad year) 3,719. What the abolition of the slate and improvements in the sanitary conditions of the schools and homes[2] had done to reduce epidemics, the sixpenny toothbrush, the school dental clinic, and the demonstrators employed by the Dental Board of the United Kingdom had done for dental hygiene. 314 out of the 316 L.E.A.s were providing dental treatment in 1934. When the amount of ill-health which even a single seriously septic tooth can cause is remembered, this alone is sufficient to account for the fact that the children of 1935 in our photographs look so much less ethereal and delicate than their prototypes. Lethargy, 'dullness', and actual facial malformation were steadily being reduced by the treatment of nose and throat defects, notably enlarged tonsils and adenoids, operations being performed at the rate of 125,000 a year.[3]

Progress had on the whole been steady, and notable extensions of the service since the 1914-18 war had almost eliminated the severe forms of crippling by the development of orthopaedic treatment, had enabled a serious attack to be made upon the treatment of rheumatism which led to so many heart affections in later life, and had brought the aid of electrical science to the early detection of conditions likely if neglected to lead to deafness.

Finally some indication of the total result, and in particular of the success which had attended the preventive work of the school medical service in dealing with the more serious defects, may be gathered from the fact that whereas 555 children aged between 5 and 15 in every 100,000 died in 1907 from all causes (125 from tuberculosis), the number had by 1934 been reduced to 385 (43 from tuberculosis). In other words, at least 30,500 children died between these ages in 1907 (nearly 7,000 from tuberculosis) as compared with 21,175 in 1934 (2,365 from tuberculosis).[4]

[1] *C.M.O.*, 1934, p. 79.

[2] There had of course been other causes at work too, e.g. increased knowledge of epidemiology and bacteriology, increased provision for hospital treatment, and supervision of contacts by doctors and nurses.

[3] The spread of poliomyelitis was in future years to restrict the number of operations performed.

[4] I have assumed a population of 5½ millions aged 5-15 in each year. Actually the

Contemplating these figures one wonders if any nation ever spent £2,000,000 a year to better advantage.

The history of the school medical service belongs rather to a study of the awakening of the national conscience in regard to the public health than to a study of the growth of the public service of education. Moreover, no feature of our educational system is more fully documented, and anyone who wishes to study it can do so at first hand in the various accounts of its development which have been written from time to time by Sir George Newman, its author and chief architect, and by his successors.

Nevertheless the undoubted success of medical inspection and treatment when once established must raise a number of questions in the mind of any inquiring historian who is untrammelled by official discretion. Why, for example, was not the need for such a service recognized by Parliament before 1907? How had it been developed with such rapidity that it was by 1935 more complete and universal than in any other country? Had its contribution to the *education* of the people —for the cost was still borne from educational funds—been as marked as its contribution to the early detection and prevention of disease?

The answer to the first question will be clear to anyone who realizes how few had been the occasions in English social history prior to the Second World War when the Exchequer had permitted itself to look beyond the immediate cost of a new service to its ultimate potentialities as a means of national insurance.

Popular education began as a charity, extended first to those who had no parents or whose parents were indigent, later to those other classes of the population least able to look after themselves. But at every stage resistance was offered to any wider extension. Lord John Russell might charge the Committee of Council in 1839 to look to 'the general education of the people', but nearly thirty years later (1863–4) we find them still splitting hairs as to the classes to whose children the elementary school might open its doors. 'Does the parent rank and associate with the working men or with the tradesmen of the place?' was the test they employed. 'Simple policemen, coastguards, and dock and railway porters may commonly be regarded as labouring men. But petty officers in those services, excisemen, pilots and clerks of various kinds present more difficulty', they reported.

It was not, therefore, until this resistance was finally broken down, after the passage of the Education Acts of 1870 and 1876, and until the

---

population in these age-groups was rather larger in both years. The number in the elementary schools was 5,161,850 in 1907, and 5,460,904 in 1934. The expenditure quoted is that upon the school medical sevices. Other contributory factors were general health education, drainage, better housing, hospitalization, immunization, etc.

whole mass of the nation's children were assembled for the first time in surroundings more hygienic than the homes from which they came that the extent of their ills could be gauged. Even then those ills were at first apparent only to the teachers, who were hardly as yet effectively organized as a social force,[1] to H.M.I.s[2], and to a few doctors and enlightened members of School Boards. 'Day by day in East Bristol', Dr. Macnamara told the House of Commons, 'I used literally to shudder in contemplation of the fact that it was upon these rickety shoulders that the burden of the Empire in time of come would have to rest.' Moreover, the major ills had to be dealt with first. Power to segregate the blind and the deaf had to be conferred upon School Boards by the Elementary Education (Blind and Deaf Children) Act of 1893. Power to 'ascertain' the children who were mentally defective and those who were suffering from severe epilepsy had to be granted by the permissive Defective and Epileptic Children Act of 1898. Gradually, however, experience accumulated. London had appointed a school medical officer in 1890, Bradford in 1893;[3] one H.M.I.[4] translated, from the extremely technical German in which they were written, the researches of Cohn upon the eyesight of German children, thus making his findings available to English medical men and a wider public; social workers raised the cry that the national physique was being impaired by the urbanization of the population.

The Boer War was probably the turning-point. Members of Parliament might be ready to accept with a certain resignation the inevitability of a great mass of physical impairment in other people's children just as many people today accept the toll of the roads. But when they found that 4,400 potential recruits had to be rejected every year on the ground of defective teeth alone, they bestirred themselves, and in 1903 and the following year a Royal Commission on Physical Training (Scotland) and an Inter-Departmental Committee on Physical Deterioration both pointed to the need for some systematic medical examination of the school population. This need was even more clearly emphasized by a third committee appointed by the President of the Board of Education in 1905, and Mr Birrell (who had himself been condemned from the moment he was born to wear spectacles) inserted a clause in his ill-fated Education Bill of 1906 to allow the L.E.A.s to institute medical inspection if they wished and at their own cost.

[1] The National Union of Teachers had a membership of 35,000 in 1895.

[2] The general reports of H.M.I.s are of course full of references to the poor eyesight of many of the scholars and a departmental committee seems to have been appointed about 1895 to consider the question.

[3] For the campaign conducted in Bradford see my book *Margaret McMillan. The Children's Champion*, Museum Press, 1960.

[4] Mr Turnbull. I remember hearing him described, I believe by Dr Eichholz, as 'the father of the school medical service'.

The historian will follow the fate of this clause with interest. The House was more than friendly. Only one member of either party raised his voice against Mr Tennant's amendment designed to convert Mr Birrell's permissive clause into one imposing a duty upon all local education authorities 'to make arrangements for attending to the health and physical condition of the children educated in public elementary schools'. The Bill as a whole was lost and the medical inspection clause went with it. But it was revived in a Private Member's Bill of the following year and eventually passed in the Administrative Provisions Act of 1907.[1]

At the same time it would be a mistake to read into these parliamentary proceedings evidence of any real determination on the part of the legislature to establish a complete school medical service. It would probably be nearer the truth to say that Parliament welcomed the establishment of medical inspection for three principal reasons. In the first place they believed that the moment the school doctor had called the attention of a parent to her child's ailments she would at once visit the family doctor. Secondly medical inspection would at least detect those children who might otherwise suffer irreparable damage through injudicious eye-strain or physical training. Thirdly, by providing an anthropometric survey it might answer what Mr A. J. Balfour described as a 'burning question of the day', namely whether the drift from the country and the urbanization of the population was adversely affecting the public health. Mr Tennant in moving his amendment to Mr Birrell's Bill was at pains to explain that he had certainly no intention of compelling the authorities to institute schemes of *treatment* in addition to medical inspection. The fear of 'pauperizing' the parents —a legacy from the Victorian theory of 'self-help'—was fairly general. The fear of antagonizing the private practitioner was stronger still, and perhaps better founded—as the experience of the National Health Insurance Commissioners was to prove a few years later.

At this point the historian will be brought up against his second question: How was a service which began in such an uncertain atmosphere developed with such rapidity that by 1935 it was universally recognized to be one of the most valuable and least costly agents of modern educational progress and a principal foundation of the national health?

The answer can only be found in the early reports of school medical officers, dentists and nurses, and in the files of the Medical Branch of the Board of Education. The first inspections disclosed, as we have seen, a truly shocking amount of preventible defect, and all subsequent

[1] Securing the passage of this Bill during the last years of a tottering Government was one of Sir Robert Morant's greatest contributions to English education. He had fallen under the spell of Margaret McMillan whom he had visited in Bradford.

inspections tended to confirm the inability of the parents, whether through poverty or the absence of a health conscience, to obtain treatment for their children. The files of the Medical Branch of the Board show that, in the face of these disclosures and relying upon the general friendliness of all classes of parliamentary and official thought, the Board deliberately bestirred themselves to encourage the L.E.A.s to provide school clinics[1] and to enter into arrangements with local hospitals and voluntary associations to provide the major forms of treatment such as tonsil and adenoid operations and the treatment of ringworm by X-rays. In some departments of educational development the Board of Education has been accused of resembling a motor car with excellent brakes, a good steering mechanism but no engine! In the particular sphere of the school medical service it can at least claim a great deal of the credit for the astonishing developments after 1908. The annual reports of Sir George Newman on the health of the school child, the missionary work performed by the Board's medical officers during their day-to-day inspections of the work of each area, and the letters of advice sent by the administrative staff of the Board on the result of these reports have together constituted a shining example of the 'fertilizing' power of government inspection when properly employed. Service in the Medical Department of the Board proved such a severe test of administrative capacity that it came to be known as 'the grave of reputations'. In it, however, many who subsequently rose to high posts of responsibility in the Civil Service acquired a 'bedside manner' which subsequently proved invaluable to them.

Nearly every area in England and Wales was visited annually. The school medical officer was made conversant at this visit with the best work being done in other areas. Subsequently the members of the education committee were told in an official letter exactly how their service stood in relation to those of other authorities and what were the next developments which they ought to undertake. These letters, dealing as they did with a whole range of medical phraseology new to official correspondence, produced many delightful examples of official language such as 'conditions of uncleanliness associated with pediculosis'.

The State might have taken the view that its sole concern was to make a physical or anthropometric survey of the child population and a record of the defects disclosed by medical inspection and to exercise some control over infectious disease, leaving treatment to the parents and the family doctor. Had it done so the country would still have been losing many thousands of child lives now saved annually, while the

---

[1] I can recall as symptomatic of the nervousness engendered at this time by the religious controversies of the day that it was actually doubted whether Catholic children could be expected to use the clinics if they were provided by the L.E.A.s.

direct educational gains in improved attendance and the industrial gains in the prevention of future loss of working time would have been wantonly jettisoned. As a people we have hitherto been taught to pay honour almost exclusively to our politicians, our proconsuls, our diplomats, our generals, and our admirals. Perhaps the future historian will recognize in Sir George Newman—who retired on 31 March 1935—a public servant who by his work saved more lives than were ever lost in our national wars.

Thirdly, there is no doubt that the school medical service made its own distinctive contribution to the *education* of the people. It taught the country to look upon the child, not as a unit for statistical record or clinical data, but as an individual to be trained in a hygienic way of life, preserved in health where he possessed it or restored to health where he did not. It taught the parents of the first generation of children to be subjected to school medical inspection that ailments could not with impunity be treated as trifling in an urbanized population.[1] It created in that generation, when they became parents in their turn, a health conscience which abolished the 'Mother Gamp' of the slums and endowed the young mother of the 1930s with a fund of common sense and a readiness to seek advice which her prototype of forty years before rarely possessed.

The growth of the remaining special services of education constitute a story which, if fully told, would upset the balance of a book designed to give a picture of educational advance on a much wider front. Moreover, like that of the school medical service, it has been so fully told and documented by Sir George Newman's annual reports that there is practically nothing to add to what he has written.

About half the blind and deaf children for whom education in a special school would now be regarded as essential had been sent to such schools by 1895. By 1910 nearly all were probably in school, and the numbers have remained fairly constant ever since. Partially blind and partially deaf have taken the places rendered vacant by the reduction of the number of those suffering from preventible blindness and deafness. The teaching has of course improved to a remarkable degree. The first school for the mentally defective[2] was started in Leicester in 1892, anticipating a school in London by a few months. In this case also the

---

[1] It is interesting to notice how very old people still tended to regard such matters as tuberculous glands, scarlet fever, and whooping cough as inevitable childish ailments not to be taken too seriously. The theory that the human body is normally in a state of health and normally tends to return to it after illness may have been satisfactory when it was evolved by the ancient Greeks (see article on Greek medicine in *The Legacy of Greece*), but it is surely of more doubtful application to a modern urbanized population.

[2] Now described as educationally subnormal.

number of schools and scholars remained fairly constant between 1910 and 1935, although less warrantably so, for it is probably still true to say that a considerable number of borderline cases, who could more profitably have been educated in these schools, remained in the schools. No school for cripples was recognized before that established at the Passmore Edwards Settlement in 1899. A residential school for convalescent children was recognized in 1902, and the first open-air schools were started in 1908.

While a proportion—although no great proportion—of the school population will always require special treatment in such schools, whatever progress is made in the public health services, two major developments deserve mention.

In 1895 a child born a cripple was condemned to remain a cripple for life. Similarly in 1895 a child born deaf was condemned to remain not only deaf but probably mute as well for life. Oral instruction, by lip-reading, was beginning to be taught to the older children, but silent instruction, 'talking on the fingers', was still widespread. The child born a cripple in the 1930s could in a great number of cases be subjected to orthopaedic treatment and partially if not wholly cured, thanks to the development of schemes of orthopaedic treatment in which the L.E.A. for Shropshire took the lead. By the 1930s the child born deaf but having any residual power of hearing (and it has been discovered that most deaf children have some residual power of hearing at some pitch or frequency) could be taught orally like an ordinary child and learn to speak with a natural intonation. This was effected by the use of an instrument resembling an inverted wireless set into which the class teacher could speak. Each child wore headphones and had an independent volume-control and frequency-control which enabled him to adjust his 'phones until he heard the teacher's actual voice. The improvement in intonation by this method as compared to lip-reading was of course remarkable.[1]

It had already begun to appear that the time might not be far distant when the deaf person who revealed his affliction by his speech, or the girl or youth whose limbs were twisted by a congenital crippling complaint, would be regarded as a reproach to the education authority in whose area they were brought up.

The determination of social reformers of the first decade of the twentieth century to put all children so far as possible on equal terms in respect of their capacity to benefit from the education provided by the State led to another special service—the provision-of-meals service. The provision of penny dinners for the hungry with the assistance of voluntary funds had been a feature in many of the poorest schools for

---

[1] Since 1946 most schools for the deaf have been equipped with electronic aids which enable the children to move about freely.

An early cleanliness inspection in 1908, at the commencement of school medical inspection.

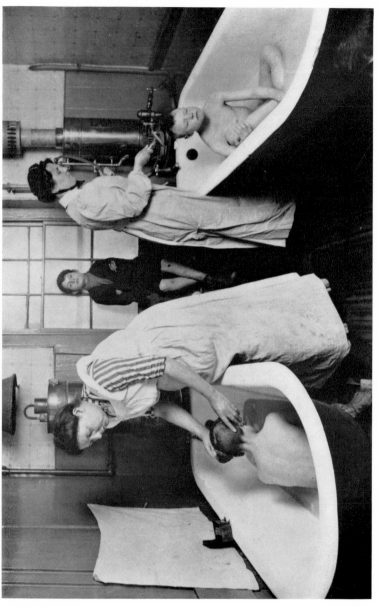

The appeal to cleanliness in practice, 1918

years. It was actively in operation in London, at Liverpool, Bradford, and elsewhere in 1886. In 1906 by one of the first successful Private Member's Bills sponsored by the earliest Labour Members to be elected to Parliament, the education authorities were empowered to put premises and facilities at the disposal of voluntary associations to provide meals for children 'unable by reason of lack of food to take full advantage of the education provided for them'. If the funds of the voluntary association were insufficient, the authority might, with the approval of the Board of Education, expend up to the produce of a halfpenny rate on providing such meals themselves.

In 1914 a further successful Private Member's Bill removed the halfpenny rate limitation, abolished the necessity of obtaining the sanction of the Board of Education, and legalized the provision of meals during school holidays.

The Acts undoubtedly achieved much to diminish the misery, wretchedness, and poverty due to the empty cupboard. They acted as a safety valve in the prevention of disorder arising from the desperation of those who saw their children hungry in periods of unemployment or industrial stoppage. They avoided the traditional association of the Poor Law, and they were often the means of valuable training in good social habits. Their contribution towards the reduction of malnutrition was, however, less obvious. A single meal a day could hardly have been expected to effect a revolution in nutrition, although other agencies of social amelioration had gone some way to achieve it. The rapidity of the development of school milk clubs since the reduction of price effected by years of continuous effort, associated with the National Milk Publicity Council and the Milk Marketing Board, were in later years to sustain and enlarge the improvement effected. As we shall see in Chapter XIII the 1939–45 war led to a vast improvement in both the scale and effectiveness of school meals and milk.

CHAPTER XI

THE SILENT SOCIAL REVOLUTION ACHIEVED BY PUBLIC EDUCATION BETWEEN 1876 AND 1935

THE years 1876–1935 saw the transformation of the inhabitants of England and Wales as a whole into a school-taught and substantially literate people.[1]

Moreover, in addition to that immense feat of nation-wide organization which provided a school place for every child up to 10 years of age they also witnessed a substantial advance towards 'the formation of manners'[2] in a child population previously sadly uncivilized, and a considerable awakening of the national conscience in relation to the child.

The school attendance officer who wished to penetrate one of those slums from which a far from negligible proportion of the children were drawn in the 1880s and 1890s had often been compelled to take a police officer with him. Moreover, as one of them told the Cross Inquiry Commission, 'the streets of London and other large cities were swarming with waifs and strays who had never attended school, and slept together in gangs in such places as the Adelphi Arches, on barges, on the steps of London Bridge, in empty boxes or boilers covered with tarpaulins and old sacks'.

The development of the national conscience towards the child had been gradually gathering force through the work of such men as Sir William Osler, the fourth Lord Shaftesbury, Dr Barnardo, and women like the McMillan sisters, Mary MacArthur and Mrs Humphrey Ward. By 1907 it had hardly permeated to the 'top people' of the day, as the following passage from the annual report for that year of the chairman of the L.C.C. education committee illustrates: 'Undoubtedly the best method of disposal for the majority of the boys is to place them in Army bands where the discipline carries on the work of the school in steadying the character of the boys. Other satisfactory methods of disposal are to farm and sea services. Work is also found in the mines. The chief method of disposal of girls is to domestic service while emigration offers an excellent opening for both boys and girls.' As a contrast

---

[1] Out of the 2,416,272 voters at the general election of 1886 only 38,587 were literate although the proportion among adults who had not attained the vote was probably higher.

[2] 'Formation of manners in youth'—Dr Johnson's definition of education.

a mere twenty years later one finds Professor F. G. Parsons in his presidential address to the British Association reminding his audience of 'the poor little half-starved bodies, so common thirty years ago, shivering coatless and hatless in the depth of winter, their miserable limbs maimed by rickets, their ears streaming with matter from middle ear disease, and their eyelids red with ophthalmia'.

Anybody who studies at first hand the annual reports of the superintendents of school attendance to a large education authority,[1] or the answers of teacher witnesses to questions put to them by Royal Commissions in the 1880s and 1890s, will recognize in these humble social servants the pioneers of a new and more enlightened age. For the most part their names go unremembered and their work forgotten, but its effect on the social history of England and Wales was profound. The name of one of these witnesses, however, is now fittingly recorded in that of a London school—Elizabeth Burgwin—and her testimony to the Cross Commission is so much in point as to justify quotation in full.[2] She was asked if she considered that the existence of her school and the work she had described had left any mark on the condition of the people of the neighbourhood. In the course of her reply she said:

I think that no voluntary agency could ever have grappled with such a large amount of poverty. Neither church nor chapel, until we opened that school, had touched that particular part, and I do not think that any voluntary agency alone could have done the work, because so much money is required to work a district of that kind. Little things of seven would begin to earn money for their parents, and we had to face the opposition which resulted. I feel most strongly that the girls that I turn out of that school will never be content to live the same kind of life as that which their mothers have led.

You could hardly, in years gone by, bring a person down that street without a blush of shame; the people did not think of putting window blinds up; they pitched everything out of the windows into the street, regardless of passers by, and made, in fact, the street the dustbin of the place, and their language was shocking. Now I can confidently say that whatever quarrel may be going on, and whatever bad language, if they see a teacher coming up the street it is instantly stopped and they would not give me a vile word as I pass them.

Some Christmases ago I sent a new short curtain to every house to give it a

---

[1] To take an example at random: 'Girl aged seven. When charged this child was with her mother who was playing a concertina outside a public house at 11.30 p.m. The mother had her head wrapped in bandages and the child was accosting passers by for money. Enquiries proved that the woman had had no home for years. The child was found to be illegitimate and medical examination showed that she was suffering from a spinal complaint and was also deaf. A large cut on the head was alleged to be the result of a blow from the mother. No industrial school would receive the child but arrangements were made with the Southwark Board of Guardians whose Chairman attended the Court and promised the Guardians would adopt her' (1905).

[2] Cross Inquiry Commission. Answers 17,310, 17,312, 17,401 and 17,298.

bright appearance for Christmas day, and now the people feel a sense of shame in various ways. If they attempt to come near me dirty they would even apologize. I felt it my duty to tell any woman who came up to me dirty that she should have enough self-respect to wash her face before she came to see me.

To anyone who has read himself back into the atmosphere and environment of those days so that he can construct in his mind's eye a cavalcade of public education, the contribution which a set of good schools under teachers of the stamp of Mrs Burgwin could make to the civilization, health, cleanliness, orderliness, sobriety, and self-respect of the population must always, perhaps, seem to outweigh all other gains.

But there were further gains too. For it is readily demonstrable that every widening of educational opportunity over these years from 1876 to 1935 (the years of the First World War excepted) in the long run repaid its cost by a commensurate increase in the national wealth and prosperity; and that the population as a whole became healthier, better able to utilize its leisure, more adaptable. The Consultative Committee of the Board of Education expressed the matter in 1909: 'A rising level of education among the mass of the workers increases the real level of their wages, though this may not be accompanied by a rise in their nominal amount. It conduces to wise expenditure of income and to the avoidance of thoughtless or hurtful waste.' Moreover, 'improvements in educational opportunity strengthen that power of organization and combination which enables the workers to secure a just share of the produce of those operations in which their labour is an indispensable factor'.

The part the schools played and still play in the indirect inculcation of thrift is liable to be overlooked or underestimated. Immediately the fees in board schools were stabilized or abolished and those in church schools reduced by the Act of 1891, school savings banks began to spring up like mushrooms everywhere. By 1935 there were already 22,000 groups based on schools known to the National Savings Association. This was twice the number in industrial undertakings. Some indication of the cumulative result can be gathered from the following figures.

Amount of national savings at various dates:

1913	...	...	£285,000,000
1919	...	...	£710,000,000
1936	...	...	£1,336,000,000

Adding the amount standing to the credit of small investors in other forms such as the building societies, the small savings of the people were by 1936 standing at £3,000,000,000, a figure which was increasing at the rate of £100,000,000 a year.

Great as had been the direct work and influence of the school savings schemes, it is doubtful if they could have achieved such results had it not been for the indirect work of the schools in teaching children to avoid unnecessary expenditure. The boys in their handicraft centres were learning to make, for example, cheap but lasting furniture and objects for their home, or to face up in a business-like way to household decorations and fitting. The girls in their domestic subjects courses were learning to make simple clothes and to plan their weekly budgets. Both boys and girls in their hygiene lessons, and through example, were getting a more balanced view than their parents had ever had of expenditure on alcohol.[1] The cumulative result was that the margin between weekly wages and weekly outgoings was then tending to grow a little bit wider with each generation which passed through the schools. In each generation too a slightly higher proportion of the age-group were leaving school with that marginally better training which would enable them to lay out the narrow family income of the working-class household to better advantage and to avoid a little more success-fully the frittering away of the balance on perishable extravagances.

Again, a public system of education, which has been built up from the primary school and not down from the universities (a consum-mation which so many emergent countries have essayed to achieve), creates, so long as it teaches each generation to become progressively more adaptable but progressively less superficial, a continuously ex-panding series of skilled occupations and posts of responsibility throughout the whole range of industry and commerce. Such a society is, in fact, continuously moving, like a biological species, from the un-specialized and undifferentiated to the specialized and differentiated.

This can be seen most clearly in a survey of those occupations largely unprotected before 1935, upon which this country ultimately depends for its continued economic health. For, despite the remarkable con-tribution which British agriculture has made during the first two-thirds of the twentieth century to our balance of payments, our existence as an industrial and banking nation still substantially depends upon our educational standards. It is essential that we should continue to enlist from our schools a supply of recruits who can produce and market at competitive prices goods of better quality, craftmanship, and design, greater durability and precision, than those of our industrial rivals.

Finally, nobody whose imagination enables him to put himself back into the atmosphere of the cramped nineties can fail to realize that, just as the school medical and dental services had by 1935 become a principal foundation of the national health, so the expansion of the public system of education was becoming a principal foundation for innumerable new forms of cultural, scientific, and physical activity.

[1] It is interesting to recall the attacks which the Brewers' lobby in Parliament made upon Sir George Newman's 'Syllabus of the Hygiene of Food and Drink'.

Comparative indices of the sum total of mental or intellectual activity in a community are not easy to obtain, but it is surely not without significance that the first halfpenny newspaper came into being (and was an immediate success) in 1897; and that by 1935 a more literate people was already sustaining more than 100 principal newspapers published daily, and 500 appearing weekly if one includes trade and professional publications. In addition 2 million copies of children's newspapers were being bought every week. Again the volume of postal business, including advertisement matter (but without substantial benefit as yet from football pools) passing through the Post Office increased over the same years from 2,850 million to 6,935 million, representing 148 postal packets per head of the population in 1935 as compared with 73 per head in 1895. As a further index of that insatiable desire for reading material which (before the days of television) already rendered our consumption of newspapers and our publication of new books as high as that in any country in the world, our population was by 1935 borrowing 240 million books from the public libraries every year.

Passing from indices of mental and intellectual activity to evidences of developing cultural and physical activities, the mid-thirties witnessed new societies and clubs springing up to foster every type of leisure-time pursuit. Moreover, older societies, such as the British Drama League, the Women's Institutes, the Co-operative Guilds, the Arts League of Service, and the English Folk Dance and Song Society, were annually increasing their membership and the scope of their activities. Leadership for such activities which forty years before had had to be drawn from the better-endowed sections of the community was now beginning to spring from the people themselves; for example the university settlement movement, which had relied upon socially responsible undergraduates for its successful maintenance in the early days of the century, was being reinforced by those 'Piers Plowman' settlements, the new local community centres, at which character and powers of leadership were being formed in preparation for citizenship and public service.

In the early days of the century there was no sadder sight than to ride on the top deck of a tram through south London on a hot Sunday evening and see at every window tired and utterly bored folk, old and young, listlessly watching the passing traffic. The homes of England had always been too small for the average family to live recreatively. The spread of education made them smaller still, but it pointed a way to relief. By the mid-thirties the weekend exodus from the big cities by the young folk on foot or on cycles, the growth of camping and swimming, the rise in a few years of the Youth Hostels Association, were already beginning to render the Victorian Sunday a thing of the past.

The local authorities were being compelled to spend a million pounds a year on the purchase of land for playing-fields, open spaces, and swimming-baths. In short visions conjured up by activities enjoyed at school were building up a demand which, but for the interruption caused by the coming war, would have carried us far further towards a genuinely recreative society than we have as yet attained.

By 1935 then, considering how much had had to be accomplished, the task of creating a school-taught and school-conditioned democracy had been worthily begun. It will, however, be necessary in succeeding chapters to reveal how many gaps still remained to be filled before England and Wales could claim to be, in any true sense, an educated democracy. The millennium was still a very long way in the future. There were still many thousands of children who were failing to obtain the precise educational treatment their individuality required; there were still children who were hungry, had nowhere to play, failed to secure the medical treatment they needed. There were still children thought of (and actually described by elderly Poor Law officials) as 'workhouse babies'. There were still far too few fully trained teachers and the training of new entrants to the teaching profession was still far too short. The country was still largely unprepared for the 'third industrial revolution' which would sweep over her after a war from which she would emerge exhausted.

PART III

Retrogression, Reconstruction, Resurgence

CHAPTER XII

1935–1939. THE EDUCATIONAL HORIZON DARKENS

Damage to children's lives in England and Wales during the First and Second World Wars—some points of difference.—Loss of formal education the dominant risk between 1939 and 1945.—Reactions of the public, the Services advisers, and the psychologists to the threat of possible air attack on Britain's cities.—Unreliable forecasts of casualties and loss of morale lead to over-insurance.—Air Raid Precautions and the schools.—How the idea of school evacuation began.—The Anderson Committee.—London gives a lead in preparation.—Munich.—The Government Evacuation Scheme.—Order, counter-order, disorder.

DURING the 'Kaiser's War' of 1914–18 most of the children of school age in England and Wales suffered grievously. Their fathers were killed and maimed in far greater numbers during those four bitter years than in the six years of the Second World War. They had to exist on near-starvation rations through years when the science of nutrition was in its infancy. Their clothing became threadbare and, as old photographs reveal only too clearly, their footwear in far too many instances reverted to the conditions of the 1890s. Their physique suffered proportionately. Rather surprisingly a contemporary estimate by H.M.I.s did not put the educational retardation of the school population at a higher figure than three months.

By contrast during Hitler's War of 1939–45 there was a general improvement in child health, after some recession in the first year. This was undoubtedly assisted by the spread of knowledge of the bases of sound nutrition and the supplements which could be given to these.

The gradual achievement of full employment and the policy of fair shares as exemplified by clothes rationing, together with the clothing schemes operated by the local authorities, kept children's clothing in reasonable condition. Fathers and elder brothers, too, were usually able to get home to visit their families much more readily than in the First World War.

Loss of formal education therefore became the dominant risk.

This did not arise, as might be too readily assumed, solely through the Government Evacuation Scheme. Other factors contributed. Damaged houses numbered 3,500,000 and 222,000 were completely destroyed, 1,250,000 people were rendered homeless for a month or

more. Periods spent in the shelters and rest centres became for many
children a bleak substitute for the family fireside. This was particularly
the case before Mr Malcolm MacDonald's new broom at the Ministry
of Health, at the end of 1941, swept the soulless and inhospitable Poor
Law standards out of the rest centres' battered doors and broken
windows. The building of new schools and the replacement or improvement of old schools ceased abruptly. Twenty per cent of the
23,000 schools in England and Wales were destroyed by enemy action
or severely damaged, while the vast programme of shelter and canteen
construction, together with window protection, seriously diminished
the efficiency and convenience of those that remained. Another factor
is perhaps little appreciated today: the immense wartime movement of
population, the scale of which was without parallel in Britain's history.
Nearly 35 million changes of address were recorded by the food
rationing organization during the years of war. Nearly every change of
home from one food district to another probably involved a change of
school for the children of the family, and such moves must inevitably
have had a serious effect upon the continuity of their education. Moreover, all too often they broke up the pre-war cohesion of the worker's
family with its reliance upon Granny and Grandpa as stand-bys and
shock-absorbers.

It seems probable, therefore, that few children in the country can
have suffered no educational disadvantage, and that at least a third of
the school population (fortunately a population 200,000 smaller than
in the previous war) suffered a potentially serious educational setback.
To understand how and why this came about it is necessary to appreciate what appears to have been the climate of opinion in the pre-war
Committee of Imperial Defence in Whitehall. It was this that led in
many directions to exaggerated over-insurance against a scale of attack
which never did occur, and probably never could have done so.
Coupled with this there was, initially, considerable under-insurance in
providing for many of those near-essentials which would be of special
importance for the child population.

In retrospect an inexplicable psychological phenomenon of the
years between the rise of Hitler in 1931 and the outbreak of the Second
World War in September 1939 is the ostrich-like attitude of large
numbers of ordinary people in Britain, who brushed aside the notion
that another war was inevitable. This attitude was not held by those in
Whitehall whose concern it was to keep the nation's 'War Book' up to
date. Regrettably however, with few exceptions, the Service advisers
seem to have gone to the opposite extreme in too uncritical an acceptance of the Wellsian forecasts of disaster conjured up by the Air Staff.

The attitude of the Air Ministry is understandable if one recalls
that, as the junior of the three Services, they had to compete con-

tinually with the other two for the Treasury resources which were so soon to prove our salvation in the Battle of Britain. At the same time, however, they were endeavouring to establish the much more questionable thesis that the bomber could perform tasks which neither the Army nor the naval air services could attempt. It is easy to forget today that the bomber of 1939, whether German or British, was a far less efficient weapon in loading capacity, in performance, and in defence against air and ground attack, than the Stirlings, Lancasters, and Halifaxes of the later war years, with their radar and electronic bombing aids and their immense bomb loads. Thus to say (as the Rt Hon. Sir Charles Trevelyan said in a message to teachers as early as 1924) that air power for the first time in the history of the world had put it into the hands of man to destroy civilization itself was simply not true, either in 1924 or 1939. Moreover, such statistics as were available from 1917 and up to the time of the Spanish Civil War appear to have been seriously inflated by the occurrence of what, in the terminology of 1940, came to be called 'incidents', in which a single Zeppelin or Gotha bomb had caused a number of casualties out of all proportion to its size.

The starting-point for all these calculations (or miscalculations) appears to have been some figures from the First World War: 300 metric tons of bombs dropped on Britain had caused 4,820 casualties, 1,413 of which proved fatal. The Committee of Imperial Defence in 1924 drew the conclusion that 100 tons of bombs could be dropped in the first twenty-four hours of a war, 75 on the second day and 50 tons a day thereafter, three-quarters of the total falling in daytime raids. Ten years later (1934), with the known rapid expansion of the German Air Force, the estimate had risen to 150 tons a day. Mr Winston Churchill, no doubt as a result of his contacts with senior members of the Services, had already two years (10 November 1932) before warned the House of Commons that 3 or 4 million people might be driven out into the open country round the Metropolis. Now he was voicing the opinion—one much more realistic as events proved—that 'the most dangerous form of air attack is the attack by incendiary bombs'.[1] By 1937 the Air Staff were expressing the view that with their well-known predilection for a 'kolossal' blitz at the outset of a war the Nazi Air Force might attempt to drop 3,500 tons of bombs in the first twenty-four hours as a knock-out blow directed at the 9 million people living within the 750 square miles of the Metropolitan area. By 1939 they had settled for 700 tons a day for the first fortnight.

Nor were their forecasts as to the accuracy of bomb-aiming any less

[1] He had, on Mr Baldwin's invitation, joined the newly formed Committee on Air Defence Research in July 1935, making it a condition that Professor Lindemann should be a member of the Technical Sub-Committee.

alarmist. They asserted that 40 tons of bombs dropped from a height of 20,000 feet would fall within less than 200,000 square yards (a square with $\frac{1}{4}$-mile sides). No doubt in this calculation they were imagining a daylight raid in good visibility unimpeded by anti-aircraft fire or fighter defence. Nevertheless it is an interesting commentary upon such an estimate that, of all the bombs dropped (mainly of course by night) on German targets up to the time of our first 1,000-bomber raid on Cologne on May 30th 1942, only one in ten had fallen within five miles of its target. Moreover, our bomber losses up to that point had averaged 5 per cent per raid. The German figures, we now know, were comparable.

The estimates of casualties, physical and psychological, which would result from attack on such a fantastic scale, and the calls which would arise for hospital beds and manpower to staff the rescue services and aid posts, were similarly astronomical. By 1937 the Committee of Imperial Defence were estimating that 600,000 people would be killed, creating a need for mass burials in cardboard coffins, and that 1,200,000 would be injured. The need for hospital beds was put at anything between 1 million and 2,800,000. By 1938 these forecasts had been reduced to a formula of 24 dead, 24 seriously injured, and 24 slightly injured per ton of bombs dropped. A Committee of Psychologists went even further. They reported that psychiatric casualties might exceed physical casualties by three to one, and that the most probable cause of chaos in the community would be the moral collapse of the personnel employed in the working of the vital services and a considerable volume of disorderly flight from London.

In the light of these opinions it should be recalled that, although Britain suffered a larger number of casualties among civilians through air attack than any other member of the Allied Nations, the morale of the civil population, man, woman, and child, never once faltered.

The actual casualty figures over nearly six years of war, on the British estimate of 71,000 tons of bombs dropped on these islands, worked out at 0·88 killed, 1·2 admitted to hospital, and 2·1 slightly injured per ton. (If one accepts the German claim of 174,000 tons the figures become even smaller.) Particular areas, of course, suffered more heavily. London was continuously bombed for seventy-six nights and subsequently intermittently, and in the later stages of the war had to bear the brunt of the V1 and V2 rocket attacks. Even so the casualties were nowhere near the pre-war forecasts; they worked out at 2·44 killed, 4·13 hospital cases, and 7·27 slightly injured per ton. In Birmingham and Coventry 4·2 were killed and 11·7 injured per ton, and some other areas, such as Bootle and Plymouth, would show similar figures. The one pre-war estimate which came anywhere near the reality was that relating to material damage. This was put at £35,000 per ton of bombs dropped, and it was suggested that 500,000 houses might be totally destroyed and 1 to 2 million substantially damaged in the first year of war. In fact fewer were destroyed, but more were damaged, as noted on p. 189.

Why, it may be asked at this interval of time, did nobody question the Air Staff's warnings or call for experiments to verify some of their claims? (One part of the answer must be that from the time of Baldwin's 'sealed lips' policy, later so vigorously denounced by Churchill, and Chamberlain's successive policy of appeasement, all such estimates and forecasts had, so far as possible, been kept secret. Another reason is that the Air Raid Precautions Department of the Home Office was not only pitifully understaffed but kept starved of funds. Moreover, it had no experience of dealing with the local authorities, who would bear the main burden of preparation. In most important matters it was limited to thinking about problems in terms of police action supplemented by the military. Mr (later Sir Wilfred) Eady, who was subsequently its head, confessed, according to *The Economist*, that it had issued 'what were probably the sloppiest regulations ever produced by any Government Department'. Nevertheless, in fairness to a much-maligned Department, it should be recalled that it did fine work in providing the country with the 'Anderson' and later the 'Morrison' shelters which saved countless lives. Had the country had the leadership which it enjoyed in such abundant measure later the public might have been much better informed and prepared. For example, no statesman aware of the diabolical films such as *Oom Paul*, which were being shown in Nazi Germany to whip up hatred against England among German youth, or even of the sums in the Nazi school arithmetic books with their problems of bomber loads and distances to British towns, could have sustained the fatuous embargo on any official mentioning of the threat of the Nazi Air Force.

There were of course honourable exceptions. While one Department of the Ministry of Health was engaged in the macabre task of issuing a million burial forms to local authorities, the Emergency Hospitals Division of the Ministry was roundly telling the Air Ministry that their estimates were ridiculous. 'I think there will be quite a lot of upper storeys still standing in London at the end of a war', remarked a senior official of the Ministry of Transport,[1] gazing wistfully out of his window high up in Northumberland Avenue in July 1939.

Unfortunately where so much of the general picture was obscured by secrecy, neither Parliament nor the Press could exercise their undoubted right to ventilate misgivings. Miss Ellen Wilkinson attempted to do so, but her choice of words was unhappy. 'Isn't there far too much talk of gas and Air Raid Precautions? Aren't we in danger of

[1] Now Lord Hurcomb.

emasculating the population?' she asked in the House. The gale of laughter which greeted Mr Churchill's growled interjection, 'The Hon. Lady means gastrating them', blew away the effect of her protest.

One result of this misguided policy of secrecy was as shocking as it was inexplicable. In mid-1939 detailed information became available about the casualties and damage caused by 735 tons of bombs dropped on Barcelona by German-built bombers. These disclosed that in this compact and crowded city, with no fighter protection, no more than 3·5 inhabitants had been killed and 13·7 injured per ton of bombs. Yet this vital information does not appear to have been passed to the Departments! Had it been made available the vast disorganization in hospitals and in houses earmarked for government use, and the immobilization of nearly a million Civil Defence workers, doctors, and nurses during the early months of the war—the 'phoney war'—might have been avoided. Even the Government Evacuation Scheme—with its corollary, the closing of every school in nearly a hundred areas—might have been recast to provide for a limited period of dispersal. This would have been sufficient to forestall any 'kolossal' initial blitz on London and the east coast ports, and the 'trickle scheme', which worked with such unfailing smoothness after bombing started in 1940, could have been substituted thereafter.[1]

But the early thinking of the Home Office on the subject of evacuation, obsessed as they were by the Wellsian visions of the Air Staff and the psychologists, today appears quite horrifying. Their first plan of 1933 (mercifully unpublished) actually envisaged the removal of 3½ million men, women, and children by families under police control from Inner London and their compulsory billeting within fifty miles of the capital! Fortunately no reference was made to the subject in the first A.R.P. circular of 1935. By November 1937, the Home Secretary (Sir Samuel Hoare) was forced by pressure in the House to amend the A.R.P. Bill to lay a duty on the local authorities to provide information against possible schemes of evacuation. Right up to the time of Munich he had clearly refused to believe in the inevitability of war. As late as 15 September 1938 he was saying to Mr Herbert Morrison, 'You tell me, Mr Morrison, that there is a crisis. I

[1] See Winston Churchill, *The Gathering Storm*, p. 265. 'We might in 1938 have had air raids on London, for which we were lamentably unprepared. There was however no possibility of a decisive Air Battle of Britain until the Germans had occupied France and the Low Countries, and thus obtained the necessary bases in close striking distance of our shores. Without these bases they could not have escorted their bombers with the fighter aircraft of those days.' As we know today, even when they had these bases the majority of the German fighters employed in the Battle of Britain only had petrol sufficient to remain over London for ten minutes, and, even more surprising, could not communicate with the bombers.

don't believe there is a crisis, or at least I think it is one which, if it comes, will develop very slowly indeed.'[1]

It has been necessary to recall, in some detail, these unreliable forecasts, and the reactions to them in Whitehall, in order to understand the circumstances which led up to the Government Evacuation Scheme as it eventually developed. The plan to disperse for the first few weeks of war the child population of London, which was in 1938 clearly the most populous and vulnerable area, arose in a curious way. In January 1938 the Board of Education issued a circular to the L.E.A.s, Circular 1461, which invited them, in mild and soporific terms, to begin thinking what they should do about A.R.P. in schools. By one of those curious twists of fate which have consequences more far-reaching than those immediately concerned would have dreamed, an Assistant Education Officer at the L.C.C., upon whom the task of reporting upon this circular to the Education Committee devolved, had three memories which appeared to him to be relevant.

On the outbreak of the First World War in 1914 a rumour had spread rapidly up the east coast that a tremendous naval battle had taken place in the North Sea. As a boy of 17 this officer had been asked by his father, who was Rector of the parish of Cottingham near Hull, to get on his bicycle, visit all the larger houses in the village, and find out how many of them would be prepared to receive and care for a wounded sailor (British or German) if the number of casualties brought into Hull was, as seemed likely, more than the local hospitals could admit. The warmth of his reception on this first 'wartime billeting survey', which resulted in offers to receive and care for no less than 150 wounded sailors in one village, had not only afforded him a remarkable insight into the innate kindliness of the British people but convinced him that, should similar circumstances ever again arise, householders would again respond to such a call.

Twenty-one years later he had been placed in charge (under Mr E. M. Rich, the Education officer for London) of the assembly of 70,000 children on Constitution Hill and the Mall to greet their Majesties King George and Queen Mary on one of their Jubilee drives through London. This experience, and that of assembling 37,000 children on the Embankment on Coronation Day 1937, had demonstrated the ease with which large bodies of children could be

[1] 15 September was the day upon which Mr Chamberlain made his first abortive visit to Hitler at Berchtesgaden. On that day, too, Henlein the Sudeten leader fled to Germany and all German radio stations broadcast his proclamation demanding the annexation of the Sudeten areas, containing the line of fortresses in Bohemia. In the words of Winston Churchill, 'The summit of the crisis was now reached.' (*The Gathering Storm*, p. 232.)

transported in school parties by bus, underground, and rail if they were under the control of their teachers.

In the third place, he had had some experience of boarding out school children in the exceptional circumstances covered by Section 24 of the Education Act 1921, and through such voluntary agencies as the Children's Country Holiday Fund and the Invalid Children's Aid Society.

The L.C.C. report which he wrote (S.O. 124 dated 24 January 1938) is perhaps worth summarizing at some length because it illustrates a realist reaction, eighteen months before the war, to the kind of problems which war might involve for the child population of great cities. (The writer, of course, knew nothing of Radar or of the Air Staff forecasts of bomb tonnages and casualties.)

The report showed that 50 tons of bombs dropped on London during the 1914–18 war had resulted in ten schools receiving direct hits, at one of which (Upper North St, Islington) nineteen children were killed. There was damage by concussion to 239 further schools (the term 'blast' was not yet current). It assumed that in any future war attack could be made on London by a very large number of aircraft; that it would be resolutely pressed home; and that, although an effective balloon barrage might restrict low-level attack, and also the cubic miles of sky in which defending fighters would have to search for the bombers, this would result in greater inaccuracy of aim and a wider scatter of bombs; moreover, it could not be assumed that any real attempt would be made to hit selected targets. The schools, many of them containing 1,000 children, could be assumed to be fairly evenly distributed over London, and all would therefore be at risk. It might perhaps be assumed that an enemy would use the hours of darkness to get to London and the children might not have arrived at school. Nevertheless it would clearly be quite impossible to continue to enforce compulsory attendance under such conditions.

If the intensive phase of a war resulted in a high wastage of pilots, machines, petrol, and ground personnel (as a result of counter-bombing of the enemy's aerodromes), after a period of say six weeks the less perishable components of the scheme of defence, e.g. listening apparatus, anti-aircraft guns, searchlights, and the balloon barrage, might obtain a greater relative advantage than in the early stage. After this six-week period raids might therefore become less frequent, more limited in their objectives, and would no longer employ such large numbers of aircraft. Clearly the schools would have to be shut during the intensive phase. Although the question of reopening could be kept under constant review it would surely be a policy of despair to turn the children into the streets for an indeterminate period. To do so would expose them not merely to the dangers of bombing, fire, and possibly gas but to the sights and experiences of modern war. This might have far-reaching psychological consequences for them. Some children would undoubtedly be sent to friends or relatives in the country, but if education was to be maintained for the great majority for the vital initial weeks then the only course would appear to be to evacuate them. The best, if not the only, way to do this would be to send them out as schools under the control of their teachers and board them out with foster-parents in the country.

Although today, in the light of history, this report may well appear an obvious, almost a jejune, appreciation of what was in store for our large cities, and the obvious remedy, it should not be supposed that at the time it was written (eighteen months before the war and two and a half years before the London Blitz) it was by any means representative of current thought. For example, at the opposite pole of opinion Mr Austen Hopkinson, M.P., was at that time voicing the sombre view that 'It is the business of the people living in the London area to be the bait drawing the enemy into a trap provided by our fighter squadrons, while balloon barrages and anti-aircraft guns drive him into the zone of battle.'

The L.C.C. approved their officer's report in principle and forwarded it to the Board of Education, who had no observations to offer upon it. The Home Office on the other hand were frankly aghast at its daring. Indeed its author derived much amusement, at a later date when the plan had been carried out without a single casualty, from reading what the officials of the Air Raid Precautions Department had written about his 'fantastic' idea. Fortunately, however, the Home Office had to some extent become committed themselves, for a booklet entitled 'The Protection of Your Home against Air Raids', which they circulated to the public at the precise time that the L.C.C.'s plan became known, contained the following rather singular advice: 'If you live in a large town children, invalids, elderly members of the household and pets should be sent to relatives or friends in the country, if this is possible.'

Since the Air Raid Precautions Department had not a single unit of staff to concentrate his whole mind on the question of evacuation, they resorted to the device beloved of civil servants who wish to put a question into cold storage—they appointed a Committee to consider and report upon the problem. This Committee, under the Chairmanship of Sir John Anderson, proved the turning-point. They got to work immediately and produced their report by 26 July 1938, although publication was withheld until after the Munich crisis of September. This report came down firmly in support of the L.C.C. plan to get schools away under the control of their teachers. A significant passage, of which, regrettably, too little notice was taken at the time, was:

'The transference of large numbers of people from their homes and accustomed surroundings to other and often unfamiliar areas is not a task to be undertaken lightly. It raises problems of great complexity and difficulty at every stage, whether it be the collection and transportation of the refugees or their reception, accommodation and feeding at the other end. All the services which are delicately adjusted to meet the needs of the community on the present distribution of the population would have to be refashioned to deal with the new situation.'

Meanwhile, as the international situation grew daily more menacing the L.C.C., under the driving force of Mr Herbert Morrison's personality, did not sit back and await a lead. With the help of the friends on the Railway Headquarters Staffs whom they had made at the time of the Jubilee and Coronation Assemblies they set in train the preparation of detailed bus, underground, and railway schedules to remove not 70,000 or 37,000 this time but 500,000 children from London.

On Thursday 15 September (the day of Sir Samuel Hoare's rebuke to Mr Herbert Morrison) Mr E. M. Rich explained the scheme, which had been prepared in complete detail by working day and night over the preceding fortnight, to the head teachers of London's 3,000 school departments. At parents' meetings 80 per cent of the parents agreed to allow their children to leave with the school, and practically every member of London's 20,000 teachers volunteered to take them. Nine other Metropolitan areas from Willesden to Ilford were brought into the scheme and other large towns such as Birmingham and Liverpool were supplied with the details. Prodigies of spontaneous organization and improvisation were performed at every school in equipping and labelling the children.[1]

About 1,200 children attending nursery schools, 2,800 in schools for the physically defective, and 1,000 blind and deaf children were actually sent out in advance on 28 and 29 September by buses and ambulances to large country houses and holiday camps, and this proved a valuable rehearsal for the evacuation of September 1939.

Mr Charles Robertson, Chairman of the L.C.C. Education Committee, said in a letter to *The Times* (3 October 1938):

'As a nation we are too much inclined to disparage our gifts for organization, yet what other nation, faced with the task of building up from nothing in a fortnight an organization capable of moving an army of well over half a million children, ranging in age from 3 to 17, divided among nearly 3,000 school departments and spread over an area

---

[1] For example half a million luggage labels were bought, broken up into the requisite numbers for each school department, and distributed over 117 square miles between 9.30 a.m. and 4.30 p.m. By Thursday 29 September 37,000 bus places were ready to carry infants to their nearest station.

of about 200 square miles, could have reduced it to a scheme so exact that every parent had been consulted, every railway timetable fixed, every school got ready to move to an appointed station at an appointed hour (the infants going by omnibus where the station was more than a mile away) to an area where the L.E.A. had been warned to expect them?

'If there are any who are still inclined to criticize the teaching profession of this country they should take note of the fact that over 20,000 teachers undertook voluntarily to take the children in their charge out into the country, to keep them together in school units, and to do everything in their power to keep the education going.'

'Pied Piper', as the scheme came to be known from the code word which was to have been used to launch it, though hastily improvised, was indeed as *The Times Educational Supplement* said, a 'daring and courageous plan'. What would have happened if all these children had actually been decanted then at stations within 100 miles of London unfortunately baffles the imagination. For right up to the eleventh hour the Home Office had retained their preference for their own plan to decant 2 million men, women, and children from central London and billet them compulsorily on the unsuspecting inhabitants of Surrey and Hertfordshire. In fact it was only on the evening of Thursday 22 September that they approved the changeover to getting the children away first, when they 'requested the London County Council to prepare immediately a scheme on the lines advocated, and to transmit it to the schools by midday on Friday' (the next day!). Their inadequate Departmental staff had at last been augmented by the appointment of a retired Colonel.

Actually it was not until 26 September that they were finally persuaded to give the movement of the children one day's priority. When the crisis subsided with the Berchtesgaden agreement of 30 September the Home Office inevitably came in for considerable criticism, and a joint memorandum at Cabinet level by the Board of Education and the Ministry of Health resulted in the subject of evacuation being taken from them.[1] The Evacuation Department, which was formed at the Ministry of Health, borrowed four senior administrative staff from the Board of Education and three from the L.C.C. and set to work with a will on the immense work of planning. Ninety-three areas were selected on account of population, density, and vulnerability to be evacuation areas, and a further list was prepared of those areas which would not be evacuated but would not receive evacuees (the 'neutral' areas). The remaining 56,000 square miles of England

[1] See particularly the open letter to Sir Samuel Hoare by Sir Frederic Mander Secretary General of the National Union of Teachers, in *The Schoolmaster*, 27 October 1938.

and Wales, with the exception of a few square miles near special targets and aerodromes, were classified as reception areas. In these a thorough billeting survey was launched on 5 January 1939. It was carried out through the agency of the local Housing Authorities. While Ribbentrop was opening Hitler's diplomatic offensive against Poland 100,000 appointed representatives visited 4 million homes occupied by 18 million people. In all offers were received to care for $2\frac{1}{4}$ million unaccompanied children.

The railway, underground, and omnibus timetables, with detailed advice on the preparation of the children and other problems which would require solution, which had been worked out for the Metropolitan Area at the time of Munich, were expanded and circulated as a model to all evacuation areas. By April, a few weeks after German troops had overrun Czechoslovakia, the actual timetables for every school in the 93 areas had been prepared, involving something like 4,000 train-loads. They had actually been refined to a point where the destination of every school was known in Whitehall and all grammar, junior technical, and similar schools had been routed to an area where a school of equivalent organization could be paired with them. Fortunately, as it proved in the event, information on destinations was not communicated to schools.

In these computer-conscious days it may be amusing to recall how the remaining task, as formidable as it was invidious, namely securing an absolutely fair distribution of train-loads to billeting accommodation in the 56,000 square miles of the reception areas, was performed. It was done in two days by a single individual (Charles Hart, O.B.E., of the L.C.C.) sitting in front of a large-scale railway map with a supply of coloured wool and pins! The maximum total of evacuees was 3 million (mothers with children under five, expectant mothers, aged persons, the blind, and severely handicapped adults had been added). The total number of unoccupied rooms in the reception areas after allowing one habitable room to each member of every family was 11 million. As the line of wool and pins moved out down the railways leading from each evacuation area, three evacuees were allotted to each eleven unoccupied rooms in each new local government area which the railway entered. The resulting distribution map stood the test of time throughout all the changes and chances of the war years. The distribution of numbers in particular areas was however gravely prejudiced, and here and there overloaded, by the fact that some 2 million individuals, a high proportion of them adults, 'stole softly away' from the towns in the weeks before the war to gain safety in accommodation which had been offered in February for those to be officially evacuated.

When the test came on 1 September 1939 the staff work was complete and the stage seemed to be set for the most carefully planned logistical operation affecting children which the world had ever witnessed. Then the Government stepped in.

The two fundamental maxims of all good staff work are that 'A good plan resolutely carried through is better than the best plan in the world fumbled', and 'Order followed by counter-order breeds disorder'. These the Government had forgotten. As soon as it was reported that the 80 per cent acceptances by parents at the time of Munich was not being achieved they ordered that the timetables must be telescoped into three days instead of four. No doubt the Air Ministry was still threatening that mass daylight air attacks might cut the scheme in two—although they must have known how high a proportion of the German bomber force was already engaged on the Polish front. No doubt the Ministry of Transport was dolefully pointing out that such a vast passenger movement might delay their coal trains. No doubt the War Office saw their troop concentrations interfered with if the co-ordinated timetables did not dovetail as planned. A resolute Minister of Health backed by a resolute President of the Board of Education could still have insisted that the scheme should be allowed to proceed as planned.

The result was, fortunately, not chaos so far as dispersal was concerned; for 1,473,000 evacuees, mainly of course children, were moved in the three days, several thousand by sea from the Thames to east coast towns. There was not a single casualty. One small boy fell out of a carriage but was picked up unhurt. It did produce chaos, however, so far as the delivery of evacuees and schools to their designated destinations was concerned. Those awaiting an infant school on many a country platform received a trainload of expectant mothers. Those awaiting a secondary grammar school received a trainload of tired mothers and under-fives who had experienced the journey from London to Devonshire in a non-corridor train. Was this perhaps the fate of the mother who some months before the war had written to the leader of her trainload a letter poignantly illustrative of the fears and perplexities which assailed the humble homes of 1939?

'Mr — — leder
I understand as you are leder of my party of mothers and under fives My little daughter Winnie as week bladder and will want to go bad in the train. In course she will have her pottie an ernamel one with her. When she wants to go she wimpers a bit and fidgetts about. I wish you could tell me whear we are going secretly of course. Of course it may never happen but in course it may. You never know what that Hitler has up his sleeve or elsewhere.'

Perhaps Winnie's mum had wisely stayed at home. For the collective wisdom of the British public had obviously summed up the difference in the preparation of the country in September 1939 as compared with what had passed for preparation at the time of Munich. Where in September 1938 they had turned out to dig trenches in the London parks many had now their Anderson shelter on order or installed down the garden. Where they had seen a solitary anti-aircraft gun precariously mounted on Westminster Bridge they sensed that there were probably now hundreds ringing the capital. Balloon sites were manned and here and there a balloon was rising, rather tentatively, into London's sky. To deal with incendiary fires 1,600 trailer pumps were ready, in place of the six which were all that had been delivered by the time of Munich. Perhaps thoughts of the cost of keeping two homes going, or of meeting fares to visit one's child in the country, or of how elder children left behind with Dad would cope with the cooking, washing, and mending, or even of what Dad might get up to if left alone, made it better to wait and see.

CHAPTER XIII

THE 1939–1945 WAR

A worthwhile task for everyone of goodwill in the reception areas.—
Evacuation reveals the black spots in Britain's social life.—The un-
recorded labours of the teachers and country housewives.—Would the
Board of Education have been more imaginative than the Ministry of
Health?—A new appreciation of the value of the trained social worker.
—Four million children and mothers moved to places of greater safety.—
The success of the Emergency Maternity Homes and the Residential
Nurseries.—How many child casualties did the Scheme prevent?—
Effect on formal education.—Cumulative damage to public education
through other facets of total war.—The credit side of the account.—
Introduction of city children to country life.—The challenge to the city
teacher.—The remarkable debt owed by the nation to wartime foster-
parents.—School meals and milk.—Provision of boots and clothing.—
The spread of Nursery School ideals.—A better understanding of child
maladjustment.—Development of new welfare services.—A contribution to the morale of civilian women, and of married men in the services,
during a dark period in Britain's history.

I т is well known that at the beginning of the 1914–18 war, although
morale was high, government organization was pitifully inadequate.
From the Dowagers in the Shires anxious for their sons to play a part
to the citizens with schemes for the discomfiture of Zeppelins, all
Britain wanted to help, but much of this potential was lost. By contrast the arrival in September 1939 of 1½ million evacuees in the reception areas (but no bombs on the evacuation areas) provided every man
and woman in those areas with a worthwhile job near at hand to be
done. Had the bombs begun to fall it is probable that everyone would
have praised the Government for their foresight in dispersing the
children in such numbers and getting other vulnerable people away
from the dangerous areas at least for the first few weeks of war, when
nervous tension was bound to be at its worst. As matters turned out the
condition of some of the children and the behaviour of a proportion
of the mothers administered a shock to the country so serious that four
years later *The Economist* described the Evacuation Scheme as 'the most
important subject in the social history of the war because it revealed
to the whole people the black spots in their social life'.

The Ministry of Health had been afforded a very short time for the

preparation of the Scheme which, it was realized, must give rise to
a vast crop of problems in human relationships. Nevertheless had
the psychologists, instead of joining with the jeremiads of the Air
Staff, given warning that many of the mothers, feeling unwanted in
other women's homes, might behave in a way in which they would
never have behaved in their own homes, there might well have been
more intensive study before 1 September of the problems likely to
arise.

The condition of some of the children, who had been out of school
for the long weeks of the summer holiday, was more readily explicable.
Skin diseases among the school population had been on the increase in
1938 as compared with previous years. At least ten children in every
thousand would have started their journey with scabies, a most infectious complaint which might well be passed on to a number of
other children in a crowded railway carriage. Elder sisters in many a
family were proving so reluctant to disturb their hair-sets, by combing,
that dirty heads were being passed down with increasing frequency to
younger sisters. The School Medical Officers in the evacuation areas
knew these things, but there was no time for routine medical inspections
and cleanliness surveys after the evacuation was set in motion, and it
was too late in the day to delay the transfer to billets by examining the
children when they arrived.

A proportion of the mothers felt themselves unwanted and had little
to do but drift around window-shopping, without prams for their
young children, in an unfamiliar environment. These soon decided
that to endure the inconveniences of country life might well be worse
than the blackout and the shadow of the bomber, and by Christmas
80 per cent of them had returned home; and so the thick file of correspondence between the Ministry and the railways, accumulated in the
endeavour to persuade them to accept the prams for delivery, was
closed with the two-word minute 'solvitur perambulando'!

The work accomplished by the evacuated teachers and helpers in
tracing their children to their billets (which could in extreme cases be
spread over several hundred square miles) and in starting school
activities for them was beyond praise. Beyond praise, too, was the un-
recorded work of countless country housewives in cleaning up their
evacuees, coping with their bedwetting, repairing their clothes, and
replacing their plimsolls with boots. Countless others showed the
greatest forbearance and kindliness in trying to make mothers feel
more at home, in organizing day nurseries for their under-fives and
'make and mend' sessions to help them with their clothing problems.
Our treatment of the evacuees may be contrasted with the hostile
reaction of the population to evacuees in at least one other European
country. Unfortunately it was not these unselfish heroines of the

comb, the wash-tub, and the village hall but the individual instances of shocking behaviour on the part of their wartime guests which hit the headlines in the newspapers. Those who settled down to make the best of an unfamiliar way of life were not news. As Margaret Bondfield remarked, 'married couples do not write to the Divorce Courts to say that they are settling down together quite nicely'.

The Commons debate of 14 September 1939 was a shameful affair, although the psychological situation at the time should be remembered.

Much of the criticism was naturally directed at the Ministry of Health,[1] and the suggestion has sometimes since been put forward that had the responsibility for the Government Evacuation Scheme been placed upon the Board of Education they would probably have exercised it more imaginatively.

They would clearly have entrusted the preparations to the L.E.A.s instead of the Housing Authorities, many of which were too small and inadequately staffed to deal with what was essentially a problem concerned primarily with children. They and the L.E.A.s would have understood and anticipated the urgent needs which would arise for footwear, clothing, and so on better than the Ministry, and would have been less inclined to accept the embargo placed by the Treasury on any expenditure in advance of the scheme being launched. For the Ministry of Health, as successor to the Local Government Board, had never quite succeeded, during the twenty years of its existence, in emancipating itself from the chill atmosphere of the Poor Law. Moreover, the Ministry had always conceived of its function as restraining rather than stimulating local initiative. The proportion of children who would not have adequate footwear or possess a coat or mackintosh was known exactly as a result of counts made at the Jubilee and Coronation Assemblies. Yet in approaching the Treasury for money the Ministry only mentioned these vital needs in an apologetic postscript. The provision of boots and clothing for children who could not attend school warm and dry had been on the Statute Book in Scotland for many years, and the Board of Education would certainly not have been content to accept the niggardly £1 per 200 children ($1\frac{1}{2}d$. per child) wrung out of a reluctant Treasury at the eleventh hour a few days before evacuation commenced.

Again, the Board of Education might have anticipated the need, which was bound to arise immediately the scheme was launched, for day nursery or nursery school provision for the children under five. They did in fact endeavour to repair this omission, as soon as they

[1] It was suggested, rather crudely, that the telegraphic address of the Department ought to be changed to 'Incontinence London' (*O.E.D.* Incontinence. Inability to control evacuation).

could, by their remarkable Nursery Centres Pamphlet; but by the time it could be written and published, it was too late.

They would certainly, too, have to put up a better fight to preserve their policy that 'The local school and the visiting school should each retain its own individuality', by preventing the telescoping of the time-tables.

They might also have devised some intermediate plan comparable to that which they later established for children attending schools con-ducted by a L.E.A. other than that of the area to which they belonged (extra district children). This would have saved some at least of the millions of man-hours spent in local offices in attempting to trace back evacuees to the area of origin in order to establish Poor Law charge-ability. They would not, as the Ministry of Health did, have prevented children who won scholarships from joining the grammar schools of their parents' choice in the reception areas.

On the credit side, the Ministry of Health was the only Department which in 1939 possessed any substantial knowledge of the problems, medical and hygienic, likely to arise in making residential provision for children, mothers with young children, and expectant mothers. This body of experience, channelled through their Medical Officers and General Inspectorate, a remarkably practical body of men and women, became of vital importance as evacuation stretched into its second and subsequent years. As early as July 1941 660 hostels had been opened, accommodating 10,000 children (mainly those awaiting transfer to billets or difficult to billet). There were in addition 731 hostels for mothers with young children, 150 sick bays for children, 90 emergency maternity homes, 55 ante- and post-natal clinics, and 230 residential nurseries for babies and children under five who had become without parental care in the evacuation areas. Moreover, the Ministry was less 'closed shop' minded than many of the other White-hall Departments in the matter of taking on additional staff for specific duties.[1]

At the time of Munich the L.C.C. had despatched their Divisional Organizers of Children's Care, a body of trained social workers of great experience, to assist in any way possible in the areas due to receive children from London. In 1940 it was decided to appoint Welfare Officers to the staffs of each of the Ministry's Regional Offices and to ask the L.C.C. to second many of their Care Committee Organizers for this purpose. (Incidentally the conference at which this decision was taken must have been one of the most macabre which can ever have taken place in a Cabinet Minister's room. For London lay under a cloud of low fog over which intruder Messerschmitt 110s zoomed,

[1] Although, as one of them remarked wryly to the author, 'it takes ten years to become a member of this club'.

dropping an occasional light bomb, and the messengers had not had time to remove from the Minister's table a huge specimen coffin, fabricated from cardboard, which had been placed there for his inspection!)

This decision was to have far-reaching results, for it marked the beginning of a much more general appreciation of the value of the trained social worker over wide fields of government and local authority activity. Hitherto this field had too often been covered—in so far as it had been covered at all—by those who had grown up under the arid conception that the only proper sphere of government intervention was to ward off distress (thought of as a kind of symbol of social incapacity), in the case of the poorest citizens.

The ebb and flow of the Government Evacuation Scheme, the reactions of town mothers and children to the country, and the upsets and sense of intrusion caused by billeting in private houses when no bombs were falling, are subjects only marginally relevant to the study of the impact of war on the Public Educational System. Moreover, all such problems have been brilliantly covered in Professor Titmuss's *Problems of Social Policy* in the official histories of the war, and in nearly 200 private studies of individual aspects of the Scheme.

Before an attempt is made, however, to strike a balance of profit and loss for the educational and related social services which arose from the Scheme, the modern reader should perhaps be reminded of a few salient facts.

Many people today are, for example, under the impression that it was no more than a considerable, though only partially successful, attempt to remove certain vulnerable classes, the largest of which was the school population, from the big towns at the outbreak of the war. In fact it persisted throughout nearly six years of war and enabled something over 4 million people in Britain, the great majority of them mothers and children, to stay for a time in the safer areas of the country. This 4 million was made up of the 1,450,000 who went out at the beginning of the war; 300,000 who were moved from the east coast and the Medway towns on the fall of France; $1\frac{1}{4}$ million who were evacuated during the period of intensive air attacks; and a further 1 million who were moved during the V1 (flying bomb) and V2 (rocket) attacks. At the darkest period of the war 13,600 children were sent to Canada and other overseas countries, 2,600 of them under government auspices.

The Scheme remained voluntary throughout the war. No legislation could have enforced compulsory separation of families or compulsory billeting while at the same time ensuring proper care for the children so billeted. This may in part explain why, when the children were finally brought home, only 29 cases occurred in which parents were thought to be attempting to avoid resuming care of their children.

Both from the human and the organizational point of view the two classes of evacuee who caused the greatest initial anxieties were the expectant mothers and the babies and children under five who became without parental care in an evacuation area. (The usual circumstances in which this occurred were the death or disablement of the mother either through bombing or natural causes while the father was on service.) Yet, to the credit of the Ministry, these two aspects of the Scheme proved among the most successful. Apart from the Ministry's emergency maternity homes, which dealt with 170,450 confinements, by the end of the war the Ministry had built up 450 nurseries with about 14,000 places, and in all some 60,000 babies and children under five had been cared for in this way. The discovery that healthy babies and toddlers could remain healthy under the fine conditions and devoted care provided for them in the large country houses given over to them, and that they would not develop those psychological symptoms of deprivation about which the psychologists constantly uttered such gloomy warnings, was one of the welcome legacies of the war.[1]

Anyone who reads the scores of studies of the Government Evacuation Scheme which were produced during or shortly after the war would do well to ask himself two questions. First, was this written at a date when the Scheme could be seen in balanced perspective against the background of new social services which arose directly from it, or were quickened into new life by the shock it administered to society; second, was it written with a full appreciation of the climate of Service opinion which lent such an atmosphere of desperate urgency to its preparation?

Initially its object was twofold: first to save the lives of as many children as possible; second to preserve so far as possible their chance of continuing their education.

If the Barcelona figures for deaths and injuries per ton of bombs (see p. 194) had been equalled in the Second World War the expectation of casualties in Britain would have been more than 17,000 children killed and 84,000 injured. The total number of children who actually became casualties in the age groups 0–14, throughout nearly four and a half years of air raids, attack by flying bombs, and attack by rockets, was 7,778 killed and about an equivalent number injured. Had children been killed and injured in the same proportions as the

---

[1] The view that maternal deprivation or separation in infancy is an important cause of personality disorder in later life was not modified by the psychiatrists until 1956. See article by Dr Bowlby in *British Journal of Medical Psychology*, Vol. 299, p. 211.

population *over* 14, the numbers would have been about 12,000 killed, 17,000 hospital cases, and 30,000 slightly injured.

It would, of course, be quite wrong to look at such figures as a simple exercise in statistical analysis and infer that the Government Evacuation Scheme saved so many thousand children from death, head injuries, open wounds, crushing, chromatic amputations, fractures, dislocations, shock, burns, and all the other forms of injury listed in the horrific statistical tables. Undoubtedly many children would have found their way privately to friends or relatives in the safer areas; many, too, would have been sent to the shelters while their fathers and mothers were killed or disabled in the streets. Nevertheless it should be remembered that the towns in wartime were by no means safe for young children even when no bombs were falling. Thus those who think of children as individuals and not as mere statistical units, those who assess the saving of even one child's life above the financial cost, however heavy, can look back on what was achieved with a measure of pride that a country, locked in a life-and-death struggle for survival, displayed the courage to initiate such a scheme and maintain it despite its mounting unpopularity.

Passing to the second initial objective of the Scheme—the preservation of the chance of continuing these children's education if they could be moved out of the vulnerable areas—it must be admitted that the record is considerably less satisfactory.

The initial blunder of the telescoping of the railway timetables led to such a dispersal of schools over large areas of the countryside as to cause a widespread breakdown of the sound principle enunciated by the Board of Education that 'the local school and the visiting school should each retain its own individuality'. Other government Departments might think of schools as mere aggregations of children working along a broadly similar curriculum. The Board on the other hand knew that a substantial proportion of the work of every school was still primarily social, resting on the civilizing influence exercised by its staff upon children known to them as individuals and on the mutual confidence and understanding between teachers and taught.

To some of those observing the movement from office desks in Whitehall during the first few weeks of the war it began to appear that, without launching a single bomb, the enemy had achieved a complete dislocation of the English educational system, and a substantial disruption of the Maternity, Child Welfare, and Poor Law services.

Fortunately order was much more quickly restored in most areas than had at first appeared possible, through the devoted efforts of head and assistant teachers, billeting officers, H.M.I.s, and the staffs of the L.E.A.s, both at the sending and the receiving ends, aided by the serene autumn weather of 1939. For example virtually all the secondary grammar schools from the London area were receiving education in reasonably adequate buildings for some hours every week very soon after the date for the normal beginning of their autumn term. They had taken out 60 per cent of their pupils and were joined by 10 per cent more who had been on holiday. After six months most of them were linked with similar types of school and working very nearly pre-war hours, albeit in accommodation which was often cramped, cold, or badly ventilated, and short of practical work rooms, laboratories, and gymnasia. Again many of the smaller evacuation areas and those in the north had avoided the disruption of the telescoped timetables and had been able to make useful contact with their reception areas (e.g. Newcastle and Westmorland) before the scheme was launched.

The worst educational losses were inevitably experienced by those children whose parents had kept them back in the 93 evacuation areas. For in these, initially, every school automatically closed and about 1,500 schools were invaded by the military and other services including the swollen army of Civil Defence workers. In most of these areas, too, the school medical and dental services, the school meals centres and milk schemes, and the reception homes for children who became without parental care, had been abruptly discontinued, and their staffs of doctors, nurses, dentists, and even midwives were often 'marking time' in hospitals and first-aid posts awaiting casualties.

At first no doubt it was thought that a few weeks' extension of the summer holiday could do no irreparable harm to these children left in the towns. When the bombs began to fall their parents would no doubt think better of their decision and discover some relative in the country who would take them. However, if any demonstration had been needed of the influence of the schools it soon became apparent in the rapid deterioration of this far from negligible army of evacuation castaways. Gallant efforts were made in some towns, notably Liverpool, to organize them into small, and therefore dispersed, groups working in homes with a room large enough to assemble a group, often under the supervision of a training college student. (Such improvisations may appear makeshift in retrospect, but experienced teachers were not slow to draw from them lessons for the future. As one such teacher put the matter: 'Many of the groups, particularly the 7 and 8 year olds, established a daily routine of school where they worked without teacher help during the morning. Tasks were set on the child's own rate of progress and interest and we were amazed to find how well the work went forward. When normal school working was at last re-established a subtle change had come over the whole relationship of teacher to child, and parent to teacher, and quite unnoticeably the more formal attitudes of the past were found to have been discarded, and the work habits of the Home-teaching era were not lost.')

For hundreds of thousands of children the wartime evacuation
meant an introduction to the life of the countryside

To Special Parties in Camps and Mansions
September 1939 - July 1945.

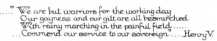

....." We are but warriors for the working day
Our gayness and our gilt are all besmirched.
With rainy marching in the painful field.....
...Commend our service to our sovereign"....Henry V.

When you are old and grey, remember these
Years lost to youth, yet giving you increase .
The inkstained, baffled hours you wrote, and toyed
With envious visions of the "form-less void.",
"The cost of living", milk rebate, and meals
"Subsidiary and main", toys without wheels
Odd socks, elusive Wellingtons and lice .
Ancestral marble busts, and rats, and mice ,
Beetles and whooping cough, bombs and V^I,
V^{II} and earache, boredom, lack of fun ,
Living in crowds and sharing rooms at night,
The hasty packing for still further flight,
The telephone account, green apples, cooks
Who came, and saw, and went! – keeping the books
Blackout, and buttoned leggings, bulls and blast,
Temperatures, toadstools, lorries hurtling past
Friendship and laughter shared, toil, sweat and tears
Hardly believable in future years,
Letters to parents, all the day by day
Enduring background for the children's play;
Nights when the men you knew sailed flaming skies
And fought grim battles in the death filled air,
You crouched in cellars with unsleeping eyes
Guarding the children happy in your care .
....

For you no trumpets sound, no flags are waved ,
Because no words can tell all you have saved .

Extraordinarily fine work was done for 60,000 children under five who spent some time in 430 residential nursery schools organized under the Government Evacuation Scheme. A Christmas card designed and written by the staff of the Rommany nursery school

By the time the war was ten weeks old the Board of Education felt compelled to decide that such schools as could be made available for the education of those children whose parents desired them to attend should be reopened. This decision was a courageous one. The Services were still unshaken in their estimates of the casualties to be expected, and the reopening of schools might well have accelerated the return of children from the reception areas.

The decision did not, of course, result by any means in all children flooding back into the reopened schools at once. A vast amount of work was entailed in withdrawing sufficient teachers from the reception areas. Since nearly 100 per cent of the teaching staff of every school had accompanied the 40 per cent to 60 per cent of the children who had gone out many evacuee children were by now being taught in classes so small as to be beyond the dreams of the most fervid educational reformer! School shelters also had to be provided before most schools could reopen. Even when the war had been in progress for eight months, and the L.E.A.s had been advised (7 January 1940) to prepare to resume the enforcement of school attendance, the position in the six largest towns where there were estimated to be 628,000 children was as follows:

Receiving full-time schooling	185,268
Receiving half-time teaching	115,506
Receiving less than half-time	23,000
Home groups	165,480
Out of school	138,926

The contemplation of such figures might lead many people to the conclusion that the public educational system reached its wartime nadir in the closed and silent urban schools of 1939 and the disintegration or evacuation of so many school communities, involving the severance of stable relationships between teachers and children and the makeshift lessons in hired village halls. Yet a dispassionate examination of the evidence, now that a quarter of a century has passed, suggests that a higher proportion of the nation's children suffered cumulative damage to their formal education through other social facets of total war than through the Government Evacuation Scheme standing alone.

Most of the 1,500 schools taken over by the Services were, it is true, returned in due course; but their number was considerably exceeded by the number of schools destroyed or damaged so severely as to be out of action for prolonged periods. Mention has already been made of the unsettling changes of school made necessary for children by 35 million changes of address from one area to another. Even where no changes of the family home took place it was, all too often, necessary for the children to change to a different school under fresh teachers because the former school had become a 'rest-centre', been damaged or under-gone a change of organization. Gradually as the war developed be-tween 20,000 and 22,000 of the younger teachers were drawn into the Services. Replacements had to be sought among older teachers, often retired or less highly qualified, and the size of classes rose alarmingly despite a substantial annual decline in the school population. The special attention to backward children which had begun to assume such an important and welcome place in the schools of 1938 and 1939 became impossible under such conditions. Books, apparatus, and materials of all kinds wore out and were difficult to replace. Many schools had to be closed temporarily, or even permanently, because schoolkeepers and cleaners had been drawn into the Services or the war factories. By the time mobilization was complete 9 million out of 17 million girls and women aged 14 to 65 were engaged full-time in the national war effort. In consequence the members of their families who were still at school toiled at the week's housework, looked after younger brothers and sisters, hawked coke, delivered newspapers, waited in the food queues, or occupied the family place in the shelters until the older members of the family could join them. The relaxation by the Home Office of their 'Employment of Children Regulations' no doubt provided a necessary lubricant to the machinery of war pro-duction, but it meant more tired children unable to concentrate on their work in school or join evening classes when the doors of the school closed behind them. The records of attendance fell sharply in most areas. Indeed the enforcement of attendance became more and more difficult in conditions where for example a mother engaged full-time on shift work at weekends in one of the war factories wanted her daughter to help with the week's shopping on her mid-week rest day.

It is not therefore surprising that by the end of the war Inspectors reported a state of general retardation in which the chief losses were in reading attainment and in written work. Everywhere, too, there was evidence of unsettlement and lack of interest in the more arduous as-pects of school work.

Unfortunately no valid and reliable tests to ascertain the general level of attainment had been applied to large samples of children in the years immediately preceding the war. Thus it was necessary to go back twenty years, to 1924, when the L.C.C. Inspectorate attempted in 1943 to apply such a test in four subjects (English, Arithmetic, His-tory, and Geography) to about 3,000 children of an average age of 13 years 7 months in their last year at elementary schools. The resulting findings (Ed. No. 208, 5:7; 43) are too detailed, too long, and too full of reservations to quote fully. The general impression which may be derived from the report is that the average retardation at the date of the test was between six and twelve months.

Great as the damage done to English education during the Government Evacuation Scheme may have been, it is now possible to see that there was a great deal to be put on the credit side of the account also. For hundreds of thousands of town children it meant introduction to a wholly new life—the life of the countryside. Despite the great advances which had taken place in the school curriculum in the 1930s teachers and social workers were often astonished when they suddenly encountered wholly unsuspected blind spots in the general knowledge of the underprivileged children of the back streets: the child who had never seen a cow or a sheep, certainly not a pheasant; who was scared out of his wits by an owl; even the child encountered by Mrs Quennell (who did such fine work at the Geffrye Museum) who would not believe that the logs placed in one of the fire-grates were wood— 'Garn wood's boxes'!

As the inspectors who conducted the L.C.C. test noted, 'children in 1943 have certain advantages over those of earlier years which appear very clearly. Many a boy or girl who has been evacuated to Cornwall or South Wales and is required to write on "A Train Journey" or "A Smuggler's Cave" is provided with a chance for utilizing observations denied to most children of the same social class in the past, and they made good use of it, drawing more on personal experience and less on fancy, and so violating probability less than the 1924 children.' 'Most of the children have some facility in expression. All the writing, however crude, is natural and sincere.' As Alec Hay, Chief Inspector of the L.C.C., was to put the matter some years later: 'The content of the children's free composition was so much more real and original that the gain clearly outweighed the loss.'

Many teachers, too, were honest enough to testify to the stimulating effect on their teaching of finding themselves compelled to keep education going without the usual resources. The movement towards 'freedom and activity', to be dealt with in a later chapter, undoubtedly derived new impetus from the challenge presented by the hedgerows and farmyards as teaching material and acorns and matchsticks as aids to number. In his valuable book *Purpose in the Junior School* (1949) Mr Kenneth Richmond, looking back on the experience of those years, says: 'Judged by pre-war reckoning, the work undoubtedly suffered; but the loss in verbalism was more than compensated by the gain in realism. With the Authorities everywhere too preoccupied to be fussy the junior school was left to its own devices. Almost for the first time it was free to experiment . . . because so much had to be improvised experiment was thrust upon it. The activity approach made more headway during these six years than it had previously done in half a century.' Moreover, it was not only those concerned with elementary education who were inclined to bear witness to features on

the credit side of the Government Evacuation Scheme. For example
the headmaster of Westminster wrote: 'We return home with lessons
not to be forgotten from the years of exile—the moral value of simpler
standards—the educational value of self help, the social value of contacts with your next door neighbour whoever he happens to be. Improvised less formal athletics, at the same time academic standards have
improved.' (Quoted in the Commons during the debate on the 1944
Education Act: see *H*, Vol. 397, Col. 216.)

No reliable statistics exist to show how many children settled down
in billets with their foster-parents for lengthy periods. The number
who did so would probably, however, surprise anyone who is tempted
today to recall the scheme (in the words of an American observer) as 'a
masterpiece of logistics' marred by continual return and re-evacuation.
Those children whose parents were content to leave them in the
reception areas often experienced—perhaps for the first time in their
lives—a combination of firmness and warmth (firmness sometimes in
the larger homes exercised by the old family cook with her longest
wooden spoon!), a recognition of the emotional need of every child for
stability and family life which no alternative to private billeting on a
voluntary basis, whether in school camp or hostel, could possibly have
afforded. Nor should it be forgotten that $2\frac{1}{4}$ million people were rendered homeless during the war for a month or more, 1,400,000 of them
in London, and that the bleak alternative to country life for far too
many children became the nightly pilgrimage to the tubes and rest
centres.

So much has been written about the undesirable presence of the evacuees
from London and Greater London in the cottage homes of the countryside
[wrote the Centre Organizer of the Women's Voluntary Services at Cromer
in a letter to *The Times* (12 June 1940), when the fall of France made it
necessary to remove evacuees from the East Coast] that I should like to paint
for your readers the other side of the picture. On Sunday June 2nd a train left
Cromer station containing some 590 children from the North Norfolk villages
and 200 from Cromer itself. The station platform was a pathetic sight—
sobbing children clung to the foster parents, themselves weeping bitterly and
assuring the children that they should come back and visit Uncle and Auntie
as soon as the war was over. As I went up and down the train I was told by
my friends, the teachers from the country schools, that the same heartrending
scenes had occurred on all the village platforms. I imagine that the experience
of North Norfolk is not unique, but that everywhere—in spite of initial
difficulties—the children have found their way, as children do, to the hearts
of their foster parents.

Looking back over the years which have passed since the war ended, the
debt which the country owes to the hundreds of thousands of men and
women, from the highest in the land (including a future Prime

Minister and a future Lord Chancellor) to the humblest cottager, who shared their homes with strangers in need of shelter, must for ever be one of the most shining episodes in our history.

To quote the Official War History:

'Many householders were never without children from 1939 to the end of the war and a substantial number had the same children for the whole period of the war.

'For the authorities to impose and maintain for almost five years a policy of billeting in private homes was a severe test of the better side of human nature. A community less kindly, less self-controlled, less essentially Christian in behaviour would not have acquiesced to the same extent and for such a long period of time as this one did.

'The sacrifices of time, convenience and privacy were accepted for many reasons; compassion, love of children and the example of neighbours were the most important.'

A personal message of thanks from the Queen went to 320,000 householders in May 1940, stressing the importance of their help.

The shock which the first evacuation movement administered to those who had tended to discount, or brush under the carpet, what they might have read of life as it still existed in some of the darker purlieus of our great cities set in train in our social services much the same astringent reappraisal as Dunkirk did for our arms. It exposed ruthlessly, almost brutally, weaknesses which called for fundamental rethinking about our pre-war conception of the appropriate role of Government.

Thus the hastily improvised provision of communal meals for the evacuated children was the forerunner of the joint action, at Cabinet level, in September 1941 by the President of the Board of Education, the Minister of Food, and the Secretary of State for Scotland to convert the provision of school meals from a quasi-Poor Law service to one universally available. The milk in schools scheme, too, though in force before 1939, was greatly expanded. In 1940 one child in 30 received school meals; by 1945 it had become one child in three. The equally hastily devised scheme to supplement the clothing and footwear of evacuees widened out, as second-hand children's shoes and clothing disappeared from the market, into the clothing schemes operated by most of the larger Evacuation Authorities by the third year of the war. Once conceded the principle became statutory in the Education Act of 1944. The attempt to relieve the evacuated mothers by providing Nursery Centres for their under-fives, which should be something more than 'cloak rooms for healthy babies' and should absorb and put into practice some at least of the ideas developed in the pre-war Nursery Schools, exercised a healthy influence on the widespread provision of day nurseries later set up for the children of war-workers.

The Youth Welfare Centres, established to deal with the difficulties of young people and be placed where they could find friendship and help when air attack developed, became the forerunners of our modern Service of Youth. The appointment of Regional Welfare Officers in June 1940 led to a considerable expansion of hostels for children who had proved misfits in billets. In the provision and staffing of these hostels many of the 6,000 evacuation helpers, who had remained out of the 20,000 who helped the teachers to take the children out, found a new vocation. Child maladjustment, little understood outside a handful of Child Guidance clinics before 1939, became a recognized handicap calling for skilled treatment by the psychiatric and psychological services established by L.E.A.s after the war.

Many other examples can, of course, be cited, although most of them were to bear more directly on the future school population than that already in school. For example the National Milk Scheme, which was approved five days after Dunkirk, supplied a pint of milk daily for every child under five and for all expectant and nursing mothers in Britain, free or at reduced cost; vitamins and orange juice became available for expectant and nursing mothers; the diphtheria immunization scheme raised the percentage of the child population immunized from the 2 per cent of 1939 to 58 per cent by the end of 1945. This cut down the number of cases from 65,000 a year, resulting in 3,000 preventable deaths, to 18,600 and only 722 deaths. Ten years later the annual number of cases had fallen below the 100 mark and the deaths below ten!

In these and countless other ways a scheme, originally conceived as a bold measure to preserve the lives, limbs, morale, and continued education of hundreds of thousands of children during the vital first six weeks of a war gradually took on the nature of a welfare service. Moreover, because bombs and rockets were no respecters of persons, and because the war became a total preoccupation in which every single citizen had a part to play, it was inevitable that this welfare service should become universally available to all as a right, not as a concession.

As the war dragged on it was inevitable that a growing body of complaints should arise from housewives, tied to the rural areas by their husbands' work, that the State was expecting too much of them. For a mere pittance[1] they were looking after the child of a townswoman

---

[1] The allowance paid weekly at the outbreak of the war for billeting one child was 10s. 6d. and 8s. 6d. each for two or more children. This was in fact the rate paid by the L.C.C. to foster-parents who received children boarded-out under the 1921 Education Act. As the war progressed the amount was raised at intervals. In June 1940 12s. 6d. was paid for children aged 14–16 and 15s. for those over 16. In May 1942 10s. 6d. was paid for each child under 11; 11s. for those aged 11–12; 12s. for

who was free to earn a high wage in one of the war factories. It is easy today to say that this complaint was a valid one. To do so, however, would be to forget that in truth Britain's battle for survival from her 'finest hour' in 1940 till she was able to 'reach out with the long arm of retributive justice' demanded the deployment of every able-bodied citizen. Moreover, the service demanded of every such citizen was precisely that which they could most readily perform. This was the 'dusty answer' to such complaints, although it was seldom given.

Those who conceived, planned, and later controlled, the Government Evacuation Scheme could never for a moment allow themselves to forget that it should be the birthright of every child to be the sole object of someone's love and attention for some part of every twenty-four hours; and that such love and attention when given by parents (even not especially satisfactory parents) is worth far more than the shared love and attention of any camp, hostel, nursery, or even foster-home. In this respect the scheme was psychologically an unnatural one. Nevertheless, weighed against the restricted life and dangers of our cities under the 'black-out', actual and psychological, of total war, it was one which had, despite all criticism, to be maintained. For the knowledge at the back of every husband's mind that if the pressures and anxieties of life in an evacuation area became unendurable for his wife and children they could get away to the country, if only for a few weeks, had, by the time our manpower was fully deployed, become one of the most potent elements in the preservation of national morale.

---

those aged 12–14; 13s. for those aged 14–16; 15s. 6d. for those aged 16–17; 16s. 6d. for those aged 17 or over. In July 1944 all rates were raised by 1s.

Today those rates appear parsimonious to a degree. It should be remembered however that the purchasing power of 10s. 6d. in 1939 was equivalent to about 35s. in 1965. In fact in some parts of northern England they were in 1939 considered to be on the generous side.

CHAPTER XIV

THE MOVEMENTS OF PUBLIC OPINION LEADING UP TO THE EDUCATION BILL OF 1943

The 1936 Education Act proposes a partial raising of the school-leaving age, and creates a modest fissure in the outworn 'dual system'; but becomes the first legislative casualty of the war.—The Board of Education at Bournemouth produce and circulate to interested bodies an imaginative blueprint for public education after the war.—A substantial measure of agreement in the sixty memoranda submitted in reply by the parties consulted.—The obvious difficulties to overcome before the school-leaving age would be raised and public system of the pre-war years could become an organic whole.—Mr R. A. Butler and Mr Chuter Ede devote two and a half years to negotiating a viable solution of the 'dual system', and attempting to rationalize local authority powers and finance.

'THERE is charm and romance in writing of "what might be" in education. There is nothing romantic in describing the dry as dust measures which legislators and administrators have to take in order to bring it about.' These words will be endorsed, with a sigh of resignation, by anyone who essays to write or lecture on the history of public education. They appeared in a memorandum, 'Education—a plan for the Future', submitted to the Board of Education by the Association of Directors and Secretaries for Education in 1942, a year when it seemed that the whole world had been plunged back into darkness, intolerance, and cruelties the like of which had not been witnessed since the Thirty Years' War.

Since the passage of the Education Act of 1944, however, it has become noticeable how many of those in other countries who study comparative education point to the social services and in particular the educational system of England and Wales as among the soundest and most logical in the world. Witness the highly erudite lecturer from the Netherlands who some years ago was bold enough to say at the Institute of the Child in Paris, 'The English social security services are logical, comprehensive and efficiently administered. All these attributes are supposed to belong peculiarly to the French. The French social services are illogical, riddled with loopholes and composed of a most complicated mixture of rigidity and dependence on vast semi-private organizations for their administration. All these attributes are supposed to belong peculiarly to the English.' Anyone who would understand why we are thought of in this way would do well to begin by an examination of the 1944 Education Act and the movement of public opinion which led up to it. For not only did it secure first place in the Government's extensive plans for reconstruction after the 1939–45 war, but the comprehensiveness of the statutory framework which it fashioned opened up a new prospect for the national system as imaginative as it was timely.

It had been the intention of the Government at the time of the Local Government Act of 1929—a measure which gave full rein to the ingenuity of its sponsor Winston Churchill, then Chancellor of the Exchequer—to produce a complementary measure dealing with education. That intention was never fulfilled, and it was not until 1936 that a major Education Bill was brought before Parliament. The Act which ensued was, in retrospect, an embodiment of the political hesitancies and chilled steel financial climate of those pre-war years. It was, in fact, a compromise between left-wing determination that the time to raise the school-leaving age was long overdue and right-wing insistence that the country was not ready for such a step and could not afford to go the whole way.

The partial raising of the school-leaving age for which it provided would probably have produced administrative chaos. For it contained the proviso that children who could produce evidence of an offer of beneficial employment could leave school during the course of their fifteenth year. As the Government were warned in no uncertain terms by the L.C.C. and other large L.E.A.s, this proviso promised to impose an administrative burden out of all proportion to the good the Act might achieve. For every L.E.A. would have found it necessary to establish machinery to deal with thousands—or even in the case of the largest authorities hundreds of thousands—of applications to leave school; applications which were often repeated throughout the year in respect of the same individual child. No two authorities could have been guaranteed to take precisely the same view as to what jobs were or were not beneficial. Thus the release of children to take up jobs in the area of an adjacent authority which had refused to treat such jobs as beneficial for its own children would probably soon have created a similar situation to that which destroyed the London continuation schools set up under Mr Fisher's Education Act of 1918. Moreover, great difficulty would have been experienced in arranging any effective schemes of work to provide a sound four years' course in senior schools.

The Act was due to come into operation on the day the 1939–45 war started, and its suspension, as the first legislative casualty of the war, tempts the comment applied by Malcolm to the Thane of Cawdor that 'nothing in his life became him like the leaving it'.

Nevertheless, the two beneficent legacies of this Act were that, by its passage through Parliament, it had laid down two firm launching platforms for the future. Clearly proposals in regard to the school-leaving age would have to be brought before Parliament once more as soon as the war situation permitted. Even more important, it had opened up the first modest fissure since 1902 in the outworn 'dual system'. It had achieved this only after interminable preliminary negotiations with the churches and those remnants of the sectarian and political interests which had obstructed the many attempts over the past thirty years to solve the problem. The device adopted had been to enable, but not compel, L.E.A.s for a limited period to pay not less than 50 per cent and not more than 75 per cent of the cost of new non-provided school buildings for senior children. The building proposals and the organization of such schools had to be of a standard acceptable to the L.E.A. and the Board of Education. The power of appointment and dismissal of teachers in a school so aided would pass from the managers to the authority, subject to the right of the managers to be satisfied as to the fitness and competence of certain of them (called reserved teachers) to give denominational religious instruction.

This douceur had appeared remarkably generous to the Church of England, obtained a measure of acquiescence from the Free Churches, and had actually been accepted by the Roman Catholic hierarchy. Only 519 proposals had been put forward by the date of the suspension of the Act. Of these, 289 were in respect of Roman Catholic schools and a mere handful (37) had materialized. Many managing bodies had been unable to raise their share of the cost, many disliked the increased control given to the L.E.A., and a few L.E.A.s had proved unwilling to subsidize denominational schools. In Liverpool the Labour Party lost five seats at the local election on this issue. Clearly in any future legislation the Government would have to make such building grants direct rather than let them depend on the chances of local elections. It is perhaps a matter for regret that more of these 519 proposals did not mature before the rise in school building costs which followed the war made it even more difficult for managers to raise their share of the cost. For the 519 proposals would in fact have provided for some 136,000 out of the 400,000 children over 11 who were in non-provided schools at the date the Act was passed; moreover, the average cost per school place in those halcyon pre-war days was about £103 for secondary and £36 for elementary schools as compared with the 1965 figure of £435 per secondary and £230 per primary place.

On the outbreak of war some 200 of the staff of the Board of Education were seconded to other government Departments. Most of the higher administrative staff moved to Bournemouth. This hegira was to have important results, for it freed them to think about the post-war reconstruction of the educational system untrammelled by the sleepless nights and difficulties in getting to work experienced by members of those Government Departments which remained in London. It was not at the time seen in this light by the cynics. An unkindly quip current among those who had remained in the firing line suggested that like other elderly and worn-out people they had probably retired to Bournemouth to die!

Now that the fifty-year rule which governs the publication of the internal cerebrations of Government Departments has been relaxed, their papers will soon be open to the public. They would probably disclose that their thinking was as imaginative, logical, and purposeful as that in the White Paper on Educational Reconstruction (Cmd. 6458), which was allowed to see the light in July 1943 and which almost immediately became a 'best seller' among government publications.

In summing up at the end of Chapter XI the development of public education in England and Wales in the first sixty years of its existence it was suggested that, considering how much had to be accomplished, the task had by 1935 been worthily begun. Probably no one who can compare in his mind's eye the educational scene as it existed in the narrow nineties with that at the outbreak of the Second World War would dissent from such a view. Nevertheless, there were many obvious gaps to be filled if the service was to be established on positive educational principles and no longer depend on what wealthy communities were willing to spend and what poor communities could afford. It had to become that 'organic whole' to which the Hadow Report of 1926 had pointed. It had to be so remodelled as to ensure that every child had the medical supervision, the shelter, the food, the footwear and clothing, and the care, necessary to its well-being. Drastic measures were needed to remove what Professor Tawney in 1941 described as 'the hereditary curse on English education—the association of educational opportunity with the vulgar irrelevancies of class and income'. The possibility that the personnel-training and not merely the plant employed by an industry might be under-capitalized had still to be driven home to most of the 40,000 small industrial concerns employing less than 100 workers in England and Wales and even to some of the larger industrial groupings. Finally, with all its merits, Mr Fisher's Education Act of 1918 had failed to face up to two outstanding problems—the dual system and the existence of 169 L.E.A.s, controlling elementary education only, most of them too small, too lacking in financial resources, and too localized to fit into a unified and progressive national system.

By June 1941, the month in which Hitler launched his ill-starred attack upon the U.S.S.R., all the principal ways in which post-war reconstruction of the educational system might proceed had been planned by the civil servants beside the seaside at Bournemouth. They had also been reduced to a tentative printed document designed to provoke and clarify discussion without necessarily committing the Government. Mr Herwald Ramsbotham was still at that date President of the Board of Education, but in July he was succeeded by Mr R. A. Butler, then aged thirty-seven. As one of Mr Ramsbotham's departing acts the document known colloquially as 'The Green Book' seems to have been circulated confidentially to a large number of bodies and associations concerned with various aspects of public education. This move, though unusual, was as it proved a wise one, for during the next two years before the publication of the White Paper in July 1942 the comments, criticisms, and collective wisdom of every body intimately concerned with public education was mobilized in reports, pamphlets, and memoranda. Owing to the wartime paper shortage these were refreshingly brief and in general followed the framework of the Civil Service document, however much they might branch out from it. Read as a whole they served as a weather-vane to indicate to the Government those proposals which, if embodied in future legislation, would find the ministerial team playing with the wind of popular opinion behind them and those where the wind would be contrary, with some evidence of its probable strength and cross-currents.

A detailed analysis of some sixty such memoranda submitted to the Board of Education between January 1942 and the appearance of the Education Bill late in 1943 shows that:

(1) The raising of the school-leaving age to 15, and to 16 as soon as it became practicable, was supported by all educational opinion.

(2) The organization of education in three progressive stages, primary, secondary, and further; the abolition of the charging of fees in all secondary schools; the completion of Hadow reorganization; and the achievement of parity of conditions in all types of secondary schools, all received overwhelming endorsement.

(3) The idea of young people's colleges to keep those who had passed out of full-time education in touch with educational influences from 16 to 18, and of healthy leisure-time training and recreation—without compulsion or regimentation—through an expanded Service of Youth, similarly attracted wide support.

The reasons for such unanimity were not far to seek.

The raising of the school-leaving age had, of course, been the principal plank in the programme of every educational thinker for nearly twenty years. It had indeed been achieved by Private Bill legislation in a few exceptional areas like Cheltenham. What was perhaps insufficiently realized by the enthusiasts, however, was that to raise the age to 15 would entail the provision of 391,000 extra school places, and to 16,797,000 extra places, even after the 151,000 places lost owing to war conditions had been replaced. Hadow reorganization, too, had now been a major objective for fifteen years and had indeed commenced in London, and a few other areas, before 1926. The degree to which it had been achieved by the outbreak of war was, however, disappointing. A survey in 1934 showed that it had been carried out in 71 per cent of the schools in the smaller urban areas and 59 per cent of those in the county boroughs but only 39 per cent of those in the counties. In Church of England, Roman Catholic, and other voluntary schools 304,000 children (nearly 200,000 of them attending small village schools) were still condemned to remain, at least till the end of the term in which their fourteenth birthday occurred, grouped with children of all ages from 5 to 14 in an average of four or at most five classes per school. A further 314,000 (38 children in every 100) were still suffering the same disability in council schools. As against this, 62 per cent of children in council schools were now able to make a new start on reaching the age of 11 in reorganized senior schools as compared with a mere 16 per cent of those attending non-provided schools. The position was particularly serious as it affected the country schools, only 20 per cent of which had been reorganized. Thus far too many children were still leaving school at 14 in photographic terminology 'under-exposed, under-developed and insufficiently fixed'.[1]

As the reader will have seen in Chapter VI, one of the most substantial achievements of the Education Act of 1902 had been to cover the country far and wide with a fine network of secondary grammar schools. For every pupil attending a grammar school in 1902 there were by 1939 six, for the attendance had risen from about 80,000 to 470,000. In terms of length of school life the figure would be more like 16 to 1. An educational ladder had, indeed, been provided but it was still a steep one and several rungs were missing. The odds against a child from an English Elementary school gaining a free place in one of the secondary schools, which had (as noted on p. 80) stood at 270 to 1 forty-five years before, had been reduced to slightly less than 10 to 1. Three-quarters of those in attendance had started their school lives in the elementary schools and 50 per cent were exempt from fees. In addition 27,000 pupils were attending junior technical schools which were already among the brightest stars in the educational firmament, although a fatuous administrative restriction still prevented the junior technical pupil passing on to a senior technological course.

---

[1] I do not know the author of this sally. It sounds like Sir Robert Wood who was Deputy Secretary of the Board of Education at this time and later became Principal of Southampton University College. His nickname among his friends was 'the head that launched a thousand quips'.

Yet the hold of these grammar schools on their pupils was still tenuous. In 1938 one in four pupils left before they were 16, representing a 'fall out' of nearly 4,000 in the fifteenth year, 10,000 in the sixteenth. The school Certificate Examination was not even attempted by 40 per cent. Only about one in ten of those selected for the privilege (as it was then regarded) of entry from the public elementary schools remained in attendance after 16. It had been calculated by Professor Gray and Miss Moshinsky in 1933–4[1] that 'when we compare children of equally high ability seven fee paying pupils will receive a higher education for every one free pupil'. No wonder that many of the bodies consulted, such as the Council for Educational Advance, the Association of Education Committees and the Workers' Educational Association, stressed the need for an adequate system of maintenance allowances to enable these children from the poorer homes to remain at school after 16.

Those concerned to defend the existing order might no doubt have dismissed these untoward facts as inevitable concomitants of rapid growth—mere growing-pains. Generally the older the school the better showing it made, and a development of sixth-form work would be bound to come as more and more of the 'mushroom' grammar schools reached maturity, as 'full employment' pushed up the wages of the worker and as the family allowances adumbrated in the Beveridge Social Security plan took effect.

The real criticisms, however, remained. First, the continued presence of 50 per cent of pupils who owed their place in the grammar schools to the willingness of their parents to pay fees (which in most cases only covered from one-seventh to one-half of the cost). This was a clear negation of the principle that the accident of parental circumstances, or place of residence, should not preclude any children from receiving the education from which they were best capable of profiting. Second, all types of post-primary education were as yet far from being regarded as on a parity whereas, under any national system logically conceived on a democratic basis, all should receive equal treatment in such matters as accommodation, staffing, size of classes, and so on. So long as the primary stage of education was followed at 11 + for more than 80 per cent of the school population by a form of education still referred to as 'elementary' the term 'secondary education' could never disengage itself wholly from an implication of caste—or at least higher esteem—instead of becoming, as it should, a genuine second stage in the education of every child. It is interesting to note that already some of the bodies which sent memoranda to the Board of Education, e.g. the T.U.C. and the Workers' Educational Association, were pointing

[1] *Ability and Opportunity in English Education* by J. L. Gray and P. Moshinsky, 1934.

to the 'multilateral' school as the solvent. A return to the day continuation schools of Mr Fisher's Education Act of 1918, but under some new name likely to sound less abrasive to the susceptibilities of young people who had left their inadequate school days behind them, was favoured by nearly all those consulted. Most of the more important bodies, however, appeared to think that the equivalent of one day's attendance a week would be inadequate and advocated at least half-time attendance. Unfortunately in the absence of prototypes, except at Rugby and in Henry Morris's admirable Village Colleges experiments in West Suffolk at Impington and elsewhere, few people had any very clear conception of the type of buildings, courses, or staff for which such an innovation would call. During the Second Reading Debate[1] Mr Kenneth Lindsay, a former Parliamentary Secretary to the Board of Education, who had obviously given more thought to the problem than most of his colleagues, threw out the interesting suggestion that the establishment of the system ought perhaps to be given the highest priority in order to retrieve some of the losses suffered by school leavers due to the effects of the war and evacuation.

It is seldom profitable to grieve over 'might have beens' in the sphere of public education but, looking back over the needs of the more 'unclubbable' types of youth in post-war England, it is not difficult to imagine how much such a move might have accomplished. For, as Kenneth Lindsay had found in the wartime youth forestry camps, young people like to feel that they are doing something of value to the country; do not want artificial work made for them; but do respond to leadership from people who have a genuine skill of their own to impart and the experience and personality to back it. There are still those who look back to the stamp of teachers attracted to London's short-lived day continuation schools, Constance Spry among them, and feel that a fine opportunity was sacrificed.

On the more strictly welfare aspects of the public educational services there was universal approbation among those consulted for the idea that a duty should be laid upon L.E.A.s to provide such nursery schools as in the opinion of the Board might be necessary, and separate schools for infants and juniors respectively with progressive reduction in the size of classes. They also approved the suggestions that the provision of school meals and milk should be laid upon authorities as a duty; that powers should be granted to provide footwear and clothing for all children and young persons attending grant-aided schools where they would otherwise be unable to arrive at school warm and dry; and that medical inspection should be extended to all children attending grant-aided schools. On this last point several bodies stressed the importance of laying down minimum standards for the provision of

[1] *H*, Vol. 396, Cols. 444 and 447.

medical treatment and the abolition of the charges still collected for such treatment—charges which often cost more to collect than the sum recovered. There was also a general welcome for the suggestion that every independent school should be open to inspection and registered; those where instruction was found to be inefficient, or where the proprietor was not a fit person, should not be allowed to continue. Most of the bodies consulted displayed some acidity towards the continued existence of such schools, attended at the time by more than half a million children, and the W.E.A. (Workers' Educational Association) suggested that the attendance of any child at any school outside the state system should require a specific approval by the L.E.A.

Almost every organization consulted displayed whole-hearted enthusiasm for the expansion of facilities for adult education—the T.U.C. and the Association of Municipal Corporations stressing the importance of persuading L.E.A.s to co-operate with each other in establishing residential colleges.

On the other hand the suggestion that major county awards to universities, hitherto a power unevenly exercised, should be expanded met with a response which might be described as acquiescent rather than enthusiastic. The explanation probably lay in the penury and niggardliness of the system of awards current up to 1939.

Since 1902 a ladder had, in theory at least, been raised up which the ablest young men and women could hope to climb into a university from the sixth forms of the grammar schools. It was no longer the case that 'it would be next to expecting a boy out of the London Board schools to take wings as to expect him to advance by his own efforts to the University'.[1] Yet the chance of many of these young men and women securing sufficient aid to carry them smoothly through a university course without suffering severe privations still varied widely according to the area in which they happened to live. Mention was, for example, made during the debates on the Act of 1944 of a brilliant boy whose talents had won for him a scholarship at Cambridge which was no doubt supplemented by his L.E.A. He was pointed out in the street to a member of the local council, whose comment was 'There goes a twopenny rate!' There were still only about 5,000 undergraduates receiving aid from their L.E.A.s and 1,150 receiving aid in the form of state scholarships from the Board of Education. The average amount of aid in the case of those assisted by the L.E.A.s worked out at £60 a year. The state scholars were slightly better off at £118. Even after conversion into today's purchasing powers, these amounts clearly still fall some way short of meeting the legitimate demands of a university

[1] One of the first to do so was F. O. Mann, who became a well-known Inspector of Schools and whose early death alone prevented him from attaining even greater distinction as a novelist.

education. Inevitably they resulted in scholarship-hunting on a wide scale and many young men and women arriving at the university academically satiated, socially unprepared, nervously exhausted, and financially unable to contemplate full participation in the corporate life of the university.

The only alternative method by which a number of individuals of high promise could achieve a university education was that of entering upon a firm commitment at the age of 17 or 18 to become teachers and taking the three-year degree and fourth-year teacher-training course. This system of earmarking was already condemned by all responsible opinion. In one of the earliest of his great broadcasts to the nation the Prime Minister had set before the country 'the social ideal of establishing a state of society where the advantages and privileges, which hitherto have been enjoyed by the few, shall be far more widely shared by the men and youth of the nation as a whole'. Here, it may be thought, was one direction in which Britain had a long way to go before she began to build a base sufficiently broad for the achievement of democracy.

Another feature of the memoranda which may appear curious to anyone who reads them today is the sparsity of the response evoked by the suggestions:

(1) that the provision of adequate facilities for technical, commercial, and art education should become a duty laid on L.E.A.s and no longer a power to be exercised at their discretion;

(2) that industry and commerce should review their arrangements for training and co-operate in associating the technical colleges and art schools more fully with the industrial and commercial life of the country.

The vital importance of further education for a country compelled to import far more than she could hope to export and to make up a third of the deficit from her shipping trade and the remaining two-thirds from overseas investments (which were bound to be drawn upon if war came) had been far too little appreciated before 1939. Some of the reasons why the development of technical and commercial education had lagged so far behind that of primary and secondary education have already been indicated (pages 149–51). In a notable passage early in the committee stage of the Bill[1] Mr Chuter Ede, who as Parliamentary Secretary to the Board of Education was Mr Butler's right hand throughout the debates, underlined the responsibility of Sir Robert Morant and his team of Wykehamist colleagues and successors for this situation. How serious the situation was may be gauged from the fact that two out of every three young people in the age range 15 to 18 had passed out of any educational influence other than those which

[1] *H*, Vol. 393, Cols. 1697–1699.

a few might experience through apprenticeship, membership of a juvenile organization, or the wireless programmes. Such conditions provided a very inadequate bridge to the technical and commercial colleges, which themselves were hedged about by a pernicious system of 'in' and 'out' county fees. These often resulted in bizarre situations; for example, students coming from Czechoslovakia to learn boot and shoe terminology might pay fees about a sixth of those charged to British students living on the opposite side of the street.

The total attendance of full-time students at the major technological institutions in 1939 was about a sixteenth of that in 1966. The number of part-time students taking day-time courses was about 2,000, plus 41,000 part-time release students; the comparable 1965 figures are 124,000 and 546,000. In another of his magnificent broadcasts (21 March 1943) Winston Churchill had reminded the country that 'The future of the world is to the highly educated races, who alone can handle the scientific apparatus necessary for pre-eminence in peace or survival in war.' These figures show how far we had to go. Mr Bevin, too, who did such remarkable work as wartime Minister of Labour, once remarked that if we had had the vision twenty years before the war to have raised the school-leaving age to 16 he would not have had the skilled labour problems which his Ministry continually had to face. Nevertheless it should not be forgotten that the country's technical colleges did, as the war progressed, make a truly remarkable contribution to the war effort, not only by training the infinite variety of specialists called for by the services and war industries, but in the actual invention and production of such special equipment as the graticule for the sights of anti-aircraft guns.

Clearly at any time after 1942 it would have been comparatively easy to secure the passage of an Act to provide for the raising of the school-leaving age without exemptions; to abolish fees in the grammar schools; to broaden the ladder to the universities; to stimulate the growth of part-time education for the 15–18 age-groups; to enable boots and clothing to be provided; to underpin the health of the school population by closing the gaps in the school medical service; and to ensure that what had hitherto been little better, in many areas, than a higher caste Poor Law service to feed the hungry child became one which provided at least one nutritionally balanced meal a day eaten in a civilized atmosphere.[1] For the climate of opinion both in the country and in Parliament was ripe for advance. As one Member of Parliament put the matter, 'The people of this country can regard themselves as

---

[1] The many families living below the poverty line in the years before the war had been gravely neglected in Whitehall. Sir John Orr had estimated that between 20 per cent and 25 per cent of children were living on diets which were defective in all respects, and a much greater proportion on diets which were defective.

having been paid back every penny they ever spent on their education rate by what happened in the skies of Britain between June and September 1940.' The war had demonstrated, not only to the British people themselves but to the free world, the resources, quality, and character of the race. Never had it been so clearly recognized as in the seventy-six nights of London's ordeal, the reactions of Birmingham, Liverpool, Coventry, and other towns to the bombing they had endured, and in the scenes on the Dunkirk beaches, that 'The bulwarks of a city are its men.'

Nevertheless such an Act would have fallen very far short of providing a framework for the development of a genuinely national system of education. For the overriding problems of reconstruction would have been left untouched. These were four in number. (1) How to enable Hadow reorganization to be completed—a process which must inevitably involve a substantial replacement or remodelling of the first generation of buildings occupied by senior elementary schools. (2) How to revise and recast the system of L.E.A.s. (3) How to attract and train enough teachers to repair the short-sighted, cynical, and parsimonious inactivity in this respect of the pre-war years. (4) How to readjust the contributions respectively payable by the central Exchequer and out of local rates to meet the extra millions of expenditure which any advance in public education on such a broad front must entail.

Any solution of the first of these three problems would involve reform of the dual system, a potential minefield of religious controversy in which one after another of Mr Butler's predecessors had foundered during the past forty years.

Any solution of the second would involve a radical shake-up of local government, and, since politics is the art of the possible, no politician— unless endowed with the 'fire and driving force of a Luther'— would willingly trample upon the boundaries, civic corns, and cherished powers of ancient boroughs without a lengthy and circuitous preliminary reconnaissance.

Any solution of the third must involve the expansion of the teaching force by at least 50,000 to meet the raising of the school leaving age to 15 and 14,000 more to make a start with young people's colleges. A complete recasting of the Burnham agreements would be essential to ensure that in future there should be one grade of teacher only and one basic scale of pay. The creation of a very substantial number of new teacher-training colleges would also be necessary to replace teachers who would retire and married women who would want to give up at the end of the war, as well as to train new entrants from the wartime services.

Any solution of the fourth problem, the financial relationship of authorities and the Exchequer, would have to iron out such anomalies as the fact that current rateable values of the thirteen counties and four county boroughs in Wales were £11,000,000 and the product of 1*d*. rate £45,000, exactly the same as for the City of Westminster alone. The average rate liability for elementary education in counties was 2*s*. 10*d*.; but it was 1*s*. 7½*d*. in wealthy counties like Surrey and the Isle of Wight, and 7*s*. 5*d*. in Carmarthen, 6*s*. in Glamorgan, 5*s*. 6½*d*. in Durham, 5*s*. 8½*d*. in Pembrokeshire, and 5*s*. 7*d*. in Monmouthshire.

It took Mr Butler and Mr Chuter Ede two and a half years of the most intricate, unremitting, and patient negotiations—upon which they were warmly congratulated by almost every Member who spoke in the debates—before they could put forward the comprehensive solution of the dual system embodied in the Education Bill, which appeared on 15 December 1943. Ministers were not immune from the difficulties and delays which so complicated the lot of more humble folk in wartime Britain. Looking back on those years they must often have felt like St Paul that they had been 'more overworked than they', 'constantly on the road', 'in danger in towns, in the country'; they had 'toiled and drudged' and 'gone without sleep hungry and thirsty'.[1]

As Mr Chuter Ede, whose sense of humour never forsook him even in the most tense moments of the debates, told the House: 'There have been moments when, before we had been in the room ten minutes, I felt that the best thing to do was for us to clear out by the door before we both left through the window. ... There were times, when we were over some of the precipices, when I thought some of our spiritual advisers, in turning over their service books, had reached the burial service; but I gathered, when I looked over their shoulders, that they were hoping for our conversion, and were studying the "form of Baptism for such as are of Riper Years".'[2]

Let us take a brief look at the dual system as it existed between 1902 and 1944, the climate of opinion in the denominations, the educational world and the general public, and some of the eddies and cross-currents which they must have encountered.

The religious settlement of 1902 had brought state aid to the maintenance of the non-provided schools to the tune of nineteen shillings in every pound of their overall running cost. It had, nevertheless, left the managers of those schools in complete control of the engagement of the teaching staffs. It had also left them in complete control of the religious instruction, provided it was given in accordance with the terms of the original trust deed and was not alterable at the whim of a new incumbent.

The right to withdraw their children from that instruction had been

[1] II Corinthians Chapter 11, New English Bible.
[2] *H*, Vol. 396, Col. 487.

preserved to parents, but this was seldom exercised; mainly, no doubt, because children dislike being made conspicuous but often, perhaps, because, however strongly the ministers of the denominations might feel on the subject, the parents did not themselves feel sufficiently denominationally minded.

As the obverse of this freedom the managers had to meet the whole cost, fair wear and tear excepted, of any repairs, alterations, or improvements to the school buildings or fabric. They had also to meet the full cost of providing new schools or enlarging existing schools.

The L.E.A.s on the other hand, although paying the salaries of the teachers, could not even transfer a teacher whose services were no longer required in one non-provided school to another of the same denomination requiring additional staff. They could do virtually nothing to ensure that adequate repairs, alterations, and improvements were carried out. Yet they had no power to close a non-provided school if it contained over 30 pupils, however much spare accommodation there might be in neighbouring schools. From time to time indeed glaring instances had occurred where for example a non-provided school had been burnt down and rebuilt—with the insurance money—although all the children could readily have been received in the council school across the street. Again instances had occurred where a new non-provided school had been built and had drawn off the whole of its intake from the local council school.

The extent to which such a dyarchy hampered all efforts to afford a new start in a senior school for all children on reaching the age of 11 has already been mentioned. Of the children over 11 in council schools 62 per cent were in separate senior schools as against only 16 per cent of those in non-provided schools.

One important change which had, however, taken place since 1902, when looked at from the denominational angle, was that whereas in 1902 there had been somewhere between 8,000 and 9,500 'single school' areas, allowing no choice of school to parents, there were now only 4,000.

As the years went by the resources of the denominations had made the task of meeting even the cost of essential repairs and alterations one which the managers found greater and greater difficulty in fulfilling. Between 1902 and 1944 3,722 non-provided schools (an average of 100 a year) unable to meet the continuing financial strain had been closed or transferred to L.E.A.s; and the average attendance in denominational schools had fallen from the 3,151,000 of 1902 to 1,374,000. Correspondingly the average attendance at council schools had risen from the 2,344,000 of 1902 to 3,074,000 and was thus now two and a half times that of the non-provided schools. The great majority of those schools which had been closed were small rural schools, 92 per cent of which had been in buildings dating from before 1902. Of the 10,553 non-provided schools still in use 541 had been placed on the 'black list' prepared by H.M.I.s fifteen years before, but had not yet been brought up to a tolerable condition. The playgrounds of such schools, which were mainly in the rural areas and were still attempting to educate about 279,000 children over 11, were often described as a 'quagmire' in winter and a 'sahara' in summer. Their lavatory provision may perhaps best be left to the imagination. As one H.M.I. reported, 'With the local squire, who is Chairman of the Managers and who was accompanied by his retriever dog, I inspected the boys' offices. The dog wisely remained outside!' One such school, indeed, achieved the distinction of being the only school in the country which was replaced by a new school during the war years. Its premises had collapsed! As Earl Winterton remarked in the debate, 'The village schools inspired Oliver Goldsmith to song but they have driven everyone else to despair ever since.'

There had probably not been any very substantial change in the relative strength of the various denominations since 1902, although the distribution of the children of Church of England parents over the rolls of council schools and of those of Free Church parents over the rolls of both council and Church of England schools renders it very difficult to arrive at firm figures. The Roman Catholic community was the one in which the preponderant majority of the children would be attending Catholic schools. Here the 1,047 schools with 253,000 children of 1902 had increased to 1,240 schools with 377,000 children. These however would represent only about 8·4 per cent of the total school population. Owing to the generally larger size of Catholic families the total Roman Catholic population, then put at about 2,400,000, represented a rather lesser proportion of the total adult population. One third of this Catholic population was concentrated in Lancashire. Where there had been a change was in a considerable attrition of the barriers, even animosities, which had still tended to divide the denominations in 1902. Several members in the debate expressed their belief that there had been a real deepening of understanding among Christian people, not only among Protestants of different denomination, but also in the deeper respect that a great number of Protestants had come to feel for their Catholic fellow-citizens.

There had been, too, some decline in church and chapel attendance, perhaps due to the rise of the light car industry, which had affected so many parental Sunday mornings, and also to the counter-attraction of Sunday evening wireless programmes. In *The Idea of a Christian Society* (1939) T. S. Eliot had recently argued that English society, though still in form Christian, was now in fact largely neutral. G. K.

Chesterton, writing in the 1920s, had gone even further: 'When a man says he is a churchman,' he remarked, 'it tells you nothing at all. The only thing you can be sure of is that he never goes to chapel.' It was affirmed, without contradiction, during the debate on the Bill that only 15 per cent of the parents in the country belonged to any denomination.

This decline in religious observance on the part of parents, however, did not by any means render them less concerned that their children should receive some form of religious instruction in school. Undoubtedly there was a great body of parents in England and Wales who, though they were hardly members of any church and might do very little more than listen to an occasional sermon by Canon Dick Sheppard from St Martin in the Fields on their wireless sets, regarded themselves as Christians and required for their children something more than secularized education.

Another considerable change had been brought about by the widespread adoption by one L.E.A. after another of Agreed Syllabuses of Religious Instruction which had enabled schools to take part in a collective act of non-denominational worship at the beginning of the school day. These syllabuses had originated in the West Riding of Yorkshire (1923) closely followed by Cambridgeshire (1924), and in their preparation representatives not only of the teachers but of virtually all the denominations, except the Roman Catholics, had joined. Their purpose had been to formulate an agreed core of Christian doctrine representing the highest common denominator of the various religious disciplines. By the time the Bill came before Parliament they were in use by two-thirds of the authorities in the country. A fervent Church of England critic might complain that they were compelled to omit beliefs central to his peculiar faith and could not, for example, include the Book of Common Prayer, the Catechism, or any of the hymn books which were not common to the denominations. The Bishop of Oxford of the day had indeed told his Diocesan Conference that 'If the present regime of undenominationalism in the schools is allowed to continue unabated, the result for the country will be disastrous.' The *Church Times* came out in opposition to the Bill. Indeed in the view of many Roman Catholics and High Anglicans, Agreed Syllabus Instruction could easily become 'the religion of nobody, taught by anybody'. On the other hand Mr Kenneth Lindsay was undoubtedly speaking for a very wide body of ordinary opinion when he asserted in the Second Reading debate: 'I hold the view that the agreed syllabuses are very remarkable documents. They cover the whole of the Old and New Testament and they are the fruit of the highest scholarship. Hymn books have been compiled. No Anglican, Congregationalist, Methodist, or member of the Society of Friends can reject the simplicity and dignity with which they tell the story of the Christian gospel.'

Opinion in the educational world as evidenced by the various memoranda and pamphlets sent to the Board of Education between 1941 and 1943 ran strongly, as did that of the more general voice of the Free Churches, in favour of the termination of the dual system. The view of the N.U.T., as expressed early in 1943, was that all grant-aided schools should come under the control of the L.E.A. The Association of Municipal Corporations (23 July 1942) also wished to see all those non-provided schools which were regarded as necessary transferred to the L.E.A., but religious instruction remain under the control of the Managers and be given by 'reserved teachers'. The W.E.A. expressed the view 'that the time is ripe for the unification of the schools under the control of the Local Education Authorities who should be given full powers to close redundant schools'. The T.U.C. initially went further (1942). They suggested that, as in the United States, Australia, and New Zealand, denominational schools should meet their full costs of maintenance like private schools and that all grant-aided schools should be placed on the same footing. The 'Council for Educational Advance', an organization which was brought into being to voice the combined views of the T.U.C., the N.U.T., the W.E.A., and the Co-operative Union, initially (early 1943) expressed the opinion that 'no useful purpose is served by the Dual system'; but in its second report, arrived at after studying the White Paper, came round to this view: 'Whether the terms offered to the non-provided schools are to be regarded as acceptable depends on two conditions (a) that they shall make possible a settlement of this vexed question (b) that they shall form part of a really effective measure of educational advance. The second is absolutely vital. Many people are uneasy about these proposals. We must not allow the progress of educational reform to be once again held up. The Government has gone very far to meet the Churches.'

The Association of Education Committees (24 April 1942) and the Association of Directors and Secretaries of Education (1942)—two bodies perhaps more intimately familiar with the administrative realities of the problem, and the probable consequences of action too radical—were rather more constructive. The first made the interesting comment that if a voluntary school could not find 50 per cent of the cost of bringing its premises up to requirements it should come under closer control of the L.E.A. The second suggested that all schools provided, or which might in future be provided, by churches or other bodies for the express purpose that denominational instruction be given should be transferred to the L.E.A. on specific terms: (1) acquisition on equitable terms; (2) all teachers to be appointed to the L.E.A. services; (3)

L.E.A. to have powers to close or alter the organization of the school subject to the approval of the Board of Education; (4) L.E.A. to have the duty of keeping the premises in repair and make any necessary alterations and improvements; (5) Denominational religious instruction by reserved teachers to be allowed.

Some day, no doubt, a future historian may be able to trace the course of the negotiations which led up to the final compromise solutions embodied in the Bill. It is much to be hoped, too, that R. A. Butler's personal notes of his meetings with the various interests—some of which are believed to have been very amusing—will become available to posterity. The most that anyone who was not involved in them—or even in the Education Service at the time—can discern from reading between the lines of the parliamentary debates and the contemporary press is, first, that the Roman Catholic Press and hierarchy at one extreme and the Rationalist press at the other were obdurate—in the one case in demanding extremely high rates of grant towards the cost of rebuilding and maintaining denominational schools, and in the other root and branch termination of the dual system. Secondly, the moderate elements in the Church of England, led by the Archbishops of Canterbury and York, the Moderator of the Free Church Council, and a number of representative Free Church leaders, 'eagerly desired to see carried into law a truly effective educational reform, creating something like equality of educational opportunities for all'. They therefore hoped that 'differences between religious bodies will be confined to a small area of the Bill' and that 'attention will not be focused too exclusively upon the controversial clauses dealing with the modification of the dual system and kindred questions and the impression thereby be created that these are the only aspects of educational reform in which the Churches are interested'.[1]

This middle of the road approach on the dual system and emphasis on the churches' paramount concern with social justice was crucial. For in contrast with the Archbishop's wise words Dr Hensley Henson, former Bishop of Durham and still the stormy petrel of the northern churches, had been saying (also in a letter to The Times): 'As things now stand, religious teaching is not treated seriously, that is, it has no secure place in the official scheme; it is not officially inspected; it is entrusted to teachers who are not adequately equipped; and in short it is treated rather as an unimportant extra than as an element of crucial importance.' Further south the Bishop of Oxford, tilting at the Agreed Syllabuses, had demanded that the Cowper Temple entail, which had survived since 1870, must be broken: 'Church children in Council schools are entitled to and must receive in those schools adequate instruction in the faith and practice of the Church of England.' As we

[1] Letter to The Times, 10 May 1943.

shall see, both bishops would find in the Bill provisions which could go some way to meet them, but these provisions could hardly have won acceptance if they had been couched in terms of such forthright advocacy.

As early as February 1941 the Archbishop of Canterbury had put forward five points, and all of these were in fact met by the Bill or subsequent decisions at the administrative level. These were:

(1) in all schools Christian teaching should be given by teachers willing and competent to give it.

(2) Religious knowledge should 'count' in the certificate for teachers' training.

(3) The religious teaching should be given at any period of the school day. (Hitherto it had been necessary for all teachers to take part in it.)

(4) Religious teaching should be inspected like other subjects.

(5) There should be an act of worship at the beginning of each school day.

Clearly the Archbishops' recognition of the paramount claim of social justice was influenced by the remarkable thinking and pamphlets issuing from the Christian Education Movement (notably 'Educational Reform and Social Justice 1943'). This body met under the chairmanship of Canon Cockin (later Bishop of Bristol) and was greatly assisted in its work by Mr Spencer Leeson (headmaster of Winchester and later Bishop of Peterborough), who had at one time been a junior member of the administrative staff of the Board of Education.

At last Mr Butler, having received stout assistance from the sterling common sense and non-alignment of Mr Chuter Ede,[1] was able to put forward his compromise solution. It is impossible to give more than a summary in the broadest outline here, but the essentials of the compromise were as follows.

(1) In every county (formerly 'council') school and in every auxiliary (formerly 'non-provided') school the school day should begin with a collective act of worship on the part of all pupils in attendance at the school (the parental right of withdrawal of their children to remain). This provision met the last of the five points put forward by the Archbishop in February 1941. It was, too, a provision the need for which had been stressed in the first of three notable reports made by a Conservative Committee on Education in September 1942. It was clearly in line with what was generally believed to be the climate of

---

[1] Mr Chuter Ede was at the time thought to be a Unitarian and thus could not be accused of favouring any of the denominations. After the Bill was through the House he did in fact mention that he had been brought up in the Congregational Church.

parental opinion in the country. Nevertheless there were a number of sincere Christians both inside and outside Parliament who felt that religious teaching in the schools should remain free from state compulsion and that religion ought to be left to win its own way by its own power. Mr J. W. H. Brown, the Education Officer of the Rationalist Press Association, went so far as to assert: 'It is difficult to find any difference in principle between the abortive Elizabethan Act of Uniformity and Mr Butler's proposals.' Later amendments in the House made it clear that where the whole school could not be assembled together in one hall the collective act could take place in several places at once.

(2) In addition to this collective act of worship religious instruction on the Agreed Syllabus should be given in every county school; and denominational teaching could also be given on county secondary school premises where specifically asked for by parents and when it was impossible to give it elsewhere. Vice versa parents might ask for Agreed Syllabus instruction for their children in (auxiliary) denominational schools. Moreover, this instruction might be given at any time during the school week, so as to allow it to be taken for different classes at different times by those members of the school staff willing and competent to give it. Where the Agreed Syllabus was being used H.M.I.s might inspect the teaching. No teacher would be required to give, or penalized for not giving, religious instruction.

These provisions were designed to allay the feelings of, for example, the ardent Church of England parent having children attending a county school, or the ardent non-conformist with children at an auxiliary school. It opened the way to the appointment of specialist teachers of religious instruction in charge of the subject throughout the school, and freed those teachers who did not feel they had any gift for religious teaching from being compelled to take it with their class. It of course met the Archbishop's points 1, 3, and 4 and, as was said in the debates, the Bill marked the first recognition by the Board of Education that the State had a responsibility for the spiritual as well as the social welfare of the children of England and Wales and that the education of the country must be built on a firmer spiritual basis.

(3) The remaining question, about which the denominations were sufficiently alarmed to make it possible that any Bill might fail (as did Sir Charles Trevelyan's Bill in 1930), was how the non-provided schools were to meet the heavy cost of Hadow reorganization. Here the compromise put forward was equally ingenious, though financially very naïve.

Those denominational schools which were prepared to raise 50 per cent of the cost were promised a 'pound for pound' contribution from the public purse. They would in future be known as 'voluntary aided' schools and could preserve their full freedom as in the past, continuing to appoint their own teachers. The 50 per cent contribution would not, however, apply to the provision of additional new schools as distinct from the replacement or enlargement of those already in existence. The cost of maintenance of the external fabric would continue to be borne by the managers on similar lines to those under the 1902 settlement, but certain costs such as those of internal repair, the schoolkeeper's house, the repair of the playground and of playing fields (though not pavilions on those playing fields) would in future be met by the L.E.A.

Where a denomination could not find 50 per cent of the cost the school would become 'voluntary controlled'. The whole bill would be payable out of public funds, the teachers would be appointed to the L.E.A. service, and denominational instruction could be given for two periods a week only, the rest of the religious instruction becoming 'Agreed Syllabus'.

The influence of the views put forward by the Association of Education Committees and the Association of Directors and Secretaries for Education can clearly be seen in these provisions. Moreover, since it was generally anticipated that the Church of England would opt for controlled status and that 'Agreed Syllabus' religious teaching would become general in the 4,000 single school areas, the solution was one which might appease Free Church opinion. It might indeed go some way to appease the teachers who equally disliked the fact that in the case of these 4,000 schools and 6,000 others appointment to headships could only be secured by individuals who professed a particular faith.

(4) Finally, as a gesture to the 482 out of 519 bodies of managers whose proposals submitted under the Act of 1936 had been stopped by the outbreak of war, the Bill permitted such proposals to be put forward once more, again with a time limit. Despite the possibility that in these 'special agreement' cases a grant of 75 per cent could be obtained as compared with the 50 per cent offered to schools accepting voluntary aided status, very little use was made of this concession. For many years there were in fact only 38 'special agreement' schools in England and Wales (16 Church of England, 21 Roman Catholic, and one other).

By a government amendment at the committee stage of the Bill it became possible for schools accepting voluntary aided or special agreement status to receive a loan direct from the Ministry through the Public Works Loan Board to carry out their share of the capital cost, after taking into account any contribution they had received from the L.E.A.

This 'fifty-fifty masterpiece of benevolent illogicality '(as it has been described by a Catholic writer) met with a very widespread welcome in the press, from the denominations, and from those members of industry and the wider public who were not wholly immersed, as so many then were, in Britain's war effort. *The Times* described the Bill as 'a masterpiece of compromise and an inspiring embodiment of educational advance'.

The Church Assembly (Church of England), where in 1942 an amendment in favour of seeking a solution on the lines of the Scottish system[1] had only been defeated by 169 votes to 94, approved at two sessions without a division a report which followed the main lines of the Bill. It is true that they added a rider that the financial proposals were put forward not as a statement of the ideal method of arranging for religious education in this country but as an outline of the terms which the Church would be wise to accept if the Government were found ready to offer them.

A majority of the representatives of the Free Churches were prepared to accept it rather than lose the Bill as a whole, while still drawing attention to the position of Free Church parents and children in the 4,000 single school areas, and asserting that if they had had their own way they would have put an end to the dual system. When Archbishop William Temple met Mr Butler and Mr Chuter Ede in company with Dr Scott Lidgett representing the great Nonconformist bodies, Dr Lidgett warned them that if they went beyond the Archbishop's five points they would find many sunken rocks in the channel.

The Catholic hierarchy of England and Wales, who had accepted the compromise of 1936, said in a joint pastoral letter: 'Let us say quite frankly that our objections are mainly on financial grounds, and that if we are given the means to make the Bill workable, so far as our Catholic schools are concerned, we shall co-operate wholeheartedly.'

In the light of this interplay of sectional interests *The Economist* was more guarded than *The Times*. 'If Mr Butler can, first, repair the omissions in his White paper and, then, pilot through Parliament a Bill which unambiguously commits him and his successors, he will be, beyond question, the most effective President the Board has ever had. Until then, a certain scepticism will be in order.' Professor Gruffydd (University of Wales) expressed the same point of view more graphically: 'I recognize the extreme difficulty of Mr Butler's position as a modern Blondin having to walk the tightrope between a host of conflicting interests.' A friend put the same thought even more bluntly: 'You have built up such a balance that you make Blondin look like a blundering fool.'

[1]In Scotland, a country predominantly Calvinistic with a small Catholic minority where only a tenth of the schools were non-provided, a concordat achieved in 1918 handed over the denominational schools to the local authorities. The authorities meet the full cost of maintenance and appoint the teachers from panels, the religious qualifications of whose members have been approved by the church concerned.

Even if Mr Butler and Mr Chuter Ede, fortified by thirty months of exploration, probing, of training and experience, could feel a reasonable hope of crossing the Niagara of the dual system, there remained the risk that the rope might be frayed or broken by a combination of those Members of Parliament who represented the 169 L.E.A.s which had hitherto exercised independent powers of control over elementary education. For these authorities would now lose all their elementary schools for senior children over 11 under the new policy of secondary education for all.

Widespread, though interested, public criticism had greeted the proposal in the White Paper that in future the 146 county and county borough councils should be the L.E.A.s for all purposes. To preserve and stimulate local interest in educational affairs, however, counties were to be required to prepare schemes for the constitution and functions of district education committees. These district committees would be entrusted with the general duty of keeping the educational needs of their area under review and making recommendations to the county education committee, and with such other functions as might be delegated to them by the county education committee. Any county district with a minimum population of 70,000, or a minimum school population of 7,000, would have the right to have a separate district committee for its own area.

These first tentative proposals had been modified by Mr Butler before the Bill appeared and as a result of a preliminary debate on the White Paper. Counties were required to prepare schemes of divisional administration which would create divisional executives appointing their own committees and sub-committees and exercising far more direct executive control over the schools than the district committees envisaged in the White Paper. Areas with a population of 60,000 or a school roll of 7,000 were permitted to become 'excepted districts' exercising executive powers similar to those of the counties, preparing their own schemes which were not alterable by the county council but only by the Ministry.

The device adopted to palliate, though it could not cure, the chronic financial inequalities existing between different L.E.A.s was to stabilize the rates of grant at their 1939 level and make fresh money (initially £900,000, later raised to £1,900,000) available to bolster up the finances of the thirty or forty poorest authorities.

The percentage grant payable by the Board of Education to L.E.A.s in 1939 was 55 per cent overall. It was, however, based and graded according to needs so that the wealthier areas, which were also normally those having the lowest proportion of children to educate, received considerably less than 55 per cent.

Bournemouth, for instance, received only 34·01 per cent as com-

pared with Merthyr's 68·28 per cent. Durham, with 1 child to every
6½ units of adult population compared with an average for other
county areas of 1 to 8, received 64·25 per cent. The country had to
wait for many more years before a reorganization of local authority
finance brought into the calculation a number of factors which made
the grant formula a less crude yardstick than the mere relation of child
to adult population—such factors for example as the number of aged
people in a county and its mileage of roads.

CHAPTER XV

THE EDUCATION ACT OF 1944

Intensive preparation, determination on all sides not to lose the Bill, and conciliatory treatment of amendments, ensure a smooth passage through the House.—Some notable speeches.—Standpoint of the different denominations on the proposals for recasting the 'dual system'.—Ingenious amendments by-pass the 'single school area' grievance.—The reduction in the number of independent L.E.A.s.—The 'direct grant' grammar schools.

Some examples of the extensions of opportunity to which the Act has led.—New school accommodation for four million children in twenty years; the remarkable response to the challenge of the Act on the part of the Roman Catholic community; the virtual disappearance of the 'single school area' grievance.—The daily act of worship emerges from the shadows on to a fully lighted stage.—The gradual improvement of 'life chances' for children of 'equal measured ability' from under-privileged homes.

THE debate on the Education Bill of 1902, despite the use of the guillotine, lasted for fifty-two days in committee of the whole House; that on the Bill of 1944 took twenty-three days in the Commons and eleven in the Lords. Anyone who has the hardihood to read and compare these two debates will note with relief the change in atmosphere which the passage of forty-two years and the agonies of two world wars had brought about. There were, of course, tense moments in the 1944 debates, but nothing to compare with the 'surge and thunder' of 1902.

Instead there was a manifest determination in every quarter of the House that however many amendments might demand discussion nothing should be allowed to wreck the ultimate passage of the Bill. There was, too, an obvious determination to surmount, with the minimum of controversy and the maximum effort to find constructive amendments, those controversial points in the Bill which were bound to run counter to the wishes of substantial sections of opinion in the country. Thus few Bills of such a length and such importance can ever have passed through all their stages in the House in less time with less controversy and so small a residue of hard feelings.

No doubt this was in part due to the intensive and careful preparation which had gone into its drafting by the Board of Education and Parliamentary Counsel. 'It is such a great change', as one M.P. put it, 'to study a Bill which is pleasant to read and easy to understand.' It was undoubtedly due, in even greater measure, to the persuasiveness of Mr R. A. Butler and Mr Chuter Ede and their invariable readiness to examine further and discuss with their movers amendments which the Government could not for the moment accept. Few Ministers in the long history of Parliament can have won such golden opinions in every quarter of the House or been greeted by such a chorus of genuinely sincere congratulations at the Third Reading stage. Nevertheless in the light of history it is clear that the progress of the Bill owed a great deal to the fact that it was the first of the great measures of national reconstruction, the finest flower of the National (Coalition) Government. It was fortunate, too, in the time of its introduction. For not only had the revelations of evacuation and the obvious deficiencies of the war-battered and understaffed schools probably rendered the country more education-conscious than it had ever been, but a feeling of growing confidence was abroad.

Indeed the war news seemed to be better than anyone could have hoped a year previously. Might not the country at last be glimpsing the light at the end of the long dark tunnel through which it had been passing? Africa had been cleared. Italy, freed from the Fascist yoke, had changed sides. Japan was passing to the defensive. The threat of invasion had been lifted from the Indian continent. The Battle of the Atlantic had restored the command of the western seas to the Allies. The power of the Luftwaffe appeared to have been substantially diminished. Vast American and British forces stood poised for the formidable undertaking of re-entry to Europe to deliver France and strike at the German homeland.

Despite the 'block buster' raids upon London of February 1944 such phrases as 'even if the war with Germany ends before April 1945' found their way into the debate. The Government found themselves faced with constant pressure to advance the dates for bringing into operation the raising of the school-leaving age not merely to 15 but to 16, the setting up of young people's colleges and a simultaneous surge forward in adult and further education.

The Bill had passed through all its stages in the Commons by 12 May 1944. The Second Reading debate in the Lords coincided with the liberation of Rome and the successful opening of the Second Front on the Normandy beaches. Then the skies dramatically darkened once more as the flying bombs began to fall. On 13 June the first four flying bombs (V1s) fell on Greater London, to be followed by the launching of 200 more on 15 June, the delivery of 3,000 in the next few weeks and 8,000 before our armies had overrun the launching sites, by which time 1,300 rockets (V2s) were being launched from Holland. Civilian casualties, which had stood at 49,730 killed and 59,371 admitted to hospital at the end of 1943, rose by 12,734 deaths and 26,133 hospital cases, a great majority of these being directly due to the V1 and V2 attacks. Three-quarters of a million houses and a corresponding proportion of schools were damaged. 23,000 of those houses went to swell the total of 200,000 already beyond possibility of repair, and the number of school classrooms destroyed rose to 150,000. A million evacuees were sent out once more into the country. The sweep of the Allied armies through France and into Germany encountered exasperating and costly checks and delays around Caen and later at Arnhem and in the Ardennes with vast wastage and consumption of material resources. Even when victory was finally won, the abrupt cutting off of Lease-Lend and Britain's fall from the gold standard left a war-weary country in urgent need of a minimum of 1 million new houses and hardly knowing from where its next meal would come.

No one could foresee that the $4\frac{1}{2}$ million school population of 1944 would by 1955 have risen to nearly 7 million, or that the cost of secondary school building, assumed during the debates to be likely to be 34 per cent higher than in 1939, would in fact increase by more than 400 per cent. Thus many of those Members who were so assiduous in attendance at the debates and so insistent upon quick action to implement the Bill might well have had second thoughts if they had been able to look into the future. Today the wise words in the Third Reading debate of Mr Cove, Member for Aberavon, stand out like a beacon in a war-scarred world: 'For the economic necessities of this nation in the hard world that we shall have to face, for the equipment of the nation to meet that hard world, we shall have to depend largely upon the efficiency of our education service.'

It would be pleasant to be able to record that a comparison of the speeches delivered in the two debates of 1902 and 1944 bore witness to the benefits of forty years' improvement in public education. In fact, of course, the educational background of Members who spoke differed very little in 1944 from what it had been in 1902. Perhaps it was less than fair of Professor Gruffydd (University of Wales) to assert, 'Some of us believe in Democracy but we go on educating the democrats of the future in separate cages and still regard our "mute inglorious Miltons" with all the aristocratic tolerance of the early eighteenth century.' Nevertheless 56 per cent of the Members of the wartime House of Commons had been at the public schools, 21 per cent at state secondary schools and a mere 22 per cent at elementary schools only.

The debate was, however, relieved by a number of notable speeches of extraordinary sincerity. An unprejudiced observer would probably select as outstanding Mr Maxton's plea for the establishment of adult education colleges,[1] Commander Bower's statement of the Roman Catholic standpoint,[2] Mr Magnay's plea, as a leading Nonconformist,

[1] *H*, Vol. 398, Cols. 803–806.   [2] *H*, Vol. 396, Col. 425.

for a better financial deal for the Roman Catholics,[1] and the Third Reading speeches of Mr Chuter Ede and Mr Butler.

A curious incident occurred during the committee stage at a late hour on 28 March. Only two-fifths of the Members were present and the Government sustained a snap defeat by one vote (117–116). This was on an amendment which would have written into the Bill a requirement of equal pay for men and women teachers. The clause thus amended was immediately withdrawn by the Government and reinstated in its previous form on a vote of confidence by 394 votes to 28. Thus both the Government and the Burnham Salary Committee were saved from embarrassment, and the principle of equal pay, which affected many other professions besides teachers, was later dealt with as a separate and national issue. Apart from this the main weight of the debate centred around four questions. These were:

(1) The proposals embodied in the Bill to reform the dual system and facilitate the separation of the new secondary schools from the former 'all age' elementary schools.

(2) The concentration of the powers of raising an education rate and borrowing money into the hands of the 146 county and county borough councils as Local Education Authorities, involving the replacement of the 173 authorities hitherto exercising independent powers to control elementary education by a smaller number of 'excepted districts' and 'divisional executives'.

(3) The early raising of the school-leaving age to 15 and then 16.

(4) The abolition of fees in the 232 secondary grammar schools which received direct grants from the Board of Education.

The subsequent history of English education demands that the climate of parliamentary opinion on each of these questions should be briefly reviewed.

(1) The Debate on the dual system illustrated with great clarity, first, the existence side by side in English education of 'a faith once for all delivered and a faith progressive and widening as the thoughts of men widen'; and second, the continued bitterness of many Free Churchmen (although every speaker on the subject represented a Welsh constituency) on the score of the children of Free Church parents being compelled to attend Church of England schools in the 4,000 single school areas. In one county, for example, it was affirmed that whereas not a single assistant teacher had applied for transfer from council schools, 200 had applied for such transfer from denominational schools in single school villages. This, it was asserted, was due to 'the niggling interference of the vicar and his wife'.

[1] H, Vol. 396, Col. 299.

For the Roman Catholic community the most sober, and therefore the most effective, statement of the Catholic viewpoint was that delivered by Commander Bower (Cleveland) in the Second Reading debate.

We have to be fair and freely admit that the present system of State education with an agreed syllabus and a collective act of so-called non-Denominational worship at the beginning of the school day has found general acceptance amongst Christian parents. I think that many do not quite like it but at any rate their conscience is not in any way affronted and they are able and willing to compromise. Those of us who are unable to compromise in this way admire these people for their spirit of self sacrifice and we ardently wish that we, too, could enter fully and unhampered into the national system of education. But there is a considerable minority who are, very unfortunately, unable to take this view, including a large number of members of the Church of England, some others, and the entire Roman Catholic community numbering between 2½ million and 3 million souls.

The Council of Trent, by crystallizing and fixing some of our doctrines, made a gulf between Roman Catholic and Protestant thought which is absolutely unbridgeable.

The belief of Protestants in free judgment, emphatically rejected by us, allows them considerable latitude in their creeds and adherence to the old principle of authority, emphatically rejected by them, allows us none in the spheres of Faith and Morals.

Religion must permeate the whole of our curriculum. All subjects must be taught from the Roman Catholic angle. We hold in conscience that—on this point there can be no compromise—parents have a definite primacy in determining the kind of education their children should have and we are bound to regard teachers as in loco parentis.

We are only being offered in some respects a higher contribution towards a very much higher liability.

We do not intend to oppose the Second Reading. We do not abandon our principles but we realize the virtues of this great educational advance.

To the historian, exercising the privilege of hindsight, it must seem a matter for regret that the many Catholic Members, instead of continuing throughout the debate to demand grants of up to 100 per cent both towards the reorganization of their existing schools and the erection of new schools, did not take up and build upon the interesting suggestion of Mr Magnay, a leading Nonconformist and one of two laymen on the Methodist Council: 'There are 35 hours a week for secular education, 15 hours for the religious body (5 hours Religious Instruction, 3 hours on Saturday night to clean the building up for Sunday and 7 hours on Sunday). Therefore the proportions should be 70–30 per cent.'[1]

Had a compromise been sought on these lines it might have prevented the unwise campaign conducted outside the House to influence

[1] *H*, Vol. 396, Col. 299.

Members by shoals of postcards, pamphlets, leaflets, and letters from servicemen abroad (who obviously believed that the maintenance grants to Catholic schools and not merely building grants were in future to be 50 per cent only).

As Member after Member indicated during the debate, such a procedure was more calculated to harden the heart of any Member than to influence him, especially when it descended in Kipling's words to 'twisting the words' a Minister had spoken 'to lay a trap for fools'. Mr Butler's words, 'Therefore I have been unable to concede the full demand of those who desire complete liberty of conscience', were twisted in one leaflet circulated to Members into a suggestion that he was opposed to liberty of conscience. Mr Silverman summed the matter up very justly—'It has happened time after time here and in other places that good causes lose some part of their appeal by being recommended for bad reasons'—and the Catholic community had to wait until 1957 to obtain what Mr Magnay advocated.

It was an interesting sidelight on the debate that, in contrast to the opinions voiced by every other organ of the Catholic Press, that of the English Dominican Order used the following words: 'Catholics will do well to console or fortify themselves by considering the disadvantages which would have accompanied the 100 per cent if we got it. The buildings would not belong to us and we should have to rent them for use in the evenings or holidays. Also every other denomination that could get enough parents to sign a requisition would be able to get a school. Methodist and Baptist schools would soon be multiplying, spiritualist or Christadelphian in some places perhaps, no doubt Communist schools too under some religion-of-humanity camouflage.'

It is difficult for anyone who has studied the debate as a whole to believe that the views of the Catholic Members could have prevailed if carried to a division against the National Government (as happened in the wrecking amendment moved by Mr Scurr against Sir Charles Trevelyan's Party Government Bill of 1930). It is even more difficult to believe that Mr Butler could have given way without imperilling the delicate balance which, as we have seen, he had built up.

Nevertheless the greatest ingenuity was displayed by the Government in devising additions and amendments to the Bill which left that balance largely undisturbed while simultaneously pleasing all sides, Catholic, Church of England, and Free Churches. Their effects were as follows.

(a) They enabled any denomination, in addition to receiving the direct government grant of 50 per cent of their actual site and building costs for schools transferred to new sites or established in substitution for former schools, to obtain a loan for the balance of the cost on the same terms as L.E.A.s could get such loans from the Public Works Loan Board. This loan concession appeared at the time to be of immense importance to the Catholics, as it would reduce the interest and amortisation charges which they were expecting to have to meet—at the school buildings costs then assumed to be involved—from £590,000 to £430,000 a year.

(b) They enabled any denomination to obtain the 50 per cent direct grant on all accommodation added to a new voluntary aided school (which would not itself attract any building grant) if that additional accommodation was designed to provide for a substantial number of pupils displaced, e.g., from some other aided school through reorganization.

(c) They enabled the parents of children of any denomination to ask for free transport for a reasonable distance to attend a school of the denomination they desired. This was welcomed by the Catholics, and in particular by the Free Churches, as enabling Nonconformist children in single school areas to attend the nearest county or controlled school.

(d) They applied a brake upon single school area schools, which might wish to perpetuate themselves as aided schools by seeking a loan to add to or improve their premises instead of becoming 'controlled' schools. The diocesan authorities had first to be satisfied by the managers that 'aided' rather than 'controlled' status was appropriate; and Nonconformist parents whose children attended the school could ask for a public inquiry by the Minister if they were dissatisfied with the diocesan decision. This amendment went a very long way to take the steam out of the 'single school area' grievance.

By such amendments as these the denominations obtained not only what they had been promised on the first publication of the Bill but a good deal in addition. No one section of opinion obtained all its desires, but all sections were bound to recognize that a very real attempt had been made to meet the wishes of all parties. The debate, too, was remarkable for the good humour and moderation shown on all sides. Only one envenomed shaft marred the millions of words uttered and led to cries of 'Withdraw!' This was an attack on the Church of England by Mr Aneurin Bevan, an outright secularist, who, as he said, regarded the Agreed Syllabuses as an attempt to put the Deity in commission. 'What is desired is to sustain, promote, and foster the Toryism which centres on the Church school in a single school area—the Church of England gets the biggest bite out of this Bill everywhere. I suggest that the Church of England, not by any positive emotional organization but by the enormous influence it has on Members on that side of the Committee—secret, furtive influence ....' (Interruption from Hon. Members) 'Withdraw!'

The incident well illustrates the impossibility, for anyone who was not actually present, of assessing what a Member genuinely felt. Quite possibly Mr Bevan was merely plagiarizing Bernard Shaw's 'The Church of England is the Tory party at prayer.' Mr Chuter Ede evidently thought so, for he said of Mr Bevan, 'I know that threatening as his attitude may be, he has a kindly heart under a frowning exterior.' If Mr Bevan was quoting Shaw, Mr Chuter Ede was obviously quoting *Hymns Ancient and Modern*—'Behind a frowning Providence he hides a smiling face.'

(2) It is becoming increasingly difficult at this distance of time to evaluate the arguments which were used in support of retaining as independent L.E.A.s the 173 urban district councils which before 1944 exercised powers of control over elementary education. In the twenty-one years (up to 1965) during which the local finance of public education has been concentrated in the hands of the county and county borough councils, the country has witnessed the building of 7,500 new schools providing places for 3,750,000 children at a cost of some £1,300 millions; the vast post-war expansion of further education; and the great broadening of the ladder to the universities and higher technological education. Could such rapid advance on so wide a front have been achieved by the former 319 authorities, many of them possessing neither the population, the financial resources, nor the breadth of vision to make a proper contribution to a unified and progressive national system? Indeed today, some of the keenest minds in the service of education are beginning to speculate whether the county and county borough authorities are any longer large enough to cope with the economic problems and results of such widespread advance, and whether, ideally, fewer education authorities with a population of about a million each might not be a better ultimate administrative set-up.

It is a truism of crowd psychology that no crowd likes to decrease its numbers. Similarly members of public bodies invested by Parliament with specific powers resist any suggestion that those powers should be taken away. Moreover, such bodies as the Association of Education Committees, which had given valuable help in arriving at the religious compromise, when faced by the loss of half their members were obliged to adopt a neutral attitude.

In 1944, moreover, there were plenty of Members of Parliament representing the small authorities, doomed as they saw it to extinction, who were ready to speak (sometimes with some justice as in the case of Cheltenham which had raised the school age to 15 in 1934) on their behalf. They argued that urban areas which had built up a fine education service would be absorbed by rural counties where the pace had been much slower; that as in the wartime convoy system the speed of the convoy would become the speed of its slowest members; that there was never the same local interest in the proceedings at the distant county hall as there was in those of the local borough council; that the smaller authorities had given a lead in Hadow reorganization; that there were 17 non-county boroughs with populations exceeding 75,000, 12 of which exceeded 100,000, whereas there were 12 county boroughs with populations less than 60,000; and that a little more time spent in selection of the areas to be constituted as education authorities might be amply repaid in obtaining a better administration, on the analogy that the tailor-made suit lasts longer and wears better than a ready-made 'reach-me-down'.

The Labour Party came out strongly at this point in Mr Butler's support: 'We feel it is desirable to have a wide area for the levying of the education rate, the recruitment and promotion of teachers and for planning and carrying out the full national system of education.' This enabled Mr Butler to take a strong line: 'After two and a half years of close study of the problem I have come to the conclusion that the proposal before the House, though a severe one, represents the best chance of getting a proper education service.' 'Am I to attempt in an Education Bill to remedy the anomalies created by the Local Government Act 1888?' Mr Chuter Ede was more picturesque: 'The inbreeding of the teaching service of this country is one of its worst aspects. People who are born in an area go to the elementary school in the area, pass to the secondary school, go to the nearest Training College, come back to the area, serve for forty-four years in the area and take their annual holiday for a fortnight in the same seaside town.'

(3) A motion in committee that the school-leaving age should be raised to 16 twelve months after it had been raised to 15 was defeated after a prolonged debate by 172–137 votes. As has already been suggested, the situation which faced the country when the war eventually ended would certainly have rendered any such action impossible, if not actually untimely, for some years. In the optimistic atmosphere of the early months of 1944, however, such an amendment was more difficult for the Government to resist.

The question of the recruitment and training of teachers was, however, recognized by all the wiser members of the House to be the crux of the whole Bill. From among those on active service, 20,000 might return, but wastage was amounting to 6 per cent annually; so 12,000 teachers a year would be lost, and yet the intake to those colleges which had remained in action was no more than 6,000 or 7,000 a year. If the size of classes was to be reduced—even with a total school population lower than it had ever been before—and if the damage and destruction in existing schools was to be repaired, perhaps to many Members the balance of advantage seemed to lie in raising the age to 15 and then as soon as possible enrolling the 15–16 age group in young people's colleges until the housing shortage for the population as a whole could be relieved.

(4) The amendment to abolish fees in the 232 secondary grammar schools which received a direct grant from the Board of Education was eventually defeated by 183–95 votes.

Nevertheless this amendment probably caused considerable anxiety to the National Government because its Labour supporters obviously set much store by the statement in the White Paper: 'A system under which fees are charged in one type of post-primary school and pro-hibited in the others offends against the canon that the nature of a child's education should be determined by his capacity and promise and not by the financial circumstances of his parents.' Again, a section of the McNair Committee which was due to produce its report before the Bill was through the House had submitted an interim report advocating the abolition of fees in every secondary school without distinction— and this section had included the headmaster of Cheltenham and the headmistress of Roedean.

Members were also concerned that in certain areas direct grant schools provided the only form of secondary grammar school available and that, in those areas where there was a choice, the continuance of a secondary school charging fees might lead parents to attach a mistaken value to it as compared with the publicly provided secondary schools. Thus it would tend to cream off the ablest pupils. The 232 schools at that time contained 84,055 pupils, equivalent to nearly 18 per cent of the total grammar school population, although a mere 4 per cent of the school population who would become 'secondary' through the Act. Many of the 232 were not local schools but drew their pupils from a wide area, another complicating factor. Fees ranged from £4. 10s. to £75 and the cost of abolishing them was put at £1,100,000. The pupils who in fact had free places numbered 23,398.

The government argument for retaining the direct grant was that, although the schools must be accessible to all and the L.E.A.s must be able to count on continuing to secure places in them, to attempt a clean sweep might well drive some governors to refuse to accept any more grant and become independent. This would deprive the public educa-tional system of the 25 per cent of free places and tend to accentuate social distinctions. On the other hand, if they were left in continued receipt of direct grants many governors might in due course decide to avail themselves of the liberal rebuilding grants which they could look for if they accepted 'aided' status. Probably this latter argument weighed with Members; but as an alternative to 'aided status' has since presented itself to many of the schools in the form of new science buildings and equipment provided by the Industrial Fund,[1] the problem is still with us.

'I rose merely to say', remarked Mr Cove in the Third Reading debate, 'how often I have observed during the debates on this Bill that many Members know little of the actual work which is being done in the ordinary schools of this country.' This feature, unfortunately common to most debates on Education Bills, was matched by its corollary, the number of Members who appeared to have very little understanding of the children for whom they were legislating. For example, several members produced, as shocking evidence of the low level to which religious teaching had fallen, the story of a clergyman who on questioning thirty-one evacuee children was distressed to find that nineteen of them could not tell him whose birthday occurred on the first Christmas day. Any experienced teacher could have set the reverend gentleman's mind at rest on the point. For a proportion of the children in any group—not even necessarily evacuees, who would probably be uncomfortable in a strange environment—when questioned perhaps in unfamiliar language by an imposing visitor in unusual black garments would become completely incommunicado. Another Member produced the old story which gained currency in 1934 of the group who could not tell him the name of their local M.P. (Sir Anthony Eden). Yet another appeared shocked that the children in a rural school could not name five British birds which hovered.[2]

Nevertheless, to the credit of all Members, what Mr Foster wrote to Charles Kingsley in 1870, and what his successors could have written of every subsequent debate on the dual system before 1943, could no longer be said of this one: 'I wish parsons, Church and other, would all remember that children are growing into savages while they are trying to prevent one another from helping them.'

It is interesting to recall that the debate began in the week set aside annually for prayers for Christian Unity. Mr Magnay—the Methodist—was not so wide of the mark when, looking into the future of a war-torn world, he said: 'If I can read the signs of the times, there is looming before us a fight in the spiritual world. It may not be in my time, but it will certainly be in the next twenty years. We shall not then want to ask Christians whether they are Methodist or Baptist or

[1] A fund of about £2,000,000 raised voluntarily by industry to improve the buildings, particularly for science, at the public and direct grant schools.

[2] Hovering has no exact meaning. The kestrel is always taken as an example of true hovering when it seems to hang in the air with infrequent movement of the wings. Some shrikes, kingfishers, nightjars, and terns can remain in the air in more or less one place by flutterings of the wings.

Church of England. We shall get together and fight it out against the Satanic forces which want to down us as a free Christian nation.'

The two main objects of educational reform are, first, extension of opportunity, and second, improvement of quality. An attempt will be made in the remaining chapters of this book to indicate some of the directions in which the three partners in the educational system of England and Wales—the Ministry, the L.E.A.s, and the teachers—have improved quality. The extent to which the Act has extended opportunity in the first twenty-one years of its operation can perhaps best be realized from a brief comparison of the situation in 1965 with that in 1939, as described in the previous chapter.

The Board of Education was a body which had never met. In racing parlance it had been brought into being by the Duke of Devonshire out of some nameless constitutional lawyer, but his Grace when questioned could never remember how its name had been chosen. Its powers were limited and obscure. Mr Butler's Act replaced it by a Minister charged with the duty 'to promote the education of the people of England and Wales and the progressive development of institutions devoted to that purpose, and to secure the effective execution by local authorities, under his control and direction, of the national policy for providing a varied and comprehensive educational service in every area'. Mr Butler thus became the country's first Minister of Education. Mr Messer (South Tottenham), who moved the Amendment at the committee stage, remarked at the Report stage that he had never attended obsequies with such pleasure. Mr Morgan (Stourbridge) went further: 'I am quite sure that we shall take such a step forward that generations of children yet unborn will come to bless the name of Butler for giving them such a good start.'

Four million children are now enjoying the amenities of the 7,500 new schools built since the Act was passed; 15,000 students can look forward to obtaining the equivalent of an honours degree in Colleges of Advanced Technology; 187,427 students are in enjoyment of university awards (as compared with the 6,100 of 1939). How many of all this multitude, one wonders, are ever encouraged to reflect what their condition might have been if Mr Butler had failed to pilot his Bill through Parliament? Unfortunately our national proclivity to underrate our achievements while exaggerating our mistakes tends to make too many of us think of post-war educational expansion in terms of a vast game of 'Snakes and Ladders' conducted on a countrywide board, to which new Snakes are added every time there is a run on sterling.

Only those Members who, like Mr Kenneth Lindsay, had held office at the Board of Education seemed during the debates to appreciate that an Education Act so comprehensive should be regarded in the light of a book of blank cheques to be filled in over a period of perhaps forty years. 'Everyone knows', he said, 'that to carry out the Bill will take decades of reconstruction.' A close study of the debates hardly bears witness to the prevalence of such knowledge among other Members who took part. How far then has the country succeeded during the twenty-one years in which the Act has attained its majority in fulfilling the hopes which were held out by its sponsors? Has it completed Hadow reorganization? Has it effectively separated the primary and secondary stages of education? Has it opened up a broad avenue of opportunity to the universities, to further education, to adult education? How far has it succeeded in stilling or satisfying the consciences of those who hoped to see an end to the dual system, and those who hold that the future of the country depends upon the teachings of the Old and the New Testaments being absorbed by, and applied in the individual lives of, the nation's children? How far has it underpinned the health, mental and physical, of the rising generation during their schooldays and after through an expanded Service of Youth?

Volumes have been written on each of these questions. Here it is only possible to pinpoint a few of the more salient facts.

Since the Hadow Report of 1926 new accommodation has been provided for 5 million children (1 million between the wars and 4 million since 1946). Thus if the school population had remained at the $4\frac{1}{2}$ million at which it stood when the Act reached the Statute Book, every child in England and Wales, including the 14–15 age-group added by the raising of the school-leaving age, might now, theoretically at least, have had the chance of receiving education in a 'second generation' school, that is one planned and built within the last forty years to conform with the Hadow principle. That this is by no means the case is due first to the fact that in the same period we have re-housed nearly two-thirds of the 15 million families in England and Wales and that much of this new housing has been centrifugal, requiring new schools to be built on the housing estates; and second, to the largely unforeseen 'population explosion' which had already raised the school roll to 7 millions in 1965 and is likely (so far as projections can be accepted) to raise it by at least another 2 millions by 1975. Our school planners and architects have in fact for years been trying to run up the 'down' stairway of a moving staircase, attempting to keep level with a school population riding up the 'up' staircase. Nevertheless the 'all age' school has slowly over the years become a relic of the past. Even as late as 1961 there were still 220,128 pupils (50 per cent of them Catholics) still attending 'all age' schools. By January 1965 however the number in senior classes of 'all age' schools had been brought down to 9,376, and the proportion aged 13 represented only 0·5 per cent.

A feature to which these figures draw attention is that, in the nation-wide reappraisal of their schools and resources upon which every denomination was immediately forced to concentrate by the Act, that of the Catholics was, and still is, by far the most 'agonizing'.

When the Bill was before the House it was naïvely estimated that the Catholic community, which had raised about £3,500,000 for its schools since the Act of 1902, would have to find another £10,000,000 to meet the requirements of the new Act. This, in itself, seemed alarming enough to the Catholic Members who took part in the debate. Not one of them appeared to realize, however, that other difficulties, more imponderable but none the less disturbing, would have to be resolutely faced before the Catholic schools could make the best use of the new prospect opened up by the Bill.

In the first place, the Act would impose the reorganization of some 1,300 schools containing 400,000 children in order to separate those children over 11 from those of primary age. For those over 11 would now become 'secondary pupils' instead of, as hitherto, senior pupils in 'all age' schools.

Secondly, these 'all age' schools had mainly been provided, particularly in the north-western and north-eastern areas of England, on a parochial basis out of the 'pennies of the poor' in general to serve the poorest sections of the community. Catholics living in the suburban and middle class areas had become accustomed to sending their children to private schools of the 'convent school' type where the fees were moderate, ranging from 6 to 15 guineas a year. Many such schools had been established in this country since the expulsion of the Teaching Orders from France in 1900. Similarly the old Catholic families and the wealthier sections of the community normally attempted to gain admission for their children to the Catholic public schools. Obviously the senior departments of the parochial 'all age' schools would now have to be replaced by large inter-parochial secondary schools; but might not the parish priests, who had worked so hard to establish and maintain them, express grave pastoral objections to such 'decapitation'? Might this not indeed nullify, or at least slow down, the efforts of the diocesan authorities?

Thirdly, over and above the cost of providing these new inter-parochial secondary schools (for which the 50 per cent—later 75 per cent—grant and preferential loan terms might be expected from the Ministry), a further extensive building programme would be required to provide, in new schools for which no capital grants would be obtainable, for the Catholic share of the 'population explosion'. This was likely to be nearly twice as serious proportionately as that with which the L.E.A.s would be faced. Indeed projections suggested that between December 1959 and December 1969 the Catholic child population aged 5–14 would rise by 300,000, as against a net increase of 177,000 to be provided for in non-Catholic schools.

Lastly—although this prospect was still over the horizon—the reorganization of secondary education on comprehensive lines would call for yet further expenditure and renewed concentration of Catholic secondary pupils, if the principle of 'believing child taught by believing parents and believing teachers' was to be maintained.[1]

The resolution with which the Catholic community has risen to these challenges over the post-war years should evoke the admiration of all Christians of whatever persuasion. Under the strong lead of Cardinal Griffin the Catholic Education Council was revivified, and Diocesan Schools Commissions were brought into being to survey the educational needs and financial resources of the dioceses. A National Catholic Building Office was established to control building costs and obtain value for money. Priority was given to school building over everything else. Several new Catholic teacher-training colleges were established. As against the naïve 1944 estimate of £10,000,000 the gross cost of the Catholic building programme in maintained schools since 1944 is now put at over £100,000,000. Of this the net cost to the Catholic community after deducting direct grants from the Ministry will probably be upwards of £40,000,000, after allowing for interest and redemption charges on loan expenditure.

For the Church of England, with about five times as many schools as the Catholics (9,204 C. of E. and 1,826 R.C. in 1947) the re-appraisal, though severe, was not as difficult. In the first place 4,141 of their 9,204 schools were in single school areas, and in the light of the promises made to the Free Churches during the debate, and advice given by the Church Assembly itself, many of these could obviously not expect preferential loan terms where substantial rebuilding was involved. Moreover, except in the case of the Anglo-Catholic minority, the conscience of the Church of England was not affronted by the prospect of religious instruction on the Agreed Syllabuses in the preparation of which it had taken so large a share. Indeed both Archbishop Temple of Canterbury, who had recognized the validity of the Free Churches' single school area grievance, and Archbishop Lang of York had expressed the view that the Church of England schools would do well voluntarily to use Agreed Syllabuses for three days a week and would find the remaining two days sufficient for distinctively

---

[1] In the comprehensive secondary schools of the British Families Education Service in Germany the Catholic children are withdrawn for a separate Morning Assembly taken by Catholic members of the staff, but they work with the rest of the school for all the secular subjects.

Nearly 8 per cent of the teaching staff in Catholic maintained schools in January 1964 were non-Catholics (1,935 out of 24,368).

Anglican teaching. These views had in fact been expressed before it became known that a new Education Act was contemplated.

An examination of the single school areas had revealed that the grievance, though genuine enough in certain areas, notably Wales, was not universal. Nevertheless the desire of the Church of England to concentrate its financial resources where they were most needed, for example in producing a greater supply of teachers whose sincerity of conviction would render the religious instruction more lasting and real, resulted in practically all the single school areas accepting 'controlled' status for their schools. In Wales for example the number of Church in Wales schools, which stood at 501 (572 Departments) before the war, had fallen by 1964 to well under 100 preserving 'aided' status, over 250 having become 'controlled'. Apart from this wise settlement of the single school area grievance the Church has shown a resilience, unexpected during the debates, in its reorganization of existing schools and provision of new ones. Building programmes between 1945 and 1965 have included 214 projects providing 53,790 places in 'aided' and 'special agreement' schools, at a cost of some £7,000,000; of which the net cost falling on the Church has probably been of the order of £4,000,000. At the end of 1964 there were some 3,000 'aided' and 'special agreement' Church of England schools, and some 4,000 'controlled'.

In the first fifteen years after the Act came into force (1945–60) the use by the denominations of the 50 per cent building grant to assist reorganization resulted in the provision in round figures of about 150,000 school places in aided and special agreement schools (Roman Catholic 120,385; Church of England 23,145; Other 5,705). Grants totalled £15,848,224. It might be inferred from these figures that the cost per place amounted to about £212; this would be misleading, however, because the provision included the generally less expensive primary and the generally more expensive secondary places. Moreover, substantial contributions were made by the L.E.A.s for certain types of specialized accommodation (kitchen and dining arrangements, playing-fields, medical inspection, and treatment rooms and so on).

One purpose of the amending Act of 1959[1] was to enable the voluntary bodies to play a full part in a new drive for improved provision for secondary schools. Besides raising the basic rate of grant from 50 per cent to 75 per cent the Act introduced a new category, i.e. the secondary schools provided in order to redress the balance between primary provision by the voluntary bodies and secondary provision as it then existed. As a consequence the rate of secondary provision undertaken after 1960 increased to such an extent that in the five years 1960–5 nearly as many places (142,000) were brought into use as in

[1] Secondary education for all. A new drive (Cmd. 604).

the previous fifteen years (Roman Catholic 104,000; Church of England 30,645; Other 5,670). Total grant expenditure during these years was £40,033,774. Of this all but £2,062,725 attracted grant at 75 per cent.

There is little doubt that considerable advantages have flowed from the improved opportunities opened up by the Act for developing religious education in the schools. It should be emphasized, however, that 'extension of opportunity' does not necessarily imply 'improvement of quality'. The extent to which quality has improved can more conveniently be examined in later chapters, because the wholly distinct treatment required by infants, juniors, modern streams in comprehensive and secondary schools, grammar streams, and sixth forms was little appreciated when the Act was before Parliament. Its passage created a new era in which the great majority of Britain's children would in future receive their principal personal Christian teaching and their principal personal experience of worship in the nation's own schools— not from the clergy and the Sunday Schools. Regrettably, however, it is still (1965) doubtful if the education authorities and the schools as a whole have yet provided the conditions essential for the great improvement in quality which should have followed the Act.

Before 1944 there was, of course, no statutory requirement that religion should be taught at all, although virtually all schools provided for it. The Act, which would probably have experienced a much more difficult passage but for the by-passing of the dormant but still potential religious controversies provided by the Agreed Syllabuses, converted religious knowledge from an optional extra into a statutory obligation. It also freed a number of teachers who did not feel competent, or perhaps inclined, to give religious instruction from the sense of obligation to their colleagues to make the attempt.

The myth that a large proportion of the teaching profession consists of atheists, agnostics, or secular humanists dies hard; as does the corresponding myth that such teachers, where they exist, are still compelled to give religious instruction instead of availing themselves of the conscience clause. Early in 1944 'Mass Observation' found that in a representative sample of 1,900 teachers from varied types of primary and secondary schools 90 per cent were in favour of religious education in state schools, although 71 per cent were opposed to merely denominational instruction.[1]

Some reduction might be expected today in the percentage of teachers who in 1944 were so forthright in their support of religious education in state schools. In common with the other years of war,

[1] *The Times Educational Supplement*, 11 March 1944. The sample may be objected to as too small, but it is the general experience of opinion surveys that the percentages do not vary substantially after the first 2,000 answers have been recorded.

1944 was a year of high national purpose and idealism when, as we have seen, the ordinary people of the country had, in their care for the children from the evacuation areas, given one of the most remarkable demonstrations of practical Christianity which any country can ever have witnessed. Fear, determination, and a feeling (largely inarticulate) that Christianity was fighting for its existence against the dark forces of Fascism and a Satanic Nazi ideology had sent vast congregations, many members of which had not entered Church or Chapel for years, to the country-wide Services of Intercession arranged at the time of the fall of France. We felt that in truth we were fighting 'the Devil and all his works'. In the intervening twenty years we have seen what a *Times* leader has described as 'bafflement, uncertainty, a lack of a national consensus of opinion'; television speaking with what Bishop Spencer Leeson (one of the finest Christians and educationalists of his generation) described as 'the thin and acid voice of ridicule'; the results of the social wastage of the war years; and the exploitation by mass media of the 'debunking' mood fostered by that wastage. In view of this it is perhaps surprising that a national opinion poll carried out in May 1965 disclosed that only 1·1 per cent of those approached claimed to be agnostics or atheists, 1·8 per cent professed no religion, and 92·9 per cent described themselves as Christians. Ninety per cent expressed the view that religious education in schools should continue.

As regards compulsion to give religious teaching the myth appears to be equally ill-founded, because only about one teacher in seven in county secondary schools, one in five in modern schools and one in twenty in comprehensive schools was teaching religion in 1965. How rapid the change has been is illustrated by the fact that, whereas in 1955 virtually every form master in a third of the secondary modern schools was taking his own form for religious instruction, in 1965 only about 2 per cent of them were doing so. In the primary schools it is still usual to find class teachers taking their class in all subjects, but here too a movement appears to be on foot to allow some specialization by groups of subjects where the size of the school allows.

This situation has been brought about by the additional freedom which the Act conferred to distribute the religious instruction periods throughout the weekly timetable, thus opening the way to the appointment of individual (usually specialist) teachers who could act as heads of the religious education department in a school, and who could themselves take a major part in the giving of that instruction instead of the teacher of each class doing so. No one, looking back on his school days, is likely to forget that the teacher who was most successful in unlocking his mind to the truths of religion was the most sincere and convinced believer on the staff and the one who had obviously undergone a training which had given him a sound academic knowledge of religion. Surprisingly perhaps the most significant pointer to a desire to take full advantage of the new prospect opened up by the Act is the great demand which has arisen for improvements and additions to the various Agreed Syllabuses themselves. Although the general run of teachers probably welcome the help the syllabuses give, many of them seem to be aware that a great deal of thought and research is still required to adapt them to the requirements of different age-groups and different levels of intelligence.

A charming H.M.I. of the old school, Jasper More, whose irrepressible flashes of humour lightened so many of the dusty files of the Board of Education, once reported: 'Unfortunately the Rev. Correspondent of this school exhausted all his energy in his early 20s between Putney and Mortlake.' Reading some of the early Agreed Syllabuses leads to an inescapable feeling that too many of those who took part in framing them exhausted all their youthful energy over Davidson's Hebrew Grammar!

The teacher qualified to undertake the immensely important but undoubtedly immensely difficult task of giving children a core of enlightenment so that they do not leave school ignorant of what Christianity stands for, interpreting it attractively and meeting their spiritual needs, is at present far too rare. The demand for them has in fact created an acute staffing crisis, to which the colleges of education and departments of education and those of theology in the universities have begun, in some cases rather tardily, to respond. There is no doubt that religious knowledge is taken more seriously and taught better in the colleges of education than it was in the teacher-training colleges of pre-1944 days and that the lecturers are better equipped to help the students to master the appropriate approach. Nevertheless, as the deficiency of specialist teachers is estimated at 40 per cent (a deficiency not approached by that in the case of any other subject in the school curriculum) and as less than 200 come from the universities each year, it may be many years before the crisis is surmounted, and before all students taking religious subjects as their main course at colleges of education can hope to receive a training from which the over-linguistic and over-academic features inherited from the old style university theology courses have been exorcized. It may be longer still before L.E.A.s recognize the vital importance of appointing Advisers of Religious Instruction (as the West Riding and Norfolk have done), who by organizing teachers' courses, contact with the churches, and visits to schools could effect improvements in quality as marked as those which their organizers of other subjects have achieved.

Some day, too, it may come to be realized that young men and women whose sense of vocation leads them to want to devote their life to religious education and learn to teach from the Bible instead of teaching the Bible ought to be afforded the same opportunities for travel as, for example, the teacher of foreign languages. In their case it might be well that they should begin by a period of voluntary service overseas or, at least, a visit to the Holy Land. Perhaps the horizon is not so dark, however, as it must have seemed even a few years ago. Out of 37,607 students nearly 9 per cent (3,540) were in 1964 taking religious subjects as the main subject of their course at colleges of education. This was a possibility at eighty-two colleges. Moreover, the number of sixth-form pupils offering Divinity at 'A' level has shown a fairly steady increase in recent years. It was 1,193 in 1956 and had risen to 3,301 by 1963.

Those who hold (to quote the Ministry of Education Pamphlet No. 16) that 'Christian belief and practice are the most secure foundations for the building of a true and enduring citizenship' can take heart from the widespread improvement, which certainly seems to have taken place, in the daily act of worship at morning assembly. Christian psychologists suggest that the experience of participation in worship can form the first introduction to belief and that belief will lead to action. If this is so the extent to which the morning assembly has emerged on to a fully lighted stage, instead of the former discreet half-lighting imposed by a desire to avoid contentious publicity, so that it is now treated in more and more schools as the chief event of the school day, is one of the most welcome developments to which the Act has contributed. For not a few Members during the debates opposed the requirement that 'The school day in every county school and in every voluntary school shall begin with collective worship on the part of all pupils' on the ground that religion 'should be allowed to grow by the power of religion'. The danger of monotony and the need for variety, vitality, and freshness seems now to be constantly in the minds of a substantial proportion of heads, with the result that no two assemblies follow exactly the same pattern. It is often the small things which reveal the determination of a school staff to create an impressive service—flowers from the school garden, appropriate introductory music on the school radiogram, the lectern made by the boys in the handicraft room, pupils coming in silently carrying their chairs.

How far the improvement is due to the light and well-found halls in our 7,500 new schools, to the more ample provision of chairs, radiograms, pianos, hymn books, and school gardens, and how far to a new spirit among school staffs, it is impossible to say. In theory the convinced Christian should be able to exclude from his worship discomfort in his material surroundings. But children barely on the first rung of the ladder to convinced Christianity can hardly be expected to tolerate the continual 'up' and 'down' of standing and kneeling on a hard school floor, attempting to sing well-worn hymns to one finger on a piano at least a tone out of tune, and the droning of prayers followed by dinner lists and homilies on the moral obliquity of wearing bell-bottomed trousers in school! Only the most purblind optimist would deny that such cases of uninspiring and formal observance are still to be found. There are still, too, far too many schools presenting such difficulties as an inadequate or shared school hall, insufficient chairs, children arriving late from their trains, or school notices given out at assembly because there is no other convenient time. Considerable ingenuity is required to create an atmosphere of quiet reverence in the face of such handicaps.

Not unnaturally from time to time groups claiming to represent sects which did not share in the preparation of the Agreed Syllabuses, or more commonly agnosticism or secular humanism, tilt at the extent to which Christian worship and the teaching of religion is now a statutory feature of English education and demand repeal of the religious clauses of the Act. The National Opinion Poll of May 1965 suggests that this is assuredly not yet a live issue.

Their argument usually runs along a track so well worn that any student of educational history could probably quote half a dozen examples from parliamentary debates or the press of each decade since 1870. In Holland, it is claimed, any body of parents can approach the authorities and ask to be provided with a school run according to their ideas if they can put down a modest proportion of the cost. Why should not we in England display the same sensitivity to the wishes of minorities?[1] The answer must surely be that England and Wales have taken nearly a century to get rid of a mass of tiny, uneconomic, 'all age', and single school area schools originally provided to meet the tenets of the denominations. These have in general been replaced by reorganized primary and secondary schools of a size affording amenities which no school asked for by a secular minority group could match. In county and controlled schools the school worship and religious instruction enshrines that body of Christian belief which is accepted by practically all denominations. Whether they are county, controlled, or aided, the agnostic or secular humanist parent can withdraw his child from religious instruction. He may say that he does not want to render his child conspicuous, but if he genuinely believes that the school assembly and religious instruction periods are harmful to that child's development he has a clear duty to withdraw him. In fact, when a questionnaire was circulated by the Joint Four Secondary Associations in November 1951 to parents of children at 908 grammar schools, only three parents were found to be withdrawing their children on the grounds of

[1] A good example can be found in *The Times* of 23 April 1966, under the title 'What sort of religious teaching in schools?'

agnosticism. Moreover, the difficulty which any L.E.A. would experience in providing a school for a small minority of parents who
wanted something special is well illustrated by the fact that the L.C.C.,
with all its resources of transport, some years ago found quite insuperable difficulties in organizing a school for Welsh-speaking
children in the Metropolis. To be fair to the secular humanists it
should, of course, be remembered that they are as keen as, or keener
than, many professed Christians that the 'ethos' of every school should
be built upon what can be shown to be good in terms of considered
human experience. Probably most of them would agree with the Norwood Report that 'Education cannot stop short of recognizing the
ideas of truth, beauty, and goodness as final and binding for all times
and in all places as ultimate values'. Where they would cease to go
along with Dr Norwood would be in his next sentence: 'The recognition of such values implies, for most people at least, a religious interpretation of life.'

Finally, one welcome result of the solution (or by-passing) of the
dual system by the Act of 1944 has been the spread of understanding
and periodic joint action in educational matters by the churches. For
example the chairmen of the Church of England Schools Council and
the Catholic Education Council went together to meet a large group
of Members of both Houses of Parliament to explain their reasons for
believing that a new category of grant-aidable projects, the so-called
'matching schools', should be introduced; and they were in fact introduced by the amending Act of 1959. That Act, with its provision
for a 75 per cent grant, was passed without any of the hard feelings
which had characterized previous education debates. A Central Joint
Education Policy Committee of the Church of England, the Church
in Wales, and the Free Church Federal Council came into being in
October 1959, and there is little doubt that the replacement of suspicion by understanding and joint action has played its part in the
growth of the ecumenical movement.

How far has the Education Act of 1944 extended opportunity for
those sections of the school population upon whose doors opportunity
too seldom knocked before 1939? Anyone who asks this apparently
simple question will soon find himself surrounded by a truly intimidating pile of material—statistics, psychological monographs, and
learned papers. Probably the wisest thing he can do before reading
them is to start by reminding himself of two facts. First, the supersession of the 'public elementary school' with its connotations,
whether implicit or explicit, of lower caste and lower scale of provision,
and its replacement by 'secondary education for all', was one of the
most significant and hopeful advances which had ever been made in

English education. Second, the abolition of fees in the secondary grammar schools held out the prospect to many more children of 'equal measured ability' that they might now achieve an education which would prove more suitable to their aptitudes and attainments than that which the old senior elementary school could offer.

It should not, unfortunately, be too readily assumed that this abolition immediately provided them everywhere in the country with an equal chance of attaining that education, owing to the wide differences between one area and another (from 30 per cent to less than 10 per cent) in the provision of grammar school places. It was even further, of course, from offering to every child the same opportunity of developing his or her potential. In 1946 the lower manual working-class children in 20 per cent areas were getting only 52 per cent of the places that might be expected from their measured ability at 8 years. In those areas of high provision they were getting up to 72 per cent. The upper middle-class children were getting virtually the same proportion of places in relation to their ability whether they lived in areas of good or poor provision.[1]

The first ten years after the Act came into operation no doubt proved a disappointment to those who may have expected it to result immediately in a great broadening out of what, in educational jargon, is usually termed 'social mobility' or 'life opportunity'. The leeway of the war years had to be made up. Immense sources of ability were known still to lie untapped, owing to economic, social, and health factors and lack of incentives. The relative levels, social class by social class, of access to grammar schools appeared to show no dramatic change despite the liberation of the places previously occupied by fee-payers. A parallel case was the remarkable fall in the infant mortality rate: the unskilled worker group unexpectedly seemed to be little better off proportionately to the professional, clerical, and skilled worker classes than they had been before. As had so often happened in the past where some social service had been greatly expanded or improved, the first classes to benefit seemed to be those where need was less than that of others more under-privileged.

By 1953, however, a detailed examination[2] into various aspects of the relations between social class and educational opportunity in two comparable but contrasting urban localities, one in the north and the other in the south of England, did at least show that access to grammar schools on equal measured terms at 11 + regardless of social origins was being achieved.

[1] Address delivered by J. W. B. Douglas, Director of the Medical Research Council Unit at the London School of Economics, 31 December 1964.

[2] *Social Class and Educational Opportunity* (Heinemann, 1955). Jean Floud (ed.), with A. H. Halsey and F. M. Martin.

The second decade has witnessed some marked changes in the direction of equal opportunity for youth of all social origins. In the first place the country has seen what has aptly been described as 'the Mums' revolution'—that remarkable increase which has taken place in parental aspirations for their children. This is spread over the older 'mums' as well as the younger ones and no doubt derives much of its strength from the fact that we are now in the fourth generation of public education. The broadly educational influence of wireless and television programmes, and the gradual seeping downwards of the realization that our third industrial revolution is going to call for a much greater supply of skilled and responsible manpower, have also been at work. A further factor has been the gradual transformation and reorientation of so many of our secondary modern schools. In the early days these were too often thought of by parents as schools 'where they play all day', 'where the lessons are easy', 'schools for those who are good with their hands'—but offering little in the way of opportunity. The number of G.C.E. candidates from secondary modern schools multiplied by ten between 1953 (4,068) and 1960 (41,621).[1] Other factors have been the spread and the well-publicized success of comprehensive schools, which are now enabling the '11 +' examination and 'streaming' in the primary schools to be modified or dropped. Both the comprehensive and the secondary modern schools are adept at discovering courses leading to examinations which, though not so well known as the G.C.E., enjoy a national currency.

Up to the end of the first decade which followed the Act few educational thinkers were ready to believe that the pool of untapped ability was so large that we could probably double our intake to grammar schools, junior technical schools, and universities without accepting entrants of inferior quality. Yet between 1954 and 1961, although the standards of examinations have remained constant, the number of English and Welsh students with university entrance qualifications rose by 50 per cent; and if these rates of increase are maintained some 14 per cent of each annual group should qualify by 1980.

In this matter of 'social mobility' education is the handmaid of biology. Nature appears to maintain something like a 'steady state' in each occupational class by means of constant movement in and out of it. As Galton postulated in his law of regression, and as Sir Cyril Burt has shown by experiment, if one takes the mean of the I.Q.s of mothers and fathers, those of the lower means are likely to produce children with a higher I.Q. than the mean, and those parents with a higher mean are likely to produce children with a lower I.Q. For example parents with a mean I.Q. of about 84 will tend to produce children

---

[1] The new G.C.E. system, whereby examinations for one or more subjects could be taken separately, was instituted in 1951.

with an I.Q. of about 92 and parents with a mean I.Q. of 140 are likely to produce children with an I.Q. of about 120. Thus if one accepts the thesis that the stratification of occupations (e.g. professional, lower professional, clerical, skilled, semi-skilled, unskilled) is broadly paralleled by a corresponding stratification of I.Q.s (remembering, however, that I.Q. is not a static given characteristic but to some extent a developed attribute), this biological see-saw must constantly be bringing up to the brink of the grammar school stream children whose parents probably left school at 15.

It is at this point that serious difficulties may begin to crowd in upon the boy or girl from a humble home who is thus pushed forward by nature. There are many other factors which may hold them back. Provided their home is uncrowded by too many brothers and sisters, provided the parents are keen that their children should rise to occupations superior to those to which they ever aspired, and see that they receive the stimulation of talk at mealtimes and watch the best of the children's programmes on the 'telly'; provided, too, that they gain admission to a good primary school and are not thrust into the B stream on the basis of reading ability at the age of 7 or 8,[1] and are encouraged to cope with tasks which stretch them; again provided that they live in an area where the grammar school entry is above the 18 per cent average for the country, or can enter a good comprehensive school: in these favourable circumstances children of lower-paid manual workers will be just as likely to be doing grammar school work as children of the same intelligence from better homes; and at 14 their intelligence rating is likely to be seven points higher than it might have been had they passed into a secondary modern school. If some or all of these advantages are lacking the children will be less likely to reach grammar school standards.

At 16 when they have passed their 'O' levels another anxiety lies ahead. Should they proceed to their 'A' levels and possible university entry? Once accepted by a university they will be financially assisted more generously than anywhere else in the world; but, even though this country is now spending £1,300,000 a year on maintenance allowances for those who stay on at school, the maximum amount those children of even the poorest parents can receive when they are 16 and 17 is very far from equalling the wages they could command in industry or commerce. At the end of their university course, however, they will probably reward their parents' self-denial by securing a position in our stratified society very much higher than their mother and father ever dreamed of, and will enjoy a chance (rather better than

[1] J. C. Daniels (*British Journal of Educational Psychology*, February and June 1961) produced much thought-provoking material on the possible side-effects of 'streaming' in junior schools.

one in three) of marrying a wife or husband with a similar or at least a grammar school background.[1]

It is true that the after careers of some university leavers still disappoint those who expect all to reach professional or managerial posts. This was brought out clearly in the penetrating study by Jackson and Marsden of 88 working-class students in the thinly disguised town of Marburton.[2] Indeed one reviewer of their book summed up his reaction in what must surely have been the most brilliant headline since 'Hitler rattles the olive branch' of pre-war days. His review was headed 'Per ardua ad Aspidistera'! Nevertheless circumstances alter cases. Many of us can call to mind the young man or woman who on attaining a degree has preferred to seek an outlet in the service of the local community, while entering some valuable though possibly undervalued occupation, perhaps involving an inherited or traditional skill such as saddlery or thatching, because it has been in the family for 300 years.

Despite the degree to which the scales of opportunity must still seem to be weighted against the child from the poorest home,[3] the extent today of what our Victorian ancestors would no doubt have described as 'social promotion' would probably astonish many people. If one takes as a yardstick the sons of manual workers who become

[1] Those wishing to follow up this discussion can do so in the following publications.

1. 'Life Opportunity and Personality: Some consequences of stratified secondary education in Great Britain', Glen. H. Elder. *Sociology of Education*, Vol. 38, No. 3, Spring 1965.

2. 'Unequal Opportunities at School', J. W. B. Douglas. *Higher Education Journal*, Spring 1965.

3. *Home School and Work*, M. P. Carter. 1962.

4. *Culture and the Grammar School*, Harry Davies. 1965.

5. *Down Stream Failure in the Grammar School*, R. R. Dale and S. Griffith. Routledge & Kegan Paul, 1965.

6. *Social Mobility and Education: Biological Aspects of Social Problems*, edited by J. E. Meade and A. S. Parkes. Symposium held by the Eugenics Society in October 1964.

7. *The Family, Education and Society*, F. Musgrave. Routledge & Kegan Paul, 1966.

8. 'In search of an Explanation of Social Mobility'. *British Journal of Statistical Psychology*, Vol. XVI, Part I, May 1963, page 27.

[2] Brian Jackson and Denis Marsden, *Education and the Working Class* (some general themes raised by the study of eighty-eight working-class children in a northern industrial city). Routledge & Kegan Paul, 1962.

[3] The proportion of children reaching full-time higher education was at the time of the Robbins Report on Higher Education (Cmnd. 2154, 1963, pages 49–53) four times as high from families with one or two children as those where five or more children have claims on the family's resources; and the proportion is eight times as high among children whose fathers continued their own education to the age of 18 or over as among those whose fathers left school under 18.

non-manual, the proportion has been put at 35 per cent in the urban areas of France, 26–30 per cent in Germany, 44 per cent in Switzerland, 29 per cent in Sweden, 33 per cent in Japan, and 31–35 per cent in the U.S.A. Probably a survey similar to those which have been carried out in these countries would yield at least comparable results in Britain but, up to the present, only one such survey seems to have taken place.[1]

The most serious stain on the bright hopes which Parliament entertained in passing the Act of 1944 has undoubtedly been the failure hitherto to implement the 'county colleges' clauses. This must be assessed in a later chapter in the light of the expansion which has been achieved in the provision for 'day-time release' of young workers.

[1] Peter Willmott and Brian Young, *Family and Class in a London Suburb*, Routledge & Kegan Paul, 1962. By the date of the Robbins Committee over a quarter of the British university population were the sons or daughters of manual workers. In Sweden it was 14 per cent, in France 8·3 per cent, and in West Germany 5·3 per cent.

CHAPTER XVI

PRIMARY EDUCATION ON THE MOVE

Growing interest in child growth and behaviour influences the planning
of education for young children.—The country's tardy provision for
children under five.—Pioneers in this field and the important place in it
of the McMillan sisters.—A German visits an English nursery school.—
The wartime residential and day nurseries and their post-war fate.—
Characteristics of children of nursery-school age and the adaptation of
methods to fit them.—The need for an increased provision of nursery
education on a selective basis for children who have to face special
difficulties.—'Activity and experience' replaces 'knowledge to be
acquired and facts to be stored' at the primary school stage.—Little
gained and much lost in attempting to teach a child things he is not ready
to learn.—Streaming.—The pitfalls of syllabus religious instruction at
the primary ages.—The importance of play.—Children see things differently from adults.—The fallibility of intelligence testing.—Discipline.

THE history of the infant and junior elementary schools from 1935 to
1944 and of primary education in England and Wales between 1944
and 1965 is that of a steady and increasingly successful attempt to improve upon traditional methods by synthesizing a growing volume of
knowledge of child growth and behaviour into a properly conceived
educational plan.

In the gradual building up of this synthesis there have been three
main phases. The first has been the correlation of the experience and
adventurous practice of enlightened observers, and of those with an
instinctive understanding of child psychology in the teaching profession, with the knowledge accumulated by psychiatrists, psychologists, and social workers in the child guidance clinics, children's wards
in hospitals, children's homes, residential nurseries, and orphanages.
The second phase has been the slow process of demonstration by
measurable facts, gathered under objective conditions by psychological
and educational research teams and aided by the departments of child
development in several of the universities, that—in the words of Dr
Gesell, the noted American psychologist—'The findings of modern
science have confirmed the verdict of common sense.' The third phase
has been the dissemination of proved theses, and their practical application by the colleges of education in the case of intending teachers
and by H.M.I.s and others conducting refresher courses for serving
teachers.

As Sir George Newman, the first Chief Medical Officer of the Ministry of Health and the Board of Education, once wrote in his great series of reports on 'The Health of the School Child': 'The child under five stands at the gateway of our educational system. What happens to him before he is five is bound inevitably to have results for good or evil.' Much the same thought was expressed by Bishop Stopford Brook when he said, 'The world moves forward on the feet of little children.' It should surely therefore be sound national economy to safeguard potential human wealth and prevent the serious consequences of human neglect by ensuring that those little children are well shod to face the roughness of life's highway.

It may therefore be appropriate to commence this chapter by taking a look at the country's all too tardy provision for her 'under fives'.

To anyone who examines the statistics of the School population in 1895 and compares them with those for 1965 it will probably come as a surprise to find that the number of children aged two, three, and four in the schools of 1895 was 634,785—nearly three times the present number. Contemporary students of comparative education in those days saw in our infant schools England's most distinctive contribution to educational science. There can be little doubt that this was due to the substantial proportion of sound natural observers of child psychology among our infant teachers of those days. These 'natural psychologists' may not have been highly trained teachers in the modern sense; but in their daily contact with the children some of them would probably look back to the work and writings of eighteenth- and nineteenth-century idealists of the stamp of Robert Owen and David Stow, who preached the doctrine that education must be grounded on the sound basis of social training, drawing upon the desire of the young child for activity. They had no doubt, too, been influenced by Froebel's philosophy of 'self activity', kindergartens, and the importance of play. Indeed there must still be many elderly people alive who can recall the mats which as infants they so laboriously wove from strips of coloured paper, or how they learnt to fold a paper square into the shape of a pig. They may even regret that they no longer remember the foldings required for the more complicated paper box, in which water used to sizzle so excitingly without the paper catching alight when it was held on a poker over the schoolroom fire!

John Dewey did much to unfreeze the rather formal pattern and practices into which the kindergarten routine eventually tended to solidify. Dr Montessori, too, in the early days of the century stated her conviction that the child would grow spontaneously through 'auto education', driven on by forces arising within himself if supplied with material suited to his developmental needs. 'We must', she used to say, 'liberate the child.' But it is to the views and insight of Margaret

McMillan and their practical application by Margaret (the seer) and her sister Rachel (the doer) in their shoestring Lamborene, the Open Air Nursery School at Deptford opened in 1914, that the English nursery school system owes its real genesis, lasting success, and revolutionary influence. For the ideas and principles pioneered by the McMillan sisters, and later developed by others, percolated first into the infant schools and later into the junior schools; and it is these ideas and principles which have been largely responsible for the transformation which the education of young children has undergone since the First World War.

In the parliamentary debates of 1944 Margaret McMillan was described with some justice as 'the greatest educationist this country ever produced'. It was said also in those same debates that 'What Margaret McMillan proved to the few, war experience has proved to the country'. Now that her life has been fully documented it is clear that she was by no means merely a passionate advocate of good social causes who was goaded into white-hot action by the appalling conditions affecting the plentiful but unprized toddlers[1] in the slums of our northern cities and the east and south-east areas of London. It is true that her origins were humble, her initial opportunities for education restricted. Nevertheless she possessed a remarkably alert brain and she had an uncanny knack of seizing upon the one thing which was both urgent and practicable in the current social scene. Moreover, she achieved her entry to the Hall of Fame not, as so many others did in those days, by the door marked PUSH, still less by that marked PULL. She entered it by the door marked SERVICE. Sir Cyril Burt, England's leading child psychologist of her day, who knew her well, has said of her: 'She somehow managed to integrate in a kind of synoptic vision a practical synthesis of child psychology, child medicine and child training in an inspired educational plan.' This achievement must appear the more remarkable to anyone who appreciates how few books on the social and emotional development of the child can have been available to her before she wrote her *Early Childhood* (1912), *The Nursery School* (1919), and *Education through the Imagination* (1923). Fortunately she was fluent in both German and French and had mastered Rousseau, Pestalozzi, and Froebel, the works of neurologists like Donaldson and Lombroso and of psychologists like Mosso and Claporede, and, though not an exact scientist, was familiar with almost every scientific textbook on mental deficiency from Seguin onwards.

It was in fact from Seguin that both she and Dr Montessori got the principle of the 'form board' which both used in connection with some

---

[1] The word toddlers is used advisedly, for so many of them were bow-legged as a result of rickets, or their shoes—if they had any—did not fit. The word would rarely apply to nursery school children of today.

of their apparatus. There, however, the similarity ceased. For whereas in the hands of nursery staffs the Montessori apparatus too readily tended to become teacher-dispensed and directed, in the McMillan nursery schools the function of the good teacher can be summed up in the phrase 'skilled non-intervention'. Unskilled non-intervention is, of course, a very different matter. To let a child do as he likes without regard for persons and property may very readily result in chaos and unhappiness. Independence must be socially directed. Children must be surrounded with love but allowed to *be*, to live as fully as they can at each stage of development.

The following extract from an article written by a well-known German woman journalist, Brigitte Beer, after a visit to an English nursery school, goes to the heart of the matter. 'A marked difference in principle as compared with the German Kindergarten is noticeable at this point, namely that the initiative in every matter is made to rest upon the children themselves. The commencement of a combined game, a story telling period, a singing period will be at the suggestion of the children; and, even so, merely for those children who combine together to ask for it. The rest of the group are allowed to continue their play occupations quietly without interruption in the room or playground. Without doubt one sees here the beginning of that training in self sufficiency and independence, though certainly not without proper consideration for the feelings of others, which permeates the air of England and renders it so pleasant to breathe.'

Between March 1914, when the Deptford Open Air Nursery School opened, and Margaret McMillan's death in 1931 the nursery school movement gathered momentum slowly. Between 1931 and 1939 it went ahead more rapidly, and by September 1939 114 nursery schools had been opened (58 by L.E.A.s and 56 by voluntary bodies), with 10,000 children on their rolls, although the average attendance would be considerably lower.

As we have seen in Chapter XII, most of these were moved into the country under the Government Evacuation Scheme and became residential nurseries. By the end of the war the number of such residential nurseries had increased to over 400, with 14,000 beds for children under five who had become without parental care in the evacuation areas. Every effort was made to provide each of these nurseries, which were, of course, staffed by trained nurses and large numbers of nursery helpers, with a teacher or teachers trained in pre-war nursery school ideas. Simultaneously the Ministry of Health set on foot a campaign to persuade the Maternity and Child Welfare authorities to open day nurseries for the children under five of women war-workers, and by September 1944 nearly 1,000 such nurseries had been opened with places for 71,806 children.

It seems probable that when the 1944 archives become available to historians they will disclose that the branch of the Board of Education concerned with the development of nursery schools put in a strong plea that the promised Bill should impose a duty on the L.E.A.s in considering the needs of their areas to make generous provision for such schools. If any such plea was in fact put forward it fell on deaf ears. No doubt it was thought that the L.E.A.s would not accept any such clause, and the wording of the Bill was watered down to render the provision of nursery schools permissive rather than obligatory. The result has been the inevitable game of 'Snakes and Ladders', with four successive Governments careful to pay lip service to the nursery school but equally careful to check its expansion.

At the time of writing (1966) new nursery schools can be provided only if they satisfy a tortuous formula designed to bring back married teachers into service. Nevertheless the 1944 Education Act did at least ensure that the existing nursery schools should remain alive after the end of the war and possibly be added to if and when economic conditions and the supply of teachers improved.

The fate of the 1,000 wartime day nurseries was far otherwise. As soon as possible after the end of the war the Ministry of Health withdrew their 100 per cent grant and, by administrative action, set about reducing their number drastically. As the Ministry were to lose to the Home Office their responsibility for 'Poor Law children' and might, on that account, have been expected to concern themselves more sedulously with their continuing responsibility for children under five, their action seems difficult to understand. As mentioned earlier, however, they had always since their Local Government Board days considered it their function to live up to the dictum attributed to one of their former Permanent Secretaries that 'Money saved is always better than money expended whatever the circumstances'. In the difficult financial circumstances of the immediate post-war years the Poor Law mentality found little difficulty in reasserting itself and the number of day nurseries was soon brought down to 455 with 21,000 places, at all of which fully economic charges were levelled on the parents. Inevitably one is reminded of the lines of Clough:

> Thou shall not kill but needst not strive
> Officiously to keep alive.

Although about 227 of these former wartime nurseries were taken over eventually by L.E.A.s, and became nursery schools, in the year 1948 less than 5 per cent[1] of the child population aged between two and five were able to attend a nursery school or class.

---

[1] 20,722, i.e. 1·03 per cent in nursery schools; 70,985, i.e. 3·55 per cent in nursery classes.

In the original White Paper on Educational Reconstruction after the war which, substantially, formed the basis for the Education Act of 1944, it was clearly recognized that the gap between the upper limit of effective provision by the Maternity and Child Welfare authorities (about one year of age) and the lower limit of provision by L.E.A.s (five years) must be bridged. To secure this it was suggested that the responsibilities of L.E.A.s should be extended downward to include all children from, say, the age of two. To the social historian it is one of the saddest 'might have beens' that this suggestion became sidetracked in the flood of legislation which ushered in the welfare state.

For in viewing the situation today (1966) one is inevitably reminded of the words used by Lord Goschen before the creation of the county councils by the Act of 1888: 'There is a chaos as regards Authorities, a chaos as regards rates and a worse chaos than all as regards areas of taxation.' There were in 1964 22,678 children attending full-time in maintained, direct grant, and independent nursery schools; a further 8,712 attending part-time; and 13,500 in Ministry of Health day nurseries. If to this total one adds the children under five attending independent and 'all age' primary schools (11,265), maintained primary schools (67,333), registered private day nurseries (25,000), or being looked after by registered child-minders (15,000), the sum total (163,488) still represents a mere 7·7 per cent of the 2,001,000 children between two and five to which the 'population explosion' had raised the number in these age-groups since 1948.

The 'chaos' consists in the multiplicity of actual or virtually inoperative authorities responsible for this group. Those in the nursery schools proper are the responsibility of the L.E.A.s and the Department of Education and Science; those in the day nurseries, the private nursery schools, and in the care of the child-minders are the responsibility of the Ministry of Health. The rapidly expanding 'play groups' are sponsored by voluntary organizations such as the Save the Children Fund and the Pre-school Play Groups Association. A small band of enthusiasts keep them viable, but grants from the local authorities are spasmodic and regular income an ideal seldom attained. As regards responsibility the Ministry of Health appears to stand on the sidelines.[1]

Owing to the length of the waiting lists which have built up few parents can hope to secure admission to a nursery school for their child much before he is three and a half. By this age he should have passed out of the first stage of life, that of biological unity with his mother, and the second, that of close and unbroken contact with her in which she may not be so much loved as 'needed', into the third, where he is able to reach out to new people; although wise nursery school superintendents encourage the mother to play an active part in the process of

[1] See Ministry of Health Circular No. 56/5.

'In the country areas courses based on rural science render those schools among the happiest and most pleasant to visit.' Rural science in a Wiltshire school, 1962

'Every day is full of new experiences.' 1953

'School journeys reach out from the north of Scotland to the south of France.' The London Schools Symphony Orchestra performing in Rotterdam, 1954

weaning from home to school. He will have reached the stage of independent movement; he will have some speech, some degree of toilet training; the ability to eat without much help; some capacity for orientation to new surroundings; although still largely egocentric, he will have begun to accept and enjoy playmates and the ability to use toys with some degree of skill or imagination or both.

By the time he is passed on to the infant school he will no longer be content to enjoy the noise he makes knocking pegs into a perforated board with a child-sized mallet or pushing down his own (or another child's) pile of bricks. He will be asking for nails to knock in and wood to saw. Moreover, the steam-roller he makes with two cotton reels, a couple of match boxes, and a bit of wire will probably remain in his memory as the most 'real' steam-roller in his life. His shop-play will be moving out from the few minutes of 'make believe' with a chair serving as counter and anything as goods and money. He will have come near to genuinely setting up shop and playing at buying and selling, even demanding cardboard money, scales, weights, and a tape measure to make his imitation of the adult world more real, although exact measurement, the giving of change and persistence in the game for more than say half an hour will still be in the future. The give and take of group play—which may have begun with the tea set—will be coming more naturally to him, although some slight indisposition or disappointment may still cause him to throw back to an earlier and more infantile level of behaviour.

The experienced nursery school staff know only too well that it is unwise to attempt to make children share things and play together before they have emerged from egocentricity; and that continuous anti-social behaviour—sometimes even experienced in the overbright child who is merely bored—is best met by isolating him from the group. It must, however, always be isolation with occupation. 'Stand in the corner', like the 'dunce's cap', has vanished as completely as the Dodo. He will be talking readily; greatly interested in such things as motor cars and aeroplanes; bursting to relate new experiences. He will be asking innumerable questions some of which may be disconcertingly original—'Oo looked after them sheep Miss when the shepherds went down to Beflehem?' 'Oh I expect the angels did Tommy.' 'Ow did they get there?' Jimmy: 'I spect they crash landed Miss?' Moreover, he will be displaying an almost psychic capacity for detecting whether his questions are answered faithfully and truthfully. The attempt to answer a child's questions faithfully while saying no more than the child's age and comprehension can assimilate sometimes produces a reaction as delightful as it is unexpected. One of the most charming recent instances of this was the little girl who kept on saying that everyone would tell her where she came from but nobody would tell her how she began. At last the teacher told her, quite naturally and without emphasis, that before she began her father had to plant a little seed. The child's face became radiant: 'How wonderful, how lovely! Was my picture on the packet?'

The child's life in the nursery school will have been a rhythm of activity and repose; of play periods of purposeful activity guided unobtrusively into the right channels by an observant and self-effacing staff who will have encouraged him to do for himself everything he appears ready to move on to; of quiet times for informal conversation, stories, a simple thanksgiving. Such abstract conceptions as unselfishness, truthfulness, kindliness, and constancy will still be beyond him, but he will have assimilated all those qualities from a staff to whom in a good nursery school they should be second nature.

Although the 'simple thanksgiving' at the 'morning circle' is a feature in most nursery schools, some experienced observers believe that it is extremely difficult for the young child, unless exceptional, to conceive of God beyond grasping that 'God is Love'; and that the attempt to teach religion to them, as it used to be thought possible to do, may merely tend to evoke the kind of reaction so well illustrated by the small girl who was found reflectively muttering 'Fiddling business for God making fleas'; or that of the little boy who asked 'If you polished a piece of hilver [he was only four and still had difficulty with his S's] for a hundred hundred years would it be as bright as God's face?'

All responsible educational opinion today appears to be agreed that the child who has been lucky enough to attend a nursery school has a better than average chance, by the time he is ready to pass on to the next stage, of being stable and well adjusted in his emotional life and outlook. He will certainly have a far better understanding of his small world and the place he occupies in it as an individual than if he had remained at home, perhaps in a sixth storey flat or accompanying his mother 'window-shopping', with his personal vision bounded by damp umbrellas and skirted or trousered legs. Unfortunately the fact has to be faced that, at £135 per head annually, nursery school education is nearly as expensive as post-G.C.E. 'O' level secondary education (although if a child becomes maladjusted who might have been saved by nursery school education, he will cost far more ultimately). Moreover, while the secondary age-groups are staying longer and longer at school the supply of trained nursery school teachers will probably never be sufficient to expand the service as a wise ordering of society would postulate.

Nevertheless, harking back to the words of Sir George Newman quoted at the commencement of this chapter, an increasing number of magistrates, psychiatrists, psychologists, marriage guidance councillors, social workers, and responsible head teachers are beginning to glance backwards to the 1890s. If we still had the same proportion of our under-fives in school as we had in those days, but under the care of the much more highly trained teachers of today employing modern nursery school techniques, might we not be saving a substantial part of the great sums which the nation has to bear today for mental ill-health, delinquency, legal aid in the matrimonial courts, and the care of children of broken marriages? For today over 46 per cent of all hospital beds are occupied by mental patients and in the opinion of psychiatrists the genesis of 80–90 per cent of these cases lay in the pre-school years. Again, legal aid for those appearing before the matrimonial courts is costing more than £1,000,000 a year and delinquency and the care of children from broken homes many millions. To quote the very wise words of the panel of H.M.I.s to the Advisory Council on Education in Scotland in 1946: 'The nurture of the nursery school is of special value to children living in industrial areas, in flats and houses without gardens, in homes where the mother is delicate, where only one parent is alive, where the relationship between the parents is an unhappy one, where the mother is overwhelmed with domestic duties or has to go out to work or is desirous of practising her profession. Such and similar conditions are not likely to decrease in the post-war years and will intensify the need for nursery schools.' Might not a selective extension of nursery schools to cover these and similar categories go some way to reduce the population of our mental hospitals, our homes for children deprived of parental care, and even our prisons?

The primary schools

By 1935 it had begun to appear to a few observers, and by the end of the war to many, that the time was ripe for a thorough overhaul of the traditional and formal system of primary education as it had developed hitherto.

While the war spread its dark mantle over educational experiment, or, perhaps more accurately, over its dissemination, the Government Evacuation Scheme, as we have seen in Chapter XIII, produced lessons which were not lost on alert teachers. In the reception areas, despite all the difficulties of accommodation and frustrations arising from deficiencies of equipment, perhaps indeed as a result of the determination of adventurous teachers to surmount those difficulties, schemes and activities of obvious value had been planned and carried out with infant and junior children. In particular it became obvious to a number of inspectors and teachers that the content of the children's free compositions was so much more real and original than before that the gain clearly outweighed the loss. In the evacuation areas themselves, in the period during which the schools remained closed, many of the small groups of ten or twelve children who had been assembled in different parents' homes were found to have established a daily routine despite having to work without the help of a teacher for some part of each day. Tasks had been set based on the individual child's own interest and rate of progress, and teachers had been astonished to find how well the work went forward. When the schools reopened a subtle change seemed to have spread over the whole teacher–child–parent relationship, and it was seen that the more formal attitudes of the past could be discarded and the work habits of the era of home groups preserved. It was realized that education might be better and more effective if organized to facilitate self-learning.

Obviously the old conception of 'knowledge to be acquired and facts to be stored' must be looked at again. While it ruled educational thought it was too easy for the tidy-minded administrator to sit back and think of the primary school as so many children divided into more or less equal classes in neat rows at standard-pattern desks in classrooms painted in dark green or mud-coloured paint; each class in charge of a teacher who was a unit interchangeable at will with any other teacher. By the end of the war all schools would be overdue for a repaint and much school furniture would be superannuated. Might not bright colours bring some sunlight into school life; and might not the new tubular stackable furniture (already provided by some of the more advanced L.E.A.s) enable classrooms to be cleared for various activities? It might, of course, be many years before the staffs of primary schools could become balanced and specialized teams, with the more psychologically mature members of such staffs in charge of the youngest children, but this was obviously a goal at which to aim.

Already some years before the war adventurous teachers had been beginning to experiment, first in the infant schools, with the ideas which had been proved in the nursery schools. Gradually these ideas and the practical application of them to children of different age-groups extended upwards into the junior schools. It is, however, extraordinarily difficult to assess what proportion of the schools of any particular type had changed over completely to orienting the whole of their work in terms of 'activity and experience'.

During these same years the 'new psychology', as exemplified by Sigmund Freud and his daughter Anna, Jung, Adler, Gesell, Karl and Charlotte Bühler, Susan Isaacs, Schonell, and many others, and confirmatory evidence from paediatricians of the stamp of Dr John Bowlby, was beginning to percolate widely in educational circles and the university departments of child development. At first it had perhaps been regarded rather quizzically by an educational world brought up on the old 'instinct psychology', the theory of faculty training, and those charming studies which, for example, explained 'play' as a necessary preparation for life through recapitulation of racial experience in children and fox cubs, but unnecessary in those sections of the world of nature which emerges fully fledged and capable of escape from their enemies. But Dr Gesell's remark that 'the findings of modern science have confirmed the verdict of common sense' was at once an invitation and a challenge to the educational world to translate those findings from the cautious and scientific language of psychology into terms which could be 'understanded of the people', however much they might lose in precision in the process.

Let us look at some of them and at some of the ways in which they have affected or been translated into practice in the primary schools.

The Advisory Council on Education in Scotland said in their fascinating report of 1946 on primary education: 'These seven years are among the most vivid of our existence. Every day is full of new experiences; the relatively static seems permanent; time seems to last much longer; events and individuals leave deeper impressions and more lasting memories than in later life.' It is during the earliest years that the art of living with people is cultivated with the least effort. It therefore becomes a pre-eminent task of the good primary school to help every child to develop his own personality as a member of a group and achieve self-discipline by sharing with children of his own age and by learning to co-operate with adults, whether those adults are his teachers, his parents or, in some homes, that important individual, 'big sister'. This unfolding of personality will obviously occur more satisfactorily where the school provides an environment as rich in opportunity for varied occupation and interest as possible; and where the teachers regard their function as giving unobtrusive guidance to lead the child step by step from one challenge and achievement to the next rather than imposing any artificial pattern by their own personality. As few orders as possible will be given, but the individual child must always be expected to remember and respect the needs of the greater number, and rules of safety and of health must be obeyed without question. These childhood years cannot come again. Fun and laughter, a sense of wonder, and a sense of security derived from the loving understanding of adults are as necessary as food and sunshine to the growing child.

Because every day is full of new experiences the enquiring minds of primary age children are constantly agog to relate the excitement of those experiences to their teachers and other children. The traditional pattern of rows of children sitting silently listening to the teacher's voice will have little place in the modern primary school. Although as they get older primary children must clearly be expected to spend an increasing proportion of the school day quietly cutting their teeth on the hard subjects, the good primary school will go to great lengths to afford them the opportunity of talk and movement whenever the activity on which they are concentrating allows. To draw out knowledge, creativity, and powers of speech is education. Chalk and talk by the teacher may be one of the essential vitamins of education, but only in so far as it vivifies and supplements the children's own actions.

Fortunately the craft, art, physical education, and other practical activities which now occupy such a prominent place in the primary school curriculum allow abundant opportunities for real education in this respect. A middle-aged German teacher was asked in 1951, in one of the primary schools of the British Families Education Service in Germany: 'Do you find much difference between this school and those you have worked in before?' 'Oh yes, very much so indeed,' he replied in a shocked voice: 'Why in this school the children are actually allowed to talk and sometimes they even laugh!' Perhaps, however, he belonged to a tradition which was already on the way out. For the very erudite young German teachers who by that date were being given the opportunity to attend the holiday courses for British teachers conducted by H.M.Is, and may by this time be head teachers themselves, were very ready to say, 'We cannot imagine what our headmaster would say if we tried to put your ideas and methods into practice when we get back to our own school, but we are convinced that they are absolutely right!'

All modern research points to the conclusion that to attempt to foreshorten the educational process by attempting to teach a child things that he is not really ready to learn is a waste of energy for both the child and the teacher; and that in the long run little is gained and much lost by doing so. The experienced primary teacher of today is not so much surprised as shocked when he reads, for example, that Thomas Arnold of Rugby presented his son Matthew Arnold with Gibbon's *Decline and Fall of the Roman Empire* in eight volumes for proficiency in reading at the age of two. He is aware that quite a number of the more highly gifted children could be taught to read, much as a puppy can be taught tricks, by constant repetition, at an age when their natural development should find them acquiring and enjoying much more appropriate skills and experiences. He knows, however, that such tricks are really, by the drill involved, absorbing time which could be much more profitably employed in the all-round development of the complete child; and that a child who has been encouraged to follow his successive interests until he has passed through each and on to a more difficult one will quite naturally, if presented with the appropriate stimuli, want to start mastering the skills of reading, writing and arithmetic when he is ready for them. Some observers, it should be noted, doubt if there are many children who can pass from the more elementary concepts of number to arithmetic proper before they are seven or eight years of age. Unwise insistence on mastering the rules of arithmetic before children are ready for them may well account for the unpopularity of the subject. An extensive inquiry made some years ago disclosed that it was the most unpopular subject with 40 per cent of the children questioned.

To anyone who has even a limited acquaintance with the volume and ramifications of modern biochemical and endocrinological research it will be obvious that no two children could possibly be identical any more than their fingerprints could be. Glandular functioning, the mixture of the genes at conception, and the influence of environment combine to present an infinite series of differences. These are bound to produce a wide variation in the time and intensity of different children's 'sensitive periods' of mental and physical growth. It follows that the kind of generalization so common in earlier writings on education, which began 'All children of such and such an age should etc.', has largely and very properly been abandoned. The modern educator will be very chary about suggesting the age at which particular skills should be established, still less about the intelligence of individual children. His ideal—however seldom he can hope to attain it while primary classes remain so large—will be that the uniqueness of the personality of every child should be preserved and that each should be presented with suitable challenges and experiences at the precise moment he is seen to be ready for them.

Moreover, this ebb and flow of the sensitive periods would appear to reinforce the objection felt by many teachers to attempting to divide primary schools into fast and slow streams. In the kind of group activities and projects, e.g. constructing a zoo, now so common in the best primary schools the teacher who knows her class can normally divide up the tasks in such a way as to give those children who are, for the time being, the brightest the more difficult jobs to do, while distributing the easier ones among those children who are, perhaps temporarily, passing through a less alert phase.

Even before the '11 +' reckoning children are probably much more sensitive to the estimation in which they are held by the adult world than is generally realized. The child who feels that he has been labelled 'B stream' may well react by finding the intelligence to defeat the most skilful of teachers! Correspondingly a child in the unstreamed primary school whose confidence has been built up into a firm belief that he can do a job stands a much better chance of achieving it than the child of twice the ability who distrusts his powers.

Actually, of course, the division of the primary school curriculum into subjects—mathematics, science, art, craft, music, etc.—however convenient and indeed necessary it may be from the adult point of view to make sure that every quarter of the field is explored, does not bear much relation to the vision of the child. For the child of primary age there is really only one subject, the world in which he lives: a world expanding with every day's experience. The good primary school recognizes that, for example, the construction of a puppet theatre can be made to involve *inter alia* measurement, craft, art, speech, music, mime, composition, and the elements of history.

A sense of history, as understood by the adult, is normally a matter of slow growth in the minds of children of primary age. Their minds have as much as they can absorb in the expanding world of their present adventures. Anyone who examines the earliest of the Agreed Syllabuses of Religious Instruction and follows their modification through successive revisions will detect the gradually widening appreciation of the need for a psychological approach which recognizes this difficulty. The success of one new kind of syllabus was mentioned in a report of the Research Committee of the Institute of Christian Education in 1957: 'The Durham syllabus sets the example of beginning with the story of the Church in the neighbourhood. Several others have followed and have devoted a large amount of space to it. In most places the parish church may offer a starting point, however modest the building and its contents in contrast to the great cathedral or other monument of faith, worship and service. Developed as an aspect of local studies, which it really is, or used in "teaching history backwards", this obviously has value.'

The pitfalls of attempting to follow a syllabus of Religious Instruction based on teaching from the Bible as distinct from teaching the moral lessons of the Bible will be familiar to all junior teachers. The story of the small boy who was told to illustrate a lesson on 'the flight into Egypt' and drew an aeroplane with a pilot appropriately labelled PONTIUS may well be apocryphal. That of another boy who was found carefully inserting a small black dot behind the donkey and, when asked what it represented, replied that it was the '*flea*' because the Bible said 'Take the mother and the young child and *flee* into Egypt'—is perfectly true. So is that of the other small boy who, told to illustrate a lesson on Abraham and Sarah, included a row of flower pots outside the tent which he explained were for 'the seed of Abraham'.

The value of full and rich play usually passing from sand and water play through building play, on to drawing and painting, shop play or play concentrating on other centres of interest, the construction of a zoo, the making and dressing of puppets for a puppet theatre, the local harbour, the medieval village and so on is today accepted almost universally. It is recognized as an essential element not only in intellectual growth but, equally important, in imaginative and emotional growth. The intellectual development of a child whose need for play is inhibited may be delayed, his emotional energy absorbed, and his creativity dammed. The child who has nothing to play with develops neither manually nor mentally. Similarly a child who receives no mental stimulus at home tends to remain infantile and the child who hears little or no human speech might remain dumb. Those who were brought up on Kipling's *Jungle Books* will now realize that the capacity for human speech of their beloved Mowgli would probably have atrophied completely long before he returned to the world of men —a fact that has unhappily been established in the case of the few genuine Romulus and Remus children who have been rescued.

Moreover, children see things differently from adults. As Marion Richardson, whose work as an art inspector of the London County Council opened up such new vistas for children's art, used to say, 'Art is bound up with the child's existence'; but it is not adult art, for they see things according to their interests. This is well illustrated by the following phonetic composition: 'My cat Smut is a cleva cat at home: he has four legs: wen he runs on top of the wall he has mor legs: wen he runs fast he has so meni legs i can not cownt: how he makes his legs like this i do not kno i cud tell you lotsa bout smut but not his legs: its a misteri.' (This is incidentally a good illustration of the break-away from the set compositions and formal exercises in grammar and punctuation which wore out so many red pencils and stulti-fied the capacity for lively composition of so many children in the past.)

In the early days of intelligence-testing, which in the early 1920s was usually by the Binet-Simon method and applied to mentally retarded children, it used to be too readily assumed that science had provided the educational world with a tool capable of determining once for all the probable capacity of a child for education. The extremes to which this assumption led are well illustrated by the case of the young and en-thusiastic American teacher who taught her class for a whole term by reference to the intelligence quotients which she had copied from a list on the school superintendent's desk, only to find, at the end of the term, that they were in fact the children's locker numbers!

With the development of alternative systems of testing and their in-creasingly widespread use it was soon realized that the range and differing varieties of intellectual capacity were much wider than had hitherto been supposed. Moreover, rifts began to appear in what had seemed to be a neat and foolproof pattern. For example children who had been notified to the Local Control Authority as ineducable, some-times before the age of five, were discovered to possess quite respectable intelligence ratings after a few years away from their homes, where they had probably heard little speech and enjoyed little or no mental stimulation. Today it is widely recognized that operational intelligence, as disclosed by such tests in educational attainment and in everyday living, tends to improve in childhood and adolescence in relation to such factors as parental encouragement, the quality of the educational stimulus given, and other characteristics of the child's environment. Determination in a child to achieve something he really wants to do can also be a potent factor.

Finally we should consider the question which the world of education has become increasingly concerned in recent years to ask itself: whether greater freedom and the relaxation of the older traditions of discipline in the primary schools can be held to bear any responsibility for the much-publicized problem of lawlessness in teenage youth. Can it be justly claimed, for example, that the proliferation of material, the free use of which by the child of primary age in school hours is such an important factor in the process of challenge and achievement, may have stimulated children to 'acquire' such materials for their activities outside school hours. If so does 'open display' in shops put too great temptations in their way?

Most teachers would probably reply that, so far as the life of children in school is concerned, interest has been proved to be the best disciplinarian. Many, however, would probably add that the task of inculcating respect for the sanctity of property in the children of a limited number of the parents with whom they have to deal has become more difficult than it used to be before the war. Nevertheless they would point to the very small proportion in each age-group among boys, and the almost negligible proportion of each age-group among girls who ever get into trouble with the police. Some might suggest that if the country could do more to stabilize the emotional development of its 'under fives' there might be a corresponding decline in the statistics of juvenile delinquency.

Modern psychology introduces the temptation to explain aggressiveness and destructiveness in the post-school years as the result of failure to sublimate and socialize the feelings of aggression and destruction which many experience as children. There is indeed a school of psychological thought which holds that the modern child is too well protected, owing to such factors as the decline in the size of families, restrictions on free movement due to increased road traffic and high tenement blocks, or repression by parents who have moved to a new housing area and are concerned with what the neighbours will think. Factors such as these, they argue, too often combine to inhibit the young child from exploring feelings of danger, aggression, destruction, and anger and learning to surmount them while his muscles are undeveloped. Unless he has lived through them as a child, it is suggested, they may lie submerged and burst out again in his teens. Or it may be that if he finds the local community incomprehensible and indifferent to him as a person he is likely to grow up imagining it is hostile.

A recent visitor to Great Britain, Dr Donald Hornung, one of President Johnson's special assistants, remarked on leaving that he had been particularly impressed by the experimentation in education which he had seen in England. Whereas on the Continent a variety of things were being considered, more was being done in this country. Although what he had seen was probably mainly in the sphere of science and technology his remark would probably apply with equal or even greater force to that of primary education. The ferment of ideas based on 'measurable facts gathered under objective conditions' is annually sweeping away more and more of the formal curricula of the past, with remarkably successful results in increasing the pace of learning (which will be considered in the next chapter). Experiment is being made with totally new practices such as the new mathematics, the initial teaching alphabet, and, where there are teachers well qualified both as linguists and in methods suited to the teaching of junior children, the teaching of French.

The design of our new primary school buildings since the war has also deservedly won an international reputation, although very heavy expenditure is still needed to replace those nineteenth-century relics in the crowded hearts of many of our industrial towns and in country districts.

The attempt made in this chapter to show the gradual development of thought up to 1965 in relation to the education of young children was written in its entirety before the publication in January 1967 of the massive 556-page report of the Central Advisory Council Committee for England, 'Children and their Primary Schools', the Plowden Report. That report, with the one still awaited from the Welsh council, will set the course of primary education in the country for a generation as surely as the report of the Robbins Committee on Higher Education has done so for university and further education; but at the date when this historical study covering the years 1935 to 1965 must go to the printer its recommendations are still substantially at the stage of consideration by the Government and the L.E.A.s. Moreover, so many excellent summaries of its contents have appeared in the national and the educational press that a further effort to outline them here would be a work of supererogation. Everyone who has the interests of public education at heart will wish that the advice of Lady Plowden and her colleagues may be translated into effective action as quickly as that of Lord Robbins.

CHAPTER XVII

SECONDARY EDUCATION 1935–1965

The 'Butler Act' frees all forms of public secondary education and raises the age of compulsion to attend school to 15 from 1 April 1947.—The achievements of the tripartite division of secondary education prior to 1944.—The new prospect and challenge which faced the former senior elementary schools as a result of the 1944 Act.—Their remarkable response.—A rapid decline in the number of 'all age' schools.—The intrusion of a demand by parents and employers for an examination for secondary modern schools.—Misgivings over the validity of selection procedures at 11+.—The evils of coaching for the 11+ examinations. —The palliative suggested by the Spens Report.—Changes in the social and occupational structure of Britain in the 1950s as compared with earlier decades.—Factors in the widespread experimentation in secondary school reorganization.—The lead given by Anglesey and the Isle of Wight to the rural areas and by London to the urban areas.—The debate about comprehensive schools: arguments in favour and against.— The remarkable growth of sixth-form work in the secondary schools.— The steady improvement in the scores of children and pupils submitted to the periodic 'standards of reading' tests conducted by H.M.I.s.

FUTURE historians in dealing with the expansion of public education in England and Wales will probably single out four salient features of these three decades so far as the sphere of secondary education is concerned.

(1) The growth and achievements of the system of secondary modern schools which replaced the senior elementary schools and the 'all age' schools following the Education Act of 1944.

(2) The growing awareness of the fallibility of selective procedures, leading to progressive questioning of the tripartite division of schools into secondary grammar, secondary technical, and secondary modern, and the widespread experiments in new types of secondary school organization to free the junior schools from the shadow of the 11+ examination and provide a greater wealth of choice in the curriculum of all secondary schools.

(3) The remarkable growth of sixth-form work in the secondary schools and its by-product, the '18+ problem'.

(4) The evidence of steady progress in the pace of learning and standards of reading and arithmetic.

Mr Butler's Education Act for the first time in English educational history conferred on every child the right to a free secondary education. In this England, war-torn as she was at the time, was in many respects in advance of other countries. France, however, has subsequently raised the school-leaving age to 16 and the United States has for many years retained its school population (for the most part) at school till 16 or 17.

With the passage of the Act the situation in which a certain proportion of the nation's children were selected for state grammar school education not on the basis of their ability but because their parents were able to pay fees irrevocably disappeared. As we have seen, these fees were an illogical anachronism and often represented only a small fraction of the cost to the British ratepayer and taxpayer. It should be noted, however, that the relative proportions of fee-payers to others had been falling for some years. In 1938 the majority (53 per cent) of pupils were being educated free, 16 per cent had qualified by selection but their parents were assessed to pay something, and 31 per cent were ordinary fee-payers. The abolition of fees was also coupled with the declared intention to bring all secondary schools up to the same level as regards staffing and accommodation.

A few days after the Bill had passed through its committee stages in the House of Commons, but before it went to the House of Lords, Mr Chuter Ede underlined this point publicly. 'I can find in the Bill only one form of school for senior pupils and that is the Secondary school. Clause 34 of the Bill is the "Block Buster" that reduces to ruins the old structure.' This was in direct opposition to the thesis so long prevalent among the self-styled economists in Britain that although in theory all children were equal 'some were more equal than others': and that it was therefore a proper policy to save money by arranging a cheaper and shorter form of education for those children who at 11 were apparently less able than others. It was also to have marked repercussions on the related thesis that the tripartite division of public education was the only form of secondary organization which suited the facts. Once the Act was on the Statute Book and the school-leaving age had been raised to 15 (a move which had to be deferred until 1 April 1947), secondary education must of necessity become for every individual (and not merely the 25 per cent of very able children) a genuinely liberal education. Such an education, besides imparting knowledge, must endeavour to arouse in each individual three types of interest—cultural interests for the enrichment of personal leisure, vocational interests in preparation for the successful gaining of a livelihood, and community interests leading to responsible participation in the duties of citizenship. It followed that it must become the objective of every school not only to broaden the range but to enrich the content of its curriculum.

The curriculum of those grammar schools which had been revived or brought into existence after the Education Act of 1902 still followed, in its general lines, the subjects which convention had supported in the nineteenth century. It was a curriculum which had produced civilized, intelligent, and responsible men and women in the universities, an admirable civil and local government service, and a professional class which was recognized, almost universally, to have few equals in honourable dealing and breadth of vision. Nevertheless, great as had been its service to administration and the professions, its contribution to industry and commerce had been considerably less conspicuous. The expansion described in Chapter VI had not been marked by any substantial corresponding innovations or new conceptions in the field of studies. Indeed the work of the Secondary Schools Examinations Council, however necessary it may have been, in the reduction and standardization of the number of external examinations had tended to stereotype the grammar school curriculum.

It is true that the parallel development of the junior technical school had struck a new note. These schools had shown that sound mental growth could clearly be fostered among those who had not responded particularly well to the conventional methods and curriculum. Their development had, however, been hampered by regulation and suspicion and they only accounted for about 4 per cent of the pupils of secondary school age.

So far as the senior elementary schools were concerned, the tardy progress of Hadow reorganization meant that most of them had only been in existence for a comparatively short time.[1] In the best of them there could be found a praiseworthy degree of imagination and sympathetic insight into the needs of their pupils. Their existence had, however, been bedevilled by the tendency of Governments between the wars to make educational development look like a glorified game of 'Snakes and Ladders'. Few senior schools had ever experienced a clear run of five years without encountering frustration in the shape of an economic crisis or the need to adjust themselves to some further reorganization and, finally, the war and evacuation. They had, moreover, been given very little in the way of libraries and equipment. Even when an individual school had been lucky enough to become established in good buildings with similar amenities to those enjoyed by other secondary schools it had too often found it impossible to build up for itself 'parity of esteem' in the eyes of parents. An even greater handicap was the fact that it could so rarely rely on retaining its pupils for more than two years and a bit, only one of these years lying in the teens. The date of the last compulsory lesson for the great majority of boys and

---

[1] At the date of the raising of the school-leaving age to 15 (1947) there were over 8,000 'all age' schools containing (in round figures) 380,000 pupils over 11, as compared with 3,000 secondary modern schools with 770,000 pupils.

girls varied between 13 years and 11 months and 14 years and 3 months. Not surprisingly such conditions had led many of the older heads (imposing figures and conscientious to a degree) to seek safety and preserve the reputation of the school with local employers by adhering to the traditional formal methods and the mechanical grinding-in of the three R's. This was understandable enough if one recalls that their own school days had been spent in the era of 'payment by results'. Moreover, their apprenticeship to teaching had for the most part taken place in the era when the adolescent was still regarded primarily as a little wage-earner, a subject for economic exploitation. We tend to forget today that the conception of all children as individuals who must be guided to a point where they should be relied upon to make the best of their own lives and, by the quality of their living, to bring up their own children to do the same, was slow to permeate the educational world. When nearly all his contemporaries during his most formative years think of education in terms of filling up empty pots, it is a bold and unusual man who will be inspired throughout a long teaching career by the knowledge that his role is more comparable to that of a water-diviner or a skilled lighter of fires!

In a speech delivered at the meeting of The British Association on 12 September 1913 Sir James Yoxhall, the secretary general of the N.U.T., made the following remarkable prediction: 'Fifty years hence everybody will be educated up to secondary school level and the number of university graduates will be increased ten times. Why should England wait fifty years for what she needs and can have today? The revolution can be accomplished. The compulsory school age will be raised to 15; cheap labour will cease; and an outfit for life will be in the grasp of every child. That is an economy which England needs.'

Exactly a third of a century later (1 April 1947) the means of realizing this prediction were provided when all the senior elementary schools changed their name to 'secondary modern schools'. The Ministry, His Majesty's Inspectorate, and the teaching profession then had first to discover the principles upon which a secondary education, which would not only be effective but would be seen to be effective, could be provided for nearly 400,000 adolescents whose brothers, sisters, and forebears had never remained so long at school before.

This undertaking was rendered the more formidable in many areas by the disorganization caused by the war. Much of the accumulated wisdom of the pre-war senior elementary schools had been shattered with their bomb-blasted buildings[1] and the dispersal of their former pupils; parental support for the added year was an unpredictable quantity; and, unlike the grammar schools, they could rarely call in aid any collective tradition or past reputation. Many newly appointed

---

[1] One school in five in the country as a whole had sustained war damage.

head teachers, however enthusiastic they might feel for the pioneering job they saw ahead, when faced with the unpromising countenances of several hundred children swept into their pre-fabricated classroom huts from decapitated 'all age' schools, might well have recalled Winston Churchill's mule—'without pride of ancestry or hope of posterity'. Perhaps even more would have had their doubts if they had been able to look forward eighteen years to the Government's declared intention to absorb them all into an organization of comprehensive schools![1]

Fortunately, over their years of teaching, these new heads had had ample opportunity to appreciate the central truth of the Hadow Report (1926) that all sound teaching must be based on the pupils' interests—on the attraction and challenge to every boy and girl of his or her immediate surroundings. In the Air Training Corps and other wartime organizations they had seen boys grinding through courses of mathematics and mechanical drawing which might, taken as single subjects, have repelled them if they had not seen, or thought they had seen, their usefulness. As the work of adolescents of quite moderate attainments in pursuit of the Duke of Edinburgh's Awards is still proving today, interest is a key which can unlock the most unpromising mind. The Advisory Council for Education in Scotland put the matter thus: 'Not until the vital spirit which informs our best infant departments has taken possession of Primary education as a whole will the secondary school in its turn be regenerated.'

The process of learning how to convert the formal and didactic curricula and timetables of the past into an approach by way of experience and creative activities took several years. Inevitably some schools went too far in their pursuit of the new prospect, overworking the 'project method' and 'centres of interest', until they awoke to find that the capacity to be adaptable without becoming superficial is as important in the life of a school as it is in the school of life. They then returned to teaching the academic subjects in much the same way as the grammar schools (though of course not at the same pace) and using the time saved for instance on languages for additional handcrafts, art, clubs of many kinds, and hobbies.

Other schools, again, fearing that if they launched out too precipitately into uncharted seas, with 'children's interests' as their only compass, they might never be able to complete their voyage, focused their aims on securing a balance between 'drills' and 'exploration'. Ten years before this might have appeared to be highly effective senior elementary work, but it no longer measured up to the new prospect.

A number of surveys, official and private, afford evidence of the progress that was being made in raising the prestige of the secondary modern sector. H.M.I.s who were constantly in the schools and could

[1] Ministry of Education Circular No. 10/65.

draw on pre-war experiences were by 1949 finding many encouraging signs. They made no attempt to gloss over some deterioration in some of the more formal subjects, notably in science and mathematics and to some extent in English, which was partly due to the upheavals of the war years. On the credit side, however, they noticed a more human atmosphere in the schools, their increased spiritual awareness, the greater attention paid to the needs of the individual child, and the growing co-operation between the schools and the surrounding community, especially, too, with the homes.[1]

In the summer of 1952 Professor H. C. Dent, newly appointed at the time to the post of educational correspondent to *The Times* after eleven years in which he had done fine work in rejuvenating *The Times Educational Supplement*, visited a large number of secondary modern schools. His experience as head of the Gateway School, set up by Leicester as a secondary school for boys with a strong practical bent, rendered him an exceptionally well-qualified observer. His classification in that year put about one third of the schools visited as doing good original work or sound work showing touches of originality. The great majority of the rest seemed to be doing sound but unoriginal work. Only 5 per cent seemed to be definitely poor. A similar survey covering a new group of schools made four years later (1956) found 16 per cent of the schools visited doing good original work, 36 per cent doing sound work showing touches of originality, 43 per cent doing sound but unremarkable work, and again only 5 per cent definitely poor.[2] During the middle fifties too, reports were written by H.M.I.s on about one eighth of the 3,500 secondary modern schools in England and Wales. On the evidence available about three-quarters of them were doing consistently sound and successful work in the basic subjects despite the fact that the surroundings of so many of them were often discouraging and the pupils of poor ability.

The schools during these years, years which witnessed an ever-mounting interest in education, were moving into a period when they could plan their programmes as a four-year course with some pupils dropping out at Christmas or Easter, or even as a four-year course with an additional year for a substantial number of pupils. By the end of the 1950–60 decade there was a growing realization of what the ordinary boy or girl could achieve if he did not, as in the past, leave school before his potentialities had become apparent—potentialities which had often been masked by inadequate powers of speech and limitations of home background. The schools were in fact beginning to look like the first blueprints of what secondary education for all should be.

Many schools were discovering that one way of marking the ap-

---

[1] Ministry of Education Report 1949, pp. 21–6.
[2] H. C. Dent, *Secondary Modern Schools*. Routledge, 1958.

proach to adult status was to give the curriculum a new look for the last two years of school life and to allow the pupils some choice in the subjects they studied and the programme they wished to follow. A wide range of occupational interests could now be organized in the best of the modern schools where they were large enough (e.g. three-form entry in the case of a single-sex school and four- or five-form entry in the case of mixed schools). A considerable variety of 'technical' courses were organized for boys aiming at skilled apprenticeships in industry, particularly the engineering and building branches. Courses for girls in catering, dressmaking, nursing, needlecrafts, retail distribution, and commercial subjects accompanied the boys' courses to prove that the schools had definite aims and could provide genuine incentives. In the country areas courses based on rural science and agricultural occupations were rendering these schools among the happiest and most pleasant to visit anywhere. In seaside towns courses were often started in seamanship and navigation.

As more and more secondary modern schools found it possible to develop good fifth-year courses there became less and less need to worry about quite able boys and girls finding themselves at a dead end. This, however, underlined the importance of re-energizing the dis-heartened by ensuring that the less able elements got a fair deal in the matter of the best staff, the best rooms, and the most interesting special jobs. For all modern schools have a far wider range of ability than any grammar school, and no special course should be allowed to impinge too severely upon the genuine secondary education of the less able children who are generally considered to form at least 12 per cent of the roll.

By 1963 just under one third of the modern schools (noted in the Newsom survey of that year) were providing some modern language teaching and, in doing so, were finding that it could be a stimulus to those pupils whose confidence needed a lift and a means to encourage them to apply fresh energy to learning their native tongue. Schools which pioneered these extended courses, often despite a static or worsening staffing position, soon demonstrated how much pupils of average ability can achieve in an academic course if they are given the chance and the desire: far more than would have been believed when the school-leaving age was raised. Moreover, those who had stayed on till 16 not only knew more than they did at 15 but were proving far more ready to take their place in the world as responsible and balanced individuals. So far from marking time they advanced with unexpected rapidity.

One result of this surge forward—an unhappy result in the opinion of many experienced head teachers and administrators[1]—was an ever-

[1] This point of view was expressed by Sir James J. Robertson in his presidential

increasing demand for a leaving examination. The first ten years of the secondary modern schools were largely free of external examinations. The opportunity for independent initiative and experiment, and variety of syllabus content and teaching methods, had rendered every school community unique in itself while producing a remarkable unity in variety in the education of the secondary modern child. By the mid-fifties, however, this unity was being threatened by a complex of pressures which heads could neither sufficiently control nor influence.

Performance in a single examination test obviously cannot reveal a great many qualities of the utmost importance, whether in employment or in personal life. Pleasant manners, general attitudes to learning, persistence in seeing a job through where care matters more than speed,[1] honesty, cheerfulness, a sense of humour, and the kind of leadership which ensures co-operation by inspiring it, are all qualities which a wise examiner would wish to bring into his final assessment but can rarely detect in the scripts. Those who remember from their schooldays the sheer frustration of being compelled to parse 'Crack went the whip, round went the wheels', when they wanted to write in freedom about the things that interested them, will realize how far a demand for correct punctuation, spelling, and grammar can cripple mental flow.

Yet however justly they might stress these points, one head after another was finding his hands forced—by parents and sometimes school governors brought up in the academic tradition, who refused to believe that what they saw in the secondary modern schools was education at all, by parents who could no longer buy a place in a grammar schoool, by parents who thought the be-all and end-all of education was the 'Matric', and, worst of all, by the discovery that his school was now the odd man out in the rat-race for minor qualifications admitting to lowly occupations. Such attitudes as these have helped to make Britain the most examination-ridden country in Europe.

By 1955 half the secondary modern schools were preparing pupils for external examinations. Yet there is no sadder sight for anyone interested in education for all, whether they are 'flyers' or in the lower ability ranges, than to find thirty children who have been turned out to weed the school garden while their class teacher coaches three children for G.C.E. Biology!

Finally by 1960 the Ministry of Education, whose attitude hitherto

---

address to the education section of the British Association a few years ago. The invasion of the secondary modern school by G.C.E. and other examinations ('educationally it is folly, but by other criteria amply justified') had, he regretted to say, resulted in much of the morning glory of the secondary modern school having faded by noonday.

[1] Scrapped or rejected work is currently believed to account for a national loss of £650,000,000 a year in British industry.

had varied between complete negation and blanket discouragement, were persuaded that rather than continuing to allow the schools to suffer untold harm by letting independent examinations proliferate unchecked, they must exercise some degree of co-ordination. This they have attempted by the institution of the Certificate of Secondary Education (C.S.E.), an examination at a lower level than the General Certificate of Education (G.C.E.) at 'O' level. This new examination is controlled by fourteen or more regional examining bodies with extensive teacher representation. The plan provides three choices: schools may submit individual pupils for the regional bodies' examinations; or they may put up their own examination scheme for the approval of the regional body; or they may ask the body to examine candidates upon their own syllabus. What the long-term results will be remains to be seen, for the first of the examinations only took place in 1965 when nine regional boards examined 66,000 candidates. Despite the obvious care taken and guidance given to ensure that passes in the subjects examined attain a national currency, it will probably be some years before it becomes possible to assess whether the admitted gain to the few is only achieved at the expense of the many.

The comprehensive schools and the largest modern schools situated in areas where selective schools do not cream off too high a proportion of the 11 + age-group can no doubt provide for both G.C.E. and C.S.E. examinations. Nevertheless it is important not to forget the reactions of the pupil of 16 who may still be suffering from a sense of inferiority at having failed his 11 + when he experiences a second failure in the C.S.E. or is not allowed to sit for it. It is important to remember, too, the schools in slum areas which even today ought to be small schools because half their work is still essentially social. As the Crowther Committee so wisely remarked, examinations can be valuable in showing pupils where they stand, in providing them with an incentive to continue, and in fostering good habits of work and standards of attainment. What is all-important, however, is that they should fulfil the role of helpful servant, not that of dominating master.

One of the best of the contributions which the good modern school made to the science of education—in the pre-examination period—was the ingenuity it so often displayed in securing a balanced interaction between curricular and extra-curricular activities. This balance derived from the growing realization that intellectual growth is merely one facet of a full education and was of particular importance in relation to children of normal or below normal ability. Undoubtedly these extra-curricular activities threw a considerable burden of extra work on the teaching staffs, particularly perhaps in those schools where poultry and farm stock had to be cared for during holidays as well as in term time.

It was the normal practice in the best of the modern schools to try to ensure that everything which could be fabricated in the school should be made there—garden frames, the extra greenhouse, pigsties, sundials, lily ponds, wrought-iron gates, even simple sports pavilions and open-air swimming pools. Individual schools secured camping locations, even disused railway stations, for residential courses from which the girls would return, as one head put it, 'having a kind of glow about them'. Similarly the boys would develop confidence and attitudes of responsibility almost unknown in schools of the past, probably because they had experienced something of the self-dependence, in, for example, having to make decisions and plans without reliance on their parents, which is distinctive of boarding-school routine. School journeys reached out from the north of Scotland to the south of France, some even further afield. The formal invitation to privileged visitors to lunch in the housecraft flat branched out in some schools into inviting younger brothers and sisters or a group from a nearby infant school for a whole school day, to be entertained, played with, read to, and provided with dinner.

Time will show how far the extra preparation, evening marking of papers, blackboard work, and note dictation involved for the school staffs to prepare the middle 20 per cent of children for the C.S.E. impinges upon such extra-curricular activities. The number of children in each annual age-group in Britain is remorselessly moving towards the million mark against a stationary or even slightly worsening staffing position. Young married teaching staff often feel impelled to undertake evening institute or other secondary jobs. Marriage, promotions, and reorganizations are constantly involving staff changes, so that few heads are able over a settled period of years to provide all the activities they would wish to offer. In the face of these and similar difficulties known to all teachers it may be remarkable if the enterprise and enthusiasm of the early years is to remain fresh and unimpaired by the imposition of a new annual cycle of examinations. Will the television periods, for example, which now keep 8,000 sets in use in schools bringing the outside world into the classroom, have to be curtailed? They have broken much new ground by enabling teachers to take part in criticism and dissection of the science, geography, current affairs, and vocational guidance programmes after viewing. Will examining bodies be willing to assess a candidate's command of spoken English, control of the local vernacular, understanding of argument, and ability to put a point of view—all important elements in literacy—if they can only do so by listening to thousands of tape-recordings?

Let us hope that this is too gloomy a view of the ultimate results of the surrender to parental importunities and public demand for documented results. Unfortunately by the time the sum total of the results can be assessed there may be few assessors left who remember what schools achieved before the examination octopus gripped them.

One of the most heartening results of the growth of modern schools has, of course, been the gradual absorption into them of those pockets of children over 11 who before the 1944 Act formed the top section of 'all age' elementary schools. In 1935 there were still 13,208 'all age' or 'all standard' departments without senior divisions containing 847,605 pupils over 11, and a further 150,000 pupils in 'all age' or 'all standard' departments in which a senior division had been organized. By 1965 the number of pupils in senior classes of 'all age' schools had been reduced to 9,376. To put the matter in another way, in 1965 only 3·3 pupils in every thousand could be found in 'all age' schools by the age of 13. In 1935 the number must have been over 500 in every thousand.

Next to the growth and achievements of the system of secondary modern schools (prior to the gradual absorption of many of them into a 'comprehensive' organization in the late 1950s and following the Ministry Circular No.10/65 of 12 July 1965) a future historian of English education will probably single out as distinctive of the period from 1935 to 1965 the growing recognition of the inadequacy of a tripartite division of secondary schools into secondary grammar, secondary technical, and secondary modern. This indeed was one of the principal factors which led to the Government's decision to invite L.E.A.s to adopt some form of comprehensive or bilateral organization in all future planning.

He will examine the roles played in this growing awareness by parental aspirations (Archbishop Beck's 'revolt of the Mums'); the growing misgivings among psychologists, teachers, and administrators as they came to a clearer and clearer realization that the only answer to this revolt—the production of an infallible selective procedure—did not and never could exist; and the ever-widening conception of the need for forms of secondary organization which could meet rapidly changing economic and social trends and the impact of mass media in the second half of the twentieth century.

He will probably ask himself initially what led to such a general acceptance for so many years of such an early age as 11 for properly applying selective procedures. He may not find the answer easy to discover. It seems probable, however, that it was taken over by the L.E.A.s for higher education, created by the Education Act of 1902, along with the 'Junior County Scholarship schemes', inherited from those Technical Education Boards which had established such schemes with their 'Whiskey Money'. The first such scheme—that started by Sidney Webb and Sir Herbert Llewellyn Smith in 1897—had awarded 2,167 scholarships to a group of 75,000 London children aged 11 (about one scholarship to thirty-five children). These children would have been free to leave their elementary schools at 12 by passing the '7th Standard' at a special examination held by H.M.I.s, and in fact about 1,000 London children were doing this every year. 'If we want to catch the brightest children from our elementary schools', it was probably argued, 'we must catch them a full year before they can escape.' As they represented only 3 per cent of their age-group all of them would probably have had a mental age of about 13 (although mental ages, still less intelligence ratings, were rarely, if ever, calculated in 1897). Sad to relate, nearly 20 per cent, having won their scholarships, left the grammar schools to which they had been admitted by the time they reached 14. If this was in fact the origin of the 11 + it can only be described as 'administrative psychology', which combined with early leaving from the grammar schools to stabilize the age of transfer at 11.

Successive reports—Hadow (1926), Norwood (1943), Spens, and so on—justified or even attempted to rationalize the 11 + examination. The Crowther Report (1959) cast a baleful eye upon it and the Newsom Report (1963) obviously disliked it; but only today (1967) is it being directly called in question by the Plowden Report,[1] in the light of the prospect of a school-leaving age of 16 after 1972.

It would be easy for our future historian, studying the emotionally charged tirades against the 11 + examination in newspaper articles and editorials of the 1950s and 1960s, to exaggerate the width and depth of public feeling on the matter. Nevertheless it was probably always the most responsible and best-educated sections of the parents in England and Wales which were the more vocal in their criticism of the system. Some would themselves have been among the first generation to achieve grammar school places. Many would be those most determined that their children, growing up into a changed world, should receive the best education apparently available. Others again—perhaps less worthily—would be concerned because the modern schools locally available still appeared to them to carry a stigma of social and educational inferiority. All these classes of parents had reason to believe that the 1944 Education Act had held out a promise to them that their children would receive a secondary education suited to their 'age, ability and aptitude', and that the authorities (the mysterious 'they') were cynically going back on the promise. The passage of the swollen post-war age-groups through the narrows of the 11 + examination inevitably increased both their numbers and their agitation. The amount of private coaching and cramming against the dreaded day of the examination which the children of such parents were forced to endure became a sorry blot on English education.

[1] 'Children and their Primary Schools' (1967), Vol. 1, Chapter 11.

On the other hand there were always a few parents, wiser than their generation, who realized that the best school for any child is that at which he will be encouraged to work at his own best pace on a curriculum that evokes his interest. There were others who did not really care, who did not understand, who were dull or unambitious for their children or who wanted them to be able to leave school and get to work at the first legal opportunity. There were even a few parents who feared that a grammar school education might result in their children becoming too 'superior' for their humble home.

Momentarily it looked as though a palliative might be in prospect when the Spens Committee, after studying the contribution of technical subjects to a general education, made a praiseworthy attempt to dispel the apathy in the public regard for the remarkable work of the junior technical schools. 'We have come to the conclusion', they reported, 'that although these junior technical schools may have as their general aim the provision of a liberal education for those who intend to enter industrial occupations nevertheless their curriculum and the methods of its treatment will also develop best the ability of certain types of pupil whatever occupation they may subsequently adopt.' Starting from this point they went on to advocate the development of the junior technical school idea, in the direction of the establishment of technical high schools recruiting at 11—recruiting which would be in every way parallel to the existing grammar schools. Had this suggestion been adopted it would no doubt have drawn off some of the potential agitation against the 11 + by doubling the intake to selective secondary education. Fortunately perhaps it remained a dead letter. Such a solution could only have reduced the secondary modern schools still more markedly to communities from which all the abler pupils had been drawn off, schools occupied only by the intellectually slower children or those who had the misfortune to have unambitious parents. Could such schools have attracted a fair share of the ablest teachers? Below-average children (as the Crowther Committee remarked) make above-average demands on the educational system, or, as that great schoolmaster Thring put it, 'a dull boy is a wise man's problem'.

A great volume of literature in the form of investigations, monographs, papers in psychological journals, and the records of experimental work on examination systems over the years under review,[1] inexorably pointed to the conclusion that no selective procedure could be devised which would infallibly detect those children who at 11 were, and would remain, abler than a borderline of others. Health, nervousness, social background, streaming in the junior school, and other similar factors all play a part in the result of an examination conducted

[1] A list of the more important of these is given at the end of Chapter 11 of the Plowden Report, Vol. 1.

at so early an age. Exceptional cases abound and can readily be called to mind—e.g. the boy who registered an I.Q. of 109 and 112 before failing the 11 + examination but subsequently 134, when he had been admitted to a grammar school. Far more serious, however, were those investigations which suggested, for example, that a rigidly academic form of education proved unsuitable for between six and seven children out of every twenty admitted to a grammar school; that a fresh classification at 15 would have redistributed about 14 per cent of the pupils, and at 18, between 22 per cent and 29 per cent; that 122 children in every 1,000 were probably wrongly allocated.[1] Anyone who has acted as a chief examiner will know the immense pains and ingenuity expended in endeavouring to design papers in English and Arithmetic which will supplement the Moray House intelligence tests; to equate the marking of a team of examiners; to re-examine the borderline candidates; and to bring the assessment of the junior schools into the final account. A high tribute was in fact paid to our selection methods in the World Survey of Education in 1962 carried out by U.N.E.S.C.O. As the Crowther Committee felt bound to admit, however, 'We cannot hope to avoid further error by additional refinements in the process of selection.'

By the late fifties the educational world had become increasingly concerned over such findings and, in addition, readier to accept the stubborn facts: first, that the kind of qualities which are measured by intelligence tests may be in part acquired characteristics, dependent to some degree on influences of physical and social environment; secondly, that the causes of lack of progress, in the kaleidoscopic period of adolescence, may be personal and complex and are not solely bounded by limited intelligence or inappropriate teaching: thirdly, that the growth of abilities is like a rising tide which may momentarily recede only to come back a little higher up the beach; finally, that the adolescent world (like the adult world) does not and never has fallen into the two neat divisions of those who need books and those who only need tools!

Even before the war a few far-sighted educational thinkers were beginning to see the shape of things to come. For example in a paper read to the North of England Education Conference as early as 1936, on the need for L.E.A.s to establish a psychological service, Dr. A. G. Hughes said: 'The education of junior children is at present dominated by the scholarship system. It is generally agreed that the system is bad and ought to be abolished, and I have little doubt that it will in due course be relegated to the limbo of educational blunders, there to join such shameful relics as child factory labour and payment by results. The

[1] Robin Pedley, *The Comprehensive School*, (1963), pp. 15–20. Pelican Series. See also Plowden Report, Vol. 1, para. 413.

solution must be sought by a raising of the school-leaving age to 16 and a unification of secondary education. There must be the equivalent of scholarships for all who need financial help so that at the age of 11 there will be not the fierce competitive examination but a carefully regulated choice among a number of alternative secondary school courses of equal status.'[1]

The post-war world clearly presented Britain with what Anthony Sampson, in his brilliant examination *The Anatomy of Britain* (1962), described in the vivid phrase 'the painful transition from Imperial splendour to competitive trading'. In this, as he went on to say, what the schools had to learn was 'to turn the sons of gentlemen into business-men; the sons of amateurs into professionals'. By the early sixties, the secondary modern schools had shown that reserves of talent wholly or only partially suspected before the raising of the school-leaving age were still awaiting the key to unlock them. Conscription had revealed that half the National Service recruits to the Army who were rated in the two highest intelligence groups had left school at 15. The develop-ment of 'extended courses' was producing scores of thousands of boys and girls who had a specific qualification of one kind or another in view.

If an increasing number of pupils who had not been deemed able enough to enter the grammar schools at 11 + were demonstrating that they could—given the right educational help—achieve so much more than had been expected of them, then it was clearly in the economic interest of the country to provide that help, apart altogether from the postulates of human justice and the creation of a much wider 'aris-tocracy'—of those who excel in social living. Obviously, however, the kind of help which they required was not a watered-down imitation of the grammar school curriculum. Secondary education for all was a challenge to the educational world in its thinking to get right outside those categories of thought relating to the adolescent in which it had grown up hitherto. Even in the grammar schools themselves, as the report of the Consultative Committee on 'Early Leaving' showed, 37 per cent of the intake was failing to secure at least three passes at 'O' level.

The England of the fifties and early sixties had become a country so different in its social, economic, and cultural aspects from that of the decades which followed the Education Acts of 1902 and 1918 that it would have been hardly recognizable to those who controlled her destinies in those decades, particularly, of course, those who did so before the First World War. As the Crowther Report reminded the educational world in 1959, the population was better housed, living

---

[1] Dr Hughes, author of *Learning and Teaching*, subsequently became Chief Inspector of Schools to the L.C.C. As such he played a notable part in the prepar-ation of the reports upon which the comprehensive solution was adopted.

longer, marrying earlier, having smaller families. Women were work-ing after marriage in far greater numbers. The 'freedom of the latch-key at 21' had given way to a situation in which, although 90 per cent of adolescents were still living at home two years after leaving school, a third of them had only spent two evenings a week at home, and 26 per cent of the boys and 6 per cent of the girls had been out every evening. The continual subdivision of the industrial and commercial hierarchy (already at work before 1935 as mentioned on p. 183) had reached a point where intelligent workers who might in past generations have been found doing a job at some quite humble level were now two or three rungs up the ladder. The late S. H. Wood, when taxed by an ignorant employer with the time-worn accusation that the population was writing worse, spelling worse and speaking worse in every succes-sive generation, would reply, 'I quite agree—they always have ever since 1870.' What he meant was that the employer was comparing the quality of labour he could get for his lowest-paid and least attractive jobs with that which his forebears could obtain thirty years before—men whose intelligence and education would now have promoted them to jobs several stages up in the hierarchy. In fact the manual skill and craftsmanship which used to be devoted to a product has now often moved from the shop floor to the desks of the draughtsmen, planning, development and production engineers, the design staff, metallurgists and so forth. Correspondingly the proportion of unskilled workers in the community has fallen to about 12 per cent.

In 1908 only 12 per cent of the country's 48 million acres of agricultural land was farmed by owner-occupiers. By 1960 more than 50 per cent of the best of these acres had passed into their ownership, and the value of such land which had remained more or less stationary in terms of real money values over the 900 years since the Doomsday record was now going up sharply every year.

All these changed features in the national life had obvious reper-cussions on educational needs. Half the girls leaving school would be married by the age of 25 and should obviously no longer be treated as adolescents in uniform at the age of 17 or 18. They would have their families at an earlier age and be able, if they had secured some market-able qualification at school, to re-enter employment when their children reached school age. Smaller families ought to mean the ability to support a longer school life for the children. Moreover, the redistri-bution of wealth arising from a total real output a third greater than twenty years earlier had benefited the lower-paid worker.

Every five or six years there would be a turnover into employment of half a million grammar school pupils who in perhaps fifteen years' time would be demanding a similar standard of education for their own children. Both boys and girls would need an education redirected towards general mechanical intelligence to meet the inevitable changes of occupation as the scientific and technological revolution surges forward on its way to the twenty-first century. Yet despite the raising of the school-leaving age in 1947 the proportion of the gross national product devoted to education ($1\frac{1}{2}$ per cent in 1921, $2\frac{3}{4}$ per cent in 1938, $3\frac{1}{2}$ per cent in 1955, 4·3 per cent in 1960, and 5·4 per cent in 1965) has barely kept pace, if one excludes the expansion of higher education and the health services, with the expansion of the national income.

As the Venetian Ambassador to the Court of St James explained to his Government as early as the year 1500, no people are more ready than the English to direct their efforts to the securing of anything which they realize it is to their immediate advantage to secure. The need to bring increasing freedom to the junior school curriculum; the urgent need to complete Hadow reorganization; the replacement of the first generation of school buildings; the revolt of the Mums against the 11 + examination; the realization by the educational world that no additional refinements in the process of selection could render it less haphazard; the importance of concentrating the stationary or slightly falling supply of honours degree graduate teaching power to the advantage of the maximum number of pupils in the secondary schools; the rapidly mounting cost of adequate land for school sites in built-up urban areas combined with the equally rapid improvement and diminishing cost of school transport (which made it so much cheaper to build large schools on the periphery of towns); the success of the fourth- and fifth-year courses in the secondary modern schools in unlocking previously concealed talent; the challenge of the 'Third Industrial Revolution', automation and the discernible future pattern of industrial, commercial, and agricultural employment; all these factors, and many more considerations of a local character, played their part in the widespread experiments in secondary school organization which have been taking place up and down the country since the end of Hitler's war.

Already before the war various experiments had been conducted by leading Education Authorities, such as the West Riding of Yorkshire, in the establishment of bilateral schools: e.g. the combination of a grammar with a junior technical school, or multilateral schools divided into distinct, separately organized sides, 'grammar', 'technical', and 'modern'. The Board of Education in the White Paper which ushered in the Education Act of 1944 left the door open for the continuation of such experiments in the future without, however, enunciating any new educational principle or philosophy. 'It would be wrong', they said, 'to suppose that the three main types of secondary schools will remain separate and apart. Different types may be combined in one building as considerations of convenience and efficiency may suggest. In any

case the free interchange of pupils from one type of education to another must be facilitated.'

The earliest true comprehensive schools, that is schools drawing all
the junior school leavers from the surrounding area into their organization and not labelling them into different categories at the start, were
brought into being in the two large islands Anglesey and the Isle of
Man. They represented a common-sense solution of the problem
presented by small pockets of children over 11 in 'all age' elementary
schools which, as a result of the 1944 Education Act, could no longer
be treated as senior elementary pupils but had to be provided with
secondary education. Similar though partial concentrations were
effected in such predominantly rural Welsh counties as Brecon,
Cardigan, and Montgomery, and comparable English counties such as
the East and North Ridings of Yorkshire and the county of Westmorland.

So far as the largest built-up areas were concerned a strong lead
came from London, which at the end of the war found itself faced with
an enormous building and reconstruction programme as a result of
bomb damage to its existing school buildings. This meant having to
find 1,080 acres of sites to replace 360 schools, or a much more modest
700–800 acres if they were replaced by large schools on the comprehensive pattern; and further, the provision of new premises for many of
the junior technical schools which had hitherto worked in the buildings of senior technical colleges whose normal daytime students had
been absorbed for the past few years in the wartime industries or the
Services.

As early as July 1944, when the ink was hardly yet dry on the 1944
Education Act, the Education Committee of the L.C.C. decided in
favour of including in their development plan, which they would be
required by the Act to prepare, a fully comprehensive organization.
This decision was not, however, based solely on such practical considerations as those outlined in previous pages. All or nearly all such
considerations played a part, but the majority party on the Council had
even in pre-war days been strongly influenced by the policy of the
Labour party, which ever since 1911 had been demanding genuine
secondary education for all children in schools offering equally genuine
parity of esteem. Their educational advisers had, moreover, been
considerably impressed by certain aspects of the comprehensive schools
they had visited in the U.S.A. and particularly in Canada.

Anyone reading these old reports today, whether he is an advocate
of the comprehensive school or still one of its opponents, will perhaps
be tempted to permit himself a wry smile—although for very different
reasons depending on which side of the fence he stands—when he
finds that the political argument for what was proposed was drawn

from a document already forty or more years old! This was a quotation from the words of the headmaster of a public school. As a member of the Moseley Commission he studied the multilateral schools of the U.S.A. as early as 1903, that is long before the attrition of class barriers caused by two world wars and the growth of our fine network of grammar schools, and at a time when the normal leaving age in this country was still twelve. He no doubt knew the limited and too often class-conscious and clannish public school product of 1903, but might he not have found a much sounder ethos in Britain's schools of 1944? What he actually commented on was 'the absence of those well defined social barriers which in England separate class from class and which even when broken down in individual cases are built up again with other material; and further, the absence of laws of primogeniture and the pre-conceived traditions and "invidious bars" which, abounding unconsciously in our English training, prevent the unrestrained development of even the most ambitious spirits of our own people. Social emergence, often stifled by birth and circumstances in our close insular atmosphere, is a plant which has never been nipped or dwarfed in the ampler oxygen of the United States.'

As more and more chairmen and members of provincial education committees and their educational advisers visited and observed the success of the purpose-built comprehensive schools in London and elsewhere the movement spread rapidly. It was undoubtedly fanned by the publicity which attended the somewhat ill-advised attempts by two Conservative Ministers to check it prior to the partial conversion of H.M.I.s to the possible merits of the comprehensive solution.

By the end of 1964 a survey by the *Sunday Times* showed that, of the 146 L.E.A.s, 49 (29 counties and 20 county boroughs) had pronounced in favour of the comprehensive principle; 52 (17 counties and 35 county boroughs) were actively considering the question; 17 (7 counties and 10 county boroughs) had adopted some other form of organization, for example the junior and senior high school plan pioneered by Leicestershire; and 28 (9 counties and 19 county boroughs) were not proposing any change.

On 21 January 1965, the House of Commons endorsed the Labour Government's declared objective to end selection at 11 + and to eliminate separatism in secondary education; noted with approval the efforts of local authorities to reorganize secondary education on comprehensive lines; and called for a declaration of national policy. This declaration took the form of a Circular (No. 10/65, already mentioned above) issued on 12 July 1965, to L.E.A.s and the governors of direct grant, voluntary aided, and special agreement schools, setting out six main forms of comprehensive organization which had so far emerged from experience and discussion.

Sir Fred Clarke, the first chairman of the Ministry's Central Advisory Council set up under the Act of 1944, once expressed the view that only after a diagnostic twenty years would it be possible to decide whether a particular structure of secondary education was likely to be beneficial. True, many comprehensive schools are already in operation, and some of them have been in existence for a sufficient number of years to have surmounted their initial teething troubles (apart from those occasioned by loss of key members of their staffs on promotion to new schools now opening). Nevertheless those who agree with Sir Fred Clarke's dictum will be interested, if still alive, to assess its validity in 1985. For the Government's declaration certainly represents one of the most important and far-reaching ventures in English educational history. The most that any educational historian writing today (1967) can safely attempt is some review of the arguments which have hitherto been advanced for and against the comprehensive school and the tentative opinions formed by those who have already spent some years at work as teachers in such schools. For the debate still continues and may do so for some years to come.

In theory a countrywide system of comprehensive schools universally applied should set the junior schools free to work out their own curricula in terms of activity and experience (without the shadow of a final competitive examination as distinct from diagnostic tests). This should bring immensely welcome relief to heads and administrators in no longer having to deal with over-anxious parents, over-pressure on 10-year-old children, and hostile and largely unanswerable criticism of the examination itself.

At present, however, the number of areas which have achieved such a consummation is very small indeed. Where the L.E.A. has been able to persuade the governors of a direct grant or an established voluntary aided grammar school to accept expansion into a comprehensive school the new organization has usually got off to a flying start. The local reputation, traditions, and ethos of the grammar school are absorbed and such schools soon achieve popularity with parents and the local community. No parent can feel that his child is being treated as an educational guinea-pig, and no pupil can feel that he is not being given the same chance as his brother, sister, or cousin. Local esteem of an equivalent order can only be built up gradually in the case of the purpose-built comprehensive school formed by the admission of successive annual intakes. Either method has, however, generally proved considerably more successful than the school formed by the amalgamation of two or more non-selective schools and the subsequent attempt to build up an intake of selected pupils. So long as the direct grant and voluntary aided grammar schools of any given area are able to remain outside the development of a comprehensive school organization by the L.E.A. some form of competitive selective entry, with all that it implies in parental pressure on the junior schools, must persist.

Again in theory the comprehensive school should be able to ensure that the minimum number of children of high intelligence, or of those possessing some highly developed flair for a particular group of studies, fall by the wayside through getting into the wrong stream at 11, or through the poverty—actual or cultural—of their home background. Already considerable evidence has become available in support of this theory, particularly perhaps from those schools serving the rural areas. The pupil of average ability finds himself in an environment which in the past has normally only been available to a privileged minority. He wears the same school uniform, enjoys the same library and craft rooms, sings in the same choir, plays in the same teams and joins the same school journey or camping parties as his brother, sister or cousins who have always been held up to him as the brighter ones in the family. He is encouraged to stay on for some special fourth- or fifth-year course where he will become aware of the number of positions of responsibility which are open to him if he works hard and completes the course satisfactorily.[1] He can become a school prefect, thus enjoying opportunities for leadership for which his more academic brother, absorbed in his work for 'A' levels in the G.C.E., cannot always find time.

Whether these benefits are experienced to an equivalent degree by the pupil of high intelligence is probably still something of an open question. He should certainly, in course of time as the school develops if not already, have as wide a choice of subjects at 'O' and 'A' level in his G.C.E. as he would have done had he secured a place in the largest grammar school. For example one of the earliest-established comprehensive schools is already offering 25 subjects at 'O' and 14 at 'A' level. If, however, the local direct grant or grammar schools have creamed off the majority of those children whose performance at eleven plus was slightly better than his he may find himself lacking the stimulus of adequate competition—that burnishing achieved by the rub of mind on mind in the grammar school sixth form. Although there will probably be a considerably greater allocation of time for sixth-form teaching than he would have enjoyed in a small grammar school, his direct contact with the headmaster will probably not be so close and continuous. For the head of a comprehensive school must parcel out his time over a much wider number of classes.

---

[1] A survey by the National Foundation for Educational Research published early in 1967 revealed that only one in five of those pupils who leave school at 15 get jobs of skilled status as compared with two out of three of those who obtain ordinary passes in the G.C.E. and more than 90 per cent of those who stay on at school till 17 or 18.

New activities are constantly arising in secondary schools. Fencing at a London school, 1963

'What Sea power was to Britain up to 1918, and Air power up to 1946, scientific school power has now become.' Science Laboratory at Ifield County Grammar School, Crawley

Part-time release arouses a sense of purpose and reality in the recipient. A mechanical engineering craft practice course at Southwark College of Further Education

Science and Technology have become the upper and nether millstones for Britain's daily bread

No doubt it is such considerations as these that have led the critics of comprehensive schools (despite the evidence to the contrary gradually becoming available from pilot studies here and abroad) to describe their approach as a calculated lowering of what hitherto has been offered to the talented minority for the benefit of the average majority: that one should not judge the influence of the comprehensive schools' specialist staff on the average pupil by the admittedly remarkable academic and other results achieved by the earliest of such schools to be formed. They have been so desperately concerned, the critic will allege, 'to keep up with the grammar school Joneses' that they have probably spent thousands of pounds worth of specialist time and energy on every pupil they have groomed up to the winning of an 'Open' award at a university. Moreover, he will probably add, the London comprehensive schools from which such academic achievements are usually quoted have 60 per cent to 70 per cent graduate staffs. This ratio cannot be reproduced over a countrywide spread of comprehensive schools, for the percentage of all graduates in maintained secondary schools in England and Wales as a whole is no more than 37 per cent.

The special facilities which a comprehensive school can offer can be of great benefit to the 'below average' group. This is usually put at about 12 per cent of the intake. The intelligence ratings of the pupils in the group at eleven plus would probably be found to lie in the 70 to 85 waveband, and in the secondary modern school the group would constitute the 40 per cent for whom the Beloe Committee thought examinations undesirable. It is much easier, despite timetabling difficulties for a large school with a staff of 80 to 100, to arrange a remedial department for such pupils than it has proved in the case of the smaller secondary modern school. Here those who are merely retarded or backward can be sorted out from the genuinely dull. Such emotional or social factors as the death of a parent, a broken home, bad health, the influence of bad companions, loss of interest at the onset of adolescence account for many children, who are not in reality dull, failing for a time to do themselves justice. However backward this sector of the pupils may be, there will still be more clubs and societies which they can join than they would normally find in most secondary modern schools. They can work with the best in the school garden, greenhouses, potting sheds, or with the livestock and can be encouraged to take pride in anything they can do well, even though in the more formal aspects of school work their teachers may not be able to do more for them than bring them up to the limit of their potential.

There is a long-standing tradition in English education that no school should be so large as to prevent the head knowing every pupil. The real strength of British schools, it is often argued by the critics of the comprehensive plan, has been the pastoral care bestowed on the pupils.

To build up a school which can cater properly for the whole ability range and produce a viable sixth form, the annual intake should be one of at least six or seven forms (180–210 pupils), thus producing eventually a school of 1,500 or more as pupils are encouraged to extend their school life. Will not this, the critics ask, result in the country being covered by a network of schools resembling impersonal factories, 'streamed and streamlined communities grooming everyone for some meritocratic millennium on the "1984" pattern?' In such a school, it is alleged, there is little movement between streams.[1] The children from favourable home backgrounds, where they hear conversation at mealtimes and critical discussion of films and television programmes and their homework is not outside the ken of their parents, will always feature prominently in the promotion lists. Those of the less skilled or unskilled workers will rarely enjoy the same opportunities. The short answer to this, the advocates of the system reply, is that to detect or allege that they can detect social inequalities at work is not an argument for remaining content with a tripartite system which is demonstrably more unequal.

Actually there is already a great deal of evidence that in the good comprehensive school the vast majority of the pupils work happily together irrespective of their streams and abilities. Moreover, if the declared aim of the comprehensive form of organization 'to promote a feeling of social unity among adolescents of all kinds and degrees of ability' is to be realized, it is predominantly the social life of the school which will become the unifying force.

Most of the valid criticism has been focused on the division of the catchment areas of comprehensive schools in certain areas into 'neighbourhoods'. Such a practice, it is alleged, may well exacerbate class differences between schools and, in addition, will deprive parents of virtually any choice of school. The Ministry has reacted to this criticism, and Mr Crosland when Minister made it known in Parliament that he was most anxious that comprehensive schools should not develop into purely neighbourhood schools, and that he would support the widest possible range of choice for parents. If this threat to the promotion of social unity can be overcome clearly the large school can offer far more opportunities and stimuli, both curricular and extra-curricular, than a small one. With its large staff representing the widest variety of interests it will surely enjoy far better opportunities to develop extra-curricular amenities, for example camping locations (even disused Lakeland railway stations) for residential courses. The visitor will find the widest variety of activities at 'House' or 'tutorial group' level taking place in the lunch hour, small games, chess clubs, debates, even car-cleaning to raise funds for Oxfam. He will learn that twenty

[1] Cf. Plowden Report, Vol. 1, para. 372.

or more parties have enjoyed school journeys in the past year. In the craft rooms he will find pupils spending many hours in preparation for such outside activities; making rucksacks and equipment for light-weight camping, climbing, walking, or cycling expeditions; construct-ing sailing dinghies, canoes and paddles for adventure trips, even water skis.

Obviously no head of a comprehensive school can know constantly, intimately, and personally every pupil in the school. Nevertheless it is at least possible for him to secure that every pupil should know him or her personally and feel the effect of his personality. He would fail in his function if this did not occur. However, he should never become a mere administrator and he should certainly be provided with competent administrative and clerical support and the help at least on a part-time basis of a trained social worker to assist with the multiplicity of 'wel-fare' problems arising between the school and the pupils' homes. The preservation of the 'family spirit' will be secured by the delegation of certain functions to a number of deputies, heads of departments, house-masters, and house-tutors in daily personal touch with smaller groups. The head should remain the inspiration and driving force of a great organization, the creator of its ethos and the leader and mentor of his colleagues. Although he will naturally work to a large extent through his housemasters and heads of departments he will be careful to remain accessible to the most junior members of the staff. In particular he will be concerned so to direct the moral influence of the school as to elimin-ate once and for all the residual conception in the minds of so many adolescents in the past that morality seems to be primarily concerned with 'not scribbling on lavatory walls'. In its place he must somehow continue to substitute the more difficult conception that morality means a self-imposed code of moral and social behaviour, the distin-guishing features of which are kindliness, tolerance, service to others, chastity before marriage, and fidelity within it.

Thus it has already become plain to the most casual observer that the headship of a comprehensive school postulates the appointment of a man or woman of absolutely outstanding calibre backed by immense reserves of energy.

By 1985, when the school population of England and Wales will on present projections have risen by 2 million from the 1965 figure of $7\frac{1}{2}$ million, the number of secondary schools of all types may have been reduced, by the change-over to comprehensive schools, from the 9,608 of today to perhaps 3,500–4,000. Already there have been a few critics—usually outside the teaching profession itself—who have been bold enough to express doubts whether sufficient men and women of the outstanding quality required will be found to take charge of so many comprehensive schools.

Apart from the strictly educational arguments for and against the comprehensive principle it has, of course, many attractive features from the point of view of the administrator or sociologist.

Two which seldom appear in the already extensive literature on the subject are economy of scarce teaching resources and economy of land.

If we are to succeed in the painful transition from imperial splendour to competitive trading (whether within the Common Market or outside it) we must so adapt our educational system as to bring the highest possible proportion of our adolescent population during their school life into living contact with specialist teachers who are enthusiasts for their particular speciality. For our industry and commerce must integrate if they are not to disintegrate, and public education has always provided the main instrument of social change and social mobility. We are on a stationary or indeed slightly falling market in this matter of the supply of specialist and graduate teachers, and it seems vital not to dissipate them in thousands of schools but to concentrate them in large schools where they can influence as many pupils, sixth formers and others, as possible. The small grammar school with an average sixth form made up of, say, 25 first-year pupils, 14 second-year, and 4 third-year, perhaps only able to take English and French to 'A' level, with no music and only one laboratory, is an anachronism today.

Nobody appears as yet to have worked out the savings in specialist teaching power and numbers which might result from a universal spread of comprehensive schools. It may, however, be a significant pointer that the cost per pupil of teachers' salaries in comprehensive schools is at present £65–£70 as compared with £80 in grammar and £100 in independent schools.

Again, the agricultural scientists and sociologists concerned at the loss of the country's resources of productive land in the face of the 'population explosion'—a loss put by certain experts at the agricultural average of a moderate-sized county such as Oxfordshire every ten years—can point to the fact that 4,000 comprehensive schools (even ones of 2,000) could be properly sited, at 8 or 9 acres apiece, on 30,000 to 36,000 acres (an area rather larger than Salisbury Plain). Since a secondary school of 500 is not properly sited on much less than three acres the comparable figures in their case might be nearly 50,000 acres. Few people realize that, even at the very moderate estimate of an average site (including playgrounds and playing fields) of an acre, the 32,408 schools of all types in England and Wales must already cover an area of 50 square miles. We have only 32 million acres of land not built upon, less than three-quarters of an acre per person as compared with America's 12½ acres and France's four acres.

In October 1965, the Ministry of Education offered a grant of £200,000 to the National Foundation for Educational Research to conduct a six-year evaluation of the quality of different types of comprehensive schools to see what they are trying to do and how competently they are doing it. During the six years the Foundation will no doubt attempt to measure such factors as how heads visualize their aims and the purpose of their school; how it is organized internally; its teaching methods; the curricular and extra-curricular facilities it offers; the attitude of parents, pupils, and staff, their enthusiasm for particular activities, and dislike of others.

Although in twenty years' time educational thinkers may very well wonder why the opposition to the comprehensive principle was so long-drawn and bitter, it is to be hoped that not too many comprehensive schools will have been irrevocably formed by the fusion of existing schools before the National Foundation's report becomes generally available. A purpose-built school in the planning of which the L.E.A., the head-designate, and the staff will have had time to study and digest the findings of the National Foundation should be a very different and probably far superior community to some of those schools already formed by the compulsory marriage of separate schools. One is reminded that in his work on Medieval Europe the late A. L. Smith described the union of Italy with the Austro-German complex to form the Holy Roman Empire as 'a Mezentian union'. Anyone who has the curiosity to look up Mezentius will find that he was a king of a Tyrrhennian city who had the unpleasant habit of tying his living captives to the bodies of the dead and throwing them into a common grave!

No account of the development of secondary education during the years 1935 to 1965 should fail to take account of two features each of which represents a 'success story' in itself: first the remarkable growth of sixth-form work in the grammar, comprehensive, and independent schools, and second the evidence of steady progress in the pace of learning as shown by the periodic 'standards of reading' surveys carried out by H.M.I.s.

In 1935 the number of pupils aged 17 and over in secondary schools on the grant list in England and Wales stood at 29,861 or, adding the same proportion of the total school role for independent schools not on the grant list, say 35,000.

In 1965 the number aged 17 in schools on the grant list had risen to 130,671 with a further 20,930 in independent schools recognized as efficient and 2,470 in other independent schools, making 154,071 in all.

This is not the whole story, of course, because the average size of the three age-groups from which the 35,000 of 1935 came was 606,000 whereas the 154,071 of 1965 were drawn from average age-groups of 751,000. Although in the absence of precise figures the number of pupils aged 17 and over had to be used by the Crowther Committee in their assessment of the growth of sixth forms (from 1947 to 1958) the Department of Education and Science's annual report for 1965 gives the sixth-form population in maintained schools in that year as 169,000, that is 15,000 higher than the number shown as aged 17 and over on 1 January 1965. The 15,000 extra pupils are probably accounted for by those 'flyers' who had entered upon sixth-form courses before their seventeenth birthday. Adding the 23,020 in direct grant schools and the 37,374 in independent schools recognized as efficient, one arrives at a grand total of 229,400 sixth-form pupils.

The main reasons for this remarkable increase have no doubt been the encouragement given to promising pupils to stay on (or transfer from the top forms of secondary modern schools) to work for 'A' level subjects in the G.C.E.; the availability of more generous maintenance allowances which have undoubtedly been a factor in building up the increased proportion of boys and girls from the homes of manual workers who now represent upwards of half the total; the self-perpetuating character of secondary education in that parents who were themselves at grammar and independent schools normally insist on their offspring having the same advantages; and a more general realization by the public that the chances of entering upon a skilled occupation is up to 90 per cent for those who have extended their school life in this way.

The most reassuring aspect of these figures is that many sociologists and educational thinkers have in recent years wondered whether the country's social advance may not be checked by the inadequate proportion of young people, particularly girls, staying on at school to complete a full course of secondary education. In the early post-war years there were undoubtedly too many good jobs chasing too few good girls! Great efforts were being made to persuade six or seven out of every ten girls who had completed a full secondary course to enter teacher-training colleges. The three or four out of every ten who did not do so formed a very inadequate recruiting area for the needs of the Civil and Local Government services, nursing and the welfare services, commerce, industry, and agriculture.

The steady improvement in the scores achieved by children and pupils submitted to the 'standards of reading' tests carried out at intervals since 1948, with samples now numbering 18,000 children, in schools covering all parts of the country is an equally remarkable 'success story'.

The booklet in which the inspector's findings were set out, namely 'Progress in Reading' (Education Pamphlet No. 50, H.M.S.O.), is a statistician's bonanza, but an intimidating comprehension test to anyone who classes himself among the literate but innumerate section of the population! Here, however, it is only necessary to concern ourselves with the principal findings. These are that in 1964 boys and girls of 11 reached on the average the standard of pupils 17 months older in 1948, representing, over the 72 months of schooling since they entered school, a 24 per cent increase in the pace of learning; the standard reached or exceeded by half the boys and girls in 1948 was reached or exceeded by three-quarters of their successors in 1964; and a corresponding advance has taken place among boys and girls aged 15. Over the years the pace of learning appears to have increased between 16 per cent and 32 per cent for juniors and between 14 per cent and 24 per cent for seniors.

Two striking discoveries which the 1964 tests revealed were that 4 per cent of the children of 11 were in advance of 50 per cent of the children of 15, and that 8 per cent of the children attending secondary modern schools were in advance of 50 per cent of those in grammar schools.

The student of constitutional change might note with interest that the Secretary of State for Education himself wrote the Foreword to the statistical pamphlet. He might reflect with amusement what the old Duke of Devonshire, his predecessor of sixty-five years before (who complained so bitterly that he could never understand 'all those damned dots' in the Department's estimates),[1] would have made of it!

[1] I know that this story is normally told of Lord Randolph Churchill when he was Chancellor of the Exchequer, but I certainly heard it attributed to the Duke of Devonshire by one who was serving in the Education Department of the Privy Council when the Duke was Lord President.

CHAPTER XVIII

THE EXPANSION OF TECHNICAL, TECHNOLOGICAL, AND HIGHER EDUCATION IN ENGLAND, AND WALES, 1935–65: 1

Science, technology, higher education at university level, and the training of adequate technical supporting staff now the millstones for Britain's daily bread.—The remarkable increase in numbers entering upon full-time and part-time courses by 1965.—The conversion of Whitehall from resignation to leadership.—Some distinctive features of technical, technological, and further education in England and Wales.— The country's poor showing in this field between 1902 and 1935.— The contribution made by the technical colleges during the war years 1939–46.—The awakening interest in many forms of further education created by wartime conditions.—The years of cheeseparing and frustration 1945–55.—The years of advance in technological education 1955–65.

COMPASSION, romance, humour (all those ingredients which appear to be anathema to the compilers of government reports, with the honourable exceptions of Sir John Newsom's 'Half our Future' and Lady Plowden's 'Children and their Primary Schools') offer no hand- or toe-hold to anyone who is brave enough to attempt a survey at once accurate and readable of the foothills, the uplands, even the exciting peaks of technological and higher education. He must be prepared, before starting the ascent, not only to find his way through a dense jungle of blue books, scientific and technical articles, statistical projections, and learned papers, but also to realize, as he emerges into what for the moment seems to be clearer air, that his choice seems to lie between producing either a sizeable volume or a small blue book so condensed as to be almost unreadable.

The impact on Britain of the new industrial revolution foreshadowed by scientific discovery

Yet in a world daily bending more and more of the secrets of nature to its service Britain's future, as well as the contribution she can make to the less-developed areas of the world and the Commonwealth,[1] is at

[1] There are 71,000 full-time students and trainees from abroad studying in the U.K. (16,000 are student nurses and midwives, another 16,000 attending full-time

stake. Successful effort and research in technology and higher education—which includes work in the science, physics, and biological
laboratories and the engineering departments of her universities, her
regional colleges of technology, and the industrial design departments
of her colleges of art—are more vital to her economic survival
(whether within or outside the Common Market) than any other facet
of her public education.

This was not always so. In the 1880s we were the 'workshop of the
world', with few competitors. Our craftsmen and technicians could,
to a considerable extent, learn their skills by starting as apprentices on
the workshop floor. The universities and a handful of polytechnics
provided the scientists and technologists we required. Before the
Second World War automation, computers, cybernetics, ultrasonics,
cryogenics, electronics, isotopes, lasers, chromosomes, tetraploid
grasses, even plastics and X-ray crystallography had not reached, or
had only barely reached, the scientific textbooks. The most up-to-date
exhibit in the annual exhibition at the local college of technology of
those days might well be an oscillograph or a sand-blasting machine.
Today it might be an electronic microscope, the hovercraft principle
of levitation applied to a hospital bed, or a chart illustrating the com-
puter calculations involved in the building of the roof of the Sydney
Opera House.

Increase in numbers

In a mere matter of three decades the 12 universities in England
and Wales in 1935 grew to 44, their full-time students from 40,000
to 140,000, and their full-time teaching staffs from 3,079 to over
20,000; the 12,336 full-time students of 1935[1] in the technical, commercial, and art colleges of England and Wales increased by 1965 to
187,000;[2] the part-time day students from 67,416 to 681,000; those
attending evening institutes from 437,367 to 1,252,518; and those
following adult education courses of all types from 50,796 to 218,881.

The conversion of Whitehall

From the languid resignation expressed in so many of the annual
reports of the Board of Education during the years up to 1935,
Whitehall was converted to the challenging leadership to be found in
so many quarters today.

Take, for example, the following resigned thoughts from the Board
of Education annual report for 1935: 'technical education in this

---

and sandwich courses in colleges of technology, and probably another 13,000
attending universities).
[1] Men 18 and over, 4,399; women, 3,533. Men 16 and 17, 2,126; women, 2,178
[2] Excluding the colleges of advanced technology.

country has been, and so far as can be foreseen is likely to remain, mainly on a part-time basis'. 'Much admirable work has been done in unsuitable and inconvenient surroundings. Experience shows that there is a potential supply of students of the right type whose needs can only be satisfied where buildings are available adequate in size, convenient in arrangement and suitably equipped.' Contrast with these the following quotations. 'Economic growth is dependent upon a high and advancing level of education because of the improvement that education brings in human skills and the greater spread of knowledge' (National Economic Development Council on 'Conditions Favourable to Faster Growth', 1963). Again, 'New initiatives were being taken throughout the country to implement the Alexander Report'. (This report, of 1964, on 'The Public Relations of Further Education' led to the appointment within two years of sixty industrial liaison officers to stimulate the interest of local industries in securing training for their staffs.) 'The resources of the Colleges were also being given a hard look by the National Advisory Council on Education for Industry and Commerce in the context of the Industrial Training Act' (Ministry of Education and Science Report 1965). In this and the succeeding chapter we shall study the results of this conversion, and attempt to show in which spheres our universities and colleges of technology have been successful or unsuccessful in achieving the successive targets set by an unending series of Reports, e.g. Barlow, Percy, Crowther, Carr, Robbins, and the five studies made between 1956 and 1965 by the Committee on Manpower Resources for Science and Technology.

Some distinctive features of technical, technological, and further education in England and Wales. Advantages and impediments

Let us first take a broad look at some of those characteristics which distinguish the field of further education from other departments of the educational system of England and Wales, at any special advantages it enjoys, and at certain features which have too often constituted an impediment to nation-wide progress.

As a starting-point it might be well to recall words used by Mr Norman Cole, M.P. for Bedfordshire, in the debate of 21 June 1956. In this, Parliament gave approval to the White Paper of February 1956 setting out a programme for the development of scientific and technological education.[1] 'Technical education is a matter in which there must never be a time gap, not only because we shall fall behind other nations but because it is vital to the life of a country with so few tangible assets in the way of natural resources to support the position it has built up for itself. The only thing that is indigenous to this

[1] *H*, 554, Cols. 1639–1762.

country is our "know how". We turn that "know how" into products which the world wants. It is the product of latent talent stimulated and given direction by technical education.'

In the case of our first Industrial Revolution the real addition to the wealth of the nation did not come immediately after some new invention but often some twenty years later. The gap was due to the need to train a generation of people who could master and work on new processes. By contrast the present Industrial Revolution swept almost with the force of a hurricane into a country ill-prepared after the financial and economic exhaustion of the Second World War. It was not indeed until the early 1960s that all sections of opinion, educational, industrial, and commercial, were at last beginning to realize that all education, and particularly technological and technical education, is a service where the more that is done the clearer becomes the need to advance, expand, and diversify still further. Correspondingly they had to realize that versatility is essential to the young men and women going into technical industry today. They must have a good general education apart from being trained for the particular job their employer has in mind for them at the moment. In an age of such swift change, although technical education must be brought within the reach of all it must never be allowed to become too narrowly vocational, and the tempo of retraining must be continuously accelerated. What the nation needs is cultivated men and women capable of being adaptable without being superficial—not mere specialists.

The work of the technical colleges in England and Wales ranges from courses comparable to those provided in the senior forms of secondary schools to those at graduate or post-graduate level complementary to the provision in the universities. It is in many respects markedly different from the rest of the English educational systems, and from the systems of most other countries, in the sense that it is more 'open-ended' and the normal selective arrangements play a considerably less part in it. Thus students can start their careers at all ages and all stages in their development and transfer from one level to another without losing the progress they have made. England never closes the door or refuses a second chance to anyone who has the persistence to continue and the ability to succeed. This system is not perfect but it is there, and it is a tradition which sometimes evokes the admiration of observers from abroad. In Britain technical education got away to an early start by part-time courses. In other countries the tendency was to start with full-time courses. It is probably this characteristic which creates so much difficulty for those who have not lived, as teachers or administrators, with the growth of the service in understanding the variety of terms they will encounter. It may be well therefore to indicate that in this and the succeeding chapter an attempt has been made to refer to the work of students aiming at some professional (as distinct from a mainly cultural or recreational) target below advanced level, as *technical education*; the work of students in scientific or technological courses at advanced level as *scientific* or *technological education*; the work of students in the universities, colleges of education (for teachers in training) and adult education courses as *higher education*; and the work of students in courses at all levels (outside the universities, colleges of education, and long-term adult education) where such courses are mainly cultural or recreational as *further education*. These categories are, however, by no means rigid. They intermingle and are not mutually exclusive.

Another asset which our colleges enjoy as compared to those in other less densely populated countries is that of accessibility. A country with a population of 583 to the square mile, possessing 44 universities, 24 regional colleges of technology, 160 area colleges, and 270 local colleges, must obviously present far fewer problems, for example in providing for the student who comes from a distance, than, say, the United States with a population of 53 to the square mile or European Russia with one of 63.[1]

A major feature which has militated against a more rapid development of further education, until quite recent years, has been the inability of most smaller firms in industry and commerce to take collective responsibility for the technical education of staff and workers at all levels. As we saw in Chapter IX, already by 1935 certain of the larger firms were beginning to encourage their younger workers and office staff to use the local facilities, and their managerial staff to serve on advisory committees. Regrettably the movement was of slower growth than appeared probable in the years immediately before the war. Mr Ernest Bevin, as wartime Minister of Labour, gave a pronounced impetus in 1942 to the movement for daytime release by his approach to the Employers' Federation and the Trades Union Council, which resulted in the establishment of the National and Regional Apprenticeship Councils. Nevertheless even as late as 1956 it was stated that 96 per cent of the factories in our manufacturing industries were employing less than 500 people; and recent figures (1965) show that despite amalgamations and 'take-overs' there are still, out of the total of 8,070,000 employees, 663,000 working in manufacturing firms with less than 50 employees, 1,748,000 in firms with less than 100, and 4,011,000 in firms with less than 500.[2]

[1] As the Robbins Report indicated (Cmnd. 2154, p. 39), in Russia part-time courses play a leading role; only 50 per cent of the students were studying full time. About 10 per cent of the part-time students were in evening classes; the remaining 40 per cent were taking correspondence courses supervised by institutions of higher education.

[2] 1965 Manpower Survey, Cmnd. 3103, Table 8, p. 61.

As the statistics in the Manpower Surveys also demonstrate, it is the small firms which employ less trained scientists, engineers, and technologists than the larger ones. Partly no doubt this has in the past been due to the cost to a firm of training an employee to one of the higher levels (at least £1,200). Unfortunately, however, until recent years there have probably been far too many small employers who, while paying lip-service to technical education at company meetings and dinners, have admitted in moments of resignation (or honest appraisal) that 'the demand for my product may provide me with an income for the remainder of my working life but I cannot see further than that'. Again, most people interested in education will have encountered the type of employer's wife who asserts that she cannot see the need for educating women and girls. 'Far better to spend the money on buying them some pretty dresses to get them married off earlier,' as one of them put it.

Boards representing each separate industry were set up under the Industrial Training Act of 1964, to see that sufficient training is done in their respective industries; to publish recommendations on the nature and length of training, the standards to be reached and the further education to be associated with training; and to share out of a national pool the costs of training more evenly among firms. It is greatly to be hoped that they will create a new atmosphere. If this happens it may, in combination with the activities of the industrial liaison officers appointed as a result of the Alexander Report, and the wider availability of county major awards as a result of the Anderson Report (1962), achieve that sufficiency of trained man- and woman-power right the way down the line, which is an essential preliminary to the revolution everyone hopes to see in our exporting industries. For a sufficiency of trained man- and woman-power has become for a country situated as we are the millstone for our daily bread.

The organization of any system of technical or further education for the agricultural industry has always presented peculiar difficulties. The total working population of 467,000 was in 1965 spread over 399,603 holdings, 61 per cent of which were of under 50 acres, and 78 per cent under 100 acres. This must mean that a very large proportion of these holdings, in an industry which normally works seven days a week, must either have no employee or not more than one worker other than the farmer and his wife. The proportion of holdings in this category was actually 66 per cent in 1949; and by 1957 half the agricultural workers were still employed on farms where there were less than five workers, 75 per cent on farms with less than ten.

Yet the technological revolution has affected agriculture as dramatically as any other industry. At home we probably enjoy the most mechanized agricultural industry and certainly we possess the highest tractor density in the world. Over 90 per cent of all farms are now provided with a mains supply of electricity. Research has improved both crops and stock out of all recognition during the lifetime of the average farmer; indeed the industry is increasing its productivity per acre by about 3 per cent a year. Rising output and a contracting labour force compel the farmer to possess more than a superficial knowledge of engineering, the science of soils and fertilizers, some acquaintance with electricity, a knowledge of accountancy, and the ability to diagnose ailments in his stock and know those which he can deal with person-ally and those for which he would be wise to call in the veterinary surgeon.

Abroad we ought—if we are to fulfil our responsibilities to the under-developed areas of the world—to be able to send out an ever-increasing flow of agricultural engineers, soil scientists, forestry and grass-land experts, and veterinary surgeons. Yet New Zealand is now looking to Holland for those who possess these skills, and Russia is now offering extensive technical aid to the Middle East and the undeveloped countries.

The development of rural science courses in our secondary schools, if and when fortified by the raising of the school-leaving age to 16; the agricultural apprentice scheme instituted in 1953 and re-cast since the Industrial Training Act; the development of block-release schemes involving a period of boarding at farm institutes; the encouragement of Young Farmers' Clubs; the extended provision of 'village colleges'; and the provision of county major awards to those who are accepted by farm institutes and the agricultural disciplines of our universities at 18 (on their showing over a period of practical experience in farming rather than their amassing of 'O' and 'A' levels) may lead, in the years to come, to the improvement of a situation which still in 1965 pre-sented far too few bright aspects.

The most difficult task which confronts anyone who attempts within the confines of two chapters to outline the principal factors in the growth of technological and further education over thirty years is to divide the subject into intelligible and self-contained sections without constant repetition. For the field is so wide that it ranges from, say, attendance for two hours on one evening a week throughout the winter months at a class on the restoration of antique furniture to the three-year full-time training of an airline pilot. The questions to which I have attempted to address myself in the remainder of this chapter are:

(1) Why the development of scientific, technological, and further education in England and Wales made such a comparatively poor showing in the years between 1902 and 1935.

(2) The contribution made by the system during the years of war 1939–45.

(3) The years of cheeseparing and frustration 1945–55.

(4) The years of advance 1955–65 and the national drive to produce sufficient scientists, technologists, and technical supporting staff for the new technological age.

In the succeeding chapter I shall attempt to describe the methods and machinery by which that advance was achieved, and other advances in higher education; and, finally, the special problems of continuative education for the 15s to 18s.

The country's poor showing in the field of technical and further education between 1902 and 1935

As we have seen in Chapter IX (pp. 151–68), it was already recognized by the end of the nineteenth century that Great Britain was falling behind her industrial competitors abroad and that their advance was primarily due to superior technical education. The closing years of the century saw a remarkable advance through the city parochial Charities Act and the 'Whiskey Money'. The latter was instrumental in bringing to birth 12 polytechnics in London, 13 in the provinces, and more than 100 science schools.

Anyone, therefore, who passes in review the course of further education in Britain from 1902 to 1955 cannot but regard the greatest misfortunes that have befallen it, as (a) the destruction, by the Cockerton judgment of 1899, of the higher-grade schools (one of which produced one of England's Nobel Prize winners), and (b) the inability of Britain's war-scarred and nearly bankrupt economy to take full advantage of the rising tide of interest in technical education which followed Hitler's war.

The Cockerton judgment of 1899 and the blight on development from 1902 to 1935

If Sir Michael Sadler, who really understood the potentialities for sound mental growth of courses other than those sanctified by the conventional methods and syllabuses of the public schools, had become Permanent Secretary of the newly formed Board of Education in 1902, the country might well have developed a system of junior and senior technical schools parallel to the new secondary grammar schools. For Sir Michael was many years in advance of his time in recognizing that, as has so often been demonstrated since by such work as that of Dr Ethel C. Venables on non-verbal tests,[1] technical and scientific activities are not alien to the human spirit. Moreover, the constantly reiterated burden of his 'Special Reports on Educational Subjects' was

[1] See in particular the Crowther Report, pp. 15–18, & para. 543.

that in the modern world the United Kingdom could maintain and improve her standard of living only by keeping a leading place in international trade through superior education. Mention has already been made of the experience of the Air Training Corps with the most unlikely non-verbal intelligences, which suddenly took an interest in trigonometry provided it was called 'air navigation'.

Sir Robert Morant, who jumped over the head of his official superior to become the first Permanent Secretary in 1902, has been referred to by one who knew him[1] as a 'Titan among Civil Servants'. This he certainly was, and no one can fairly deprive him of the credit for his contribution to the successful passage of the Education Act of 1902, his rescue of that clause in Mr Birrell's abortive Bill of 1906 which became the foundation stone of the School Medical Service, and his part in the initiation of school meals.

Unfortunately his conception of secondary education looked backwards to William of Wykeham. The new secondary schools, instead of being built up on broad lines in which the modern and technical curricula would have played their full part, were planned on the traditional basis of a 'general education', designed for the lucky few who could afford the privilege and a moderate infiltration of 'free place' pupils (after 1907). Even more unfortunately, he was bitterly determined to reduce to 'elementary status' the seventy higher-grade schools with 32,300 pupils which were already in existence and others which were in formation. They must, he insisted, be confined to an age range of 11 to 15 instead of 12 to 16 plus. This confinement cast a blight upon curricula based upon science and technical studies, which persisted for many years after Morant's resignation in 1911 and was only too apparent in the regulations for the first junior technical schools.[2] The words used by Mr I. J. Pitman, M.P. for Bath, speaking in the 'White Paper' debate on 21 June 1956, came too near the truth for comfort: 'The real trouble that the Minister is up against is the spiritual one that technical education is "non-U", whereas academic education is "U". Technical education is "servants' hall" if not scullery, whereas academic education is "drawing-room" or "upstairs". Of course the Winchester and New College men would fervently deny it just as the best chaperons in the best drawing-rooms deny that they are snobs or are in any way class-conscious.'

Mr Chuter Ede, also under the cover of Parliamentary Privilege, had said very much the same in the debate on the Education Act of 1944. Later in this 1956 debate Mr Butler, quite rightly so far as opinion had moved by the second half of the century, replying for the

[1] By Dr J. J. Mallon in his preface to *Margaret McMillan, The Children's Champion*, Museum Press, 1960.
[2] See footnote on page 149.

Government said: 'I reject absolutely any arguments which would lay at the feet of this Government the idea that there is any difference in social status between the technician and the man of arts.'

Now that the minutes and memoranda of the early 1900s are available[1] historians can judge the matter for themselves.[2] What they may not so readily understand, for they will not find it in the minutes, is that, by persuading the Civil Service Commission that the Board of Education must be staffed not from the normal administrative class examination entry but by the selection of older and mature individuals, Morant and his successor were able to staff the Department with their own nominees. Many of these were men of the highest distinction who made a name for themselves in many literary spheres, but they were almost without exception men of the academic school. Indeed young men entering the Department after the First World War—when at long last the Treasury and the Civil Service Commission, after a bitter struggle, had insisted on the normal entry by examination—found that the Minister, the Permanent Secretary, the Accountant General, the head of the Elementary Branch, and a number of other high officials, were all, as Morant had been, products of Winchester. Three Harrovians, one Etonian, and one Marlburian filled the remaining top administrative posts. Inevitably this 'academic' conception of education at the top permeated the grammar schools. It became quite unusual for a scientist or a mathematician to be appointed to a headship, and there must be many of those who passed through their local grammar school between 1900 and 1935 who would echo the words of a speaker in the 1956 debate: 'Recently I went to a school which I left thirty years ago, and I found the physics laboratory and the chemistry laboratory were exactly as they were when I left.'

Even as late as 1934, all policy decisions in the sphere of technical and further education were in the hands of two charming though elderly officials. In that year a third official (now too becoming an old man!) was added, but his assignment was to review the fees charged for technical education by every L.E.A. and persuade them to raise them, an assignment which was not only invidious but far from congenial. For there were still, as an aftermath of the 'economic blizzard' of 1931, 418 classes in operation of a therapeutic type for unemployed adults, and as one H.M.I. reported, 'I found it rather difficult to urge that the fees of certain courses should be substantially raised when I noticed that so many of those in attendance had been unable to provide themselves with weatherproof footwear.'

A short-lived attempt was made by Lord Eustace Percy, when

[1] Public Record Office Folio ED, 24/39.
[2] For a fuller account see Schools Council Curriculum Bulletin No. 2, 'A School Approach to Technology', H.M.S.O., 1967, pp. 3-8.

President of the Board[1] from 1926 to 1929, to initiate a new drive in technical education for the engineering industry and for salesmanship. He was among the first individuals in England (as a result of a report made by the then Principal of the Manchester College of Technology) to appreciate how vast the development and competition of technical and technological education in Russia might become when their plans were completed. Unfortunately he was rather unkindly described by a contemporary as 'The only Minister who is his own Permanent Secretary' and with his departure the drive tended to peter out.

Thus all that the Ministry in a review of technical education in their annual report for 1950 could say of these years was: 'The Education Act 1902 did not lead to any great immediate increase in the material facilities available for technical education. Indeed for some thirty years after the passing of the Act the developments were less in the field of new provision than in the reform of existing facilities.'

The contribution made by the technical colleges during the years of war 1939–46 and the awakening interest in many forms of further education created by wartime conditions

By 1937 the dawn of the new Industrial Revolution was at last becoming recognized and it was clear that educational neglect, particularly on the technical side, was proving a serious drawback to industrial efficiency. Provision was accordingly made by the Government for a programme of expansion to cost £12,000,000 (equivalent to nearly £40,000,000 at the building costs of 1965). This, had it been carried out, would have brought the country forward, so far as its technical college buildings were concerned, to a point not in fact reached till 1955. It was too late. The war intervened and some 80 projects for new buildings and extensions, which had been approved in detail or in general outline, were held up. Worse still, about 20 institutions had their premises destroyed or seriously damaged by enemy action.

Nevertheless the way in which the existing technical colleges and other institutions for further education rose to the challenge of war was beyond praise. Special training was provided for nearly 300,000 men and women in the armed forces and war industries, and a system of state bursaries was instituted to supply the needs of the services and of industry for technologists and other personnel at university level.

A survey by the chairman of the Education Committee of the L.C.C. in February 1948 provided an illuminating illustration of this aspect of the war effort—one which could no doubt be reproduced by an examination of the wartime records of many other L.E.As.

[1] See page 151.

'The direct contribution which the Council, in co-operation with Government Departments was able to make to the war effort through its Technical Colleges and Institutes will probably strike the historian in time to come as one of the most interesting achievements in its history. Expressed in terms of mere statistics, they trained, between Dunkirk and the end of the war in Europe, 100,000 members of the forces and skilled war workers. During some of the war years the total volume of work exceeded any recorded before the war, and, in fact, these trainees and war workers together put in 20,000,000 hours of training.

'If the playing fields of Eton officered our army at Waterloo, and if the battles of the Somme, Gaza and Passchendaele were won on the little asphalt playgrounds of the School Boards, it was the country's technical colleges and evening institutes which between 1940 and 1944 sent forth the unending stream of experts needed to win those of El Alamein, Sicily, Normandy and the Rhine. In their classrooms were trained the men behind the guns, radar and degaussing installations; the electricians, coppersmiths and signallers; the engineers on landing craft, the life-boat workers, the sea and army cooks, the skilled cinema operators and modern language experts. Here were assembled in the darkest hours of Dunkirk the gauges and drills so vital to the means of production of weapons for our defence. From here came those who broke the bottle-neck in fine precision workers, the prototype for instruments such as the graticule for the gyro-gunsight, which was described as "the eyes of the instrument which would blast the Luftwaffe from the skies".

'Women's Evening Institutes, too, played their part, notably in the food production campaign, the provision of classes in first-aid and home nursing for the civil nursing reserve, in the provision of the welfare workers for the reception areas and in child care reserve courses for nursery workers.'

To millions of men and women in the services who had lost all touch with education since their school days the war proved an educational stimulus, because through the Forces Educational Services they were afforded a chance to discover what education at the adult level could offer them. To government departments and parliamentary circles it proved a severe shock; for it revealed the country's desperate shortage of scientists, technologists, and technicians. To the economists and a number of forward-looking industrialists in the exporting industries it brought the realization that any investment of labour and materials in improving the country's facilities for technical education would pay early and handsome dividends; for the dangers of our economic situation were clear to every thinking person and our future salvation must be sought in higher production and lower costs. To the rationed housewife, the retired banker perforce turned market gardener, and those substantial sections of the community where restriction and improvisation had become the order of the day, it posed the question where and how could they learn to cope with their daily problems more efficiently.

By the later years of the war practically all women's departments and evening institutes had built up long waiting-lists for day and evening classes in crafts of all kinds, especially dressmaking and millinery, simple renovations, and cookery with special emphasis on the preservation of home-produced food. All these activities helped to meet shortages of food and materials and to maintain standards of home life. To quote an illuminating passage from the Ministry of Education annual report for 1948: 'Classes overflowed into huts, schools, factories and workshops. Laboratories became classrooms, classrooms laboratories, according to the exigencies of inflated timetables; classes started early and continued to all hours; corridors became store rooms and store rooms teaching spaces; by 1949 it became a rarity to find a college or technical school where accommodation was adequate. The war had taught the British people to improvise and here improvisation became the order of the day, even in one college to using an architectural drawing office during part of the day for practical classes in confectionery and cake decoration. Students fortunate enough to find a chair carried it round with them all day!'

Mr Bevin's initiative had by the end of the war raised from 42,000 to some 150,000 the number of workers enjoying daytime release by their employers without loss of wages, to take for one full day or two half days over a 36-week year subjects usually related to their particular occupation. Indeed the tradition of part-time evening instruction relying for its growth on local and often haphazard demand was beginning to give way to a more planned system with an emphasis on training during the daytime. This had gathered momentum during the war.

Day work had increased significantly. By 1947 there were 680 establishments providing full or part-time courses, nearly twice as many as in 1938; the number of full-time students had risen from 13,727 to 31,512; the number of part-time students had risen to 177,975 from 51,276. The number of art students had shown a similar rise; full-time, from 6,010 to 13,309, part-time, from 61,673 to 96,901.

Unfortunately one feature of the post-war world which proved a handicap—and a very severe one—to the smooth development of the system was the National Service requirement. Nobody could hazard a guess today how many young men who in the years 1938–60 seemed likely to become valuable technicians or craftsmen (having reached a point in day or evening classes by 18 where they were ready to pass to the next stage after two or more years in the services) lost the desire to continue. Undoubtedly this interruption of the careers of young men caused by National Service resulted in many of them going elsewhere to make more money in some blind-alley job. Worse still, it caused too many employers to feel that it was not worth while to spend money on training them when their future loyalty seemed so uncertain. (As the other side of the medal it should, however, be noted that a large number of forward-looking employers had taken on additional juvenile staff in 1938 and 1939 and offered them day release. In doing so they were anticipating the shortage of juvenile labour which would arise when the school-leaving age was raised to 15 in September 1939.[1]) Finally some 3,000 trained science graduates (practically a whole year's output at that time) were caught up in the services when they might have been more usefully employed getting our industries back on to their feet once more.

The years of cheeseparing and frustration 1945–55

As we have seen, in the years immediately before Hitler's war the Ministry had clearly become convinced that the provision of adequate facilities to enable the technical and art schools to develop to the full their contribution to the national life would be the most pressing task of the next few years. A substantial programme of developments had been drawn up. The plans and specifications had in many cases been prepared, only to lie, alas, in their wartime pigeon-holes till 1945. Immediately building became possible once more there was obviously an overwhelming case for the initiation of a great drive forward backed not only by the Ministry but by the Treasury, on the ground that a small investment of labour and materials in improving the country's facilities for technical education might pay handsome dividends in a much shorter space of time than equivalent expenditure on other facets of the educational system.

Instead the Ministry clamped down on practically every proposal which was submitted to them except about thirty projects to meet the most desperately urgent needs, such as the extension of the Manchester College of Technology, instalments of deferred projects at Bedford, Luton, and Watford each costing about £30,000, and the purchase of 42 sites for future building and of 33 existing buildings for eventual adaptation.

It was certainly not the L.E.A.s which held back. As Sir David Eccles admitted in the parliamentary debate of 21 July 1955: 'I believe there is a misapprehension in some quarters that L.E.A.s may hang back and not provide their share of the money. Our experience is quite contrary. Our difficulty has not been in having to stimulate L.E.A.s to put up their share of the cost of expanding technical education but exactly the opposite. They have always been willing to do a great deal more than the Ministry has been able to recognize'.[2]

[1] As we have seen (p. 219), the raising of the school-leaving age became the first casualty of the war.
[2] H, Vol. 544, Col. 651.

The Education Act of 1944 had required the 146 authorities, in association with local employers, to examine the educational needs (as distinct from the ephemeral predilections) of their constituents, and to submit by 31 March 1948 schemes of further education for a post-war world in which the country would have to face the stern climb back from lease-lend to economic independence. They were not slow to do so. Indeed by the date fixed by the Act 119 out of the 146 authorities had put forward plans which estimated their requirements for vocational education alone at £31½ million for buildings and £2·6 million for sites, with a further £77 million for buildings, £9 million for equipment and £3½ million for sites for day continuation schools (county colleges). Yet during the ten years which followed the war, while Russia for example was securing a 500 per cent increase in the number of young people in training as technologists and technicians, England and Wales only completed buildings for further education to a value of £21 million (out of £38 million approved) as compared with £208 million (out of £326 million approved) on primary and secondary schools, £9 million (out of £15 million approved) on teacher-training and special schools, and spent £16 million approved for school meals projects. Nor was this the whole story, for it was not until 1958 that the first candidates for the Diploma in Technology from the C.A.T.s (colleges of advanced technology) qualified to supplement the product of the universities. Well might a speaker (Mr Lee) in the parliamentary debate of 21 July 1955 complain: 'We have not got half a century in which to adapt our thinking to the new conditions. This Industrial Revolution will not be gradual like the last when competition was non-existent or practically non-existent.'

In the debate a year later (21 June 1956) Mr Ian Mikardo put the matter even more trenchantly: 'Our post-war interest in technical and technological education derives from the shock which we all got during the war when we discovered how desperately short we were of scientists, technologists, and technicians. We therefore set up the Percy committee which stated that "Hitherto the development of technical education has not been systematically planned. It was abundantly clear even before the war that the whole system requires overhauling". That was written in 1945. Now we are in 1956 and not one ha'porth advanced from where the Percy committee said we were then.'

It is difficult to comprehend the reasons why progress in such a vital department of the educational field was so slow during these ten years. True, the Labour Governments during their two periods of office from July 1945 to October 1951 had to contend with the abrupt cessation of lease-lend, the devaluation of sterling, the Korean war, and the Berlin airlift. Nevertheless one recalls Mr Attlee's challenging statement which related the Government's decision to go ahead with the raising of the school-leaving age to the economic difficulties through which the country was passing. Surely this should have embraced an equivalent move forward in that sector of the educational field which above all others might have blunted, if not forestalled, some at least of the country's economic difficulties.

Immediately after the war more people than ever before were seeking admission to all types of further education. Did the Minister's advisers make the mistake of assuming that many of these students were merely trying to make good deficiencies of technical or commercial education due to the war and that this development, however encouraging, might be no more than a temporary 'flash in the pan'? Or was it perhaps the case that the Government were in two minds which was the right policy to pursue next—preparation to implement the day continuation school clauses of the Education Act or a drive to develop further education for those who were keen enough to seek it?

The devaluation of sterling in September 1949 created an increased awareness of the practical importance to industry of further education. It was one of those periods of national crisis in which the economy has to be saved by productivity combined with the curtailment of home consumption and a vigorous export drive. The nation must stand or fall by higher production and lower costs. The need for more highly trained workers to support that drive, an intensification of the educational activities of industrial and professional organizations, and a renewed interest in the development of technological education at its higher levels were the educational by-products.

Not only among educational thinkers but in the board-rooms of industry the courses offered by the local technical colleges, hitherto regarded as a useful social amenity, were gradually becoming recognized as a vital ally of production. Very soon the statistics began to show that even before 1948 a permanent expansion had been achieved. The demand for part-time education, both day and evening, continued to expand, and in spite of the run-down of the further education and training scheme[1] there was even a slight upward movement in the numbers of full-time technical students. In the sphere of adult education it became clear that there had been an increase since before the war from about 60,000 to a stable figure approaching 160,000 students.

This growth of demand taxed the accommodation of many technical colleges almost beyond reason. How serious this could be in particular areas can be inferred from a contemporary report by one H.M.I.

[1] Under this scheme 52,000 members of the forces had been enabled to complete their education which had been interrupted by the war.

'In this area disused and ancient structures are common. Premises in one place have literally fallen down. In another the technical institute is established in the railway station offices, and is getting ever nearer to the railway itself. There is now a class in one of the waiting-rooms.' The Select Committee on Estimates said in the 1952 session, referring to Birmingham: 'Every practicable place has been allocated for teaching, in the corridors, and, in fact, underneath the platform of one of the lecture theatres. Lack of air and the necessity to use artificial light in so many of the rooms add to the difficulties of those responsible for the college.'

Up to the end of 1948 the L.E.A.s had only succeeded in wringing approvals of just under £3 million for further education projects from the Ministry. The year 1949, however, at last saw a rift in the clouds. Work was started on 83 major projects estimated to cost £5,044,000, although so far as availability for students was concerned the actual leeway made up during the year only amounted to 2 new colleges and 36 extensions opened. The total estimated cost of the 1950 programme was over £7 million. Unfortunately the stringency of the limitations imposed on planning meant that much of the new accommodation provided was deficient in dining-rooms, halls, common rooms, and other facilities needed for the proper development of the common life of students under training. Accommodation for commerce, industrial art, catering, and other forms of training was still short of what was necessary and it was anticipated that the shortage might well increase.

During the next four years of the Conservative administration (October 1951 to April 1955) the general picture was still one of acute pressure on accommodation owing largely to the time-lag between the approval of new buildings and their readiness to admit students. For example, although the value of all new work authorized since the beginning of 1948 amounted to £24 million only £5 million of this had been completed by 1952. Although this new construction undoubtedly improved conditions substantially in some areas there were still many places where conditions which had been unsatisfactory before 1939 were even less satisfactory by 1952. Moreover, even though the annual approvals on paper averaged £4½ million, what has justly been described as 'the long dreary "stop-go" slide' of those years too often operated to set back starting dates.

Anyone who studies the annual chapters on further education in the Ministry of Education reports for these ten years and knows the efforts which were being made by this country's industrial competitors to meet the challenge of the new Industrial Revolution can hardly fail to find them depressing reading. They began with the loss by the Ministry to the university world, in circumstances uncomfortably reminiscent of the fate of Sir Michael Sadler in 1902, of the individual who above all others knew the needs of further education. They ended with the exclusion of the Minister of Education from a Cabinet which slashed the school building programme and made painful and unpopular decisions on education which she had to defend.

Nevertheless there were some achievements: over these years the universities, in response to the recommendation of the Barlow Committee of 1946,[1] doubled in four years their output of scientists and technologists and instituted a special programme of technological building projects to be completed by 1957; plans were laid for a massive expansion of the Imperial College of Science and Technology in London; and in 1952 special grants at the rate of 75 per cent were introduced to encourage advanced work and research at the major colleges of technology.

In addition national colleges of monotechnic type were established to train to the highest level a few thousand individuals in certain industries or sections of industry which were of importance to the national economy, but did not employ sufficient personnel to justify the formation of advanced classes in more than one college. All these monotechnics were borne as a direct 100 per cent charge on the State. They were: the College of Aeronautics at Cranleigh (1946); the National College of Horology and Instrument Technology (1947); the National Foundry College at Wolverhampton and the Stafford Technical College (1947); the National College of Heating, Ventilating, and Fan Engineering (1948); the National College of Rubber Technology (1948); the National College of Food Technology (1951); and the National Leathersellers College (1951).

The success of the universities in implementing the main recommendations of the Barlow Committee had raised the number of full-time university students of science and technology from the pre-war figure of 12,949 to 27,759 by 1950–1. This achievement may have temporarily engendered a false sense of well-being in those circles, parliamentary and academic, which did not fully appreciate the competition which was building up in all industrialized countries to apply the fruits of new scientific and engineering discoveries to production and commerce. Fortunately there were by this time many bodies and individuals in Great Britain who were becoming alarmed by the shortage of practically all kinds of trained scientists and engineers. They appreciated that it was far too serious and far too widespread to be overtaken by a mere strengthening of the engineering and scientific departments of the universities and a projected expansion of the student numbers at the Imperial College of Science and Technology from 1,650 to 3,000.

[1] Cmnd. 6824.

Moreover, in 1950 the University Grants Committee had reported an overall decline of 2 per cent in the science departments and of more than 6·6 per cent in the technological departments of the universities, a decline which was to continue in steady progression till 1954.[1] A similar decline was experienced in the number of students from technical colleges obtaining external degrees of London University in applied science.[2] Although the passing out of ex-service students may in part have accounted for these movements the Scientific Manpower Committee of the Advisory Council on Scientific Policy in 1952 submitted a report (Cmnd. 8561) reiterating a warning that every effort must be made to reverse the trend and to increase the supply.

In February of that year the Treasury grant to the universities was increased progressively from £16·6 million to £25 million for the next quinquennium, to enable the balance of the faculties to allow for a greater proportion of scientists and technologists. In July of the same year the Ministry of Education introduced the special rate of 75 per cent grant to foster the development of those colleges of technology in which a large proportion of their activities would consist of advanced work and research in technology, including courses in advanced technology at graduate and post-graduate levels. Competition to qualify for the 'status symbol' represented by these grants at once became keen. For example by 1953, 22 colleges had qualified in respect of 400 courses (out of more than 1,000 courses submitted by 79 colleges). By 1955, 25 colleges had received approval for 616 courses. By 1956 the number rose to 686 courses at 26 colleges. In 1957, 176 additional courses were recognized.

In November 1953 Lord Glynn initiated a debate in the House of Lords on scientific manpower. He said: 'It has been my good fortune in connection with my work to visit a great many research stations. I think that this country is probably more fortunate than any other in possessing people of outstanding ability who have, by fundamental research at Govt Establishments, put our country in the lead above all others. But what is lacking, and seriously lacking, is technical engineers to reinforce the knowledge of the scientists, especially when the research work is brought to that stage where it can be applied to Industry. I feel that we have now reached a stage where it is absolutely essential to appreciate that unless something is done very rapidly we cannot possibly implement the Government's intention to expand the export of goods on which our whole standard of life depends.'

The Parliamentary and Scientific Committee of the Lower House

---

[1] 1950: 3,593 technological degrees and diplomas awarded; 1951: 3,481; 1952: 3,442; 1953: 3,364; 1954: 3,359. Quoted by Lord Simon of Wythenshawe in article in the *Universities Quarterly*, Feb. 1956.

[2] 1951: 504; 1952: 327; 1953: 333; 1954: 263; 1955: 218.

were in no doubt what should be done. They were in fact about a dozen years ahead of their time, for they had reported in favour of some 20 of the larger technical colleges being converted into Royal Chartered Colleges of Technology, financed by the Treasury, with a council to co-ordinate their work and a technological degree as their award to successful students.[1] The response of the Government, as represented by Lord Salisbury, who replied as Lord President of the Council, seems somewhat surprising in the light of the rather modest steps which had been taken publicly up to that date. 'This question of technological education', he asserted, 'seems to me to be one which may, in the years to come, make the whole difference between prosperity and ruin for the country. I can assure Lord Glynn that the whole Government appreciate fully the importance of it.' Despite this profession he resisted strongly on behalf of the Government the suggestions of the Parliamentary and Scientific Committee on the grounds that the Government 'preferred revolutionary progress to revolutionary change'.

The scientific press during these years was becoming more and more caustic. Paragraphs from *Nature* and the *Financial Times* 'Review of British Industry' may be selected as typical.

'There must be an end to the policy of drift which is hindering the development of technological education. Nowhere was there a hint that the Government has a policy for technical education and that this has been thought out in regard to the needs of technological education and the resources available.' (*Nature*, 24 July 1953.)

'The really disturbing aspect of the situation is that the supply of scientists and technologists is falling considerably below the overall national demand for them, and that it is seriously retarding the necessary expansion of our industrial potential. The number of entrants to the University Departments of Technology during the last two sessions failed to keep pace with the additional places made available in them.' (*Financial Times*, 24 July 1953).

Nevertheless in fairness to the Ministry of Education it should be recorded that during 1953 they had at least taken the initiative in two respects within the financial limits imposed upon them. In the first place they had pressed L.E.A.s to extend the provision of advanced short courses to help scientists and technologists already employed in industry to keep abreast of developments and new techniques. Within eighteen months 45 full-time and 829 part-time courses with this object were in operation.

This initiative they followed up in 1954, in consultation with the British Productivity Council, the Federation of British Industries, the British Institute of Management, and the Trades Union Congress, by

[1] *H*, H. of L., Vol. 184, Cols. 58 & 59.

arranging new three months' courses in 'work study'. The object of these courses, which included work simplification, effective use of personnel, material and machines, time and motion studies, and factory and shop layout, was to increase productivity and reduce losses arising from waste of materials[1] and physical fatigue.

The years of advance in technological education 1955–65

In April 1955 Sir Winston Churchill resigned the premiership and the General Election held at the end of May confirmed Sir Anthony Eden in office with Sir David Eccles as Minister of Education. Almost at once the whole atmosphere, which to all appearances had hitherto been one of half-measures, 'stop-go', palliative and drift, appeared to change overnight.

The Queen's Speech on the opening of the new Parliament contained a reference to the intention of the new Government to take measures to develop technical education, and in the debate on 9 June[2] Sir Anthony Eden used the following words: 'The pace at which the new discoveries of science can be turned to account largely depends on whether we can create a supply of young men with the necessary technical qualifications. Without that education we shall never be able to compete successfully in the markets of the world in the new industries, and I give notice that in that connection we shall go ahead.' A few months later (18 January 1956) at Bradford he reverted even more emphatically to the same theme. 'The prizes will not go to the countries with the largest population. Those with the best systems of education will win. Science and technical skill give a dozen men the power to do as much as thousands did fifty years ago. Our scientists are doing brilliant work, but if we are to make full use of what we are learning, we shall need more scientists, engineers, and technicians. I am determined that this shortage shall be made good.' At last the omens were propitious, employment was at a higher level than it had been since the war, and for once the balance of payments problem was not causing anxiety.

The Queen's Speech debate of 9 June was followed six weeks later (21 November 1955)[3] by one on the subject of scientific and technical manpower, which afforded Sir David Eccles an opportunity to outline the new Government's policy for the expansion of education outside the universities.

The time honoured way to the top of the technical tree hitherto [he explained] had been that through the grammar and independent schools to the Universities.

This academic route, even when widened as planned by the Government,

---

[1] See footnote to p. 293. Waste of materials is estimated to cost the country £650 million a year.   [2] *H*, Vol. 542, Col. 64.   [3] *H*, Vol. 544, Cols. 579 & 694.

would still be far too narrow to carry the numbers needed not only to open up new scientific discoveries but also to make them serviceable to the public. The education system must therefore be shaped to meet the call, not merely for more technologists, but also for a large number of men and women trained to support the top-flight workers and make possible their application of their discoveries to industrial, commercial, and other purposes. For this reason it was necessary to construct an alternative and much broader route than that which led to a University degree. This route must be through the technical colleges. Very bold plans were called for. These would cost a great deal of money, and would make great demands on limited building resources. The speed with which they could be executed would depend upon the support which they commanded in the House and outside it, and also the share of scarce resources which it might be prudent to devote to them.

Among the highlights of this debate were a speech by Sir H. Linstead, chairman of the Parliamentary and Scientific Committee of the House; and one by Mr Albu which was remarkable for its mobilization of the comparable statistics for 1939 and 1953 in the number of students achieving scientific and technological qualifications in Britain as compared with the United States, and an analysis of the case for a really comprehensive review of the problem and the increased contribution which the colleges of technology must make towards it in the light of the rapidly changing needs of industry. Sir H. Linstead saw the position thus: 'We 50 million people on this small island must be in a position from now onwards to sell the products of the new machines, to sell the "know how" of new techniques, and to sell our men as specialists all over the world if we are to have anything like the prosperity and render that international service which we rendered in Victorian days. We all remember the slogan which we coined just after the war "Export or Bust". I am not at all sure that the corresponding slogan for the survival of this country from now onwards will not be "Invent or Bust". . . . We must popularize science as an interesting and exciting career to make it fashionable so that educationists, headmasters, careers masters, the Senates of Universities, Local Authorities and parents realize that science can provide good education and a good and satisfying career.'[1]

The L.E.A.s on their part were certainly not slow in responding to the new mood in Whitehall and the removal of restrictions on technical college building. Before the end of 1955 they had submitted no less than 220 projects for approval. Only 40 of these found their way into the programme for 1955–6 which was settled at about £7,000,000. A further 60 were included in the £9,000,000 programme for 1956–7. The year 1956 will undoubtedly come to be regarded by future historians as the most important in the history of technological education in

[1] *H*, Vol. 544, Col. 663.

Britain. It witnessed the publication of two outstanding documents. The first, which appeared on 29 February, was the Government's White Paper[1] setting out a comprehensive five-year programme for the development of scientific and technological education. The second, published in November, was the first scientifically compiled report on the distribution of scientists and engineers employed in Great Britain with a study of the likely trend in future demand for scientific and engineering manpower.[2]

The White Paper still deserves to be read *in extenso* by any student of technical, technological, and scientific education in England, Wales, and Scotland. Since nothing is so productive of misunderstanding and argument as a failure to define the precise meanings of the terms used in such documents, the White Paper very wisely began by shortened versions of the definitions of Technologist and Technician (or as it is now preferred to describe technicians, 'Technical Supporting Staff') which had been accepted by the Commonwealth Conference of 1954. 'A professional engineer is competent by virtue of his fundamental education and training to apply the scientific method and outlook to the analysis and solution of engineering problems. He is able to assume personal responsibility for the development and application of engineering science and knowledge, notably in research, designing, construction, manufacturing, superintending, managing and in the education of the engineer. His work is predominantly intellectual and varied, and not of a routine mental or physical character. It requires the exercise of original thought and judgement and the ability to supervise the technical and administrative work of others.'

This definition has remained unaltered over the intervening years although there has been a tendency since 1958 to add a rider to the following effect: 'Moreover the professional scientist or engineer spends much of his time in meetings and discussions and in the practice of the multifarious arts of human communication. It follows that either through adjuncts to the specialist studies (the so-called perimeter studies) or through contrasting subjects designed to broaden his interests and background he must become a man of liberal education.'

Technical supporting staff were defined as follows: 'An engineering technician is one who can apply in a responsible manner proven techniques which are commonly understood by those who are expert in a branch of engineering or those techniques specially prescribed by professional engineers; working on design and development of engineering plant and structures; erecting and commissioning of engineering equipment and structures; engineering drawings; estimating; inspecting and testing engineering construction and equipment; use of survey-

[1] Cmnd. 9763.
[2] Cmnd. 278.

ing instruments; operating maintaining and repairing engineering machinery; plant and engineering services and locating defects therein.'

The initial objective set by the White Paper was an increase from about 9,500 to 15,000 in the annual output of students from advanced courses at colleges of technology. No less important, as part of a proportionate increase at the lower levels, it called for an attempt to double the 350,000 students receiving part-time release from their employers to attend daytime courses for one whole or two half days a week, normally to receive training in the fundamentals of technical work at an educational establishment. The most arresting and, as it was eventually to prove, one of the most important of the proposals was that which announced the Government's intention to nominate as colleges of advanced technology (which in a short time became universally known as C.A.T.s) a number of those leading colleges which were prepared to divest themselves of courses below those of advanced level and concentrate vigorously upon advanced work. They would be expected to develop a substantial amount of research, particularly research sponsored by industry, and where appropriate to initiate post-graduate work. The intention at the time was that the colleges selected should remain under the local control of the L.E.A.s which had taken such pride in developing them hitherto, that they should be controlled by strong governing bodies representative of industry, that they should have power to spend within the heads of annual estimates approved by the authority, and that they should enjoy freedom to plan their own courses.

An independent National Council for Technological Awards had recently been established under the chairmanship of Lord Hives to create and administer a new educational qualification to be called the 'Diploma in Technology'. This was to enjoy the standing of a university honours degree, and it was predicted that it would become the pinnacle or terminus of arrival for the new through line in our educational system provided by the C.A.T.s. The programme envisaged by the White Paper would call for building work to be started (although it was not suggested that it would all be ready to receive students) in the five years 1956–61, to the value of £70 million with £15 million for equipment.

At this point it should be noticed that for once, very much to the credit of its authors, and unlike the fate of so many similar White Paper programmes, this one was substantially achieved and in some respects exceeded within the five years' time limit. By the end of 1959 final plans of two thirds of the 363 projects covered by the five-year plan had received approval. Indeed the Minister was able to announce a further three-year plan to follow on to the five-year plan in order to maintain the momentum. This was to cost another £45 million, and it was predicted that it would enable the target figure of 15,000 students completing advanced courses by the mid-sixties to be raised to 17,000 by 1970. By the end of March 1961 the full £70 million worth of building work had been started and by the end of that year £40·3 million worth had been completed. By the end of 1965 £91·3 million worth had been completed, £124·6 million worth started, and £180 million worth authorized.

Even more important than the achievement of these building targets was the steady improvement in the harvest of students from advanced courses. As early as 1961 this already exceeded the 15,000 which the White Paper hoped to achieve by the mid-sixties.[1] By the mid-sixties it had almost certainly reached the target of 17,000 aimed at for 1970, since the figure for Great Britain (including Scotland) in 1965 had reached 21,530. Eight Colleges of Advanced Technology were initially designated.[2] It was hoped to designate two more eventually, one to cover the south-west and the other the north-east. The Bristol College of Technology was designated from September 1960 and the Brunel College at Acton from April 1961.

The one important respect in which the developments foreshadowed in the White Paper hung fire was that relating to the doubling of the numbers receiving part-time release. This will be dealt with in Chapter XIX.

The second document of outstanding importance which appeared in November of this same year 1956 (Cmnd. 276) comprised, first, an inquiry carried out by the Ministry of Labour to discover the number and distribution of qualified scientists and engineers already employed in Great Britain and the likely increase of demand up to 1959; and, second, a study by the Committee on Scientific Manpower of the Advisory Council on Scientific Policy on the likely trend in the long-term demand for scientists and engineers.

In studying the two documents side by side it is advisable to bear in mind that the concern of the Ministry of Education as expressed in the White Paper was to raise the annual harvest from advanced courses at technical colleges in England and Wales from about 9,500 to about 15,000. The Ministry could not predict accurately how many of the 15,000 could be expected to take the further steps necessary to become qualified scientists or technologists, i.e. attain corporate or graduate

[1] Degrees 1, 125; Diploma in Technology 619; Higher National Diploma 1,054; Higher National Certificate 11,717; others 650. Total approx.: 15,150. Including Scotland and Northern Ireland, the figure newly qualifying was 17,148 (Cmnd. 3103, Table 1.).

[2] They were in London, Battersea, Chelsea, and the Northampton Polytechnic in Clerkenwell. The others were Cardiff, Birmingham, Bradford, Loughborough, and Salford. The Manchester College of Technology had just achieved a Royal Charter. It passed under the aegis of the University Grants Committee.

membership of one of the fifteen professional institutions (e.g. the Institute of Mechanical Engineers) or the educational institutes (e.g. the Royal Colleges of Science of London or Ireland). A separate section of the White Paper dealt with Scotland. The concern of the Committee on Scientific Manpower was with those who had become 'qualified scientists' or 'qualified technologists' by attaining such corporate or graduate membership not merely in England and Wales but in Great Britain as a whole. The number of scientists and engineers so qualified employed by firms with 500 or more workers and a sample of firms with 100 to 499 workers was put at 119,700. An estimate (which proved later to be a serious underestimate) was made of those employed by firms with less than 100 workers, those in the armed forces, and those in other occupations such as shipping, the distributive trades, and the non-nationalized parts of the mining and transport industries. This raised the 119,700 by 15,000 to 134,700, representing approximately 0·6 per cent of the total working population of 24 million.

The estimated demand by 1959, as returned by employers, came to 152,200, a figure which was found to have been almost exactly achieved by the repeat survey of 1959 (152,400).[1]

Among the more important findings of the Committee on Scientific Manpower in their assessment of the Ministry of Labour survey were:

(1) That modern science, whether basic or engineering science, is the source of almost all the ideas on which the development of modern industry depends, and certainly the source of all the more important ideas.

(2) That there is a definable relationship between the rate of increase of industrial production on the one hand and the number of trained scientists and engineers employed by industry on the other.

(3) That the ratio of increase in numbers of scientists and engineers employed to increase in output appears to have been in the neighbourhood of 1 : 1.

(4) That an annual growth rate of 4 per cent in total industrial output would postulate an increase in the number of qualified scientists and engineers employed from the 1956 level of 134,700 to somewhere in the region of 226,000 by 1966, an increase of rather over 65 per cent.[2]

(5) That as a minimum goal Great Britain should aim at an annual

---

[1] Cmnd. 902, p. 3.

[2] The Technical survey published in October 1966 put the estimated stock of qualified manpower available for employment in January 1966 at 328,000, for the 1961 census showed that the 1956 estimate of 134,700 was a considerable underestimate. The number shown to be economically active by the census of 1961 was 259,670, out of 287,610 qualified in all age-groups up to 70 or more.

figure of 'graduations' in pure and applied science of about 20,000 as compared with 10,000 today (November 1956) if the economy is to grow at an acceptable rate. (This figure was in fact reached in 1964 when graduations totalled 20,581, and they were estimated to rise to 26,000 by 1968.)

To the unprofessional eye of the mere academic historian the doubling of the annual harvest of qualified scientists and technologists during these ten years of achievement must appear a very notable advance indeed. Between 1958 (the year in which the first 34 candidates for the Diploma in Technology qualified) and 1964 the numbers qualifying rose to 1,221, the university quota of engineers, technologists, and scientists rose from 8,275 to 12,303, and others attaining membership of professional institutions or accepted associateships and university diplomas rose from 5,741 to 7,063; an increase in total from 14,050 to 20,587.

In the mid-1950s more than three-quarters of the students who obtained professional qualifications through colleges of technology did so by part-time study only. The important engineering group (4,000 in 1955 and about 5,500 in 1957) outnumbered the university-trained engineers by two to one and probably five out of six of these had qualified by attending part-time courses. By the later sixties about half of the men and women qualifying every year as scientists and engineers can still be expected to do so from the technical college field, but less than a third of them will have received their education in part-time courses.

Although the intake from the grammar and independent schools has always been substantial, 20 per cent of the students attending advanced courses were found as late as 1959 to have won their way up from the secondary modern schools.

To those who examine these ten years of achievement not as mere historians but with a professional eye there are obviously desiderata still to be achieved and many criticisms still to be offered. For example there is still too much 'fragmentation' in British industry. Many of the smaller firms are still slow to foresee or respond to the greater harvest of qualified manpower. It remains to be seen how far they will take advantage of the opportunities now provided by the resources available to the industrial boards set up under the Industrial Training Act of 1964. Again we are not by comparison with the U.S.A., Germany, and Japan doing nearly enough yet either to bring our existing stock of qualified manpower up to date by refresher courses or to upgrade manpower with less highly developed skills. There is likely to be a continuing shortage of mathematicians, systems designers, advanced programmers, control systems engineers, and production engineers. There is too strong a tendency for students approaching the end of their courses to attempt to stay on, for example to read for a PhD. or carry out research which may be only marginally relevant to the needs of industry. We are not persuading sufficient women to qualify outside such fields as medicine, biology, animal husbandry, and rural science.[1] There seems to be some tendency—not confined to Great Britain—for interest in science at school to flag and for a swing towards the arts subjects.

However impossible it may be for the academic historian to evaluate those criticisms, he can at least note that by 1961 the Committee on Scientific Manpower felt able to venture the hope that the number of qualified scientists and technologists could be expected to rise by the end of the decade from 7 to 13 per thousand of the working population—*a potential technological revolution in itself.*[2]

There has, however, ever since the White Paper of 1956, been great concern as to whether the country's production of technicians and other skilled supporting manpower, whose assistance is so essential to the efficient use of its professional manpower, is keeping pace. As Mr Albu stressed in the debate of 21 July 1955, there were at that date too many highly qualified people doing work which should be done by others: scientific officers constructing their own apparatus and performing routine tasks, even typing their own reports. Experience in the United States had been quoted as indicating that three to five technicians were necessary to support every professional technologist. Up to 1965 information on the employment of technical supporting manpower was only available in this country from a sample survey conducted by the Ministry of Labour in January 1960 covering two industries, the chemical and the engineering industries.[3] Fortunately a much more comprehensive survey was undertaken on a national scale in the Triennial Manpower Survey of 1965.[4] Although this had to be conducted on the basis of *function*, because a majority of those acting as technicians were found to possess no qualifications having a national currency, the results were encouraging.

The number of technical supporting staff found to be employed in 1965 was 621,860 and the forecast for 1968 was put at 707,623. 17 per cent held a degree or a Higher National Certificate or Diploma, 14 per cent the Ordinary National Certificate or Diploma, 9 per cent the Technician Certificate of the City and Guilds of London or equivalent. The remaining 60 per cent had other qualifications, training with firms, or no formal training qualification assessed by examination. This should not be understood as implying that they had no qualifications at all, for there are many other unlisted qualifications

[1] In Russia in 1956, between 20 per cent and 30 per cent of higher technician graduates were women.
[2] Cmnd 1490.
[3] Ministry of Labour Gazette, Dec. 1960.   [4] Cmnd. 3103, Ch. 5.

in this field and many employers train their own staff to a high level to meet specialized requirements. The overall ratio worked out at 3·3 technical supporting staff to every unit of professionally qualified staff; but it varied widely industry by industry, from 45 to one in the Post Office (which has excellent internal training schemes), 8 to one in transport and the airways, 1·9 to one in the chemical industries and 1·2 to one in mineral oil refining. The annual harvest of new supply of those with nationally recognized qualifications was thought to be about 40,000.

CHAPTER XIX

THE EXPANSION OF TECHNICAL, TECHNO-LOGICAL AND HIGHER EDUCATION IN ENGLAND AND WALES 1935–65: 2

The methods and machinery by which the advance described in the last chapter has been achieved, and other advances in higher education.
The Percy Committee (1945) and the Barlow Committee (1946) sow the seed.—It is germinated and propagated by the National Advisory Council on Education for Industry and Commerce and the Regional Advisory Committees.—The expansion of the teaching force.—The overhaul of the system of student grants.—The reports (1964) of the Committee on Higher Education appointed by the Prime Minister under the chairmanship of Lord Robbins radically transform the whole future aspect of university and other forms of higher education.—The industrial Training Act of the same year bids fair to achieve a similar transformation in the field of education for each separate industry and for agriculture.—The C.A.T.s achieve university status.—The future of the former teacher-training colleges.—Other recommendations of the Robbins Committee, and their reception.—Some common criticisms of the rate of University expansion.—The special problems of continuative education for the 15–18-year-olds.

I T may be difficult for anyone acquainted with the broad and rapidly expanding fields of university, technological, and technical education in the mid-sixties to appreciate how narrow and circumscribed those fields were in 1935. The number of universities in Great Britain awarding their own degrees was then 16 with a full-time student population of 50,638 and staff totalling 3,670.[1] By comparison in 1965 the number had grown to 52 university institutions receiving their grant from the University Grants Committee, with a population of 168,607 full-time students and full-time academic staffs employed in teaching departments of 25,294.

Except in London and some of the large cities, or where, as at Loughborough, some remarkable character was making his influence felt, the growth of technical education had, up to 1935, been almost entirely dependent upon the personal inclinations or ambition of young

[1] The number in England and Wales in 1935 was 12 universities with 40,392 full-time students and about 3,079 full-time academic staff employed in teaching departments.

students (which no doubt accounted for the preponderance of courses leading to accomplishments such as shorthand-typing, hairdressing, and 'ballroom dancing').

It was not in fact until 1933, when Whitehall instituted the economy drive to increase fees, that any attempt had ever been made by the Board of Education to prepare, from the detailed examination of hundreds of college prospectuses, a conspectus showing on one sheet for each L.E.A.'s area what provision actually existed in that area for full-time, part-time day, day release, and evening classes.[1]

Course and class fees, which themselves varied from area to area for courses of identical type, were complicated by the charging of differential fees for students living outside the area of the L.E.A. actually conducting the course. This relic was redolent of the time-worn 'local chargeability' principle of the Poor Law. After half a dozen L.E.A.s had tried to transfer chargeability for a particular child or student whose 'residence or permanent home' was claimed to be with the mother working in some other area, Sir W. R. Barker wearily minuted, 'I should be sorry if it became the duty of the Board's Legal Adviser to trace the Odyssey of a cook general in the 20th Century!'. It was possible, as Mr Michael Stewart complained in the debate of 9 July 1955,[2] for a young man to live in the area of one L.E.A., work in the area of another, pass through the territory of a third on his way to work, and on his return to his home to go by the doors of a technical college that was running a course of exactly the kind he wanted, but to which he could only go by paying more than he could afford by way of extra district fee.

By 1936, however, partly as a result of the surveys carried out in the previous year by H.M.I.s but more particularly owing to the success of the Yorkshire Council for Further Education instituted in 1928, followed by the South Wales Advisory Council in 1934 and the West Midlands Advisory Council in 1935, there was evidence of a growing realization that provision for technical and art education needed to be mapped out on a regional basis.

The Percy Committee and the Barlow Committee

The success of the enquiries started by the Barlow Committee, which reported in 1946, in stimulating a more adequate flow of scientific and technological manpower from the universities has already been noted.

Two years earlier one of the strongest committees which had ever,

---

[1] These sheets were jocularly known among H.M. Inspectorate as 'Lowndes' tablecloths'. However, many H.M.I.s found them very useful in the survey of accommodation and advice on the direction of further developments which they were asked to construct in 1935.   [2] *H*, Vol. 542.

up to that time, considered Britain's needs in the field of further education had been appointed. It was this committee, under the chairmanship of Lord Eustace Percy, which really set in train nearly all the subsequent developments and innovations which have in the twenty years following the report in 1945 brought about our technological revolution.

Starting from the standpoint that the position of Britain as a leading industrial nation was being endangered by a failure to secure the fullest application of science to industry and that this failure was partly due to deficiencies in education, the report made the following suggestions:

(1) That a strictly limited number of technical colleges was required in which technological courses of a standard comparable with that of university degree courses should be developed. It was this recommendation which became the starting point for the designation, eleven years later, of the 10 C.A.T.s and the institution of the Diploma of Technology.

Unfortunately, like so many government committees before and since, the committee shrank from the conclusions of their own logic. For in the eyes of young men and women the status attached to a career is closely linked to the academic qualifications required to practise it. If academic qualifications equivalent to those of a university degree were in future merely to be obtainable as diplomas awarded by designated colleges of technology, they would still carry nothing like the social prestige of a degree. For the next ten years this became the recurring theme of almost every organ of the scientific press, as well as that of papers such as the *Manchester Guardian*, and of speaker after speaker in every successive parliamentary debate on scientific and technological manpower or on technological education. The Percy Committee, it is commonly believed, was exactly equally divided on the question whether to recommend that their proposed diplomas should be convertible into degrees. Had it not been so the country might not have had to wait nearly twenty years till the Robbins Committee on Higher Education (Cmnd. 2154) recommended in its report of October 1963 the creation of a Council for National Academic Awards, a council which was formed under Royal Charter in 1964 and awarded its first degrees in 1965.

(2) The second main recommendation of the Percy Committee was that there should be single institutions for specializing in particular branches of technology.

It was no doubt this recommendation which had much to do with the formation of the National Colleges for Aeronautics, Horology and Instrument Technology, Foundry work, Heating, Ventilating and Fan Engineering, Rubber Technology, Food Technology, and Leather.

(3) Thirdly they suggested: that regional councils (on the lines of

those already established in Yorkshire, South Wales, and the West Midlands) should be brought into being to cover the whole country, with a national counterpart. It was this recommendation which led to the setting up in 1947 of the framework of a National Advisory Council on Education for Industry and Commerce, co-ordinating the Regional Advisory Councils and regional academic boards and submitting advice on national problems over the whole field of technological education.

The work of the National Advisory Council for Industry and Commerce

To do justice to the work of the National Advisory Council and the influence they have exercised upon successive development in advanced technological and commercial education would require several chapters. Here it is only possible to mention a few highlights.

Their first major report of 1950 was on the question of the development of higher technological education with special reference to the part which could be played by the major technical colleges in (a) stimulating the provision of post-graduate courses in special fields of technology in both the universities and technical colleges and (b) devising awards comparable in prestige and status to a university degree for students in technical colleges. This led to the Government's decision in 1952 to institute the 75 per cent grant for advanced courses.

During the years 1952 to 1954 much of their time was spent on the question of a national award-making body, the development of 'sandwich' courses, and the investigation of the types of technological training through flexible advanced courses which could best meet the varying needs of industry.

By 1955 they were in a position to advocate the establishment of an independent national council to create and administer awards possessing a recognized national currency for students who completed successfully courses in higher technology approved by the council. Two boards of studies, one for engineering and the other for other technologies, should, they advised, be established to assist the council. It was the acceptance by the Minister of this advice which led to the appointment of the National Council for Technological Awards under the chairmanship of Lord Hives and the institution of the Diploma in Technology, initially awarded on the result of a three-year full-time or not less than four-year sandwich course.[1] The institution of the Membership of the College of Technology award, now accepted retrospectively as a Ph.D, followed in May 1959.

[1] In 1960 students taking courses for the Diploma in Technology were required to receive industrial training either in the form of sandwich periods or by a year's intermission usually between the second and third year of their full-time course.

Such studies as these having provided a basis for the policies announced in the White Paper of 1956 and sown the seeds for future expansion, the National Advisory Council were next invited in 1957 to recommend urgently what further steps should be taken to implement the commercial aspect of these policies. To this end they set up an advisory committee composed partly of their own members with experience in this field and partly of persons outside their membership who were closely connected with commercial education.

This advisory committee, under the chairmanship of Mr J. G. McMeeking, reported in July 1957. There was, it found, an urgent need for more and better education for commercial activities of all kinds both in industry and commercial undertakings. Marketing, distribution, business techniques, salesmanship, finance, insurance, industrial design, called for the creation of educational opportunities for young people of talent parallel to those at last becoming available for those whose careers would lie in fields of science and technology. Commercial education must be overhauled and reinvigorated through an expansion of apprenticeship and day release and the development of sandwich courses with a new award of national standing as their coping-stone. Women should be given greater opportunities to attain professional status in commerce. These recommendations led to the Diploma in Management studies for students over 26 possessing graduate or equivalent professional qualifications, a new Higher National Certificate in Business Studies, and in 1960 to the creation of a U.K. Advisory Council on Education for Management.

In 1960 the National Council turned their attention to the development of block release courses in which the student, instead of attending college on one or more days a week throughout the academic year, attends full-time for varying periods, e.g. one full college term of 12 weeks each year, and the balance of the year with his firm.

In addition they set up a special sub-committee under the chairmanship of Alderman Lampard-Vachell, whose two reports of 1960 and 1961 led to a substantial increase in the enrolment figures of agricultural day release students, an improvement in the supply and training of teachers in agricultural subjects, the organization of horticultural education, poultry and forestry courses, and the provision of agricultural education for women.

Three further sub-committees set up during the years 1961–4 examined (a) the organization of sandwich courses, in particular the 'end on' arrangement of such courses with a view to using college accommodation, equipment, and staff to the best advantage (Sir Lionel Russell's committee); (b) the nature and extent of the likely demand for a further higher award in business studies broadly equivalent in length and standard to those leading to the Diploma in Technology (Mr W. F. Crick's committee); and (c) the public relations of further education.

The report of the last-named sub-committee, which was under the chairmanship of Sir William Alexander, secretary of the Association of Education Committees, recommended that an identifiable officer specifically concerned with the tasks of providing information and developing public relations should be appointed at every level, national, regional, local authority, and college. The work of these officers can already be seen to be exercising a profound influence in assuring that no school-leaver, or his parents, is left in any doubt as to the advisability of continuing his education or as to the chances and choices placed before him by the astonishing development over the past twenty years in the variety of the further education systems. To anyone who has read the thousands of pages in reports on technological and higher education produced since 1935 the 21 pages of this short report must appear to have achieved greater practical results in the increase of students than any other.

The contribution of the Regional Advisory Committees

While these activities of the National Advisory Council were developing the new structure of technical and technological education, the Regional Advisory Committees were busily engaged in co-ordinating the courses available to students in the areas each cover; devising a proliferation of new courses for technical supporting staff and operatives (ranging from press tool design to courses for stokers in nuclear plants); stimulating the interest and co-operation of industrial and commercial employers in their areas; co-operating with H.M.I.s in steps to smooth the obtaining of approvals to new courses; and endeavouring to find regional solutions to the difficulties posed by the charging of extra district fees.

Although by 1956 a considerable movement towards 'free trade' among the authorities had been achieved, it was still the case that individual authorities could reserve the right to contract out in respect of specified courses and for stated reasons. The final solution of this tiresome impediment did not come until the reforms made under the Local Government Act of 1958: these established a pool to which all L.E.A.s would contribute from April 1959 on the basis of an agreed formula to cover all advanced technical education.

Owing to the great diversity of subjects and interests which must be covered the development of technical, technological, and adult education in England and Wales has always proceeded from the report of one technically qualified group of experts to another. In the Bibliography at the end of this volume 43 such reports covering the years up to 1935 are mentioned. It would be necessary to add nearly double that number if they were not in fact now listed in more convenient forms in the sectional lists of Her Majesty's Stationery Office, covering the Department of Education and Science, and in the list of research projects and investigations bearing upon scientific manpower policy appearing as Appendix C of the 'Review of the Scope and Problems of Scientific and Technological Manpower Policy' (Cmnd. 2880, October 1965).

The review of the years since 1935 attempted in this section has endeavoured to show how the Barlow and Percy reports sowed the seed, how the interest aroused by the five national surveys of scientific and technological manpower and the work of the Advisory Councils have germinated and watered that seed, and how the years since the White Paper of 1956 have begun to reap the harvest.

The expansion of the teaching force engaged in technical, scientific, and technological education

It would, however, have been a much thinner harvest if it had not been for two further major reports: the Willis Jackson Report of 1957 which dealt with the problems of finding the supply of teachers and set a target for development; and the Anderson Report of 1962, which has since led to the tens of thousands of students of advanced technology and science obtaining assistance towards the cost of their courses on terms similar to those awarded to university students under the county major award schemes of the L.E.A.s.

The report of the special committee set up in September 1956 under the chairmanship of Dr (now Sir) Willis Jackson was published in May 1957. Its main conclusions were:

(1) The colleges would require by 1960–1 7,000 more full-time and 8,000 more part-time teachers than in 1955–6, implying an average net increase over the next five years of about 1,400 teachers.

As in the case of the targets for the increase in scientists and technologists set by the White Paper of 1956 these teacher targets too were substantially achieved, for between 31 March 1955 and 31 March 1960 the number of full-time teachers had risen from 11,555 to 19,640. The number of part-time teachers probably increased over the same period from about 47,000 to 58,000 (exact statistics are difficult to obtain). By the end of October 1965 the number of full-time teachers in further education establishments had risen to 36,500, excluding those serving in the C.A.T.s which had passed under the aegis of the University Grants Committee.

(2) The three training colleges for the production of technical teachers at Bolton, Huddersfield, and London (the Garnett College) should be enlarged from 300 to 500 places and be given new buildings including residential accommodation. Improved rates of grant should

be introduced for pre-service students, and in-service students should retain their existing teachers' salaries, and receive free tuition and an allowance towards the cost of maintenance.

(3) A residential staff college should be established to enable senior college staff to study the teaching, administrative, and technical problems of further education in conjunction with representatives of industry, universities, government establishments, and schools.

(4) Conditions of service for the staff of technological institutions should be improved in many directions, e.g. the provision of more clerical, laboratory, and research assistants, and opportunities for periodic return to industry, for carrying out remunerative consulting work, and for paid leave to pursue certain forms of studies. It was thought that improvement of the conditions of service in such ways might stimulate the recruitment of late entrants drawn from the armed services and the Scientific Civil Service, and the willingness of industry and government departments to do more to release staff for part-time teaching in the daytime.

Proposals for the extension of the three technical training colleges and the opening of a fourth such college in the West Midlands (Wolverhampton) were well advanced by 1959 and completed by 1963. The Further Education Staff College at Coombe Lodge, Blaydon, Somerset, also opened in March of that year.

The overhaul of the system of student grants

The Anderson Committee on Grants to Students,[1] which was appointed in June 1958 and reported in 1962, introduced equality of treatment for all students in higher education. It did so by establishing the principle that awards should be made automatically to all students who had two G.C.E. passes at 'A' level or the equivalent and had been admitted for the first time to first degree or comparable courses at universities or establishments of further education. To implement the recommendations of the committee, legislation was necessary (the Education Act 1962), and this imposed a duty upon L.E.A.s to make awards conforming to the conditions and amounts set out in a new body of regulations.[2]

In the year in which the Anderson Committee had been appointed (1958) 16,288 students following full-time courses of acceptable standard in colleges of technology were in receipt of major awards. Most of those following sandwich courses were paid apprentice rates by their employers during their six-month periods in industry. Many firms paid not only the students' fees but their salaries in addition during the six months in college. The Federation of British Industries has

---

[1] Cmnd. 1051.
[2] S.I. 1962/1689.

given a strong lead in the encouragement of such arrangements which they saw to be in the nation's interest.

The new arrangements for automatic awards did not result in a substantial immediate increase in university awards, a sphere in which practically all L.E.A.s had moved into line during the preceding few years. Their impact on awards for courses of further education was, however, considerable. The total currently holding awards for courses in further education by the end of 1965 had risen to 56,000 full value awards and 19,000 of lesser values.

The Robbins Committee Reports and the Industrial Training Act 1964

By the end of the period under review (1935–65) the whole future aspect of higher and post-secondary education in Great Britain was on the way to becoming radically transformed by two further events of outstanding importance.

The first was the publication in October 1964 of the report of the Committee on Higher Education appointed by the Prime Minister under the chairmanship of Lord Robbins; this was followed a year later by two further volumes, the one giving a detailed picture of higher educational life in Britain in 1962 and the other a comparative study of higher education in eleven other developed countries.

The second was the passing by Parliament of the Industrial Training Act of 1964, an Act to make further provision for industrial and commercial training.

By the end of 1965 the first had already led to the introduction of sweeping changes in the structure of university, technological, and technical education; the second had commenced to make an impact, long acknowledged to be essential, on some of the most stubborn impediments to the preparation of the whole man- and woman-power of the nation for the technological revolution of the next forty years.

The reports of the Robbins Committee on Higher Education leave anyone industrious enough to study them carefully with the strong impression that it is impossible to think of any question relating to British higher education, as it existed in 1962, and comparable progress in other developed countries, which they did not answer.

The reports appear to be informed throughout by eight constantly recurring principles which the committee no doubt accepted as axiomatic.

(1) That the emergence and success of the C.A.T.s, the amount of full-time advanced work in the regional colleges of technology, and the lengthening of the training courses for teaching from two to three years, combined with the rising educational standards of entry, had by 1963 produced a situation in which the universities could no longer be looked upon as the sole providers of full-time higher education.

(2) That courses of higher education should be available for all

those who are qualified by ability and attainment to pursue them and wish to do so. The growth of the school population and the proportions reaching the minimum standard of attainment for entry to higher education must postulate startling increases in university, technological and teacher-training facilities up to 1980. The old idea that there exists a 'pool of ability' more or less constant in each age-group must be abandoned in the light of our new knowledge of the fallibility of performance in general intelligence testing and the much greater importance which must be attached to the influences of 'nurture' on measurable ability.

(3) That equal academic awards should ensue upon equal academic performances.

(4) That distinctions based on adventitious grounds, whether historical or social, are wholly alien to the spirit that should inform higher education. (Those who have dealt for many years with applicants for county major awards know how readily a species of 'stock-market' can grow up in the estimation in which higher education institutions are regarded.) It is not merely by providing places for students from all classes that those institutions will achieve the ideals of producing cultivated and adaptable men and women who have learnt to become searchers for truth; but by providing, where they live and work as students, influences which in some measure compensate for inequalities of home background.

(5) That in terms of annual public expenditure per graduate British higher education is more costly than that in most other developed countries. Our tutorial systems, classes and seminars have led to a staffing ratio of 1 : 8 as compared with 1 : 30 in France, 1 : 35 in Western Germany, 1 : 14 in the Netherlands and 1 : 12 or 1 : 13 in Sweden, the U.S.A., and the U.S.S.R. Only Russia makes provision from public funds to assist as high a proportion of students as Great Britain. A considerably lower proportion of students are home-based in Britain than is normal abroad. Nevertheless in terms of total public expenditure per graduate our system is economical because the process of sorting out abilities, no less than the high standard of work in the sixth forms of British secondary schools, leads to students entering upon university courses better prepared, shorter honours degree courses, and lower wastage rates through failure at the end of courses.[1]

(6) That strong grounds existed for the extension of post-graduate work in some fields and for greater flexibility in opportunities for transfer of a student from one institution to another where appropriate to his or her intellectual attainments and educational needs. (The number of post-graduate awards has risen greatly since the Robbins Report. It was 6,254 in 1958-9 and 14,020 in 1965-6.)

[1] For wastage rates see Cmnd. 2154, paras 125-7 and Tables 17 and 18.

(7) That, as already demonstrated in the case of scientific and technological manpower by the Committee on Scientific Manpower of 1956 (Cmnd. 276), there is a broad connection between the size of the total stock of trained manpower in a community and its level of productivity. 'We do not believe that the Soviet Union is the only country that can make full use of the brains of its people.'

(8) That unless higher education could be speedily reformed there was little hope of this densely populated island with its relative lack of natural resources maintaining an adequate position in the fiercely competitive world of the future. Both in general cultural standards and in competitive intellectual power vigorous action is required to avoid the danger of a serious relative decline in this country's standing.

Working out from such premises as these, the committee examined what should be the aims and principles of any system of higher education in the social and instructional fields, in the promotion of the general powers of the mind, in the search for and discovery of truth, and in the transmission of a common culture and citizenship. They examined closely and acknowledged the educational revolution which had taken place in Great Britain since 1945; the characteristics of British universities, teacher-training colleges and institutions for further education; and comparative characteristics and statistics of the higher education of other developed countries.

This survey enabled them to suggest with some confidence targets to be aimed at for the total need for places for each decade up to 1980–1.

The principal criteria adopted in arriving at these targets were as follows. First, that the proportion of the working population who had successfully completed courses of full-time higher education must rise from the 3·4 per cent of 1960–1 to 6·2 per cent by 1980–1 and 15 per cent by A.D. 2025; and the proportion who had successfully completed courses either of full- or part-time higher education or by private study must rise from the 5 per cent of 1960–1 to 9·7 per cent in 1980–1 and 19 per cent by A.D. 2025. Secondly, that, to palliate the undesirable pressures arising in the schools and prevent the growth of an '18 + problem' more serious in its political and social implications than the '11 + problem' of the years since the war, the proportion of university places annually becoming available to the steadily growing numbers obtaining the minimum qualifications for entry must remain at about the same level (or some 6 per cent higher, 66 per cent in 1980 as compared with 60 per cent in 1962–3).

At this point, before surveying the far-reaching recommendations by which they sought to achieve these targets, and how far the acceptance of those recommendations by the Government has been modified or expanded, it may be well to set out some figures to reveal the degrees of success or failure in the few years for which they are as yet available since the committee reports.

The picture so far as England and Wales are concerned is on the whole an encouraging one. The Robbins Committee took as their point of departure a provisional estimate of 216,000 places in Great Britain in full-time higher education for home and overseas students[1] in 1962–3. The figure for England and Wales was put as 187,700. This estimate was distributed as follows.

	Universities		Teacher-Training Colleges		Full-time Technical and Art		Total	
	Robbins	Achieved	Robbins	Achieved	Robbins	Achieved	Robbins	Achieved
1962–3	110,700	108,700	48,400	48,300	28,600	28,000	187,000	185,000
1963–4	118,900	116,000	52,800	54,800	32,800	33,300	204,500	204,100
1964–5	130,100	127,200	58,900	62,800	35,700	39,600	224,700	229,600
1965–6	143,900	140,500	66,000	73,300	38,100	47,000	248,000	260,800
1966–7	155,400	154,700	71,100	84,000	40,400	54,000	266,900	292,700
1967–8	197,000	200,000	75,000	95,000	45,000	66,000	317,00	361,000

It will be noted that by 1966–7 there was a slight short-fall in the universities' achievement, but substantially better achievements in the colleges of education figures and those for full-time advanced work at colleges of further education. By 1967–8 all totals exceed those advocated by the Robbins Committee.

Unfortunately, looked at solely from the point of view of the avoidance of the growth of an '18 + problem' in relation to those failing to achieve entry to university courses, the figures are less happy. For the proportion of the age-group obtaining the minimum entry qualification from secondary sixth forms has steadily risen, so that only 55 out of every 100 of these secured university places in 1965 as compared with 63 in every 100 who did so in 1961.[2] It is probably on this account that the Minister (October 1967) asked the universities to aim at a figure of 220,000 to 225,000 university places in 1971—about 20,000 more than the Robbins target for that year.

The C.A.T.s achieve university status

Returning to the main recommendation of the report, there could by 1963 no longer be any doubt that the C.A.T.s, with over 10,000

[1] They estimated that overseas students would represent 12 per cent of the university students, 20 per cent of teacher-training, 15 per cent of advanced further education, 10 per cent of all full-time students. The total university numbers have, however, diminished since 1963.

[2] For a full discussion of these figures and their implications see an article, 'Still more expansion needed in Higher Education' in The Times of 13 October 1967.

full-time advanced students, had achieved the high standing and the goals set before them on their designation at various dates since 1956. The technological and to some extent the scientific faculties in the universities could not, without seriously upsetting the balance of their other faculties, produce anything like the number of qualified scientists and technologists seen to be required. This gap the C.A.T.s were filling, creating with the strong support of the leading industrial firms a new concept of higher education. Over 90 per cent of their students were taking advanced courses and some £10 million had been spent on their buildings and equipment. Their libraries had been greatly enlarged and were organizing a technical information service which was proving of particular assistance to small firms. They were developing 'liberal studies' in such subjects as management and administration, the history of science, the sociological impact of technological change upon social and cultural life, foreign languages, and the aesthetics of design. In 1962 they had followed a precedent set in 1952 by Loughborough in becoming institutions directly financed by the Ministry. 'Seldom in the history of higher education has so new a departure been so swiftly accomplished.'[1] Nevertheless, although their Diploma in Technology was rated as the equivalent of a university honours degree they were still, unlike the new universities (some of which had been founded since their designation), unable to award their own degrees. In this sense it was inevitable that they should feel that they were being kept 'in a position of tutelage, less attractive to students and less able to attract staff'.

The Robbins Committee had no hesitation in recognizing, as nearly all forward-looking educational opinion has been urging for some years, that they should be given university status with power to award their own degrees. It was suggested that they should have from 3,000 to 4,000 students each and should be governed and financed accordingly. The committee went further. They advocated that the National Council for Technological Awards should be replaced by a Council for National Academic Awards covering the whole of Great Britain and established under Royal Charter, with the function of deciding whether, in colleges (including the six National monotechnics) whose full-time work was sufficient for its purpose, part-time students should also be eligible for a degree. This council, which received its Royal Charter in 1964, should in due course do much to eliminate the jungle of anomalies which has hitherto obscured the principle of equal academic awards for equal performances.[2]

[1] Ministry of Education annual report, 1962. p.7.
[2] For example all architects take a five-year course but only those who are accepted in university faculties of architecture (of which there are three or four) can receive a degree in architecture.

The future of the former teacher-training colleges

Hitherto the teacher-training colleges had too often felt themselves to be only doubtfully recognized as part of the system of higher education. The record of the Ministry had been a notable one, with the post-war emergency training scheme, the development of the institutes of education, the subsequent series of expansion programmes, the founding of the day colleges, the introduction of the three-year course, the clearing-house arrangements to find places for applicants for entry disappointed in their first choice of college, the ingenuity with which accommodation had been used to the maximum, and the expansion of courses for teachers already in service and for married women wishing to return to the service. Yet the colleges were still not in the main stream, despite the standards of work they had attained and a characteristic ethos that justified a claim to an appropriate place in it. Entrants automatically sacrificed the possibility of working for a degree, although 14 per cent of them had achieved three or more G.C.E. passes at 'A' level and 39 per cent two or more passes. In this field, too, as in that of the C.A.T.s, such anomalies must be swept away. First the designation 'teacher-training college' must go and be replaced by 'college of education'. Secondly a substantial proportion of intending teachers must be enabled to obtain Bachelor of Education degrees. One pattern which might emerge would be that the training qualification and the degree pass in education and one main subject would be taken in the College, and the second main subject by means of two or three years' part-time study or a fourth year of full-time study. The colleges should have independent governing bodies related generally to university schools of education, and be financed by the body responsible for university grants. First degrees obtained by teachers should be regarded as a suitable qualification for registration in universities for a higher degree. A target of 145,000 places for intending teachers in colleges of education should be set for achievement by 1980.

Other recommendations of the Robbins Committee, and their reception

In the field of university and higher technological education the report foresaw that a need would arise before 1980 for the creation of six new universities in addition to those already in process of formation and also two institutions of university status for higher education in management. One of the six would be a special Institution for Scientific and Technological Education and Research comparable to the Imperial College of Science and Technology and the Royal College of Science and Technology at Glasgow (later to become the University of Strathclyde). These should themselves be expanded to 3,500–4,500 students. A fifth such special institution should be developed from a selected C.A.T.

The question of preserving the academic freedom of the universities and the immunity they had hitherto enjoyed from interference or control by the Government of the day obviously presented the committee with one of its toughest problems. They were emphatic that the administrative invention of interposing between the Government and institutions a committee (the University Grants Committee) of persons selected for their knowledge and standing, and not for their political affiliation, had provided a buffer of inestimable value. It has always been one of the features of this system that committee members should be actively engaged in their profession, whether in academic life or in other forms of education or industry, and therefore in daily personal touch with current thought and developments in their particular fields. As a warning the rector of one of the most famous universities in Western Europe was quoted as saying, 'So long as we are subject to these [government] controls as regards finance, all talk of academic freedom is a swindle.' They therefore recommended the enlargement of the U.G.C. into a Grants Commission which, as the Treasury had made it plain that they would not assume responsibility for additional institutions, should pass from the aegis of the Chancellor of the Exchequer under that of a new Ministry of Arts and Science.

One of the chief difficulties which confront any historian in trying to assess such an outstanding signpost to future expansion as the report of the Robbins Committee so shortly after its appearance is the impossibility of distinguishing which of the 178 items in the list of recommendations are likely to have developed into burning issues regarded as of prime importance in ten or twenty years' time.

Immediately on its appearance the Conservative Government of the day under the premiership of Sir Alec Douglas Home welcomed the report as 'an opportunity to set the course of higher education in this country for a generation'. They accepted the basic assumption that courses of higher education should be available for all those who were qualified by ability and attainment to pursue them and wished to do so. They also adopted the committee's calculations for an expansion of places for 1967–8 and 1973–4, involving 197,000 places in universities and C.A.T.s by 1967–8, at an estimated cost for the ten-year programme of £3,500 million.[1] They accepted the recommendation that the C.A.T.s should have university status and that the Royal College of Art and the College of Aeronautics should also be accorded that status. One of the C.A.T.s should become a special Institution for Scientific and Technological Education and they should all be brought within the ambit of the university grants system. Prompt action was also taken to set up a Council for National Academic Awards. The Government recognized, however, that many of the detailed sugges-

[1] Ministry of Education annual report, 1963, pp. 13–14.

tions in the Robbins report were primarily a matter for the academic world and must await the views which informed opinion will wish to express.

A committee under the chairmanship of Lord Franks worked out a scheme for two schools for advanced business administration and management. The cost of these (one in Manchester and the other in London) is borne jointly by the Government and industry. They did not however become fully operative until 1965–6.

A remarkable note of reservation to the report by Mr (now Sir Harold) Shearman had forcefully questioned the division of the educational system between two Ministers—the Minister of Education and a proposed Minister of Arts and Science to be given responsibility for the University Grants Commission, the Research Councils and other autonomous state-supported activities administered on similar principles. His views evidently found favour with the Government, who in April 1964 combined the office of the Ministry of Education with that of the Ministry of Science to form the Department of Education and Science, under a Secretary of State for Education and Science assisted initially by two Ministers of State and two Joint Parliamentary Under Secretaries of State. Thus the Ministry of Education ceased to have a separate existence just twenty years after its creation by the Education Act of 1944. Its life span was even shorter than that of the secondary modern schools which that Act had also created.

The change of Government on 16 October 1964 led to some important variations in the Robbins design. In a statement on higher education made to the House of Commons on 24 February 1965 the new Minister (Mr Anthony Crosland) announced that no more universities or more accessions to university status would be needed for about ten years with the possible exception of a completely new technological university institution in the north-east. It was now clear, he affirmed, that the target of 218,000 university places by 1973–4 was within the capacity of existing universities and other institutions of university status. Subsequently, in a speech at the Woolwich Polytechnic on 27 April, he developed the concept of a dual (or 'binary') system of higher education: the autonomous sector covering institutions of university status financed through the U.G.C., and the public sector covering the regional, area and local colleges of technology and the provision for the training of teachers in the colleges of education. These proposals met with a mixed reception from the public sector (particularly from some of the colleges of education), but the U.G.C. stated that they were in full agreement with them and had discussed their implications with the committee of vice-chancellors and principals.

An even more mixed reception was given to the statement by the Chancellor of the Exchequer on 27 July 1965 postponing by six months starting dates for capital projects for higher education (other than those in development districts and areas of high unemployment). The difficulties and uncertainties which such deferments inevitably involve in relation to expansive targets and grants based on quinquennial forecasts were one of the penalties which the system of higher education had to pay for the country's balance of payments difficulties. These difficulties, as suggested earlier, might have been considerably reduced if this country had been as quick off the mark as the U.S.S.R. in developing its higher education system after the war.

It is extremely difficult for the ordinary reader who is not prepared to immerse himself in the vast literature and statistics of higher education to realize how great the expansion has been over the thirty-year period covered by this chapter. It defies illustration by any simple diagram which will do justice to the growth of standards (as distinct from mere numbers) in every sector, full-time, part-time, adult education and lastly evening institute classes—those 'Schools for Self Discovery' so brilliantly described by Mr Eric Browne in the *Readers' Digest* for January 1966. For example in the full-time advanced sector alone there were 19 students per 10,000 of the population in 1935, 35 per 10,000 in 1950 and 73 per 10,000 in 1965.[1]

Some common criticisms of the rate of university expansion

The expansion has inevitably created criticism in some quarters, hard feelings in others. Hardly a day passes without these questionings being reflected in one section or another of the press, or television, which unfortunately seems to call attention to students at their worst. Student strikes, rags and the irresponsible conduct or half-baked utterances of individuals tend to be treated as front-page news; such movements as Voluntary Service Overseas and for the underprivileged at home tend to appear on the back pages or in late night broadcasts.

Perhaps the most valid aspects of criticism are those concerned first with the ever-growing cost of student maintenance awards since they became obligatory under the Education Act of 1962; second with the high wastage rates through failure at the end of courses.

Maintenance awards, which were costing £26·1 million in 1959 for 129,000 students before the Anderson Committee reported, had increased to £88 million in respect of 307,000 students by 1965–6. Actually it does not require the mental capacity of an actuary to show that all but the lowest-paid families contribute over their life-time,

---

[1] These figures are based on the number of students in universities, teacher-training, full-time technological and art education (over 18s) and attending three-year tutorial or advanced tutorial classes in adult education.

through their education rate and also their annual expenditure on such taxed items as drink, petrol and tobacco, not only to full cost of the primary and secondary education of their children but for their university maintenance award too, if they make the grade.[1] This makes it difficult to go all the way with those who put forward as an obvious remedy the substitution of loans, repayable in easy instalments over the students' career, in place of the direct maintenance grants. The past history of student loans does little to support this solution. They often cost in staff time and salaries nearly as much to collect as the amount received; they would act as a deterrent to highly qualified candidates from poor homes; they might well increase the 'brain drain' and they would face women graduates with the prospect of a 'negative dowry' if they married. Moreover, as the Robbins Committee showed, our graduates are produced 'ready for market' more cheaply than those of other developed countries owing to their better preparation for entry to university courses, shorter honours courses, and lower failure rates.[2] An alternative might be to require all applicants to enter as their first choice a university which they could attend as a home-based student (for whom maximum grant is at present £275 a year as compared with £370 a year for resident students at Oxford, Cambridge, and London and £340 a year for other universities). Nobody who has had many years' experience of administering student awards would favour such a course, for he will know how important it is for intelligent young men or women to develop their personality by learning to stand on their own feet between 19 and 22, and the extent to which home-based students may miss the general social and cultural ends of higher education so clearly set out in the Robbins Report.[3] Away from home even the well-drilled examinee may become a cultured individual. At home he may get no further than becoming a mere specialist. As the Duke of Edinburgh once remarked, 'University education is merely so much vocational training unless it puts some fire in your belly.'

The high wastage rates (18 per cent for men and 12 per cent for women in university courses, 30 per cent for men and 25 per cent for women in colleges of further education) offer a more serious target to the critics.[4] They would not present so intractable a problem if college authorities and L.E.A.s were given more freedom than at present exists to send down students and discontinue awards in those cases where it becomes obvious in the first year that a student has reached

---

[1] Although the rise in costs of education and corresponding rises in rates and taxation render the figures out of date I have illustrated this argument on pages 151 and 152 of *The English Educational System* in Hutchinson's University Library series.

[2] An article on the question of grants versus loans by the Rt. Hon. Patrick Gordon Walker appeared in *The Times* for 13 May 1968.   [3] Cmnd. 2153, Ch. II.

[4] The National Union of Students are engaged on a factual survey analysing the wastage rates in the different disciplines (*The Times*, 12 Oct. 1967.).

his ceiling at the acquisition of two or three 'A' level passes in his G.C.E. in the sixth form.

A palliative suggestion tentatively put forward by Professor V. S. Griffiths, president of the Association of University Teachers, might be a two-year course for some, a three-year course for most, and a four-year course for yet other students. If the appeal procedure which this would postulate could be firmly controlled by the universities themselves it might prove a welcome relief; but anyone who has been concerned with the administration of county major awards will know the lengths to which members of education committees will go in supporting 'political' appeals on behalf of their constituents.

Nevertheless, although the 'failed B.A.' had become almost an object for obloquy or a butt for amusement in some superior quarters, nobody should fail to take note of the wise comment of the Robbins Committee that those who abandon higher education may yet be more useful citizens in the community on account of their experience. History abounds with cases of the 'failed B.A.' student who has made a national or even international name for himself in literature or the arts; and many a 'failed Dip. Tech.' will be found serving the community as a high-grade technician.

A further disquieting line of criticism which has begun to emerge, as the Robbins Report recedes into history but its recommendations for expansion are relentlessly implemented, is that which tends to question the value of university qualifications outside those spheres, such as science and technology, which demonstrably further the national level of productivity per head, or those which supply recruits to such socially essential callings as medicine, architecture, and teaching.

Such questioners assert that the worth of a university education, even to such traditional 'consumers' of the highest university products as the Civil Service, has never been scientifically demonstrated; that the Victorian and Edwardian obeisance to the 'grand old grind and mental discipline of the classics' can no longer be proved to develop powers of application and judgment of a superior order to those developed by other disciplines such as history and economics (they merely point, it is alleged, to the fact that tradition has always enjoined that the cleverest boys should begin on the classical side of a school); or that the country may be wasting vast sums of the taxpayers' money when alternatives such as subsidized foreign travel or sandwich courses at the factory bench and the technical college might produce equally well or even better the qualities demanded by modern industrial and commercial management.

Their opponents reply that the sweep of the modern scientific and technological revolution must rapidly render obsolete any body of information or practice which a student can attain in the sandwich course or by a period of residence abroad. What, on the contrary, a university course should confer upon him is 'an understanding of the processes whereby information is acquired, a capacity to distinguish between real information and mere prejudice or hearsay, an appreciation of the role played by theory in the coherent ordering of information, and the adoption of an attitude of sceptical inquiry towards generally accepted truths'. The kind of qualities which the management of our modern large-scale industrial and commercial undertakings require—'ambition, initiative, toughness, and self-confidence'—are equally necessary in the successful pursuit of a good university degree. These undertakings do not require mere 'go-getters' but people who can analyse and discriminate and above all carry a very large question mark above their heads throughout their career.[1]

There are of course numberless other lines of criticism, for example the acute shortage of residential accommodation for students either in hostels or lodgings; and the damage to sixth-form work in the secondary schools through the attraction of so many of the most able members of their staffs into posts in the expanding universities and colleges of technology. For the 38 per cent expansion of student members between 1961–2 and 1965–6 has been matched by a 37 per cent expansion of staffs.

These difficulties, though at present serious, will no doubt be remedied in time. Already ingenious schemes are afoot to remedy the acute shortage of residential places. For example the University of Lancaster has raised a thirty-year loan of £500,000 to build small flats for its students, and the formation of student housing co-operatives is under consideration in Liverpool, London, and elsewhere.

An increasing supply of honours degree graduates for the staffing of our secondary schools is still over the horizon, but it may be hoped that the situation will gradually improve as the need for such graduates in industry and commerce draws nearer to satisfaction—or individuals find that industry and commerce do not satisfy them and turn to teaching. It must be admitted that the drain from the schools over recent years has been serious. A recent survey by the Headmasters' Association showed that in the years 1964–7 no less than 4,700 teachers out of 40,000 in the schools have left the profession. Of the 1,888 leaving in the year 1966–7, 117 went to the universities, 149 to technical colleges, 325 into colleges of education, 458 into other posts in education; 341 left the profession on marriage, 140 went into industry and commerce and the balance emigrated.

The flight of talent (mainly to the U.S.A.) usually referred to as the

---

[1] Anyone who wishes to follow up these arguments in greater detail will find them in an article by Mr Walter James in *The Times* of 30 September 1967 and a reply by Professor A. H. Hanson of the University of Leeds a few days later.

'brain drain', after a period of years when the 'outs' were nearly balanced by the 'ins', has recently assumed alarming proportions. It probably affects the supply of scientists and technologists, who have stayed on at the university for higher research degrees followed by a period of work in industry and have reached their thirties, more than it affects the newly qualified university product.[1]

Those who have not been in close touch with university affairs or studied the reports of the University Grants Commission can hardly fail to wonder if all is well with our higher education when they find such anxieties and criticisms ventilated almost daily in their morning papers, or witness sensational television programmes illustrating Russian technical achievement. Nevertheless internal movements for reform in institutions of higher education are now both growing and welcomed as respectable. Student welfare, student representation, student discipline, student accommodation, organization and methods studies, costing of furniture, apparatus and equipment, plant utilization, admission policies, and broadening of curricula are all subject to widespread inquiry and review. We should at least be careful in exercising our innate capacity for denigration of British achievements to recall one sentence in the Robbins report. 'Our experiences abroad have confirmed some cherished beliefs about the excellence of British higher education, although they have caused us to re-examine others.'

The special problems of continuative education for the 15 to 18 age-groups

The release by enlightened employers of their young workers for one whole or two half days a week during the technical colleges' teaching year of 36 weeks had made a tentative start by 1935. It allowed about 220 hours' instruction a year (or 270 hours if an evening class was attended in addition). As yet, however, it only affected about 30,000 employees, of which 7,203 came from the engineering and allied trades, 4,140 from food, drink, and catering, and 3,029 from municipal and Civil Service employment. 53·8 per cent of them had been educated in the public elementary schools, 36 per cent in the grammar schools, 5·1 per cent in junior technical schools. This daytime release was already seen by the educational world and particularly by the principals of the technical colleges as supplying for the young employee the answer to a need little realized or expressed hitherto.[2] It had been developed as a partnership between employers, apprentices,

[1] The 'brain drain' was briefly considered by the Committee on Manpower Resources for Science and Technology in their report of October 1965 (Cmnd. 2800, para. 21). An analysis by the Ministry of Technology indicated an annual migration of 3,000–4,000 between 1958 and 1963 balanced to some extent by an immigration of 2,000–3,000. See *The Times*, 12 October 1966.

[2] See the views expressed by the principal of the Borough Polytechnic quoted on page 162.

local authorities, and the State in a field where the interests of all parties had been realized to coincide. Nevertheless it was a demand from the employees rather than any direct demand from the employers that initially fostered growth.

Although the technical aspect of these young people's studies was normally dominant, experience in this country was soon to prove, as it had proved in Germany, that vocational content aroused a sense of purpose and reality in the recipients, and that the association of work and study could sometimes produce results where nothing else could do so.

By 1938 the numbers had still only reached 36,000, but forward-looking employers saw, as we have noted already, that the threatened raising of the school-leaving age from September 1939 would take a whole age-group out of the market; that it was becoming less easy for the works to fit into their daily round the general training which ought, if possible, to be given before the inevitable spread of mechanization; and that it might be a wise course to encourage their recruits to obtain additional education in working hours rather than expecting them to give up their evening hours to study. By 1938, too, some of those employers who had opened 'Works Schools' on their own account found that the L.E.A.s were quite ready to take them over and maintain them for the benefit of all young employees in the area. As we have seen, the initiative of Mr Bevin as Minister of Labour during the war years led to the first great expansion of daytime release. By the time the statistics became available to the public once more in 1946-7 (and the educational world could again find time to study them) the number had risen to 159,000 receiving education in 400 colleges and technical institutions. Thus there were already five students for every one that there had been in 1935.

The blight which descended upon technical education during what has been described as the post-war years of frustration and cheeseparing soon filled release classes to a point where, by 1949, all districts reported that they had reached a limit in the number of those for whom they could cater. Yet the raising of the school-leaving age, National Service, and the low birth-rate of the pre-war years had led to such a reduction in the young people becoming available to industry and commerce that more and more employers came to realize the growing importance of offering training to those they could recruit.

Gradually the situation improved and between 1950 and 1955 the numbers rose from 241,000 to a peak of 355,000. This peak, which represented a twelve-fold increase since 1935, seemed to many of those Members who took part in the debates in both Houses on manpower requirements and technical education to represent one of the brightest galaxies in the firmament of technical education. Perhaps some of them took a mischievous interest in the fact that in Scotland, which had always prided herself on being a few paces ahead of England and Wales, day release had started late with 600 students in 1938 and had as yet only achieved 25,000! Nevertheless the achievement of England and Wales was not altogether without its critics, for one Member remarked in the debate of 21 June 1956, 'When day release and sandwich students go to the technical school they are taught that the empirical methods of the factory are unscientific which is perfectly true—and when they go back to the factory they are told "don't take any notice of all that pansy stuff they teach you at the college".'

As mentioned earlier, the bold intention set out in the White Paper of 1956 to double the number from 355,000 to 710,000 by 1961 unfortunately proved to be the one target which the Government failed to achieve. Indeed instead of the numbers continuing to rise by some 40,000 a year as predicted they actually slumped to 406,000 in October 1959 (having reached a new peak of 438,000 in 1958). In particular the numbers in the age-groups 15 to 17 remained virtually unaltered from 1955 to 1960, and as the size of these age-groups was increasing the proportion in receipt of part-time release fell from 14·8 per cent to 12·6 per cent.

Disappointing although this appeared to be at the time, perhaps the wistful comments to be found on the subject in the Ministry's reports for those years may not have sufficiently taken into account the fact that in these same years the numbers of 15s to 18s staying on at their secondary schools, transferring to full-time or sandwich courses in further education, or at 18 entering university or teacher-training courses, had risen from 374,000 to 600,000.

Another and perhaps more valid cause for anxiety in the middle fifties was the number of young men and women who entered (predominantly by evening study) for National Certificate and City and Guilds courses for technicians and craftsmen but, like the seed that fell upon stony ground, withered away before they completed them. The failure rates in the examinations for City and Guilds courses and those of the Regional Examining Unions were shockingly high, although it was already noticeable that where employers released their employees for part-time day courses such failures were greatly reduced.

The Crowther Committee, whose report appeared in 1959 after three years' intensive examination of every aspect of education for the 15 to 18 age-groups, took a hard look at all aspects of day and evening continuative education which were being developed as a rather meagre substitute for the 'county colleges' envisaged by the 1944 Education Act.

It would be a massive understatement to remark that they did not at all like what they found! Although they noted with satisfaction that the number of full-time students had increased by 70 per cent in five years, and that there had been a tenfold increase in the numbers in part-time day courses since the war, their main criticisms were that:

(1) Part-time day release was not yet offered by nearly enough industries.

(2) The eyes of students and staff being fixed on success in examinations, the background had become so vocationally biased that anything in the nature of general education tended to be regarded as an unwelcome intrusion, and the greatest enemy of the whole further education system was shortage of time.

(3) The width of the range of intellectual ability found in those entering upon further education courses postulated much greater efforts than had been made in the past to discriminate between entrants and fit them as individuals into courses exactly suited to their requirements.

(4) Much more thought needed to be given to ensuring a smooth transition from full-time education at school to part-time further education.

(5) Although the number of girls entering employment was about the same each year as that in the case of boys, only 8 per cent of them received a chance of day release as compared with over 30 per cent of the boys.

(6) It was doubtful whether evening education only should any longer be considered an appropriate form of education for boys and girls under 18.

(7) Full-time studies for young people of the 15–18 age range too often represented a belated form of repentance, or a retrieving mechanism, for work which could better have been done at school.

A change which becomes noticeable in the form of the reports of advisory committees on public education over the past sixty years is that, whereas they used to be anaesthetic or analgesic, they have steadily become more and more cathartic. The effect of these strictures on the further education of the 15–18 age-groups can be recognized in almost every innovation which has been introduced into the system since the Crowther Report appeared. These innovations included a great expansion of 'sandwich' courses in which students alternate between periods of full-time attendance at a technical college (totalling not less than nineteen weeks in the year) and work at the bench; 'block release' courses concentrating into, say, eight weeks' continuous study at a college a total time equivalent to one day a week, with day release for the rest of the year; 'Cox and Box' courses in which two sets of students use the same facilities in the college and the firm alternately; full-time pre-apprenticeship courses (and integrated full-time courses of training and education for those over 16), both counting as one year of apprenticeship for young people desiring to train for skilled employment; intensive surveys designed to bridge the gap between schools and technical colleges and to establish well-understood routes by which the school-leaver can move from one to the other according to his aptitudes; reduction of failure rates by increasing the variety of courses available and substituting the 'Craft Certificate' and the 'Advanced Craft Certificate' for the former 'Intermediate' and 'Advanced Level'.

By the end of 1965 the total number of students of all ages in receipt of part-time release in England and Wales had risen to 602,000, twenty times that of thirty years before. Scotland and Northern Ireland could show an additional 51,000. There were 17,000 students in sandwich courses and 33,000 in 'block release' courses. Thus although the first fruits of the Industrial Training Act of 1964 had yet to be garnered, the numbers were well on the way to the 710,000 envisaged by the White Paper of 1956. (By November 1967 the number had risen to 639,963.)

On page 352 of their report the Crowther Committee quoted a German industrialist as saying, 'We envy you your bulge', and added the rather wistful comment, 'We trust there may be no need to add—"but we are astounded at the way you have wasted the chance to build up your capital of skill".' It may therefore be in point to attempt to discover whether the young man or woman of 16, 17, or 18 had come to enjoy a better chance of being granted daytime release by an employer in 1965 than in 1958, the year used as their datum line by the Crowther Committee. The 223,000 young men and women aged 16, 17, and 18 who were enjoying day release in 1957–8 were drawn from three age-groups totalling 1,653,000. If one deducts, as one should, the numbers still at school in schools of all kinds (secondary, direct grant, independent), those who had moved on to full-time further education, and those who at 18 had entered a university or college of education, the pool of those potentially available for employment from the total of 1,653,000 must become 1,431,000. The 336,000 young men and women in the same age range in 1965 were drawn from three much larger age-groups totalling, 2,251,000. Deducting the far greater numbers still receiving full-time education in 1965, the 2,261,000 becomes 1,738,000. If therefore the percentage of the pool had remained constant at the 15·6 per cent of 1957–8 one would have expected to find 291,000 receiving day release instead of 336,000.

Unfortunately the total figures for 1966 or 1967 will not be available before this book is in print, but it is probable that they will reveal a sharp acceleration as a result of the Industrial Training Act. That Act, which was warmly welcomed by every section of parliamentary opinion, is expected to lead to a wide expansion of all forms of further education and particularly day release. The boards, industry by industry, which are being set up under its provisions will have three main duties: to see that sufficient training is done in their industry; to publish recommendations on the nature and length of the training, the standards to be reached, and the further education to be associated with the training; and to share the cost of training more evenly among firms through a levy. The Minister of Labour has stated in the House of Commons that he would not normally be prepared to approve the grant schemes of boards unless they made it a condition for the payment of grant that young people undergoing a substantial period of training were given day release. In this he has been supported by a resolution passed at the Labour Party Conference of 1967 to insist that appropriate release for further education be a requirement of all training schemes.

To many observers of the advance of public education in England and Wales on so broad a front over the past thirty years the saddest casualty has been the 'county colleges' of Mr Butler's Act of 1944, a fate in which they have repeated that of the 'day continuation schools' of Mr Fisher's Act of 1918. Had it proved possible to raise the school age to 16 as early as some sections of opinion in 1946 thought likely, all young people of 16 and 17, not still receiving full-time education or daytime education in sandwich or similar courses, would now be receiving 330 hours of general, social, physical, and recreational education, as they do in the German Berufsschulen. This would have meant that during the last stages of adolescence they might have received that help in finding their way successfully about the adult world and perhaps building up for themselves a standard of moral values which so many parents today find it so difficult to impart to their teen-age sons and daughters. Additionally they would have received encouragement to keep up the pursuits and the physical and cultural interests which had begun to possess their minds at school; and sometimes, forced by their emergence into the hard realities of the adult world, they might have begun to realize how inadequately they had been prepared by their education hitherto to face that world and determined to redress their self-realized deficiencies.

Nevertheless, looking at the enormous task which the country has had to accomplish in other facets of her educational services since Mr Butler's Act of 1944, it is difficult to disagree with the following passage in the Ministry's annual report for 1962: 'There is disappointment among some people that so much of the Education Act of 1944 is still letter and not deed. Nevertheless the nation would have been less well served if all the resources available had been channelled single-mindedly into what seemed in 1944 to be the first priorities. For example the creation of virtually a new structure for technical education could hardly have made such progress if the £100m. required for County Colleges had been permitted to receive priority.'

CHAPTER XX

EPILOGUE

How far have we succeeded during the thirty years since Parts I and II of this book were written in moving along the road to becoming an educated people?

As I have attempted to show in Chapters XV–XIX on the credit side of the account

(1) We have achieved remarkably widespread progress in the adoption of more enlightened practices in the education and nurture of young children. One result of this has been that by 1964 boys and girls aged 11 were reaching in reading tests (and probably in less measurable fields) on an average the standard only attained sixteen years before in 1948 by pupils seventeen months older. This represented a 24 per cent increase in the pace of learning over the 72 months between the age of beginning school and the age of 11.

(2) We have achieved substantial improvement in the national provision for 'unlocking' the minds of pupils of secondary school age. In this connection we have witnessed:

(a) The virtual elimination of the 'all age' school.

(b) A growing recognition that intelligence ratings at any given age are not immutable but capable of considerable modification, so that we can claim with some assurance today that a wide national pool of ability still remains capable of being tapped.

(c) The addition of at least a year to school life for all pupils. 559,090 pupils were remaining voluntarily at school in the 15–18 age groups in 1965. These represented 18·3 per cent of the sum of those age-groups, whereas in 1935 the 172,262 remaining at school in the same age-groups only represented 9·5 per cent of their sum. Nor should it be overlooked that there is now a growing volume of transfers to the full-time further education field which by January 1965 was providing for 33·6 per cent of the sum of the age-groups 15–17.

It is extraordinary to recall that up to about 1930 written permission had to be obtained from the Board of Education for every individual pupil whose parents wished him or her to be allowed to stay on at an elementary school after the end of the term in which the age of 14 was reached.

(d) An expansion of sixth-form work in the grammar and comprehensive schools which the Crowther Committee described as revolutionary.

(*e*) A similar advance in the pace of learning, as evidenced by the progress in reading ability, to that witnessed in the case of the primary schools.

(3) Over the thirty years the country has carried out a school building programme which, despite the interruption of the war years, had completed between the end of the war and 1965 4,910 new primary schools and 2,790 new secondary schools, representing 1,932,085 new places in maintained primary schools and 2,029,920 new places in maintained secondary schools. To get the full picture it is necessary to add the 402 schools affording 96,705 places brought into use in new Church of England and Church in Wales schools, the 247,340 places brought into use in 797 new Roman Catholic schools, and 20,330 places provided by 112 projects sponsored by other bodies. It is unfortunately impossible to obtain accurate details of the places provided in some 630 new maintained elementary schools, and some 80 new schools provided by the Roman Catholic community and the Church of England, in the years between 1935 and the outbreak of war. 3,740 new places in grammar schools were provided during those years. If, however, these schools were of the same average size as those provided since the war, the grand total for 1935 to 1965 cannot be far short of 4,562,950 places in 9,730 new schools. Curiously enough this number of places corresponds almost exactly with the figure to which the roll of public elementary schools had fallen by the end of the war.

(4) As we have seen in Chapters XVIII and XIX, the university population of England and Wales rose from 40,392 in 1935 to 140,490 in 1965, 154,735 in 1966 (and 200,000 in 1967), and will probably reach its target of 223,000 in 1971–2. From 1935 to 1965 the full-time student population in institutions of further education rose from 12,336 to 187,000 (221,828 in November 1967). The number of part-time day students increased from 67,416 to 681,000 (746,829 in November 1967). Those attending evening institute classes went up from 437,361 to 1,252,518 (1,419,765 in November 1967); and those following Adult Education classes of all types from 50,796 to 218,881 (236,330 in the academic year 1966–7). As indicated on page 359 there were probably 73 full-time students in the advanced sector of higher education per 10,000 of the population in 1965 as compared with 35 in 1950 and only 19 in 1935. Among those aged 20 to 24, 5·1 per cent graduated in science and technology in 1967 compared with 4·2 per cent in the United States and 3·2 per cent in France.[1] This should not, however, be interpreted as an indication that we are becoming a nation which can claim that a high proportion of its working population has enjoyed some form of higher education. For, as the Robbins Report (Cmnd. 2154, para. 183) showed, the propor-

[1] *The Times*, 1 August 1968.

tion of the total working population who had completed full-time higher education in 1960–1 stood at a mere 3·4 per cent and could not rise much beyond 6·2 per cent by 1980–1 and 15 per cent by the year A.D. 2025.[1]

(5) It must be admitted that for the first twenty-five of the thirty years under review teaching power—that sensitive barometer of educational advance which is a constant challenge to the educational administrator and too often a disappointment to his hopes—did not keep pace with the obvious expansion in other sectors of the field. Substantial progress was in fact made in the elimination of unqualified teachers and the lengthening of the training college course from two to three years, but these advances are too often overlooked. Every time, however, that some hard-won increase in recruitment seemed to promise a longed-for reduction in the size of classes some unforeseen development has appeared to postpone it. For example the raising of the school-leaving age from April 1947 added nearly 300,000 children to the rolls of 'all age' and secondary modern schools. School rolls were, of course, continually expanding as a result of the post-war birth rates. Again, the lengthening of the training college course to three years, resulting in the so-called 'year of intermission' (1962), brought few recruits into the profession until the summer of 1963. Finally the staffs of the universities, institutions of further education, and colleges of education were expanded from the 7,945 of 1935 to the 62,528 of 1965 and thus drew off many teachers from the school sector.

In these circumstances the annual harvest of additional teachers for the primary and secondary fields, while gradually overhauling the demand throughout the period under review, did not in fact show a marked upward swing until after 1960.

This can be illustrated, in a way which would no doubt present many points for criticism to the trained educational statistician, by taking a look at the number of teachers employed in relation to the number of children in all types of maintained and direct grant schools at successive intervals of five years for most of the period from 1935 to 1965. In 1935 the figure stood at 30·4 children per teacher (in round numbers 200,000 teachers for a school population of 6 million). Of these teachers, 33,000 were, however, uncertificated or supplementary. When in 1947 statistics again became available after the war the school population had fallen by 814,000 and the first 8,000 of the 46,000 students accepted for training under the emergency training scheme had qualified. The result was a reduction from 30·4 to 28 children per teacher. By 1950 the number was down to 26·8 despite a rise of 63,000 on the school rolls. Five years later (1955) it had again fallen, to 26·6, although again the school rolls had risen by 88,000. By 1960 it had

[1] See Robbins Report, Cmnd. 2154, paras. 182 and 183, and Appendix 4, Part V.

fallen to 25·9, despite the fact that the 'bulge' age-groups had resulted in 1,318,000 more children attending school. By 1965 despite a further influx of 180,000 children it had shown a marked improvement to 22·8, partly no doubt owing to the return to teaching of part-time staff, who were the equivalent of 14,000 full-time teachers.

In the light of the achievements summarized above it does not seem unreasonable to claim that during the thirty years 1935–65 the first objective of any public system of education—the extension of opportunity—had been notably furthered. It is when one endeavours to arrive at a balanced assessment of the degree to which the second objective—improvement of the quality of the products of the system and of national life—has been attained that one comes up against uncomfortable searchings of conscience. For inevitably the 'silent social revolution' of the years 1895–1935 must appear to many observers to have become an extremely noisy one. This must be particularly the case if they form their judgement solely by what they read in the daily press supplemented by the output of too many of the radio and television programmes. Pictures of young men and women battling with the police, insulting Ministers, conducting sit-down strikes, accounts of hooliganism at football matches, the proliferation of bingo halls and betting shops, casinos and their concomitant protection rackets, allegations of widespread drug addiction and sexual permissiveness, juvenile delinquency increasing where an education committee has deliberately interfered with the disciplinary powers of head teachers—surely these are symptoms of a sick society? They may well be, but surely there is another side to the coin. I was 35 when I began to write Parts I and II of this book. I am now twice that age. The temptation to become a cynical *laudator temporis acti* is to that degree stronger. Yet I am not brave enough to be a pessimist. I believe that just as the greater proportion of the school and young adult population is quite demonstrably healthier, fitter, and better educated than it was thirty years ago, it has also steadily improved in its capacity to think, speak, and act for itself, to extend sympathy in practical ways to the young, the aged, the handicapped and the underprivileged, and to display initiative and enterprise in its activities. It would be a serious mistake too to overlook the immense change that these years have witnessed in the attitude of parents to the education of their children. Families are smaller on the average and full employment has rendered it easier for the commencement of wage-earning to be postponed to allow another year or two at school. More important perhaps, the parents themselves come from the third generation to receive public education.

It has always seemed to me a thousand pities that among the vast annual output of admirable reports on every other facet of the public education and youth services the Department of Education and

Science has never, to my knowledge, presented the nation with a comprehensive picture of the volume of social service performed by the schools, the youth clubs, the young adult population and university students to meet the human needs of the community. If they were to undertake such a countrywide study they would, I am assured, find a truly remarkable volume of work being carried on, for example to help young and adult immigrants to acclimatize themselves, in the visiting and giving of practical help to the aged, in working through such agencies as 'Shelter', 'Oxfam', and 'Voluntary Service Overseas' to improve conditions for the underprivileged at home and overseas, in opening windows on the restricted lives of the blind, the deaf, and the disabled. Such a survey, attractively presented, might act as a corrective, even perhaps as a counterblast, to the noisy social revolution fostered by a small minority and regrettably supported by the least educated sections of the population by which the eyes, ears, and feelings of an essentially decent and kindly public are all too often affronted.

BIBLIOGRAPHY

PARTS I and II

In the preparation of this book I was fortunate in having at my disposal the libraries of the Board of Education, the Ministry of Health, and the London County Council as well as the Bodleian Library at Oxford. Although the lists given below do not by any means represent the full amount of reading involved, all the books in them should be obtainable by students of the history of education. I have arranged them under chapter headings for convenience of reference.

BOOKS FOR GENERAL READING

J. W. Adamson: *An Outline of English Education, 1760–1902. English Education, 1789–1902.*

Sir G. Balfour: *Educational Systems of Great Britain and Ireland.* 1903.

E. Salter Davies: *The Re-organization of Education in England.* 1933.

J. J. Findlay: *The Children of England.* A contribution to social history and to education. 1923.

G. P. McHugh: *Local Administration in English Elementary Education, 1883–1930.*

N.U.T.: *The Hadow Report and After.* 1928.

Sir L. A. Selby Bigge: *The Board of Education.* 1927.

H. Ward: *The Educational System of England and Wales and its Recent Development.* 931.

J. Dover Wilson: *The Schools of England: A Study in Renaissance.* 1930.

CHAPTER I

For further reading the inquirer cannot do better than study the evidence of witnesses, particularly teachers and school attendance officers, before the Cross Inquiry Commission, 1886–9 (5 Volumes). The Digest of Evidence renders it a comparatively simple matter to follow up particular topics.

He should also read:

(1) Edmond Holmes: *What is and What might be.* 1911.

(2) The general reports of Her Majesty's Inspectors, published annually in the Reports of the Committee of the Privy Council on Education.

(3) Report of the Board of Education, 1910–11: The curriculum of the Public Elementary School, pp. 2–40.

(4) Report of the Board of Education, 1922–3: Some account of the Origin and Growth of the Board's Inspectorate, pp. 9–45.

(5) James Runciman: *Schools and Scholars*: Chatto & Windus, 1887. This book, written by a teacher, gives a brilliant sketch of conditions in the earliest schools and training colleges.

(6) Annual report of the Education Officer to the London County Council for the year 1908–9. This contains a series of reports by teachers and inspectors whose services went back to the Act of 1870 on the changes in the intervening years in the conditions under which teachers served, the type of pupil, their educational attainments, their fitness for their future lives, their general behaviour, and the condition and good order of the streets especially as regards youths and girls under 20.

(7) The Final Report of the School Board for London also contains much interesting material.

CHAPTER II

Broadly speaking the only people who really knew the life of the schools at this time were the teachers and Her Majesty's Inspectors. Probably the only book by a contemporary teacher which survives is *Schools and Scholars*, by James Runciman, 1887. The general reports of Her Majesty's Inspectors, running to several hundred pages annually, were published in the Education Department's annual report to Parliament. They were written with great freedom and do not appear to have been subjected to 'editing'. They are therefore valuable social documents.

A good picture of what has been described as 'the great age of inspection' is given in *H.M.I. Passages in the Life of an Inspector of Schools*, by Sneyd Kinnersley.

The evidence of witnesses to the Cross Commission throws much light upon conditions in the schools at the time that the 'payment by results' system was at its worst.

For a picture of the social, economic, and political currents of the time I have found *England, 1870–1913*, by R. C. K. Ensor in the 'Oxford History of England' series and also Halévy's *History of the English People*, invaluable.

CHAPTER III

The evidence of witnesses before the Royal Commission on Secondary Education, 1894–5 (the Bryce Commission) throws a flood of light on the meagre provision for education above the elementary stage in 1895.

Students of the subject should also read:

(1) The Introductory Chapter to the Report of the Consultative Committee of the Board of Education on the Education of the Adolescent. 1926.

(2) The appropriate chapters in Halévy's *History of the English People, 1895–1905*.

(3) The chapters on secondary education in the early annual reports of the Board of Education, e.g. that for 1904 and 1911.

(4) The report made in 1893 by Mr (later Sir) H. Llewellyn Smith to the

Technical Education Board for London on the facilities for higher education in London at that date.

(5) The annual reports of the Science and Art Department and the Charity Commission prior to the Board of Education Act of 1899.

CHAPTER IV

Everything said in the notes on Chapters II and III in regard to the value of the evidence before the Cross Commission and the Bryce Commission and the picture of the times to be derived from Her Majesty's Inspectors' annual reports and Halévy's *History of the English People* is of equal application in the case of this chapter.

In the interests of brevity and clarity I have omitted any detailed account of the various abortive Government Bills. An abortive Bill makes a stir among a narrow circle for a time, but it is easy for the historian who draws his material too exclusively from *Hansard* to attribute an undue importance to it. This will readily be appreciated by anyone who takes the trouble to study the number of private members' bills, dealing with education, which have been introduced since 1902.

Dr B. M. Allen's *Life of Sir Robert Morant* and *Memoir of Dr Garnet* are important for the study of this period since he had access to much information hitherto unpublished.

The Fabian Pamphlet, No. 106, 'The Education Muddle and the way out', is invaluable to anyone who wishes to understand the chaos in educational affairs before the Act of 1902.

The Contemporary Review (1897), Vol. 71, pp. 276 *ff.* and Vol. 72, pp. 417 *ff.* may be consulted for an analysis of the state of the religious denominations.

CHAPTER V

For the Debate on the Act of 1902 I have chiefly relied upon *Hansard*, for the hundreds of columns that were written in the Press do not add many points of substance which did not eventually find expression in Parliament. In the amount of Parliamentary time it consumed, the Bill ran a close second to Gladstone's Home Rule Bill, for it took five days on First and Second Reading, forty-eight days in committee, seven days on report and Third Reading and eight days in the Lords.

An Index will be found in *Hansard*, Vol. 118.

CHAPTER VI

Some account of the growth and aims of Secondary Education in England and Wales will be found in:

(1) 'Recent Development of Secondary Schools in England and Wales', Educational Pamphlet, No. 50, H.M.S.O. (also published as a chapter in the Board of Education's annual report for 1923–4).

(2) I. L. Kandel: *The History of Secondary Education.* 1931.

(3) 'A Survey of Secondary Education in the United States and in Europe' —Bulletin 20 of the Carnegie Foundation for the Advancement of Teaching. 1927.

(4) J. G. Legge: *The Rising Tide.*

(5) F. W. Roman: *The New Education in Europe.* 1930.

The scholarship system and the questions connected with it may be studied in the following:

(6) Essay on 'The Scholarship in English Education', by Sir Michael Sadler, contained in *Essays on Examinations*, published by the International Institute Examinations Inquiry, 1936.

(7) Chapter on 'The Passage from the Elementary to the Secondary School', Board of Education annual report, 1911–12.

(8) Report of the Departmental Committee on Scholarships and Free Places. H.M.S.O., 1920.

(9) Kenneth Lindsay: *Social Progress and Educational Waste.* 1926.

(10) F. S. Marvin: *The Nation at School.* 1935.

(11) Professor R. H. Tawney, ed.: *Secondary Education for All.* 1922.

No full attempt to trace the social, economic and political forces at work has been made except briefly by Sir Michael Sadler in:

(12) 'The Outlook in Secondary Education', a course of lectures delivered at Teachers' College, Columbia University.

In my attempt to follow up these questions I found the following valuable:

(13) Carr Saunders and Caradog Jones: *Social Structure of England and Wales.*

(14) 'The Secondary School'. Report of a Commission appointed by Bradford Independent Labour Party, 1928–31.

(15) *Social Factors in Secondary Education.* University of Liverpool, 1932.

(16) *Education in Leeds. A Backward Glance and a Present View.* Published by the Leeds L.E.A., 1926.

(17) *The Education Problem in Leeds.* Published by the Leeds L.E.A., 1926.

(18) Report of the City of Birmingham Education Committee, 1914–24.

(19) *Education in Lancashire.* Handbook of Lancashire Education Authority.

(20) J. Howard Whitehouse: *Education.* 'In my time series', 1935.

(21) E. Sharwood Smith: *The Faith of a Schoolmaster.* 1935.

(22) The reports made by Mr (now Sir Michael) Sadler upon the provision for Secondary Education in a number of areas, e.g. Essex, Hants, Liverpool, etc. These are still obtainable in some libraries and are well worth careful study.

(23) *Learn and Live*, compiled for the Institute of Adult Education by Messrs Williams and Heath, 1936.

CHAPTERS VII and VIII

The following chapters in the annual reports of the Board of Education are valuable for the study of the history of elementary education:

(1) 1909–10: Staffing of Public Elementary Schools. The best discussion of the evil of over-large classes is, however, contained in the Report of the Consultative Committee on Attendance compulsory or otherwise at Continuation Schools, 1909, pp. 51–59.

(2) 1910–11: The Curriculum of the Public Elementary School, pp. 2–40.

(3) 1912–13: History of the Training of Teachers for elementary schools.

(4) 1922–3: Some account of the Origin and Growth of the Board's Inspectorate.

For the general history of elementary education the following should be studied:

(5) C. Birchenough: *History of Elementary Education in England and Wales from 1800 to the Present Day*. 1925.

(6) Report of the Consultative Committee of the Board of Education on, 'The Education of the Adolescent', Chapter I—Sketch of the development of full-time post-primary education in England and Wales from 1800–1918. H.M.S.O., 1926.

(7) Report of the Consultative Committee of the Board of Education on, 'The Primary School', Chapter I—The History of the development of the conception of primary education above the infant stage, 1800–1931. H.M.S.O., 1936.

(8) Report of the Consultative Committee of the Board of Education on 'Infant and Nursery Schools', Chapter I—Sketch of the history of the development of infant education as a distinct part of primary education in England and Wales from the beginning of the nineteenth century down to the present time. H.M.S.O., 1933.

(9) 'The New Prospect in Education'. Educational Pamphlet, No. 60, H.M.S.O., 1928.

The various issues of the Code of Regulations for Public Elementary Schools and the Board's Handbook of Suggestions for Teachers are essential in making any attempt to follow the changes in the curriculum.

No full account of the changes in the elementary schools during the ten years up to 1935, i.e. after the advent of Hadow reorganization, has yet appeared, although the Board's pamphlet on 'Education and the Countryside' (H.M.S.O., 1936), is a move in this direction. The Educational Press is, however, full of accounts of pioneer work in individual schools, and the inquirer who has access to reports upon the schools of an area can construct a good mental picture of what is going on. *Our Public Elementary Schools* by Sir Michael Sadler, 1926, although prior to the Hadow Report, still contains one of the best available discussions of the place of the elementary school in the community.

'The Hadow Report and After', National Union of Teachers, 1928, and

'The Schools at Work', National Union of Teachers, 1935, should be consulted for a picture of the possibilities opened up by reorganization.

For rural education the following should also be studied:

'Rural Education. Adaptation of Instruction to the needs of Rural Areas'. Educational Pamphlet, No. 46, H.M.S.O., 1926.

'An Experiment in Rural Reorganization'. Educational Pamphlet, No. 93, H.M.S.O., 1933.

The report of the Education Officer to the London County Council for 1935 contains a series of articles by inspectors and teachers showing the changes which have taken place in various types of schools since 1904.

CHAPTER IX

MAIN SOURCES FOR THE STUDY OF THE DEVELOPMENT OF TECHNICAL EDUCATION SINCE 1902

1. Books and articles by individuals or groups:

Lord Eustace Percy: *Education at the Cross Roads.* 1930.

A. Abbott: *Education for Industry and Commerce in England.* 1933

Report of an inquiry into the relationships of technical education to other forms of education and to industry and commerce. Emmott Committee, 1927.

The Entrance to Industry (1934), published by P.E.P., 16 Queen Anne's Gate, S.W.1.

Articles in the *Encyclopaedia Britannica*, 9th Edition—'Technical Education', by Sir Philip Magnus; 'Polytechnics', by Sir Joshua Fitch.

Address delivered to the British Association, 1930, by A. Abbott on 'The Development of Technical and Commercial Education in England'.

Address delivered at the annual meeting of the Association of Principals of Technical Institutions on 25 February 1932, by J. W. Bispham on 'The Cultural possibilities of Vocational Education'.

C. T. Millis: *Technical Education, its Development and Aims.* 1925.

C. T. Millis: *Education for Trades and Industries.* A Historical Survey. 1932.

Humanism and Technology. Lectures to a vocation school for engineering students in the University of Birmingham and Oriel College, 1924.

E. Salter Davies: *The Schools of England: A Study in Renaissance.* Chapter on Technical Education. 1930.

Learn and Live. Published by the Institute of Adult Education, 1936.

London Men and Women. Published by the Institute of Adult Education, 1937.

2. Publications by His Majesty's Stationery Office:

(*a*) For *technical education as affecting individual industries:*

Memorandum on the Teaching of Coal Mining in Part-time Schools, 1916.

Memorandum on the Teaching of Building in Evening Schools, 1916.

Memorandum on the Teaching of Cotton Spinning and Manufacture, 1917.

Engineering Training. Some Notes on Existing Facilities, 1917.

Memorandum on Commercial Instruction in Evening Schools, 1919.

Report of H.M. Inspectors on Technical Education for the Automobile Engineering Industry, 1923.

Memorandum on the Teaching of Engineering in Evening Technical Schools, 1923.

Report of H.M. Inspectors on Technical Training for the Gas Industry, 1924.

Report of H.M. Inspectors on Technical Training for the Manufacture and Application of Coal Tar products, 1924.

Report of H.M. Inspectors on Education in relation to Foundry work, 1924.

Report of H.M. Inspectors on Technical Education in England for the Paper Making industry, 1924.

Report on the provision of instruction for persons employed in the Coal Mining Industry in the Coalfields of South Wales, 1924.

Report of H.M. Inspectors on Technical Instruction in Structural Engineering, 1935.

Report of H.M. Inspectors on Instruction in England for the Manufacture of Leather, 1925.

Report of H.M. Inspectors on Instruction in surveying, 1926.

Report of H.M. Inspectors on Instruction in Pure Chemistry, 1927.

Report of H.M. Inspectors on Instruction in Commodities for persons employed in Commerce, 1927.

Report of H.M. Inspectors on Instruction for the Rail Carriage and Wagon Building Industry, 1928.

Building Science, 1928.

Electrical Machine Design, 1928.

Day Classes for Building Apprentices, 1928.

The Plumber's Trade and Training, 1928.

Day Classes for Engineering Apprentices, 1928.

(*b*) *General*

Report of the Consultative Committee on Attendance, Compulsory or otherwise, at Continuation Schools. Two volumes, 1909.

Survey of Technical and Further Education in England and Wales. Educational Pamphlet, No. 49, 1926.

Education for Industry and Commerce. Educational Pamphlet, No. 64, 1928.

The Course System in Evening Schools, 1910.

The Junior Technical Schools. Educational Pamphlet, No. 83, 1930.

Trade and Domestic Schools for Girls. Educational Pamphlet, No. 72, 1929.

London Men's (Junior) Evening Institutes. Educational Pamphlet, No. 84, 1930.

Work of Men's Institutes in London. Educational Pamphlet, No. 48, 1926.

The reports of the Science and Art Department (annual) and the annual general reports by H.M. Inspectors before 1899 also contain much interesting material.

(c) Adult education:

The following papers of the Adult Education Committee of the Board of Education:

No. 3. The Development of Adult Education in Rural Areas.

No. 4. The Development of Adult Education for Women.

No. 7. Full-time Studies.

No. 9. Pioneer work and other Developments in Adult Education.

No. 10. The Scope and Practice of Adult Education.

No. 11. Adult Education and the Local Education Authority.

(d) For the period of post-war inquiry:

Factors in Industrial and Commercial Efficiency. Part I, 1927, and Final Report, 1929, pp. 201–26, of the Balfour Committee on Industry and Trade.

Reports (two parts) of the Committee on Education and Industry (Malcolm Committee), 1927 and 1928.

Education for Salesmanship.

Education for the Engineering Industry.

CHAPTER X

SOURCES FOR FURTHER READING

1. Official publications by His Majesty's Stationary Office.

The annual reports of the Chief Medical Officer to the Board of Education, 1908–34.

For the *school medical service* see in particular:

Year of Report		Pages
1908	History of Medical Inspection of School Children ..	2–11
1909	The Physical Condition of School Children as revealed by Medical Inspection	26–69
	Action taken by the Local Education Authorities in respect of Medical Treatment	92–118
1917	A review of the work of ten years, 1908–17. Some results of the School Medical Service	

1929   The story of the School Medical Service
1931   What is the School Medical Service achieving?   ..   119
       Historical Note   5
1934   Infection and Mortality in School Children   119–125

For the *special schools:*
1908   The Special Schools for Defective Children   107–19
1909   Education of Feeble-minded Children   151–69
1910   Open-air Education   221–31
1919   The Cripple Child..   100–24
1922   Orthopaedics and the Child   89–101
1926   The Education of the Cripple Child (Shropshire Ortho-
       paedic Hospital)   140
1930   Progress in the Prevention and Treatment of Crippling
       Defects   51

For the *provision of meals:*
1910   Historical Note   245–54
1913   Retrospect of the Period 1906–14   241–63
1920   Provision of School Meals   146–52

    Also the Charts in 'Educational Administration in England and Wales', H.M.S.O., 1936.

2. Other publications.
    The annual reports of many school medical officers are available to those who can visit the Board of Education Library, but in general they are all summarized in the reports of Sir George Newman.
    The most interesting publication for the layman is *The Special Services of Education in London*, 1931.
    The following volumes of *Hansard* repay study: Vol. 160, 16 July 1906; and Cols., 1384–1394; Vol. 170, 1 March 1907.

PART III

CHAPTER XII

THE principal source available to students is the brilliant volume in the official history of the Second World War, *Problems of Social Policy* by Mr (now Professor) R. M. Titmuss, who was appointed to the staff of the Ministry of Health to write this history as the war progressed (H.M.S.O. and Longmans, 1950). Volume I of Sir Winston Churchill's history of the Second World War, *The Gathering Storm* (Cassell), should also be studied by anyone who wishes to obtain a full picture of the darkening educational scene.
    The L.C.C. report on the Board of Education Circular (1461) of 3 January 1938 is in the Record Room of the Greater London Council. It was Enclosure

D to the agenda of the General Purposes Sub-Committee dated 24 January 1938 but was watered down before presentation to the council lest it create too much alarm and despondency. The report of the Anderson Committee to the Home Secretary on Evacuation was produced by 26 July 1938 but was withheld and not published till after the Munich Crisis of September 1938.

For the rest, in writing this chapter I relied on personal recollection and the reading of all the material on the subject which appeared in the press and the educational papers, e.g.:

The Times	*The Times Educational Supplement*	*The Schoolmaster*
3:10:38	1:10:38	29:9:38
29:8:39	15:10:38	6:10:38
2:9:39		13:10:38
27:12:39		27:10:38
15:5:40		
4:6:40		

The Evening News	*The Evening Standard*	*The Star*
1:9:39	2:9:39	12:6:40

The Teachers' World	*The London Teacher*	*The London Headteacher*
28:9:38	30:9:38	Oct. 38
5:10:38	14:10:38	Nov. 38
12:10:38	Nov. 38	
26:10:38		
2:11:38		

CHAPTER XIII

The volume in the official history of the Second World War which was to have covered the fate of public education has never appeared owing to the greatly to be regretted death of the individual appointed to write it. Much of the ground is, however, covered by Professor Titmuss's *Problems of Social Policy*.

Nearly 200 private studies of the Government Evacuation Scheme appeared during the war years, but it is unlikely that many of them have survived except in the library of the Ministry of Education and Science. They included small pamphlets by such bodies as the W.E.A., The New Education Fellowship, the Fabian Society, the Liverpool University Department of Social Science, and the Barnett House Study Group (on London children in wartime Oxford).

Longer studies published are:

H. C. Dent: *Education in Transition*. Kegan Paul, Trench, Trubner & Co., 1944.

Mrs Amy Strachey: *Borrowed Children*. Murray, 1940.

Susan Isaacs, ed.: *The Cambridge Evacuation Survey*. Methuen, 1941.

Margaret Cole and R. Padley: *Evacuation Survey*. Routledge, 1940.

The report of the L.C.C. Inspectors on the attainments of 13-year-old children who had returned from the first evacuation is dated 5:7:1943 and numbered Ed. No. 208. It can be consulted in the Record Room at the Greater London Council Headquarters, County Hall, London S.E.1.

CHAPTER XIV

The 'Green Book' which was circulated by the Board of Education in June 1941 to a large number of professional and other bodies concerned with public education is still unobtainable and will no doubt remain so until 1971 when it should be released under the new thirty-year rule. A summary of its main points was given to the House of Commons on 22 October 1943. They cannot have differed very materially from those in the White Paper on Educational Reconstruction, Cmnd. 6458, presented to Parliament in July 1943. The observations submitted by sixty of the bodies consulted have been assembled in two folios in the library of the Department of Education and Science. Copies of a few of these may still be obtainable on application to the bodies concerned, although in most cases 'file copies' only have been preserved and the wartime limits on paper supplies seriously restricted the number initially printed.

Among the more important pamphlets were:

(1) 'Education. A plan for the future'. Association of Directors and Secretaries for Education 1942. Clarendon Press.

(2) 'Education after the War'. Trades Union Congress, 1942.

(3) 'A plan for education'. National Union of Teachers, 1943.

(4) 'Looking Ahead: Educational Aims'. Conservative Central Committee on Post War Reconstruction, September 1942.

(5) Association of Education Committees statement, 24 April 1942.

(6) Council for Educational Advance. Statement on the White Paper.

(7) Workers' Educational Association.
Pamphlet No 1. 'Plan for Education', 1943.
Pamphlet No 6. Professor R. H. Tawney: 'Education. The Task before us'. 1943
Pamphlet No 7. Mr (now Sir Harold) Shearman: 'The New Education Act. 1944.

(8) Grace Leybourne: 'A new charter for education'. Fabian Pamphlet No 76.

(9) British Federation of University Women. 1943.

(10) 'Educational Reform and Social Justice'. The Christian Education Movement.

(11) H. C. Dent: 'A Landmark in English Education'. Commentary on the White Paper. August 1943.

(12) Canon Barker: 'The Education Act 1944'. A general summary (National Society) S.P.C.K.

(13) H. C. Dent: 'The new Education Bill. What it contains. What it means. Why it should be supported'. 1944.

(14) Commonwealth Information Bulletin: 'Education'. 1944.

Professor H. C. Dent's *Education in Transition* (Kegan Paul, Trench, Trubner & Co) and Chapter IV of his *Secondary Education for All* (Routledge, 1949) cover much the same material as that in this chapter.

CHAPTER XV

It is extremely difficult for anyone to get a clear impression of the atmosphere of a long and closely argued debate unless he is prepared to read the whole of it with a copy of the Bill before him, interleaved to show the amendments tabled and the fate of each. This was the procedure followed in my attempt to condense the essence of this debate, although it is recognized that the condensation of the millions of words spoken will probably be thought by experts to have resulted in the omission of many important points.

To obtain an outline of the more important results which have flowed from the Act the following sources repay study.

(1) The school building programmes can best be traced through the annual reports of the Ministry of Education. These should, however, be examined against the findings of the school building survey (H.M.S.O. 1962), which revealed clearly how much more had to be accomplished. The problems and achievements of the Catholic community are discussed in the annual reports of the Catholic Education Council, particularly those for 1962–3 and 1964–5.

(2) The progress of Religious Education in the schools is very fully dealt with in the report of the Institute of Christian Education published by the S.P.C.K. in 1957; and in *Religious Education in Schools, 1944–1984* (Allen and Unwin, 1965). Pamphlet No. 16 of the Ministry of Education should also be studied.

(3) Extended educational opportunity for those formerly underprivileged has, as indicated in the text, produced an intimidating pile of volumes, statistics, psychological monographs, and learned papers.

These studies are mentioned in the text:

Jean Floud, ed., with A. H. Halsey and F. M. Martin: *Social Class and Educational Opportunity*. Heinemann, 1955.
A further examination of the subject is given by Mrs Floud in Chapter II of *Looking Forward in Education*. Faber and Faber, 1955.

D. Marsden and B. Jackson: *Education and the Working Class*. Routledge, 1962.

P. Wilmot and M. Young: *Family and Class in a London Suburb*. Routledge, 1962.

The following books and articles also deal with the subject:

M. P. Carter: *Home School and Work*. Pergamon, 1962.

'In search of an Explanation of Social Mobility', *British Journal of Statistical Psychology*, Vol. 16, Part I (May, 1963), pp. 27–36.

J. E. Meade and A. S. Parkes, eds.: *Social Mobility and Education. Biological Aspects of Social Problems.* Symposium held by the Eugenics Society, Oct. 1964.

Glen H. Elder: 'Life opportunity and Personality, some consequences of stratified education in British Secondary schools', *Sociology of Education*, Vol. 38 (1965), No. 3.

J. W. B. Douglas: 'Unequal opportunities at school', *Higher Education Journal*, Spring term issue, 1965.

Harry Davies: *Culture and the Grammar School.* Routledge & Kegan Paul, 1965.

R. R. Dale and S. Griffith: *Down Stream Failure in the Grammar School.* Routledge, 1965.

F. Musgrave: *The Family, Education and Society.* Routledge, 1966.

The social surveys carried out for the Crowther Committee, '15 to 18', Volume 2; the Newsom Committee's 'Half our Future'; and the Robbins Report on 'Higher Education' all throw considerably more light on the question.

CHAPTER XVI

As noted in the text, the Plowden Reports, 'Children and their Primary Schools', are likely to influence and perhaps transform the whole future aspect of nursery and primary education over the next thirty years. Unfortunately the first of these reports did not appear until January 1967: too late, that is, to enable any serious attempt to be made to assess their recommendations in a work confined to the thirty years 1935–65. Undoubtedly the best advice which can be given to anyone who proposes to study nursery or primary education in England or Wales—after he has read the Plowden Reports—is to make his choice of books to read from the 'Short list of selective references on Nursery and Infant education' and 'Short list of references on Primary education' compiled by the Library of the Ministry of Education and Science. The first list (June 1965) includes 72 titles, and the second (September 1965) 83 titles. The number of books on educational subjects, whether general or concerned with the techniques of teaching, increases every year.

Although anyone who has been engaged in or followed the expansion of public education for nearly fifty years will probably find that he has read most of the books enumerated, those which interested me particularly in preparing this chapter were:

Nursery and Infant education

'Not yet Five', *Ministry of Education.* November 1946. 3rd edition, 1964.

L. De Lissa: *Life in the Nursery School and in Early Babyhood.* Longmans, 1949.

Elspeth Howe: 'Under 5'. Conservative Political Centre, 1966.

D. E. M. Gardner: *Testing Results in the Infant School*. Methuen, 1953. *Long Term Results of Infant School Methods*. Methuen, 1950. *The Education of Young Children*. Methuen, 1956.

'Religious Education in the Nursery and Infants' School'. Institute of Christian Education, 1964.

Susan Isaacs: *The Psychological Aspects of Child Development*. Evans, 1949.

L.C.C. Education Committee:
'Movement education for infants'. 1963.
G. M. Goldsworthy: 'Modern trends in nursery education'. Feb. 1963.
'Entering the infant school'. May 1963.

National Froebel Foundation:
E. H. Walters: 'Activity and experience in the infant school'. 1955.

National Union of Teachers:
'Nursery infant education'. A report of a consultative committee under the chairmanship of Miss Lillian De Lissa. Evans, 1949.
Statement on the terms of reference to the Plowden Committee. 1964.

Nursery School Association:
Susan Isaacs: 'The educational value of the nursery school'.
G. M. Goldsworthy: 'Part-time nursery education'.
Dr W. D. Wall and Dr Anna Freud: 'The enrichment of childhood'.

Albert Mansbridge: *Margaret McMillan. Prophet and Pioneer*. Dent. 1932.

G. A. N. Lowndes: *Margaret McMillan. The Children's Champion*. Museum Press, 1960.

Primary Education

Ministry of Education:
Education Pamphlet No. 14. Story of a School. 1949.
Education Pamphlet No. 15. Seven to Eleven. 1949.
Education Pamphlet No. 42. Science in Primary Schools. 1951.
Suggestions for the consideration of teachers and others concerned with the work of primary schools. 1959.
Physical Education in the primary school.
Moving and Growing 1952.

L.C.C. Trends in Primary Education. 1950.

B. Ash and B. Rapaport: *Creative Work in the Junior School*. Methuen, 1957.

M. Atkinson: *Junior School Community*. Longmans, 1962.

N. Catty: *Learning and Teaching in the Junior School*. Methuen, 1952.

M. V. Daniell: *Activity in the Primary School*. Evans, 1947.

J. C. Gagg: *Common Sense in the primary school*. Evans, 1951.

W. K. Richmond: *Purpose in the Junior school*. Redman, 1949.

CHAPTER XVII

Everything said in the case of the bibliography for nursery and primary schools about the value to students of the 'Short list of references' prepared by the library of the Department for Education and Science applies with equal force to secondary education. The September 1965 list mentions 40 works, of which the ones I found most useful in the preparation of this chapter were:

For the rise and achievements of the secondary modern schools

Ministry of Education:
The New Secondary Education. Pamphlet No. 9, 1947.
'15 to 18': the Crowther Report.
'Half our Future': the Newsom Report.

J. V. Chapman: *Your Secondary Modern Schools; an Account of their Work in the 1950s.* College of Preceptors, 1959.

Bristol University Institute of Education: *The Curriculum of Secondary Schools offering Advanced Studies.* University of London Press, 1962.

Sixth Form Courses in Secondary Modern Schools. Cheshire Education Committee, 1966.

J. J. B. Dempster: *Purpose in the Modern School.* Methuen, 1956.

H. C. Dent: *Growth in English Education 1946–1952.* Routledge, 1954.
Secondary Education for All: Origins and Development in England. Routledge, 1949.
Secondary Modern Schools: an interim report. Routledge, 1958.

H. Loukes: *Secondary Modern.* Harrap, 1956.

Growing doubts about the tripartite system and demand for examinations

J. J. B. Dempster: *Selection for Secondary Education: a survey.* Methuen, 1954.

G. B. Jeffery, ed.: *External Examinations in Secondary Schools: their place and Function.* Harrap, 1958.

London University Institute of Education: *The Problems of Secondary Education Today.* Evans, 1954.

S. C. Mason: *The Leicestershire Experiment.* Councils and Education Press, 1963.

National Union of Teachers: *Guide to the Certificate of Secondary Education.* 1963.

The Comprehensive School Debate

L.C.C.: Report of the General Sub-Committee to the Education Committee. 27 June 1944.
London Comprehensive Schools; a Survey of Sixteen Schools. 1961.

National Association of Schoolmasters: *The Comprehensive School; an Appraisal from Within.* 1964.

R. Pedley: *The Comprehensive School.* Penguin, 1963.

National Union of Teachers: *Inside the Comprehensive School*. Schoolmaster
Publishing Company, 1958.

Times Educational Supplement. Some of the leading articles and letters published (out of a vast correspondence on the subject) were brought together in a pamphlet published by the Times Publishing Company in
1966.

The Department of Education and Science Circular 10/65 of 12 July 1965.

Direct Grant Schools

J. C. Dancy: *The Public Schools and the Future*. 2nd ed., Faber, 1966.

E. Allsop and G. Grugeon: *Direct Grant Grammar Schools*. Fabian research
series, No. 256, 1966.

CHAPTERS XVIII and XIX

The expansion of technical, technological, and higher education in England
and Wales in the three decades 1935–65 has been so rapid and so recent that
no general historical account of its progress is yet available. There is, of course,
a very substantial body of literature dealing with various aspects of the subject
normally related to the needs of particular industries. This is important in the
light of the provisions of the Industrial Training Act 1964.

The skeleton upon which these two chapters were formed was:

(1) A careful reading (sometimes between the lines!) and annotation of the
appropriate chapter or chapters in each of the annual reports of the
Ministry from 1935 to 1965.

(2) A study of all the reports of government or departmental committees on
aspects of technological or higher education since the Second World War,
in particular:

The Percy Report 1945.
The Barlow Report 1946. Cmnd. 6824.
The reports of the National Advisory Council on Education for Industry
and Commerce. Also the reports of the various standing sub-committees which the council has brought into being to examine various
aspects of the field. Examples are:

The Future Development of Higher Technological Education. 1950.
The Advisory Committee on Further Education for Commerce. 1959.
The Willis Jackson Report on the Supply of Teachers for Technical
Education. 1957.
The Alexander Report on the Public Relations of Further Education.

Ministry of Education reports and circulars, e.g.:

Pamphlet No. 8. Further Education. 1947.
The White Paper on Technological Education, February 1946.
Cmnd. 9703.
Better Opportunities in Technical Education. 1961.
Schools Council Curriculum Bulletin No. 2, 'A school approach to
technology'.

The Robbins Report on Higher Education. 1963. Cmnd. 2154.

The annual surveys and triennial reviews of university development issued by the University Grants Committee, e.g. Cmnd. 2846, 1964–5, and Cmnd. 3192, 1962–5.

The reports of the Scientific Manpower Committee of the Advisory Council on Scientific Policy, namely:

1952. Cmnd. 8561.
1956. Reprinted 1959, S.O. Code No. 36–227.
1959. Cmnd. 902
1961. Cmnd. 1490. Reprinted 1965.
1963. Cmnd. 2146.
1965. Cmnd. 2800.
1966. Cmnd. 3103.

(3) A perusal of the debates in both Houses of Parliament dealing with manpower and the importance of technical, technological, and higher education since 1946. These included:

The House of Lords debate on the Queen's Speech. November 1953. *H.* (Lords), Vol. 184.

The House of Commons debate on 9 June 1955. *H.* Vol. 542.

The House of Commons debate on 21 July 1955 on Scientific and Technical Manpower. *H.* Vol. 544.

The House of Commons debate on the Government White Paper (Cmnd. 9703) which took place on 21 June 1956.

(4) The study of each monthly issue of *The Times* Supplement 'Technology'.

INDEX